Understanding Flusser, Understanding Modernism

Understanding Philosophy, Understanding Modernism

The aim of each volume in **Understanding Philosophy, Understanding Modernism** is to understand a philosophical thinker more fully through literary and cultural modernism and consequently to understand literary modernism better through a key philosophical figure. In this way, the series also rethinks the limits of modernism, calling attention to lacunae in modernist studies and sometimes in the philosophical work under examination.

Series Editors:
Paul Ardoin, S. E. Gontarski, and Laci Mattison

Volumes in the Series:

Understanding Bergson, Understanding Modernism
Edited by Paul Ardoin, S. E. Gontarski, and Laci Mattison

Understanding Deleuze, Understanding Modernism
Edited by S. E. Gontarski, Paul Ardoin and Laci Mattison

Understanding Wittgenstein, Understanding Modernism
Edited by Anat Matar

Understanding Foucault, Understanding Modernism
Edited by David Scott

Understanding James, Understanding Modernism
Edited by David H. Evans

Understanding Rancière, Understanding Modernism
Edited by Patrick M. Bray

Understanding Blanchot, Understanding Modernism
Edited by Christopher Langlois

Understanding Merleau-Ponty, Understanding Modernism
Edited by Ariane Mildenberg

Understanding Nietzsche, Understanding Modernism
Edited by Douglas Burnham and Brian Pines

Understanding Derrida, Understanding Modernism
Edited by Jean-Michel Rabaté

Understanding Adorno, Understanding Modernism
Edited by Robin Truth Goodman

Understanding Marx, Understanding Modernism
Edited by Mark Steven

Understanding Flusser, Understanding Modernism
Edited by Aaron Jaffe, Rodrigo Martini, and Michael F. Miller

Understanding Cavell, Understanding Modernism (forthcoming)
Edited by Paola Marrati

Understanding Flusser, Understanding Modernism

Edited by
Aaron Jaffe, Rodrigo Martini, Michael F. Miller

BLOOMSBURY ACADEMIC
Bloomsbury Publishing Inc
1385 Broadway, New York, NY 10018, USA
50 Bedford Square, London, WC1B 3DP, UK
29 Earlsfort Terrace, Dublin 2, Ireland

BLOOMSBURY, BLOOMSBURY ACADEMIC and the Diana logo are trademarks of Bloomsbury Publishing Plc

First published in the United States of America 2022
This paperback edition published 2023

Copyright © Aaron Jaffe, Rodrigo Martini, Michael F. Miller, and contributors, 2022

For legal purposes the Acknowledgments on p. x constitute an extension of this copyright page.

Cover designer: Eleanor Rose
Cover image: "Einstein" (1974) Herbert W. Franke

All rights reserved. No part of this publication may be reproduced or transmitted in any form or by any means, electronic or mechanical, including photocopying, recording, or any information storage or retrieval system, without prior permission in writing from the publishers.

Bloomsbury Publishing Inc does not have any control over, or responsibility for, any third-party websites referred to or in this book. All internet addresses given in this book were correct at the time of going to press. The author and publisher regret any inconvenience caused if addresses have changed or sites have ceased to exist, but can accept no responsibility for any such changes.

A catalog record for this book is available from the Library of Congress.

ISBN: HB: 978-1-5013-4843-3
PB: 978-1-5013-8636-7
ePDF: 978-1-5013-4845-7
eBook: 978-1-5013-4844-0

Series: Understanding Philosophy, Understanding Modernism

Typeset by Deanta Global Publishing Services, Chennai, India

To find out more about our authors and books visit www.bloomsbury.com and sign up for our newsletters.

Series Preface

Sometime in the late twentieth century, modernism, like philosophy itself, underwent something of an unmooring from (at least) linear literary history in favor of the multi-perspectival history implicit in "new historicism" or, say, varieties of "presentism." Amid current reassessments of modernism and modernity, critics have posited various "new" or alternative modernisms—postcolonial, cosmopolitan, transatlantic, transnational, geomodernism, or even "bad" modernisms. In doing so, they have not only reassessed modernism as a category, but also, more broadly, rethought epistemology and ontology, aesthetics, metaphysics, materialism, history, and being itself, opening possibilities of rethinking not only which texts we read as modernist but also how we read those texts. Much of this new conversation constitutes something of a critique of the periodization of modernism or modernist studies in favor of modernism as mode (or mode of production) or concept. Understanding Philosophy, Understanding Modernism situates itself amid the plurality of discourses, offering collections focused on key philosophical thinkers influential both to the moment of modernism and to our current understanding of that moment's geneology, archeology, and becomings. Such critiques of modernism(s) and modernity afford opportunities to rethink and reassess the overlaps, folds, interrelationships, interleavings, or cross-pollinations of modernism and philosophy. Our goal in each volume of the series is to understand literary modernism better through philosophy as we also better understand a philosopher through literary modernism. The first two volumes of the series, those on Henri Bergson and Gilles Deleuze, have established a tripartite structure that serves to offer accessibility both to the philosopher's principal texts and to current new research. Each volume opens with a section focused on "conceptualizing" the philosopher through close readings of seminal texts in the thinker's oeuvre. A second section, on aesthetics, maps connections between modernist works and the philosophical figure, often surveying key modernist trends and shedding new light on authors and texts. The final section of each volume serves as an extended glossary of principal terms in the philosopher's work, each treated at length, allowing a fuller engagement with and examination of the many, sometimes contradictory, ways terms are deployed. The series is thus designed both to introduce philosophers and to rethink their relationship to modernist studies, revising our understandings of both modernism and philosophy, and offering resources that will be of use across disciplines, from philosophy, theory, and literature, to religion, the visual and performing arts, and often to the sciences as well.

Contents

List of Figures ... ix
Acknowledgments ... x

Introduction *Aaron Jaffe, Rodrigo Martini, Michael F. Miller* ... 1

Part I Processing Flusser

1 "Does AI Have a Future?" *Rita Raley and Russell Samolsky* ... 15
2 Design/Shape *Anke K. Finger* ... 23
3 Vilém Flusser in Open Circuits: The Dialogic Capacity of Video Images *Daniel Irrgang* ... 30
4 Flusser and Ars Electronica: Between and Beyond Cybernetics *Daniel Raschke* ... 39
5 Flusser in the Light of Radiation *Clint Wilson III* ... 49
6 Games and Play: On Being Human in the Universe of Technical Images *Nancy Roth* ... 57
7 Flusser's Philosophical Backgrounds *Martha Schwendener* ... 67
8 Vilém Flusser's Quasi-Phenomenology *Andreas Max Ströhl* ... 75
9 Migrants, Flâneurs, Critics: Flusserian Irony and the Genealogy of Modern Cynicism *Alexander B. Adkins* ... 83
10 *Vampyroteuthis Infernalis* as Media Theory *Geoffrey Winthrop-Young* ... 94
11 Posthistory Today: Historical Time and Virality after Flusser *Charles M. Tung* ... 103

Part II Flusser's Expanded Modernism

12 Demonologies *Laurence A. Rickels* ... 113
13 An Intersubjective Style *Frances McDonald* ... 123
14 "Naked Little Spasms of the Self": In Search of an Authentic Gesture in Posthistorical Times *Dominic Pettman* ... 131
15 The 'Pataphysical Span: Alfred Jarry and Vilém Flusser *Judith Roof* ... 141
16 Flusser's New Weird *Keith Leslie Johnson* ... 151
17 A Philosophy of Refraction: Vilém Flusser's Speculative Biology and the Study of Paramedia *David Bering-Porter* ... 162

18	Everything Quantizes *Kate Brideau*	172
19	Religious Telematics and the Archives of Memory *K. Merinda Simmons*	181
20	The Challenge of Vilém Flusser: Latinidad and Its Others *John D. Ribó*	190
21	On Synthesis and Synthetic Reality: Post/Modernism in Flusser's Thinking *Rainer Guldin*	198
22	Fascism, Iconoclasm, and the Global Village *Guy Stevenson*	206
23	The Future of Writing *David Golumbia*	211
24	Vilém Flusser's Linguistic Briefcase *Tatjana Soldat-Jaffe*	221
25	The Depressed Person and the Vampire Squid: Sonic Gestures in the Work of Vilém Flusser and David Foster Wallace *Edward P. Comentale*	233
26	Cannibalistic Animals: Posthuman Natures in Flusser and Benjamin *Erick Felinto*	245
27	Flusser's New World *Aaron Jaffe*	255

Part III Flusser's Toolkit

28	Anti-Apparatus *Melody Jue*	269
29	Apparatus *Blake Stricklin*	272
30	Automation *Seb Franklin*	275
31	Cybernetics *Heather A. Love*	279
32	Dasein's Design *Chris Michaels*	283
33	Ecology *Derek Woods*	286
34	Ethics *Annie Lowe*	290
35	Etymology: Methodology as Adventure in the Bochum Lectures *Andrew Battaglia*	294
36	Surface and Simulation: Vilém Flusser and Jean Baudrillard *Thomas Tooley*	298
37	Technical Image: Opaque Apparatus of Programmed Significance *Anaïs Nony*	302
38	Writing *Andrew Pilsch*	305
39	Zetetic Maneuvers: Stalking the Continuum *Adelheid Mers*	309

Epilogue: Between Languages and Without Discipline: A Twentieth-Century Intellect Drafted for the Twenty-First Century *Siegfried Zielinski, Translated by Daniel Raschke*   314

List of Contributors   329
Index   336

Figures

3.1	Vilém Flusser during his talk on "Open Circuits—The Future of Television"	35
4.1	The panelists at the Philosophies of the New Technology symposium, Ars Electronica 1988	46
18.1	Drawn after still life by Pieter Claesz	174
23.1	Distracted boyfriend meme example by Reddit user dankiger	217
39.1	Flusserian diagrammatics	310

Acknowledgements

The annus horribilis 2020 was the centenary of Vilém Flusser's birth—2021 is the thirtieth anniversary of his death. Our hope is that this book—a documentation of vibrant intellectual friendships fostered over many years, community which became crucial during these trying times when almost all social interaction was reduced to the exchange of technical images—will be a suitable tribute to the complex inheritance of Flusser's potent ideas and the audacity of their perseverance for the futures of the humanities.

While working on this collection, we have incurred many debts to friends, colleagues, and family. Above all, we wish to thank our loved ones. Aaron wishes to thank Tatjana, Elias, and Zara. He would also like to thank Anica Soldat for the subscription to *Kunstforum*. Michael thanks Ashley and his parents, Patricia and David, for their continued support. Rodrigo would like to thank Becky, Esme, and his family for the encouragement. A book like this one is years in the making and particular thanks are owed to amazing students and colleagues at Florida State University, the University of Louisville, Rice University, Salem State University, the University of Georgia, and elsewhere around the world who have listened and responded enthusiastically to bits and pieces of the essays and ideas assembled here.

Many contributors to this collection have participated in and helped coordinate events in Louisville, Houston, Tallahassee, Amsterdam, and Berlin that were explicitly or implicitly Flusserian: Paleo-futurism, Retro-presentism, Thinking Media After Flusser, Bio-Eco-Media, Ersatzism, Flusser Club's Flusserian Centenary, the *thresholds* MSA workshop, and the Society for Critical Exchange. Particular gratitude is owed to Siegfried Zielinski and Daniel Irrgang, Judith Roof, Cary Wolfe, Farès el-Dahdah and Melissa Bailar (from Rice University Humanities Research Center), and Jeffrey Di Leo. We also appreciate the tireless efforts of Clint Wilson III, Annie Lowe, and Chris Michaels. Support for various Flusser-related events was generously provided by the Alexander von Humboldt foundation, the Goethe Institute, the Commonwealth Center for Humanities and Society (at the University of Louisville), the Literature-Media-Culture Program, the English Graduate Literature Organization, the Department of English, and the Department of Modern Languages and Linguistics at Florida State University.

Special thanks go to S. E. Gontarski, Paul Ardoin, and Laci Mattison for supporting this book's inclusion in their wonderful series and the assiduous editors at Bloomsbury Academic: Haaris Naqvi, Amy Martin, Rachel Moore, Morgan Jones, and the rest of the team, for their help during a very difficult year.

In addition to all of the contributors to this book, we are grateful to Cristina Iuli, John Gibson, Susan Griffin, Susan Ryan, Paul Griner, Adam Jolles, Andrew Epstein, Barry Faulk, Robin Goodman, Eric Walker, John Mac Kilgore, Rob Stilling, Trinyan

Mariano, David Johnson, Christina Parker-Flynn, Adam Robinson, Undine Löhfelm, Sam Bowles, Daniel Conrad, Seth Morton, Dan Purdy, Alex Bowen, Elijah Pritchett, Tracy Heightchew, Kristin Howell, Lynda Mercer, Michael Pons, Heather A. Love, Emily C. Bloom, Jeffrey T. Nealon, Robert Tally, James Dufoe, Emilie Mears, Margaret Mauk, David Potsubay, Grant Farred, Alan Golding, Tom Byers, Tom McCarthy, Mark Pietralunga, Polona Tratnik, Eva Batličková, Rodrigo Duarte, Patrick Greaney, Annie Goh, Steven Connor, Whitney Trettien, Christian Haines, Christopher Breu, Jeffrey DiLeo, Julian Murphet, Baruch Gottlieb, Steffi Winkler, Katerina Krtilova, Rudolph Glitz, Anita Jóri, Rebekah Sheldon, Ali Sperling, Doug Armato, Gustavo Bernardo Krause, Peter Hitchcock, Katy Price, Laura Richardson, Alexander B. Adkins, Andrew Battaglia, Els Woudstra, Annie Lowe, Paul Burch, Clint Wilson III, Brooke Clarke, and Kelly McKisson.

Introduction

Aaron Jaffe, Rodrigo Martini, Michael F. Miller

As media studies institutes sprouted up to jockey for external funding or to attend to demands from the media industry, Flusser remained the only one who thought. When they invited him to speak—far too often for someone who outsourced his life to the Autobahn—his first words reminded us that media studies, if it were to exist, would have to take the place that philosophy once held under apparently media-less, strictly alphabetical conditions. Since alphanumerical high technology, as he called it, has been able to calculate avalanches of numbers without having to say a single word, a place would have to remain open anyway, or remain because of it, which gives what is going on its proper name.

After fascism (in his eyes just another consequence of that avalanche of numbers) had exiled him to the edge of the calculable world, a messenger returned from Old Europe, from Central Europe, to measure the topicalities of today and tomorrow through four thousand years of historical memories. And see: It was only this confrontation of technology and learning that rendered both simple, understandable, and elegant. The youngest ears could hear what a prophet with flaming glasses and a gray beard saw in the gradual formation of thoughts as he spoke.

—Friedrich Kittler, "Farewell to Flusser"[1]

In a 1996 German documentary, Slavoj Žižek, the Slovenian cultural theorist, describes his first visit to Berkeley after the publication of his first English book, *The Sublime Object of Ideology*, in 1989. Some people there, he says, appeared surprised to learn that he actually existed.[2] That a sophisticated thinker could somehow materialize sui generis on the theory scene sounded like a practical joke perpetrated by esoteric French hoaxers on gullible American academics. It says something about the telematic society that a walking Sokal Hoax, a golem spouting forth postmodern gobbledygook, would appear more plausible than the actual, material facts of a CV, a career trajectory of a young thinker, and the complex maneuvering of reading materials and networks of reception and influence that led a person from classrooms in Ljubljana to seminars in Paris to Sproul Plaza. The event of Žižek as the appearance of a new name amid bibliographies, reading lists, and archives, then, means less that a cabalistic conspiracy was afoot—and maybe it was that, too—than that it functions as a certain reality test, a proof of signal strength that someone out there might really be listening for new signals.

The intellectual-as-stranger arrives precisely when he or she is thinkable for new audiences—this message is part of an automated feedback response of an unseen apparatus. Just as with Žižek, so too with Flusser. Only perhaps, it is even more so with Vilém Flusser (1920–91), the idiosyncratic, eclectic, seminal, polyglot, peripatetic, and prescient Czech-Brazilian philosopher, Vilém Flusser, who never secured a stable academic position and who only now, thirty years after his death and a century after his birth, is ready for his far too belated close-up.

What we have in mind with *Understanding Flusser, Understanding Modernism* is the problem of the event of Vilém Flusser. If Žižek designates a suspicious blip in the complicated reception history of French post-structuralism, Flusser might be called a prolonged origin myth conjured up for media-theoretical modernism—posthistorical thinking and theorizing after the media, to borrow the title from Siegfried Zielinski's tour of the horizon for a field that is not one.[3] Flusser designates the continuation of philosophically-minded theory after literary humanism—a zetetic zone on the continuum also known as the special constellation of considerations sometimes branded German Media Theory. German Media Theory is finally an unsatisfactory rubric for a variety of different and contested posthumanist pursuits by German-speaking intellectuals, which Geoffrey Winthrop-Young has called "at best a motley crew of media-theoretical paradigms," circling the belated emergence in the 1980s of *media* as a new "fuzzy object" of preoccupation and concern roughly analogous to the energies that British cultural studies practitioners vested in their already established, controlling keyword "culture."[4] Simply put, Flusser arrived on the scene when German Media Theory happened.[5] Minimally, he signals an alternate, belated reception horizon for the educational afterlives of nineteenth-century German philosophy, disrupted and modulated by the historical catastrophes of the twentieth century.

An exile's return, who fled the Nazis from Prague to London and then to São Paulo, and then fled the Brazilian military dictatorship back to Europe, provides cover for a very different encounter with the legacies of Nietzsche, Husserl, and Heidegger, supplemented by an autodidactical absorption of Darwin, cybernetics, McLuhan, and many other ideas, different in important ways from the encounters with continental philosophy supplied by French semioticians, structuralists, and their heirs. After his return to Old Europe in 1972, Flusser began to present work at conferences and art world symposia and began seeking out assorted venues for publication, first in France and later, more influentially, in the German-language contexts. In the 1960s, by contrast, he was presenting talks on the state of philosophy in Brazil to small audiences in language departments in US universities. By the late 1970s and 1980s, Flusser was attending symposia at exhibitions and sharing the plenum with the likes of Jean Baudrillard and the founders of *October*, among others. In other words, Flusser was in the mix both as Theory gained a cosmopolitan if fitful toehold in academia and the art world and as media and technology became a going theoretical and aesthetic concern, particularly in the German-speaking world.

The artist, curator, and new media theorist Peter Weibel met Flusser when he invited him to participate in a symposium at the Vienna Secession, where Flusser presented a lecture on photography and exchange value on October 23, 1981.[6] Weibel describes an immediate sense that Flusser arrived fully formed for media theory with an "unusual sensitivity and intuition" for recognizing the over-determination of the present by the future: "His thinking was a radar system, calibrated against the experiences of what is probably the most terrible century in human history, which by midnight of this age, completely overwhelmed by its technical inventions, knew how to construct the coordinates of the human, just by marking the end of the ideology of humanism."[7] For about a decade thereafter, Flusser became a fixture in the circuits of the German academic and art worlds—the life outsourced to the Autobahn, which Kittler mentions in the extract provided earlier. Generally speaking, his fascinating biography is never far removed from the rearview mirror of his work and its reception—a paratextual feature of literary self-presentation which he himself cultivated with deliberation and design. His unusual curriculum vitae plays an outsized role in many of the essays collected here as well.

Published shortly after Flusser's death in a car accident on November 11, 1991, as he was returning from a lecture in his birth city of Prague, the special issue of *Kunstforum* provides an important occasion for an initial stocktaking, an impromptu *festschrift*, and the contours of his subsequent reception. Set up on the model of *Artforum* (where Flusser found a reliable English outlet for his writings after 1986, collected in book form as *Artforum Essays*), *Kunstforum* provided an apt place for this initial assessment.[8] (Even though Flusser has some contact with the *October* group, it is altogether fitting that the English-language organ most amenable to Flusserianism has been the transnational periodical *Leonardo* with its art, science, and technology orientations and the general Pynchonian flavor of its founding by the rocket scientist Frank J. Malina.)[9]

In the special issue of *Kunstforum* commemorating Flusser, Norbert Bolz equates Flusser with the modernist hero Ulysses, astutely noting that Flusser recognized beyond the reach of technē. Facing such a hard epistemological impasse—"the closed circuit between people and images, which constitutes our media reality"—he nonetheless avoids "the culture-critical lament about the decay of criticism, but recognizes in it rather a threshold of epochs [between] the world age of literature from the world age of algorithms."[10] Likening him to an avant-gardist of a second modernity, Bolz eulogizes Flusser for leading "an expedition into the no man's land of the new media and technologies [towards a] new aesthetic, on the one hand, derived on the basic Greek word *aisthesis* (perception), and on the other hand, based on the epitome of the improbable—aesthetic form as the state of emergency in our entropic world":

> Flusser's aesthetic is affirmative in the precise sense that it understands art as the self-affirmation of human existence. Behind this is a fascinating anthropological scheme according to which existence is divided into work, communication, and ritual. It is in these forms that people manage their relationships with the world, with others and with themselves. Flusser understands ritual as an aesthetic form and art as a category of existence—the proximity to Nietzsche's physiology of art is unmistakable. Walter Benjamin advocates the thesis that the work of art was still based on ritual up to the threshold of its technical reproducibility. With Flusser's

media analysis of the high-tech present one could answer: the other way around, it becomes a shoe!—the ritual has always been a kind of art. Aesthetics thus advanced to become the controlling epistemological method of posthistory.[11]

In typical fashion, Flusser orients the posthistorical shift to programs and informatics in a longer temporal scheme, a point of emphasis already clearly pronounced in his Portuguese output from his time in Brazil. For Flusser, the quantal turn toward calculation, in other words, takes precedence over—and also conceptually ingests—the revolutionary implications typically ascribed to printing and navigation. As Adalberto Müller writes, Flusser's modernity registers two modernities, dual processes set in motion long before computers and the internet, undercutting the supposed newness of new media: first, the brute rejection of a "theoretical model of the Church, which proposes stable Forms for all things" by "new processes of 'manufacturing' [that] create incessantly new forms to new objects," and, second, "the victory . . . of the *res cogitans* over the *res extensa*." "Bill Gates and Steve Jobs," Müller observes, with an ironic flourish that Flusser would no doubt have appreciated, "are only making faster the work Descartes and Newton created in the XVII century."[12]

* * *

This book is the first collection of English essays to attend to understanding the event of Flusser by exploring the exchanges between philosophy and literary and cultural modernism in his thinking. Similar to Édouard Glissant or Gilles Deleuze, Flusser's work limns the theoretical insides and outsides of Eurocentric modernity by placing special emphasis on questions of (un- and self-) translatability and migrancy, while his investigations into art, technology, culture, representation, and abstraction inform his pronounced theses regarding the im/possibilities of thought, language, information, and communication. Flusser's work also engages and rethinks several mythologies of modernity, devising new methodologies, experimental literary practices, and expanded hermeneutics that trouble traditional practices of literary/literate knowledge, shared experience, reception, and communication. His corpus ranges from aspects of language, etymology, and translation, to historiography and nationalisms, to stratigraphy and meta-modernism, to media, technology, and science studies. Working within an expanded concept of modernism, Flusser presciently noted the power inherent in algorithmic information apparatuses to reshape our fundamental conceptions of culture and history. In an increasingly technological world, Flusser's form of experimental theory-fiction pits philosophy against cybernetics as it forces the category of "the human" to confront the inhuman world of animals and machines.

As a composer of major treatises, as well as numerous shorter essays in German, Portuguese, English, and French, he frequently revisited, rearticulated, and indeed rewrote his ideas in variant form in these languages. As Flusser's reputation has consolidated since his death, he has increasingly become recognized as a decisive past master in the emergence of contemporary media theory and media archeology, especially in the German context. Already influential in art, visual studies, and in some quarters of media studies globally, the rapid appearance of his works in English in recent years brings his highly original media theory to bear more broadly on Anglophone literary, cultural, and new media studies. The significance and novelty of Flusser's expanded concept of media thinking is that it bridges new media studies with theory after the linguistic and cultural turns.

Writing with few footnotes and often from the institutional fringes of academic and cultural life, Flusser's work bridges the great modernist thinkers from before the catastrophes of the Second World War (Kafka, Benjamin, Einstein, and Heidegger) and the French postmodernists of 1968 (Lacan, Baudrillard, Virilio). Additionally, it seems to ingest whole and to probe/critique from afar (to borrow again Flusser's figure of a telematic media ecology) key exemplars of mid-twentieth-century modern thought (Sartre, McLuhan, Shannon, Wiener), including the Frankfurt School. In his letters and his "traveling" library—with dialogical traces through his works—one also finds Arendt, Bachelard, Barthes, Beckett, Bloch, Borges, Brecht, Buber, Heisenberg, Jaspers, Kracauer, Popper, Pound, Wittgenstein, and Werfel, among others.[13]

Adapting Foucault's line about Sartre ("a man of the nineteenth century trying to think in the twentieth"), Flusser was a man of the twentieth century trying to think the twenty-first. A Jewish refugee fortunate enough to escape the Holocaust, Flusser wrote in Brazil about immigration and nationalism as an experiential insider to dislocations, distractions, and disruptions, always attentive to the affordances of technology and limit cases of language, translation, and the aesthetic. While teaching at the engineering college of the University of São Paulo early in his career, Flusser channeled these life experiences into a provocative linguistic treatise inspired by Whorf and Wittgenstein, *Língua e Realidade* (*Language and Reality*, 1963; English translation 2017), and a playful bestiary of nationalisms, *The History of the Devil* (1965; 2014). Wrestling with the legacies of Heidegger and McLuhan and spurred on by his obsessions with the philosophy of language and translation, Flusser embarked on an idiosyncratic synthesis of existentialism and cybernetics as he turned his focus to media theory, anticipating the impact information storage machines would have on the "telematic mind" and their effect on the global production and exchange of knowledge. His media theory, as developed in *Towards a Philosophy of Photography* (1983; 1984), *Into the Universe of Technical Images* (1985; 2011), and *Does Writing Have a Future?* (1987; 2011), presciently noted the power inherent in algorithmic information apparatuses and how they would reshape our fundamental conceptions of culture and history.

In a late interview, Flusser described biography as not a lifeline but a network diagram: "A biography cannot be about some sort of 'I.' And it seems to me that anyone who tries to describe his own life history has never lived. Rather, I think that a biography consists."[14] As Flusser's position in Brazil became increasingly precarious with the rise of the dictatorial regime in 1964, he immigrated once again in 1972, this time to France, where he sought new theoretical networks in which to consist. In his experimental works on nature after the media, *Natural:Mente* (1979; 2013), *Vampyroteuthis Infernalis* (1987; 2012), and in his collaborations with European visual artists such as Louis Bec, Fred Forest, and Joan Fontcuberta, he offers a view of media as an inhuman apparatus and asks: Do we control our technologies, history, and language, or do they control us? Flusser theorizes through the inhuman and places philosophical pressure on the epistemological limits of the "Cartesian subject." From another point of view, Flusser exposes the ways in which scientific objectivity becomes ersatz, highly dependent on the embodied gestural apparatuses that constitute the human body. In that sense, his work affirms the human, only to expose variant inhuman perspectives, projectivities, and individuations, as opposed to subjectivities.

Yet for all its posthumanist potential, at its core Flusser's oeuvre remains an extremely modernist endeavor in an expanded sense, which is to say an attenuated humanism. The poetic aspect of his theories—a writing style that Abraham Moles called philosophictions—attests to the modernist impetus in his works and the inspiration he received from writers such as Franz Kafka, Bertolt Brecht, Fernando Pessoa, Guimarães Rosa (about whom he wrote extensively), and others such as Ezra Pound, whose famous discussion of the ideogram prompted furious annotations of Flusser's own reading copy. In his later collaborations with visual artists, Flusser devoted his energy to more avant-garde and 'pataphysical projects such as the imaginary Institute Scientifique de Recherche Paranaturaliste (Scientific Institute for Paranaturalist Research) and the project Le Vivant et L'Artificiel (Living and the Artificial) which brought together several artists and thinkers (including Alain Badiou) to the Festival d'Avignon in 1984 where Flusser himself gave a keynote address.

Before his untimely death, Flusser's works turned toward aesthetic concerns in re-temporalizing the present in terms of what Charles Tung has termed "heterochronia," thus anticipating affect theory, animal studies, biopolitical thought, thing-theory, object-oriented ontology, and other contemporary theoretical developments. One of Flusser's recurring ideas is the arrival of forms of zero-dimensionality, which moves beyond facile image/text dualisms into an algorithmic world "of calculated and computed technical images, a world of discrete numbers, dots, bits, and pixels."[15] In the development of communication, humanity has gone through a gradual development from a situation of complete concrete experience of simple societies and animals into a one-dimensional world of linear writing. As Flusser asserts rather controversially, "writing made historical consciousness possible in the first place."[16] For Flusser, we have now entered a world of zero-dimensionality, where (a nowhere, in fact) even writing itself is no longer graspable, where the abstraction of thought has developed into technical images. In this new posthistorical stage, technical images now program our "being-in-the-world" and reshape—because images are not linear like writing—how we produce, consume, and process history.

The format of *Understanding Flusser, Understanding Modernism* crosscuts the wide range of Flusser's interests and the interconnected nature of his ideas and works. His intellectual preoccupations pull together the related fields of translation, history, philosophy of science, and visual studies—which are all united by Flusser's concept of language as the ultimate mediator and his lifelong concern with how media apparatuses have shaped cultural discourse around the production of our collective, historical knowledges. In keeping with Flusser's style of curiously short, sometimes experimental and aphoristic, provocations, many of the contributions, especially the contributions to the Flusser lexicon, have a provocative, para-academic, Flusserian spirit. Some are by Flusser specialists but many more by leading and emerging critics and theorists outside the Flusserian orbit. We are certainly not after Flusser hagiography. We have instead gathered contributions that open up a productive dialogue between modernist studies and media theory.

The chapters of Part I "process" Flusser's thought and unpack some of the critical issues in ("German") media theory for the neophyte while providing a deeper understanding of the stakes involved in his writing. Individual chapters engage with such foundational works as *Into the Universe of Technical Images* (1985; 2011), *Does Writing Have a Future* (1987; 2011), and *Post-History* (1983; 2013), all of which provide the clearest overview of Flusser's thinking on media theory, history, and writing. It also features analyses of works such as *Gestures* (1991; 2014), *Vampyroteuthis Infernalis* (1987; 2012), and *History of the Devil* (1965; 2014) that introduce Flusser's playful, poetic, and ironic method of thinking. Finally, Part I delves into works such as *The Freedom of the Migrant* (ed. 2003) and his intellectual autobiography *Bodenlos* (1992), which outline the relationship between Flusser's method and concepts of diaspora and identity.

Part II opens up Flusser's work in relation to modernism in the expanded sense, encompassing Flusser's philosophictions (his take on theory-fiction), his collaborations with European visual artists, as well as his relationship with and annotation of modern writers and artists. This section will also review the concept of modernism itself in light of Flusser's media theory. Like the special issue of a journal, this section allows experts in the field to explore the ramifications and limits of Vilém Flusser in the various disciplines he encounters.

Part III consists of a supplemental glossary of Flusser's key terms which takes the form of short essays written by specialists in his work. As independent works, each glossary entry resonates with and expands upon the longer essays in the first two parts. Building on Siegfried Zielinski, Peter Weibel, and Daniel Irrgang's *Flusseriana: An Intellectual Toolbox* (2015), the third part engages with the key terms and concepts from Flusser's oeuvre, as well as the historical and philosophical background of each term.[17] Drawing inspiration from Flusser's method of thinking that relied on creative and expansive etymologies, contributions to Part III reconfigure Flusser's key philosophical terms in new and creative ways.

Flusser embodied the maxim from Johann Wolfgang von Goethe: "*Wer fremde Sprachen nicht kennt, weiß nichts von seiner eigenen*" ("One who knows nothing about foreign languages knows nothing of his own").[18] Translation and existential multilingualism form a crucial axis of his language theories, his polyglot literary practice and linguistic play, and they are partly responsible for his fitful, belated, and uneven reception. Similar to his network model theory of biography, one consequence of the slow dispersion of his literary remains into multiple languages and disciplines is that the coexistence of multiple versions of Flusser makes it difficult to know which Flusserian lines string all the other nodes together: Is it the German Flusser, the Portuguese Flusser, the English Flusser, or the French Flusser? Or, does one emphasize Flusser the media thinker; Flusser the media-actor; Flusser the media-phenomenologist; the photography-theorist; the secular Jew; the inhumanist; the exobiologist; the speculative anthropologist, the speculative linguist; the posthistorian; the STS prophet; the wayward literatus; the expanded modernist; and so on? In effect, we believe that the "all-possible Flussers" hypothesis goes a long way toward providing the skeleton key for *Understanding Flusser, Understanding Modernism*.

Without a summa or a single philosophical statement, the closest we have to a gesture of overview from the man himself may be the Bochum lectures, yet to appear in English. In the summer of 1991, shortly before his death, Flusser gave a series of dynamic lectures as a guest professor at the Ruhr-University Bochum at the invitation of Friedrich Kittler, which were tape-recorded, transcribed, and reconstructed by Siegfried Zielinski and Silvia Wagnermeier. Here we have less Flusser-the-philosopher summing up, or zeroing out, and more Flusser-the-teacher, an ironical sage on a stage at the end of history attempting to model possibilities through lectures on "Communication Structures," "Phenomena of Human Communication," and "Communicology as Culture Critique." As Kittler put it, Flusser found a way for thinking about "technology and learning that rendered both [domains] simple, understandable, and elegant." The task is often to clarify the most obscure and obdurate implications of technology and modernity, but for all its pedagogical drive, contextual positionality, and anti-universalism, Flusserian thinking happens despite the limits imposed by national frontiers and traditional academic faculties and their assorted functionaries. Sitting outside university with students after their classes, lectures, and seminars, and lingering afterward in symposia, conference venues, and gallery receptions, Flusser the impossible autodidactic is a paragon of the academic precariat. The future may be Deleuzian, as Foucault says, but the long now is Flusserian. Siegfried Zielinski has been helping administer Flusser's complex *Nachlässe* for more than twenty years, first in Cologne and later in Berlin. Zielinski's epilogue, the final section of this book, seizes on the polyglot and post-disciplinary possibilities in Flusserianism for future thinking and experimental practices, moving profoundly—not ponderously—between languages and without the calcifications of academicism.

The unique format of *Understanding Flusser, Understanding Modernism* departs from other volumes on Flusser's work. Only two recent English-language texts engage with Flusser's thought as primary material in a sustained manner: Anke Finger, Rainer Guldin, and Gustavo Bernardo's *Vilém Flusser: An Introduction* (2011) and the aforementioned *Flusseriana*. Both books distill the Flusserian thought via definition essays, making the quixotic world of Flusser available to a new audience. However, no book in English introduces Flusser, and engages critically with his oeuvre exclusively, and frames him as a modernist thinker. Recent Anglophone media thinkers such as Dominic Pettman, Alexander Galloway, Rita Raley, John Durham Peters, Aaron Jaffe, and renée c. hoogland have engaged Flusser to produce critical works on modernism and contemporary culture. *Understanding Flusser, Understanding Modernism* fills a gap in our critical environment by providing a series of essays by leading scholars of critical and media theory who engage with Flusser's work within the milieu of modernist studies and contemporary critical theory.

* * *

Understanding Flusser, Understanding Modernism aims to orient for an Anglophone readership Flusser's relation to other seminal twentieth-century thinkers, tracking his respective contributions to media thinking and modernism. Flusser's heterodox ideas lend themselves to the comparative approaches assembled here that engage them in dialogue with other twentieth-century thinkers/theorists/scenes as well as contributions that put his work in conversation with figures and artifacts associated with modernism. Although "theory" and "modernism" are not explicit concepts in the Flusser lexicon per se, the aim of this book (in keeping with the series) is to investigate what is implicit in both: to initiate an expansive, multiperspectival investigation about the general and specific conditions for theory and the role it plays in mediating modernism and modernity.

To this end, we are approaching this book on Flusser to expose different takes on "epistemology and ontology, aesthetics, metaphysics, materialism, history, and being itself" (as the general series description puts it)—and all-important keywords in the Flusser lexicon—through sets of alternative genealogies and affinities that converge and diverge in suggestive ways. Our controlling idea is that Flusser operates in and as a kind of alternate universe of theory and modernism. The strange oscillations are felt, for instance, in his precarious institutional scaffoldings, peculiar archives and improbable forms of productivity and generativity; weird meditations on philosophy, religion, nationalism, and language; idiosyncratic—at once premature and belated—anti-disciplinary receptions of continental philosophy, cybernetics, science and technology studies, to name three, that stretch across his work.

Flusser's role as an important if contested node in the network of German Media Theory and art theoretical and curatorial practices clearly diverges from the generally "French" trajectory of what's become known—in the Anglophone world, chiefly—as "Theory." Flusser's exile in Brazil and his career and reception in South America contrast sharply from the North American success of the Frankfurt School, despite Flusser's own furtive efforts to engage the midcentury world of expatriate intellectual culture in the United States. Upon his "exile's return" to Europe in the 1970s, his reengaging with European artistic and intellectual scenes meant he also skirted by the edges of the structuralist controversies of 1968 and plunged headlong into subsequent debates about posthistory and postmodernism. As Mark Poster has suggested, "French" theory and Frankfurt School Critical Theory give short shrift to the materiality of the media ("theorists from the 1970s onwards—such as Foucault, Lacan, Lyotard, Deleuze, Derrida, and Habermas—either ignore media culture, or approach it only through other preoccupations such as critiques of capitalism or institutions of democracy"). Flusser's approach proceeds apace without McLuhanian techno-affirmation, Baudrillardian nihilism, or Habermasian fetishizations of consensus, and it aligns well with certain aspects of exciting emergent concerns such as new materialism, systems theory, and biotheory, formulating "a way of critically seeing the material qualities of the codes lying behind the apparatuses of the media."

We see *Understanding Flusser, Understanding Modernism* as a kind of two-way valve that puts pressure on theory and method, from one side, by engaging with Flusser's form of speculative media thinking and methodological experiment, and "modernism," from the other. With his distinctive manner of problematizing the aesthetic creatures/monsters of modernity, Flusser is an excellent match for a series committed to expanding conceptions of literary, cultural, and media thinking into the twenty-first century. In similar terms, he aligns very well with the series' pronounced investment in an expansive understanding of modernism that includes literature, philosophy, religion, visual and performing arts, as well as science and technology. The contributors to *Understanding Flusser, Understanding Modernism* engage with the multiplicity of Flusserian thought as they provide a general analysis of his work, engage in comparative readings with other philosophers, and offer expanded conceptualizations of modernism.

Notes

1 Editors' translation of Friedrich Kittler, "Flusser zum Abschied," "Beiträge zum Tode von Vilém Flusser," *Kunstforum* 117 (1992), https://www.kunstforum.de/artikel/flusser-zum-abschied.
2 "Liebe Dein Symptom wie Dich selbst! / Love Thy Symptom as Thyself," directed by Claudia Willke and Katharina Höcker, 2006.
3 Siegfried Zielinski, *[After the Media . . .]: News From the Slow Fading Twentieth Century* (Minneapolis: University of Minnesota Press, 2013).
4 See Geoffrey Winthrop-Young, "Cultural Studies and German Media Theory," in *New Cultural Studies*, ed. Gary Hall and Clare Birchall (Edinburgh: Edinburgh University Press, 2006), 89, and "Silicon Sociology, or, Two Kings on Hegel's Throne?: Kittler, Luhmann, and the Posthuman Merger of German Media Theory," *The Yale Journal of Criticism* 13, no. 2 (Fall 2000): 391–420.
5 See Eva Horn, "There Are No Media," *Grey Room* 29 (Winter 2008): 8; Michael Geisler, "From Building Blocks to Radical Constructivism: West German Media Theory since 1984," *New German Critique* 78 (1999): 75–107.
6 Personal correspondence.
7 Editors' translation of Peter Weibel, "Vilém Flusser: A Brave New Man for a Cruel Old World," "Beiträge zum Tode von Vilém Flusser," *Kunstforum* 117 (1992), https://www.kunstforum.de/artikel/Vilém-flusser-3.
8 Vilém Flusser, *Artforum Essays*, ed. Martha Schwendener (Minneapolis: Metaflux, 2017).
9 See the *Leonardo* masthead for more information about Malina.
10 Editors' translation of Norbert Bolz, "Ulysses Flusser," "Beiträge zum Tode von Vilém Flusser," *Kunstforum* 117 (1992), https://www.kunstforum.de/artikel/ulysses-flusser.
11 Ibid.
12 Adalberto Müller, "The Dark Side of the Digital: On Kittler and Flusser," presented at the Dark Side of the Digital Conference, 2013, Center for 21st Century Studies, University of Wisconsin, Milwaukee, https://www.academia.edu/3430148/THE_DARK_SIDE_OF_THE_DIGITAL_ON_KITTLER_AND_FLUSSER.
13 See Flusser's Traveling Library, indexed by the Flusser Archive, at https://s3.amazonaws.com/arena-attachments/185811/81ba2234aae3864e896fc055a5d8dcfa.pdf

14 Vilém Flusser, *The Freedom of the Migrant: Objections to Nationalism* (Champaign-Urbana: University of Illinois Press, 2003), 89.
15 Anke Finger, Rainer Guldin, and Gustavo Bernardo, *Vilém Flusser: An Introduction* (Minneapolis: University of Minnesota Press, 2011), 107.
16 Vilém Flusser, *Does Writing Have a Future?* (Minneapolis: University of Minnesota Press, 2011), 8.
17 Siegfried Zielinski, Peter Weibel, and Daniel Irrgang, eds., *Flusseriana: An Intellectual Toolbox* (Minneapolis: University of Minnesota Press, 2015).
18 Johann Wolfgang von Goethe, *Maximen und Reflexionen* (Berlin: Holzinger, 2016), 15.

Part I

Processing Flusser

1

"Does AI Have a Future?"

Rita Raley and Russell Samolsky

> We are beginning to build levers equipped with simulations of our nervous system (artificial intelligence).
> —Vilém Flusser, "Backlash" (unpublished essay)[1]

Introduction

We begin where Vilém Flusser, in a characteristically strong pronouncement, advises we should and that is with the "hectic character of what is under consideration"—in this case, the field of artificial intelligence (AI).[2] What could be more hectic now, as we enter the third decade of the new millennium, than a field marked by frenetic research activity with unpredictable consequences? What about this moment was Flusser able to foresee, and how might we understand his thinking about AI from the vantage point of our present? In opening with this double gesture, reading Flusser in his moment as well as our own, we follow another of his rhetorical moves: the invocation of the future critic.

In a chapter devoted to "the digital" that appears toward the end of *Does Writing Have a Future?*, Flusser delineates the contours of the new paradigm that has begun to "reshape our lives from the ground up": "One has only to recite the words *atomic power station, thermonuclear armaments, artificial intelligence, automation,* and *electronic information revolution*."[3] The ground-shaking consequence of this emergent paradigm, he goes on to say, is that "we have to grapple existentially with the new formulations daily and hourly. They have a practical orientation and open horizons of freedom and creative potential we had never suspected; on the other hand, they put our mental and physical endurance at risk."[4] For Flusser, the apparatus of the moment of his late writings (the 1980s) continually pitches us on the fraught existential double edge of undreamt creativity and risk. If the immense destructive potential of the apparatus is represented by thermonuclear armaments, the great creative potential is surely represented by the information revolution and the development of AI. Looking beyond the antipodes of this paradigm, however, we notice that he distinguishes between AI and automation as different elements of the new apparatus. While some scholars have taken up the problem of the automaton and automation in Flusser's corpus, the complicated and vital role of AI in his writings has not to our knowledge been sufficiently addressed.[5] This chapter offers one contribution to this larger critical project.

We propose, then, to begin to examine the "hectic" role of AI as it pertains to Flusser's oracular claims for the end of writing. And it is here that the meaning of our play on Flusser's title begins to emerge for, to adumbrate briefly, it will be an open question as to whether AI ushers in or destroys the historical future in his peculiar sense. Apart from our analysis of the place of AI in Flusser's writings, we shall as future critics—future critics, that is, not only from the perspective of Flusser but also as the categorical future critics he invokes—attempt to assess his prognostications in terms of the extraordinarily rapid development of unsupervised machine learning in our moment and the significance this might have for his thought in both our present and future. Our examination will include Flusser's articulation not only of the future critic, and, indeed, of the future reader, but also of computers as aliens, even as "Martians come to earth."[6] Such an analysis needs to grapple not only with his claim for the ending of one technical paradigm or code and the emergence of another but also with AI, social alienation, and the abyss.

AI in Flusser's Corpus

One of the more notable qualities of Flusser's writing is his oracular tone. He is not shy about prophesying the end of the alphabetic code and with it the end of history, nor does he shy away from pronouncing the rise of the wholly new paradigm of the technical image. However, he is not so much a prophet or modern-day Nostradamus as he is an archaeologist or analyst of codes. It is, for Flusser, because apparatuses or codes carry with them a consequent temporality that he is able to offer his pronouncements. Consider how he derives his analysis of the alphabetic code and the consequence of its development: first, by an etymological tracing of the myriad roots and cognates of "writing"; then by analysis of writing as a concrete object (engravings in clay tablets); and, last, by an archaeological unfolding of the mechanism and temporality immanent to the writing code. He speaks of writing as engraving or digging and his writing on writing is archaeological in the sense that it is also a digging of sorts. In his digging, he not only draws out the material elements of writing but also makes the alphabetic code itself a concrete entity that is imbued with a performative linear time. It is precisely because alphabetic writing unfolds in an orderly and linear fashion that it ushers the writing of history and historical consciousness into being. As he puts it, "History is a function of writing and the consciousness that expresses itself in writing."[7]

If the oracular quality of Flusser's writing derives from his historical analysis of codes leading to a certain future that itself can be marked in relation to those codes (mythic-alphabetic, traditional-technical), so too can his prescient vision of digital media be understood in the same terms.[8] That is, his work in the technical image trilogy in particular is to analyze codes of information that are determined by inevitable, scientific development and are still to run their course. While his analysis of the consequences of digital media is somewhat prognostic, then, what he is truly doing is tracing the unfolding of a teleological structure: just as writing inaugurated an historical consciousness, supplanting the mythic consciousness ("only one who writes lines can think logically, calculate, criticize, pursue knowledge, philosophize"[9]), so the rise of the technical image and AI will supersede the historical consciousness brought into being by writing and the alphabetic code. In this regard Flusser's analysis completes an evident pattern, and he is less prophetic than he is attentive and attuned to the immanent temporality or atemporality of emergent paradigms.

It is here, however, that we find a peculiar tension with regard to the function and potential of AI in Flusser's thinking. For, if on the one hand, it belongs to the paradigm of the alphabetic code and performs its writing-of-history duties with consummate dispatch, on the other hand, AI is precisely the exemplary programming machine that is not only illustrative of the rise of technical images but also performs a creative role in post-history. In what follows, then, we shall examine what lies behind this paradox and how it plays out in his late work.

The paradox is that AI straddles—belongs to and is exemplary of—both paradigms that Flusser articulates, the alphabetic code and the technical image. The same entity, the same apparatus, in other words, is at once a super-writing machine that will outperform and exceed the human, as well as the most advanced instrument of the regime of the technical image. AI is paradoxically exemplary, then, of two warring paradigms in a moment in which the technical image begins to supervene upon the alphabetic code. This tension can partly be worked through by tracing a fluctuation in his thinking on the question of whether AI is indeed intelligent and capable of creative activity or merely an accelerated automation of prescribed programs.

A core theme that runs throughout the texts that Flusser produced in the last decade of his life is the inevitable replacement of humans by AIs, whether named as apparatus, instrument, automata, or robot. The process may be protracted but as he suggests it is almost as if one can witness the dominoes falling in real time while humans stand by, helpless to stop the revolutionary forces that have been unleashed upon the world. "The computer appears to be slowly (and inexorably) taking over one human intellectual function after another," he observes, and in no short order computational devices will proceed from numerical computation to criticality and then to prediction, from past to future, running the gamut from "calculation, logical thinking, decision making, forecasting."[10] Humans are too slow to compete, particularly in the realm of numerical calculation, so while "these intelligences are stupider," they are nonetheless "far faster," capable of adding "with a speed that approaches that of light."[11] In his schema, calculation and forecasting are both to some degree stupid operations because they now belong to the "primitive and methodical" world of digital code, the "infantile binary system" that robs numbers of their mystique and renders them as "heaps that can be picked at."[12] The alphabetic code will not escape such debasement for letters too can be heaped and sorted, combined and permutated, by word processors. Writing, in short, can be made available for symbolic computation and writers, mere functionaries, "can be replaced by automatic apparatuses in the foreseeable future."[13] Thus does AI ("automatic apparatuses") promise to dislodge humans from their command post atop the heap of alphanumeric figures. The arc of history bends, incrementally yet inexorably, toward supersession: "we will in fact be replaced, step by step, by automata as producers and critics of information."[14]

We have seen where this replacement narrative leads: toward AI freeing humans from the work of writing history, taking over from the linear regime of alphabetic scripts that inaugurated and then sustained historical consciousness. The question is whether these AIs will only ever be able to write automatically and stupidly, rather than intentionally like humans—whether, that is, they are to be regarded as "supermen" or "subhuman, obdurate automata."[15] Flusser goes one step further to project that "these mechanical and automated things" will "all make better history than we do."[16] These artificially intelligent things will thus produce something like a supra-human historical consciousness: "They will possess a historical consciousness far superior to ours. They will make better, faster, and more varied history than we ever did."[17] At this point, humans will be free to "concentrate on something else"—"something else" here left undefined but pointing toward "open horizons of freedom and creative potential."[18] These automata, Flusser speculates, will themselves not lack generative and creative capacity. Indeed, some day we can expect "artificial intelligences that speak, presenting a continuous program of new poems."[19] These poems, like the technical images that will also be produced by AIs, will exceed the author and historical consciousness. AI, then, is both that which takes over the writing of history and the force that propels humans into the paradigm of the technical image, which in a temporal sense invokes a simultaneity, what Mark Poster terms "an all-at-onceness," that is also the destruction of the future in that it is outside of linear time and movement.[20]

AI and Alienation

We have thus far examined the paradox in Flusser's thought of the AI apparatus that straddles two contrary epistemic paradigms, but we might further explore this paradox with regard to alienation, another of his crucial themes. Indeed, fleeing Prague after the Nazi invasion, and suffering the loss of all he had known, including the murder of his family in the concentration camps, alienation became his essential, and existential, theme. Commenting on this utter privation, Andreas Ströhl remarks: "Flusser experienced the collapse of his world as if it were a catastrophe that tore him out of history. This feeling of vertigo and of a complete loss of orientation was not only the key experience of his life, but also the starting point of all his future thoughts and feelings. It became his essence."[21] To this overarching alienation of the self or soul, there are two further aspects of alienation that we can trace in Flusser's work particularly as they relate to the phenomenon of AI. The first is the alienation that results as machines displace humans from the field of labor, and the second is alienation from the alphabetic apparatus itself. In his essay *Exile and Creativity*, he refers to the *expelled*, those whom we commonly call refugees, but he extends his notion of expulsion to include "even the expulsion of humanists from the world of apparatuses.

We find ourselves in a period of expulsion. If one values this situation positively, the future will appear a little less dark."[22]

By the time of *Post-History*, the apparatus, both its programs and its programming, conjures up the threat of automatic processes at work in the realms of culture, politics, science, and everyday life. In his sketch of a paradigmatic postindustrial society, Flusser imagines homes, garages, and shops, all completely equipped with "intelligent instruments... that execute specific tasks" such as "cook dinners, cut grass, write letters, and assemble cars."[23] These autonomous robots, defined as "miniature" because of the specificity and singularity of their functions, are not only themselves apparatuses, but they operate within, and in service to, a "gigantic apparatus"—the specter of which, he implies, must necessarily cast doubt on the claim that these miniaturized instruments serve a "de-alienating" purpose.[24] "Wherever they install themselves," he notes, these instruments "transform the environment into an apparatus" within which the space of human decision is itself miniaturized.[25]

If intelligent machines are doing the work of preparing meals and tending gardens, if they are in the kitchen and on the automobile factory assembly line, if, as Flusser foresees, "robots can act and exchange," then it must necessarily be the case that "human beings will be shut out of the economy" as it had been constituted.[26] Anticipating the mechanical arms to come, those that today sort objects on the conveyer belt, pack boxes, and screw bolts, he describes the inevitable impact of automation on the industrial workplace: "Whatever can still be grasped and produced is done automatically by non-things, by programs: by 'artificial intelligences' and robotic machines. In such a situation, the human being has been emancipated from grasping and productive work; he has become unemployed."[27] While robots will deliver humans from the servitude of mechanical or industrial labor, they will not simply deliver us into the realm of a telematic utopia. And this is not, as might be supposed, because, if in the past workers were alienated from their labor, they will in the future be alienated from the absence of work itself, but rather because as Flusser, wryly playing on Heidegger, states, "robots cannot do our suffering for us."[28] The rise of the universe of telematic images will afford humans great leisure: "People will neither work nor make works, and in this sense, society will approach a Platonic utopia."[29] However, as the etymology of "utopia" (Greek: *ou topos*, not place) suggests, such a Platonic utopia, as ideal form, can only ever be Platonic. For what Flusser means by "robots cannot do our suffering for us" is not that robots cannot take on our suffering (they can) or that AI cannot do our thinking for us (it can), but that a contradiction lies at the very heart of a telematic utopia itself. As Flusser asserts: "Consciousness, to be consciousness at all, is an unhappy consciousness. If all pain were relieved, all suffering numbed, the economy would be superseded.... The Platonic social model, applied to telematics, shows that the Platonic utopia... hides an internal contradiction: there can be no happiness without suffering. Utopia is impossible."[30]

If a certain suffering ineluctably subtends the very being of consciousness itself, and if the telematic future will, happily, by means of unhappiness, not anesthetize us to this, the dangers of "robotization" and the rise of the telematic universe need still to be underscored.[31] For the threat remains that we may well succumb, if not wholly, then largely, to the utopia of the telematic by becoming in a sense robots, instruments and functionaries of "programs that are alien to [us]."[32] The danger is that we will simply be programmed by post-history and become scheduled and habituated beings. But if the program poses the risk of our becoming alienated from ourselves, it is also possessed of de-alienating or defamiliarizing powers. It is with regard to this capacity for defamiliarization that Flusser conjures up an image of computers as "Martians come to earth" so as to imagine a position outside the code of writing.[33] (How better to communicate the experience of not being at home inside of language than to summon the Martian, as he does elsewhere when describing the "*un-settling*" of habituated, automated perspective, the seeing of one's hand as "an octopus-like monstrosity" through the eyes of an alien being?[34]) The regime of the technical image and the computational apparatus threatens to unground humans from all that has been implanted, even programmed, within us by the code of writing—not just historical consciousness but critical capacity and indeed written culture. Flusser's prescient fear about what the loss of writing would entail is nowhere as succinctly expressed than in his evocative, dystopic vision of humans as unthinking receptacles of all the communicative detritus to come, everything from advertising and political slogans to academic arguments: "We fear that in the future, all messages, especially models of perception and experience, will be taken in uncritically, that the informatic revolution could turn people into receivers who remix messages uncritically, that is, into robots."[35] (Ströhl's translation of these future humans as "uncritical mutant addressees" is more biting, particularly when read in terms of our present moment of disinformation.[36])

AI and the Future Reader

For all its great stores of data and its capacity for memory, it is AI that for Flusser bestows the Nietzschean lesson that some forgetting is necessary. "One advantage of artificial intelligences," he claims, "is that they have no difficulty forgetting. From them, we are learning the importance of forgetting."[37] What is crucial in this context about forgetting is that it clears a path for humans to more fully embrace an already emergent posthistory, the receding of the alphabetic code, and the history of culture it carried with it. Flusser is not without sadness for this loss—his was, after all, a life suffused with loss—but it is neither a nothingness nor a darkness, he thinks, on which one should dwell. He does not embrace the Enlightenment myth of unimpeded progress, but he does embrace the freedom, creativity, and ethical dialogue with others that posthistory promises.

As we have seen, Flusser was prescient with regard to the automation of writing, but so too did he anticipate advances in machine reading. Although he observed that AIs were as yet "too stupid (perhaps only for the time being)" to be able to decode letters, nonetheless, we can see in his notion of a "programmable" literature, one that takes "all literature back to instructions so as then to be computed by artificial intelligences," the seeds of what would become text analysis, topic modeling, and other digital humanities practices of reading.[38] At the end of *Does Writing Have a Future?* Flusser imagines the future reader sitting before a screen, accessing networks of information from something like what we now call the Internet: "It is the reader himself who actually produces the intended information from the stored information elements. To produce the information, the reader has various methods of access available, which are suggested to him by artificial intelligence . . . but he can also apply his own criteria."[39] What is crucially retained, even emphasized, in this scene is the capacity of humans to make their own decisions, to use their "own criteria." This future reader will be able to exercise the freedom to access some "bits" of historical information rather than others but, Flusser notes,

> the history that comes from such a reading is precisely not what we mean by "history." Historical consciousness—this awareness of being immersed in a dramatic and irreversible flow of time—has vanished from the future reader. He is above it, able to access his own flow of time. He doesn't read along a line but rather spins his own nets.[40]

We had left open the question of whether AI destroys the historical future and here Flusser offers us a partial answer: the future reader, in concert with AIs, draws upon a different temporality, not the linear order of history, but one that is networked and has itself been made possible by the apparatuses of the technical image. There is though a second register to our title, the future of AI itself. What is clearly of importance for Flusser is the creative, ethical dialogue between humans, a dialogue that becomes all the more possible in the space and time opened up by AIs. In this regard, he points toward a complicated reckoning (OE: *(ge)recenian*, recount; German: *rechnen*, to count up) with that which is already upon us and that which is to come. Particularly in his later writings, he takes account of an AI modeled after human cognition. What remains to be more fully thought out in his schema, however, is the possibility of a creative, ethical dialogue between humans and AIs. What then will our future readers have to say about this moment? Will unsupervised machine learning become a sinister instrument of biopolitical control, or will its future be more affirmative and its story one of contribution to the species and the planet itself? As Flusser writes of "Our School," "both virtualities are in the program," and it remains to be seen which is realized.[41]

Notes

1. Flusser, *Artforum // Essays*, ed. Martha Schwendener (São Paulo: Metaflux, 2017), 286.
2. Flusser, *Does Writing Have a Future?*, trans. Nancy Ann Roth (Minneapolis: University of Minnesota Press, 2011), 19.
3. Ibid., 141.
4. Ibid., 141–2.
5. See Vasileio Galanos, "Floridi/Flusser: Parallel Lives in Hyper/Posthistory," in *Computing and Philosophy: Selected Papers from IACAP*, ed. V. C. Müller (Cham: Springer International Publishing, 2014), 229–43; Baruch Gottlieb, "To Save

Philosophy in a Universe of Technical Images," *Flusser Studies* 22, no. 2 (December 2016), http://www.flusserstudies.net/node/616; and Roland Meyer, "Automaton," in *Flusseriana: An Intellectual Toolbox*, ed. Siegfried Zielinski, Peter Weibel, and Daniel Irrgang (Minneapolis: Univocal, 2015), 72–3.

6   Flusser, *Does Writing Have a Future?*, 88.
7   Ibid., 8.
8   Mark Poster makes the case for Flusser as a vanguard media theorist in his introduction to *Into the Universe of Technical Images*, trans. Nancy Ann Roth (Minneapolis: University of Minnesota Press, 2011) and *Does Writing Have a Future?*
9   Flusser, *Does Writing Have a Future?*, 7.
10 Ibid., 26.
11 Ibid., 27.
12 Ibid., 26, 27.
13 Ibid., 42.
14 Flusser, *Into the Universe of Technical Images*, 122.
15 Ibid., 75.
16 Flusser, *Does Writing Have a Future?*, 8.
17 Ibid.
18 Ibid., 9, 141–2.
19 Ibid., 76.
20 Ibid., xvi.
21 Andreas Ströhl, "Introduction," in Flusser, *Writings*, trans. Erik Eisel (Minneapolis: University of Minnesota Press, 2002), xix.
22 Ibid., 105.
23 Flusser, *Post-History*, trans. Rodrigo Maltez Novaes (Minneapolis: University of Minnesota Press, 2013), 76.
24 Ibid., 77.
25 Ibid.
26 Flusser, *Into the Universe of Technical Images*, 145.
27 Flusser, *The Shape of Things: A Philosophy of Design*, trans. Anthony Mathews (London: Reaktion Books, 1999), 91.
28 Flusser, *Into the Universe of Technical Images*, 145.
29 Ibid., 148.
30 Ibid., 145.
31 Flusser, *Post-History*, 10, 127, 149.
32 Flusser, "On Program," quoted in *Post-History*, ix.
33 Flusser, *Does Writing Have a Future?*, 88.
34 Flusser, *Writings*, 105.
35 Flusser, *Does Writing Have a Future?*, 77.
36 Flusser, *Writings*, xxviii.
37 Flusser, *Does Writing Have a Future?*, 149.
38 Ibid., 55, 60.
39 Ibid., 153.
40 Ibid., 154.
41 Flusser, *Post-History*, 149.

2

Design/Shape

Anke K. Finger

In his seminal essay on the word "design," Vilém Flusser, taking disposable plastic pens as his example, evokes Friedrich Nietzsche's famous battle cry of modernism, the transvaluation of all values, when he calls our attention to the ephemerality and finitude of design products by posing the following question: "How can we explain this devaluation of all values?"[1] Plastic pens, in essence representing a victory of science and ingenuity, face the reality of a short shelf life as they are mass-produced, ubiquitous, unsustainable because un-refillable, and easily disposed of. Their low to non-existent value, according to Flusser, reflects on the designer who, by Flusser's etymological distillation, is a charlatan, a trickster. The word "design," he argues, helps us realize "that all culture is trickery, that we are tricksters tricked, and that any involvement [Engagement] with culture is the same thing as self-deception."[2] He wonders: "Who and what are we deceiving when we become involved with culture (with art, with technology—in short, with Design)?"[3] Design as a concept, a process, and—given its result—as an object, has a firm place within Flusser scholarship, and I am not contributing here to the variety of discourses long in place about Flusser's different perspectives on the topic or its many appearances in his manifold oeuvre.[4] His writings on design have been embraced by numerous fields, including design studies and theory. They found their place in foundational syllabi, and they contribute substantially to disciplinary and interdisciplinary conversations and definitional landscaping. As Claudia Mareis, in her introductory chapter on the history of the design concept, has emphasized, the "limits of what is to be demarcated by design, draft/design [*Entwurf*] or composition/design [*Gestaltung*], remains subject to virulent social and cultural debate."[5] For Mareis, Flusser's essay on "design," especially his proposition of design as a bridge between art and technology, is an ideational glue for, say, the engineers and the creatives who must face the choice to frame the future: "Flusser's statement makes us profoundly aware of the 'synthesis' motif which presents a particularly productive idea for theories of design."[6] For such synthesis to happen, Mareis concludes, design research "must hazard and bear the risk of true interdisciplinary collaboration."[7] To successfully execute collaboration, with its origin in the medieval Bauhütte and with its radically modern version pursued by the Bauhaus, still remains design's idealized idea of humans thinking, working, and believing together—think of Gropius's Cathedral.

Flusser, in contrast, ends his own essay in proper Flusserian fashion, miming the trickster he himself invokes:

> A confession is called for here. This essay had a specific design in mind: It set out to expose the cunning and deceptive aspects of the word *design*. [. . .] If it had pursued another design [. . .] it would have given a different, but equally plausible, explanation of the word's contemporary situation. That's the answer, then: Everything depends on Design.[8]

With what may be flippantly designated as a cop-out, Flusser performs an oft-practiced about-face, potentially undermining, or at least questioning, the aforesaid to the point of perplexing, even alienating, his reader. This is by design. For design, in the best of its many modernist applications, is not only a material and technical enterprise and endeavor, it is political and cultural in its practical and theoretical engagement. It is design anthropology.

In the following, then, I wish to invert my own role in this contribution to Flusser scholarship by prioritizing the scholar of modernism and placing second my previous work on Flusser. For Flusser initially philosophizes about design from one vantage point, I argue, and one vantage point only: language. Such a statement may surprise at first, not only for its apparent obviousness—of course Flusser uses language to write about design/ Entwurf/Gestaltung—but because the tool may not necessarily affect the form, let alone the content. Language, after all, and in this context, is a means, not a design as such, or at least secondary for establishing theories and discourses that usually focus on concepts, objects, and materials of a different nature. His concept of design, however, emerges from a deep understanding of the classical modernist's skepticism of language as a comprehensible, unified representation of the world, and—as Flusser's most passionate tool for designing his own worlds of thought—it is language that represents his closest equivalent to the material designers use themselves to create deceptive worlds and to trick others. Design, to Flusser, presents no less than what language came to present to writers like Hofmannsthal, who, almost as famously as Nietzsche, bemoaned the catastrophic loss of meaning in his Chandos letter from 1902 and described how language falls apart:

> I have lost completely the ability to think or to speak of anything coherently. [. . .] As once, through a magnifying glass, I had seen a piece of skin on my little finger look like a field full of holes and furrows, so I now perceived human beings and their actions. I no longer succeeded in comprehending them with the simplifying eye of habit. For me everything disintegrated into parts, those parts again into parts; no longer would anything let itself be encompassed by one idea. Single words floated round me; they congealed into eyes which stared at me and into which I was forced to stare back-whirlpools which gave me vertigo and, reeling incessantly, led into the void.[9]

The voids, everything disintegrating into parts, are processes lodged within existential questions only too familiar to Flusser himself. Such voids were present early on in Brazil, following his escape from Prague, with his continued suicidality, and while acclimating himself to cultural contexts radically divergent from his adolescent environment. There is an existential connection between design and language, I propose from my perspective as a reader of modernism, and if we wish to engage with Flusser's thinking on design we should consult first his short essay "Auf der Suche nach Bedeutung," published in German in Brazil in 1975. Here, he recalls not only the vast significance of Nietzsche but also the fundamental meaning of language for the process and progress of self-design: "I am only real when I speak, write, read or when it [language] whispers within me to be expressed." To Flusser, language is "my repertoire and my structure, my game, model of all my models, [. . .] my involvement [Engagement]. [. . .] And—perhaps—also the form through which I lose myself."[10]

Contrary to design, language, for Flusser, is the last vestige left over from modernism, in defiance of the industrial design of death in Auschwitz, laboriously hauled across vast and gaping cultural chasms and into that vertigo created by the Second World War. With language (re)claimed, design, of objects and life, becomes part of the reconstitution mission, albeit not for the sake of style, invention, and technology that played central roles in the modernist understanding of design but for the purpose of seeking a "new human," for a new anthropology of design that, soon enough in Flusser's thought, also included design of and for the posthuman.

There is no need to address the simultaneously fanatic and thrilling ideologies of modernism, specifically of modernist design, by revisiting all the classic manifestos that promised newness for the future. Modernist design, for the masses and couture, by the early twentieth century, had swept into homes, households, and kitchens, touched and reshaped everyday objects, and reinvented how modern societies went about an accelerated life. They were thus buoyed—but also sent into fits of anxiety, as described in Simmel's 1903 essay—by rapid developments in technology and material science. As expertly discussed in Michael Hanke's "Vilém Flusser's Philosophy of Design" (2016), Flusser himself stood at the end of a repeated revivification of a legendary and storied Bauhaus when he delivered his "Gebrauchsgegenstände" [Objects of Use] in 1988 at the inaugural conference of the "International Forum for Design" in Ulm, a new iteration of the legendary Ulm "School of Design" which itself continued to grow from the Bauhaus seeds.[11]

What is noteworthy in Flusser's thoughts about design in this essay on "Gebrauchsgegenstände" is his explicit critique of design as an all-too-voluntary host of unquestioned teleology in the faithful continuation of modernism.[12] Influenced by Heideggerian notions of the object, Flusser's "Gegenstände" are literally "resistances," a "standing against." They are objects designed to obstruct, they are distinctly in the way, they block and resist. "*Gebrauchs*gegenstände," however, present a different ontology: they are objects of use that, by design, mediate between people, between you and me, they are media. They are supposed to initiate communication, exchange, dialog. More significantly, such objects of use are to be designed with communication, dialog, and intersubjectivity already in mind, demanding a rather acute sense of responsibility from the designer who is to think of the users before the engagement with design ("design thinking" as a concept was already in circulation at the time). Flusser, in fact, places the object of use not just between people to function as a medium, at the behest of a responsible designer; he places the object of use, the "Gebrauchsgegenstand" at a politicized center, a middle, a medium, between the "scientific and technological progress" of modernism and a "present cultural situation" that, as of yet, deems responsible design as backward. A pivotal question presents itself: Why is modernism, the unbroken faith in innovation, technology, and science, continuing to have such a stronghold on design, in Flusser's estimate? Why is it still the design ideology of choice? As presented in his essay, his hope manifests itself in the onset of immaterial objects of use, such as computer programs, and the objects' disappearance into oblivion by becoming trash, just like the plastic pens. His wish is for a culture within which objects of use obstruct less and mediate more—"a culture with a bit more freedom."

In the interest of approaching Flusser's philosophy of design from the vantage point of modernism, I propose a new trajectory: from Heidegger via Sigfried Giedion (a friend and collaborator of Gropius's) towards Bruno Latour. More precisely, Flusser, in most of his texts on design and designing as a process and as a project, addresses what amounts to the narrative of incomplete modernization that Heidegger tackles, Giedion initiates, Fredric Jameson describes—"what we call artistic or aesthetic 'modernism' essentially corresponds to a situation of incomplete modernization"—and what Latour reestablishes in his 2008 essay on his own philosophy of design.[13] The restrictions of my contribution here prevent a larger discussion of central philosophical concepts at the core of this issue in modernism and design—"Gegenstand" and "Ding"—in Latour's words, "matters of fact" and "matters of concern."[14] If we begin to position Flusser's thought on design through that lens, however, by beginning to engage "Gegenstand" as a "matter of fact," two other essays in the 1999 *The Shape of Things*, "The Submarine" and "The Factory," turn out to add substantially to an understanding of Flusser's thoughts on design and shape. Both essays will show that comparable to Latour's design philosophy, Flusser seeks to find synergy between both "matter of fact" and "matter of concern" in order to overcome the continued preeminence of a dehumanized modernism in design as a practice. For at the center of his design philosophy stands the human being as a project; the problem to be faced, in 1988 and surely before and most definitely thereafter, is how to de-singularize modernism, to take Jameson's notion, or to de-totalitarianize a perpetuity of modernism that remains within a particular political and scientific practice.

Giedion's investigation of "an anonymous history" in his 1948 *Mechanization Takes Command* begins with a remarkably Flusserian statement: "Tools and objects are outgrowths of fundamental attitudes to the world. These attitudes set the course followed by thought and action."[15] As if Flusser had Giedion in mind, in "The Factory" he suggests that we look at human history as a history of fabrication or manufacturing and designates periods based on objects: "hands, tools, machines, apparatuses/robots."[16] These objects become subjects and are joined by verbs: "purloin/entwenden, turn/umwenden, apply/anwenden, use/verwenden" such that "wenden" takes an all-encompassing "turn" or "turning" that facilitates the metamorphoses from nature to art toward mechanization and modernization with design: "Manufacturing means turning what is available in the environment to one's own advantage, turning it into something manufactured, turning it over to use and thus turning it in to account." Since, by Flusser's definition, design should embody a medium and thereby an intersubjective mutuality, factories manufacture both objects and human subjects in their environmental contingency. Human history then becomes the history of novel human types for Flusser, an evolution toward *Homo faber*: "the hand-man, then the tool-man, then the machine-man, and finally the robot-man." Complexity arrives with abstraction, however, and Flusser has little faith in a projected "immaterialization of the factory" that requires life-long learning from *Homo faber*. His dream is of a "factory of the future" in which to fabricate includes concrete and abstract creation, in the best of both senses of "fabrizieren": to make and to concoct.

Making and concocting lead to the doom of "The Submarine," a text signaling more of a Flusserian philosofiction than an essay and befitting one of the scenarios available in Flusser's film script, *Supposed/Angenommen* (2000). The submersible, an underwater-travel design emerging from the nineteenth century (with propulsion) to become the ultimate expression of modernist warfare in the First World War, presents a Flusserian imagination gone awry because it represents a nineteenth-century dream that turns into a twentieth-century nightmare. It functions as a lab for seventeen scientists, artists, and theologians who leave society for an experiment to rule the world and anchor on the bottom of the Pacific Ocean ("near the Philippines") to "enforce the military and intellectual disarmament of humanity."[17] To be brief, totalitarianism does not succeed. They fail because they set out to realize utopian ideals based on logic and control—from the narrator's perspective several hundred years prior to writing this story—not because the materials did not obey or hold up but because the people do not. Everyone turns against them. The author argues that the experimenters failed because they refused, deluded, to see an object for what it was: twentieth-century humans living in a dream world where the common "walking cane presented an electromagnetic field or a cultural product or a fabrication or a sexual symbol or a thing proving being (Dasein), in short, within which it presented everything: except a cane." According to the narrator, at the end of such a dream, or nightmare, and upon awakening, lies reality. But, he acknowledges, the experimenters valiantly sought to "merge faith, knowledge, and art" for the first time since the Middle Ages, while, in their "ephemeral world domination from within the submarine," they inadvertently missed considering the human factor.

If Flusser evokes submersibles, Latour, fittingly, conjures up dirigibles. In his "philosophy of design," he, too, describes modernists, leaning hard on Peter Sloterdijk, as living under a dome, in seclusion, away from reality, and taking for granted the world's natural resources. The powers needed for such inflation are significant, and Latour's image or metaphor compares modernism's trajectory to the brief existence of the Zeppelin or the Hindenburg. Latour accounts for five "advantages" of design: modesty, detail, meaning, redesign, and good versus bad or moral aspects of design. While each contributes to a rewriting of modernism as the guidepost for design as a practice, broadening and deepening the "spread" of design, a concept, an approach, and even an atmosphere, his focus is on the "collective life on earth" that calls for a radical, even revolutionary, redesign, in treacherous times. Latour enumerates his own "attitudes," using Giedion's term, even if they are "hard to come by: modesty, care, precautions, skills, crafts, meanings, attention to details, careful conservations, redesign, artificiality, and ever shifting transitory fashions."[18] His call, echoing Flusser to a degree, is for tools that, in Flusser's design philosophy, operate within the environment of robot/apparatus-man, tools that turn and fabricate creatively such that they uncover hidden meanings and open up new worlds: "what is needed [...] are tools that capture what have always been hidden practices of modernist innovations: objects have always been projects; matters of fact have always been matters of concern."[19]

Such tools, I suggest, also belong to the collective environment Flusser anticipates for the human as future project. How, then, do the disposable plastic pen and the common walking cane figure into this? What of the factory of the future, what of culture as trickery, what of the devaluation of all values? Flusser's philosophy of design presents, on the background of design in modernism as the most purist, or extremist, expression in Western design history, an anthropological critique of art at the mercy of logic in science and technology. Lost within is the human being determined by its environmental contingencies, whereby, in good McLuhan tradition, we can think of the pen and the cane as bodily extensions, as design enhancements—but where we really should think of them as obstructions of our communication with a much larger design, namely the disappearing world around us. That factory of the future Flusser envisions? It may be his dream for humanity to design precisely those objects as projects, keeping in mind matters as concerns, and to make sure our "attitudes" turn toward tools with which to design value for all creatures, not pens that end in landfill or canes that figure as crutches for nightmares.

Notes

1. Flusser, *The Shape of Things: A Philosophy of Design*, trans. Anthony Mathews (London: Reaktion Books, 1999), 21.
2. Ibid.
3. Ibid., 19.
4. See Christian Gänshirt, *Tools for Ideas: An Introduction to Architectural Design* (Basel: Birkhäuser, 2007). There are several articles on Flusser's idea of design in *Flusser Studies*; Chadwick T. Smith has written expertly about "The Butterfly and the Potato ~ Vilém Flusser on Design" in a 2009 issue of *artUS*, and one of the most recent contributions on the topic is by Raquel Dastre Manzanares, Ricardo Portilho Mattos, and Rita de Castro Engler in a presentation entitled "Vilém Flusser e Bruno Latour: duas abordagens à filosofia do design," presented at the Colóquio Internacional de Design in 2017 (available in PDF). Since Flusser's texts on and references about designing and drafting span his entire oeuvre in several languages (including *The Shape of Things*, *Vom Subjekt zum Projekt*, *Gesten*, *The History of the Devil*, to name but a few), a comprehensive bibliography would benefit the reader who is specifically interested in this area of Flusser's thought.
5. Claudia Mareis, *Theorien des Designs zur Einführung* (Hamburg: Junius, 2014), 61.
6. Ibid., 62.

7   Ibid., 63.
8   Flusser, *The Shape of Things*, 21.
9   Hugo von Hofmannsthal, *The Lord Chandos Letter and Other Writings* (New York: New York Review of Books, 2005), 121.
10 Author's translation, Flusser, "Auf der Suche nach Bedeutung," in *Tendenz der aktuellen Philosophie in Brasilien in Selbstbildnissen* (São Paulo: Loyola, 1975), 5. Compare Flusser, "In Search of Meaning (Philosophical Self-portrait)," in *Writings*, ed. Andreas Ströhl and trans. Erik Eisel (Minnesota: University of Minnesota Press, 2002), 197–208.
11 Michael Hanke, "Vilém Flusser's Philosophy of Design: Sketching the Outlines and Mapping the Sources," *Flusser Studies* 21 (June 2016): 1–26.
12 Flusser, "Gebrauchsgegenstände," originally written for a 1988 congress in Ulm, then published as one of ten essays in the journal *Design Report*; published in English as "Design: Obstacle for/to the Removal of Obstacles" in *The Shape of Things: A Philosophy of Design*, ed. Martin Pawley (London: Reaktion Books, 1999), 58–61.
13 Fredric Jameson, *Postmodernism, or, the Cultural Logic of Late Capitalism* (Durham: Duke University Press, 1991), 310.
14 See Bruno Latour, "Why Has Critique Run Out of Steam? From Matters of Fact to Matters of Concern," *Critical Inquiry* 30 (Winter 2004): 225–48.
15 Sigfried Giedion, *Mechanization Takes Command* (New York: W.W. Norton, 1948), 3.
16 Flusser, *The Shape of Things*, 69.
17 Ibid., 62.
18 Latour, "A Cautious Prometheus? A Few Steps Toward a Philosophy of Design (with Special Attention to Peter Sloterdijk)," keynote lecture for the *Networks of Design* meeting of the Design History Society Falmouth, Cornwall, September 3, 2008, accessed March 15, 2020, http://www.bruno-latour.fr/sites/default/files/112-DESIGN-CORNWALL-GB.pdf.
19 Ibid.

3

Vilém Flusser in Open Circuits
The Dialogic Capacity of Video Images

Daniel Irrgang[1]

I mean the mandalas of feedback, in whose graphically diagrammed illusion of alternating thrust and withdrawal, most often spiraling ambiguously like a pun of Duchamp, video confirms, finally, a generic eroticism.

Hollis Frampton, "Open Circuits," 1974[2]

Video, both as a specific form of technical image and as cultural technique, plays a pivotal role in Vilém Flusser's oeuvre. According the Flusser's definition, technical images have the potential not just to reproduce phenomena in the world but to "project" by means of technical apparatuses new ideas and abstract models into the visual domain. As technical *moving* images, video combines the "linear" logic of text or narration—the time axis—with the "synchronous" capacity of images to show ideas at a glance. This combination of linearity and synchronicity as specific characteristics of video, and film as well, is the main thesis of Flusser's 1973 paper "Line and Surface,"[3] which turned out to be central not only for his later media theoretical works in the 1980s but also for biographical reasons. The relatively broad reception of this paper in the United States earned Flusser an invitation to the now famous conference "Open Circuits—The Future of Television" at the MoMA in 1974. There he got in touch with various actors in arts, theory, and activism, experimenting with the liberating potential of the new video technology to provide an alternative to mass media's monopoly in the production and distribution of electronic images.

Flusser might be most famous for his book *Towards a Philosophy of Photography*.[4] However, he revealed in a letter to the Swiss cultural theorist Felix Philipp Ingold that this book "came about at the behest of European Photography [the publishing house]; otherwise I would rather have taken the video image, with its dialogic virtualities, as a model of a feature of the apparatus."[5] In this short investigation, I will show that Flusser's conception of video was determined by his contact to and collaboration with artists, activists, and theorists of video, mainly in the 1970s.

In 1972, Vilém Flusser and his wife Edith left São Paulo, which had become their home after the forced migration from Prague in 1939 and odyssey years in London and Rio de Janeiro, and returned to Europe.[6] At the time a member of the organizational team of the 12th São Paulo Art Biennial, Flusser established relations with various European artists who shared his vision of a "communicological"[7] redefinition of art exhibitions. In a letter to one of them, the video and performance artist Fred Forest, Flusser described his conviction "that it is not the arts themselves, but their communication to the broad public which are in a crisis. We shall therefore try to shift the emphasis from works to group effort, and from exhibition to laboratory, and thus motivate the public to active reaction."[8]

Flusser's plea for a socially engaged art was not new at the time. It had already been discussed and practiced by Fluxus artists such as Wolf Vostell and Joseph Beuys, and by video activist groups like Ant Farm and Raindance Corporation—or the French group "Art Sociologique," formed by Forest along with Hervé Fischer and Jean-Paul Thenot.[9] Flusser, however, developed his claim for participatory art as a unique mix of theory building and close observation of, and even collaboration with, artists who worked with the ideas he had in mind. Here, Forest was certainly one of Flusser's most important reference points. Among other projects, the thinker and the practitioner of the video image realized works such as "Les gestes du professeur" (1974), part of the video study series "Les gestes dans les professions et la vie sociale" (1972–4), featuring Flusser as the improvising, philosophy-talking protagonist in a quasi-dialogical interaction with the camera.[10] Another notable collaboration is "Video Troisième Âge" (1973), where residents of a retirement home in southern France could respond to each other via self-produced videos and enter into a video-based dialogue with one another. Flusser described such a dialogical capacity of the affordable—compared to film—video technology as its main political potential to "recognize the other in it, and to recognize oneself as someone else,"[11] obviously combining Martin Buber's philosophy of dialogue (a strong influence on Flusser since his teenage years, after he had attended a lecture by Buber in Prague in 1937) with at-the-time popular interactive or closed-circuit video installations. In a French essay on Forest's work published in 1973, Flusser outlined his dialectics of "discourse" (e.g., via mass media) and "dialogue" (e.g., via interactive video communication), the basic premise of his communication theory, while stressing the importance of Forest's "dialogical video" practice for the disruption of mass media power structures: "His commitment is the commitment of an artist in the radical sense of the term, this means that it can offer a possible attitude to face this conditioning environment [of mass media]."[12] The term "dialogical video," however, was coined by Forest,[13] not by Flusser himself—although it might have been, in parts, a result of the collaboration between the two.

It was in this intellectual atmosphere when Flusser wrote "Line and Surface." In this essay, the fundamental elements of his later media theory are already present: the nontrivial relation between media technologies, communication practices, cognition, and culture; the basic features of his cultural-anthropological model that developed from this relation; and the tension between writing (conceptual thinking) and image (imaginative thinking). The new video technologies that enabled the manipulation of velocity and further intervention in the image by the viewer—and not only by its producer—Flusser described as a socio-technological paradigm shift. For him, video as a new cultural technique indicated the overcoming of a perception of the moving image (film and television) that was still predominantly linear and derived from writing culture, hierarchically produced and distributed by the authority of a sender with no possibility for feedback or dialogue with the audience.

The publication of "Line and Surface" in the US journal *Main Currents in Modern Thought* proved to be a success, triggering enthusiastic responses from readers.[14] Among those readers were Fred Barzyk, Douglas Davis, Gerald O'Grady, and Willard Van Dyke, who responded by inviting Flusser to the above-mentioned conference "Open Circuits—The Future of Television": "We are acquainted with your essay on linear surface and surface thinking in *Main Currents in Modern Thought* and admire its direction. We are hoping that you will enlarge upon some of these ideas with regard to the video medium."[15] The video artists Barzyk, Davis, and Van Dkye, as well as O'Grady, a pioneering media studies scholar from the now legendary Center for Media Study at the State University of New York at Buffalo (SUNY), organized the conference. In collaboration with the artist group Electronic Arts Intermix, Inc., it was accompanied by an exhibition and resulted in a publication with MIT Press.[16] Open Circuits took place January 23–25, 1974, at MoMA in New York City.[17]

The conference title was taken from a 1966 manifesto written by Nam June Paik[18]— "We are in open circuits"—in which he adumbrates the potential of electronically based media for open practices of electronically mediated communication. Thus, the parallel between Flusser's work and the work of the organizers of Open Circuits is already manifest in the title. With regard to his communication and media theory, Flusser was especially fascinated by the potential of certain media technologies to provide an alternative to the unidirectional logic of mass media—a powerful sender transmitting information toward an anonymous audience which has no means to reply or reverse it—and is thus condemned to passivity.[19] This fascination with the productive potential of dialogue between media users—as a strategy of liberation from the closed circuits of cultural industry—was shared by many artists and activists working with electronic media at the time. The relatively new technology of video was particularly important. For the first time—or rather as with the Sony AV-3400 Portapak affordable video cameras appeared on the market by 1967—it became possible for artists and citizens to create and experiment with their own moving images on topics they chose—a privilege formerly reserved for mass media broadcasting stations and powerful actors of government and industry.[20] Furthermore, Flusser, as well as artists present at Open Circuits, imagined a future where former consumers of media become emancipated producers creatively replying, in a dialogical manner, with video images to the images made by others. A utopian hope comparable to today's narratives of social broadcasting services such as YouTube—yet minus the implications of platform capitalism which reintroduce the mechanics of cultural industry through the backdoor of data economy.[21]

Groups like the aforementioned Raindance Corporation or Ant Farm today belong to the most famous positions which employed tactics of electronic media reappropriation in the 1960s and 1970s, as do positions rooted in Fluxus or conceptual art.[22] Fluxus artists such as Nam June Paik, Allan Kaprow, Harald Szeeman and the conference organizer Gerald O'Grady discussed and presented their work during Open Circuits. Other participants included Hollis Frampton, René Berger (with whom Flusser had been maintaining a correspondence since 1972), and renowned German writer and left-wing activist Hans Magnus Enzensberger. Enzensberger's talk at Open Circuits on "Television and the Politics of Liberation" merits particular attention.

No doubt invited to speak at the conference because of his broadly recognized essay "Baukasten zu einer Theorie der Medien" (Toolkit for a Theory of the Media) published four years earlier,[23] Enzensberger's talk advocated for a reappropriation of the mass media by its receivers. The "reconstruction" of the unidirectional communication channels into dialogical structures, which Enzensberger calls for in the earlier essay, is explicitly borrowed from Bertolt Brecht's so-called radio theory (which reflected on the activities of the "German Workers Radio Movement" of the 1920s and 1930s)[24] and adapted to contemporary mass media. Flusser's communication theory exhibits astonishing parallels with Enzensberger's arguments; both are based on a dialectic of discursive (hierarchical) and dialogical (reciprocal) forms of communication media. It's not clear whether Flusser had already been familiar with Enzensberger's German "Toolkit" article before attending the Open Circuits conference. However, during the latter's talk, Flusser jotted down on the back of his copy of the conference program: "Enzensberger: Monolithic control, Simulation of lack, Censorship: Lack of Feedback."[25] Three years later, he consolidated his communication and early media theory in the manuscript "Umbruch der menschlichen Beziehungen" (Mutations in human relations), which would only be published posthumously in *Kommunikologie* and in which very similar monolithic mass media structures, in tension with dialogical circuitries, assume a central role.[26]

Flusser's time in New York had a strong influence on his relationship with the new image media, at the center of which stood video technology. In addition to the conference, he also visited the Center for Media Study at SUNY Buffalo, which O'Grady founded in 1972 and where stellar pioneering work was being done in the field of academic media-thinking and media-making, with video playing a pivotal role.[27] Here he also met the artist Woody Vasulka, who, together with his partner Steina, had a strong influence on the US video art scene.[28] In an approach that today would be called artistic or participatory research, O'Grady and his team of scholars, artists, and technicians—as well as known guest lecturers such as the French (post-)structuralists Michel Foucault and Christian Metz—combined theoretical positions from linguistics, behavioral science (most notably Jerome S. Bruner's developmental psychology), structuralist anthropology, and other fields with artistic and participatory approaches toward video production.[29] The Center for Media Study closely collaborated with two other complimentary institutions, the community center "Media Study/Buffalo" and the university's "Educational Communications Center," to realize its participatory claim in collaboration with citizens and artists.[30]

Several parallels can be found between Flusser's media epistemology and O'Grady's approach toward media analysis and production. For both thinkers, truly innovative media production is a necessary "creative and critical practice,"[31] which ought to be developed in collaboration between artists, scholars, and technicians; both start their theoretical considerations, not untypical for the time, with a linguistic apriority, rooting all human sign practice in language;[32] and, maybe most important, both follow a *nontrivial* concept of media, where there is a strong *interdependence* between technology, its cultural techniques, and the formation of cognitive functions.[33] Such an interdependence between culture and the elaborated functional artifacts it produces—and is produced by—was at this time, 1974, famously described by the British cultural studies scholar Raymond Williams as "technology and cultural form."[34] However, both Flusser and O'Grady built on the work of an even more famous author: Marshall McLuhan. O'Grady repeatedly referred to McLuhan's work, especially *Understanding Media*,[35] as theoretical basis for the Center's "multidisciplinary explorations of the ways in which new codes restructure perceptions and knowledge through the impact on old codes and other aspects of culture as well,"[36] while Flusser references McLuhan in several of his writings.[37] Of course, McLuhan was a rather popular contemporary reference in art and media discourses—and beyond. Nam June Paik's magnetic manipulation of a television interview with McLuhan in "McLuhan Caged (in Electronic Art II)" from 1968 might be one of the most famous artifacts of what Richard Barbrook has described as the "futurist ideology [of] McLuhanism,"[38] which dominated the utopian narratives of the 1960s and 1970s, especially in the United States. The interest, however, went both ways: McLuhan was quite curious about the artistic media experiments of the time. In fact, he even wrote a short essay about Fred Forest's dialogical experiments employing telephones and answering machines.[39]

Taking into account the timing of Flusser's visit at the Center for Media Study—the years when he, after returning to Europe in 1972, transformed his "Brazil" studies on language, communication, and information theory into a broader account on media—it seems reasonable to state that the early media study endeavors in Buffalo, combined with his participation in Open Circuits, significantly influenced Flusser's work moving forward. Considering Flusser's penchant for rarely referencing sources or other influences on his work, one may turn to his correspondence in the Vilém Flusser Archive to get an idea how deeply impressed he was by his experiences in New York. On his return to Europe Flusser wrote to O'Grady, endeavoring to secure a long-term collaboration: "I do not think I ever learned so much in such a short time. And let me tell you again how impressed I was by the pioneer [sic] work you are doing. . . . I am fascinated by your work and should like to contribute some of my own ideas."[40] However, according to my research results, no reply by O'Grady, or even further collaboration, followed.

Flusser's involvement in the video art (and early media studies) scene in France and the United States influenced his thinking for many years to come. The combination of the temporal linearity and image synchronicity in video is a recurring motive in his work.[41] So is, and maybe more importantly, the dialogical capacity of video, which he experienced in his work with Forest and during his encounters in New York: as opposed to film, one could experience the immediacy of "instant feedback,"[42] as Flusser put it in 1991, realizing either philosophical, "mirror-like" self-reflections or video-based dialogues with others. In fact, Flusser described the dialogical video experiments he knew from the 1970s as early manifestations of "telepresence," which is the instant connection of two or more persons in two or more different physical places by means of telematics (networked computers), creating a virtual presence of all actors.⁴³

Flusser's fascination with video sparked by his experiences in the 1970s was no temporary, aesthetic reflection but a rather significant event for his thinking. In his 1991 lecture series at the Ruhr-University Bochum in Germany, which he gave at the invitation of Friedrich Kittler, Flusser still talked enthusiastically about his time with

Figure 3.1 Vilém Flusser during his talk on "Open Circuits—The Future of Television," January 23–25, 1974, MoMA, New York City. Source: Douglas Davis and Allison Simmons (eds.), *The New Television: A Public/Private Art* (Cambridge, MA and London: The MIT Press, 1977), 231.

Forest and O'Grady in the 1970s.[44] He did however express disappointment at the forms taken by the now firmly established cultural technique of video—forms that expressed themselves primarily in the recording of television programs and the consumption of movies. Nevertheless, he had not yet lost all hope in the possibility that video could still become the generator of entirely novel images and image-dialogue—quite the opposite of his hope in the potential of film and photography: "One has to play against the machine if one wishes to photograph, to find some nooks inside the camera that have not yet been realized. But photography is likely nearing its end. And film will follow photography. . . . But possibilities are contained in video that the people do not even suspect."[45]

Notes

1. The author wishes to thank the Federal Ministry of Education and Research of Germany (BMBF) for funding this work with grant no. 16DII115 ("Deutsches Internet-Institut").
2. Hollis Frampton, "The Withering Away of the State of the Art," in *The New Television: A Public/Private Art*, ed. Douglas Davis and Allison Simmons (Cambridge, MA and London: The MIT Press, 1977), 24–35.
3. Flusser, "Line and Surface," *Main Currents in Modern Thought* 29, no. 3 (1973): 100–6.
4. Flusser's *Towards a Philosophy of Photography* (Göttingen: European Photography, 1984) has been translated into over twenty languages.
5. Flusser to Ingold, July 30, 1983 (Vilém Flusser Archive, document Cor97); quote translated from the German.
6. The biographical references in this paper are based on Daniel Irrgang and Marcel René Marburger, "Vilém Flusser: A Biography," in *Flusseriana: An Intellectual Toolbox*, ed. Siegfried Zielinski, Peter Weibel, and Daniel Irrgang (Minneapolis: University of Minnesota Press, 2015), 452–519.
7. Cf. Flusser, *Kommunikologie*, ed. Stefan Bollmann and Edith Flusser (Mannheim: Bollmann, 1996).
8. Flusser to Forest, August 7, 1972 (Vilém Flusser Archive, SP Bienal 1, document 83).
9. Cf. Jean Duvignaud, ed., *Fred Forest: Art sociologique. Vidéo* (Paris: Union Générale d'Editions, 1977).
10. In his essay "Gesten auf Videobändern. Für Fred Forest" (Gestures on Video Tapes. For Fred Forest), Flusser describes the project's concept (c. 1974, manuscript in the Vilém Flusser Archive, document 2385, also in English and French under nos. 2407 and 2424; the German version is reprinted in facsimile in *Bodenlos. Vilém Flusser und die Künste*, ed. Siegfried Zielinski and Daniel Irrgang [Berlin: Akademie der Künste, 2015], 73.).
11. Flusser, "Video als Spiegel" (1987, Vilém Flusser Archive, document 2489); quote translated from the German.
12. Flusser, "Sociologie: l'espace communicant de Fred Forest" (first published in *communication et langages* 18 [1973]), in *Fred Forest: Art sociologique*, ed. Duvignaud, 114–24, 123; quote translated from the French.

13 See Michael F. Leruth, *Fred Forest's Utopia: Media Art and Activism* (Cambridge, MA and London: The MIT Press, 2017), 55–6. Leruth emphasizes the participation of Flusser in some of Forest's works. A detailed analysis of their close collaboration is provided by Martha Schwenderer, "Vilém Flusser's Seventies: Phenomenology, Television, Cybernetics, and Video Art," *Afterimage: The Journal of Media Arts and Cultural Criticism* 45, no. 5 (2018): 22–8, see particularly pp. 24–6.
14 See the correspondence with the associate editor Patrick Milburn and readers (Vilém Flusser Archive, Cor143, documents 25 ff.).
15 Letter dated May 19, 1973 (Vilém Flusser Archive, document Cor143).
16 Davis and Simmons, eds., *The New Television*.
17 So it says in the "Project Statement" for the conference (undated); this and other materials related to the Open Circuits conference are well documented on the Electronic Arts Intermix website: http://www.eai.org/webpages/1244. According to the project statement, the original title of the conference was "Open Circuits: Art at the Beginning of the Electronic Age," which evokes a much broader perspective. On the significance of Open Circuits, see William Kaizen, *Against Immediacy: Video Art and Media Populism* (Lebanon: Dartmouth College Press, 2016), in particular the chapter "Prelude: Open Circuits," 10–24.
18 Apparently the organizers refer to Paik's manifesto "Cybernated Art," first printed in: *Manifestos: A Great Bear Pamphlet*, ed. Dick Higgins (New York: Something Else Press, 1966), 24.
19 See Flusser, *Kommunikologie*, in collaboration with Klaus Sander.
20 See Zielinski, *Zur Geschichte des Videorecorders* (Berlin: Spiess, 1986).
21 See Alexander Galloway and Eugene Thacker, *The Exploit: A Theory of Networks* (Minneapolis: University of Minnesota Press, 2007), and Nick Srnicek, *Platform Capitalism* (Cambridge and Malden: Polity Press, 2016).
22 See Zielinski, *[. . . After the Media]. News from the Slow-Fading Twentieth Century* (Minneapolis: Univocal Publishing, 2013), 135–72.
23 Hans Magnus Enzensberger, "Baukasten zu einer Theorie der Medien," *Kursbuch* 20 (1970): 159–86.
24 See Zielinski, "'To All!' The Struggle of the German Workers Radio Movement, 1918–1933," in Siegfried Zielinski, *Variations on Media Thinking* (Minneapolis: University of Minnesota Press, 2019), 207–60.
25 Handwritten on Flusser's copy of the Open Circuits "Conference Schedule Friday, January 25" (Vilém Flusser Archive, Cor 55, R, document 15).
26 Vilém Flusser, "Umbruch der menschlichen Beziehungen" (c. 1977/78), manuscript in the Vilém Flusser Archive, document 1-MHRD; also available, in part, in English and French versions (1-MHRF and 1-MHRE). German version published in Flusser, *Kommunikologie*. Parts of the texts have been translated into English and published in Flusser, *The Surprising Phenomenon of Human Communication*, ed. Rodrigo Maltez Novaes (Metaflux, 2016).
27 See the excellent documentation *Buffalo Heads: Media Study, Media Practice, Media Pioneers, 1973–1990*, ed. Woody Vasulka and Peter Weibel (Cambridge, MA and London: The MIT Press 2008).
28 Flusser, *Kommunikologie weiter denken. Die Bochumer Vorlesungen*, ed. Silvia Wagnermaier and Siegfried Zielinski (Frankfurt/Main: Fischer, 2008), 184.
29 Gerald O'Grady, "State University of New York at Buffalo Center for Media Studies," in *Buffalo Heads*, ed. Vasulka and Weibel, 56–9.

30 O'Grady, "Media Study/Buffalo," in *Buffalo Heads*, ed. Vasulka and Weibel, 41–55.
31 O'Grady, "State University of New York at Buffalo Center for Media Studies," 56.
32 Ibid.
33 Ibid., 58. For Flusser's position, see especially his media theoretical main works in the 1980s, *Into the Universe of Technical Images* (Minneapolis: University of Minnesota Press, 2011 [1985]) and *Does Writing Have a Future?* (Minneapolis: University of Minnesota Press, 2011 [1987]).
34 Raymond Williams, *Television: Technology and Cultural Form* (Hanover: Wesleyan University Press, 1974).
35 Marshall McLuhan, *Understanding Media: The Extensions of Man* (New York: McGraw-Hill, 1964).
36 O'Grady, "State University of New York at Buffalo Center for Media Studies," 58.
37 See Flusser, *Does Writing Have a Future?*
38 Richard Barbrook, *Imaginary Futures: From Thinking Machines to the Global Village* (London and Ann Arbor: Pluto, 2007), 147.
39 McLuhan, "Fred Forest et le téléphone," in *Fred Forest: Art sociologique*, ed. Duvignaud, 126–7.
40 Flusser to O'Grady, February 25, 1974 (Vilém Flusser Archive, Cor55, R, document 12).
41 See his later book *Angenommen* (Göttingen: Immatrix, 1989), which was intended as a manual for video artists to combine the scenic narration of video with the immediacy of technical images.
42 Flusser, *Kommunikologie weiter denken*, 184.
43 Ibid., 188.
44 Ibid., 184–9.
45 Ibid., 187; quote translated from German.

4

Flusser and Ars Electronica

Between and Beyond Cybernetics

Daniel Raschke

In 1988, three years before his death, Vilém Flusser participated in the Ars Electronica Festival in Linz, Austria, sharing a stage before an actual boxing ring with a notable group of media theorists avant la lettre: Hannes Böhringer, Heinz von Foerster, Friedrich Kittler, Peter Weibel, and Jean Baudrillard. In his review of the short volume of papers published following the event, Geert Lovink was decidedly underwhelmed by the title-card, consigning its contribution to what he calls a "genre . . . not characterized by brain-racking mental processes or sparkling controversies."[1] Instead, he reports that "six middle-aged gentlemen have produced quite solemn and well-balanced papers that add little to their individual works." For Lovink to label his elders "middle-aged" is a bit rich, considering that Lovink himself was almost thirty at this point. But nonetheless, in 1988, Kittler, Böhringer, and Weibel were all in their early forties, Baudrillard was fifty-eight, von Foerster was seventy-seven, and Flusser was sixty-eight. The event represents Flusser's encounter with three different generations of theory qua media: the second-order scientist-cybernetician, repatriated from a career in the United States (von Foerster), the French poststructuralist and postmodern academic celebrity (Baudrillard), and the first wave of German media-observant faculty (Kittler, Böhringer, and Weibel) who were busy instituting media as an object of study at the German university. Noting that the media-theory symposium was an anchor event at an arts festival that pitched itself in opposition to the usual academic formalities, this chapter situates Flusser's appearance at the 1988 Ars Electronica festival in these particular historical and intellectual contexts.

Flusser in Linz

Known globally for its signature pastry, the *Linzertorte*, and the International Anton Bruckner Festival, the city of Linz, at least until Ars Electronica, would likely not be counted among Europe's leading artistic innovation hubs—yet this all changed rapidly in the late 1970s. Attempting to "cast off the image of a 'steel city' that had been attached to [Linz] since the founding of a steel plant by Nazi Germany in 1938."[2] 1979 marked the year in which the Bruckner festival was supplemented by the first global large-scale festival concerned with modern media and the arts.[3] As Andreas J. Hirsch describes it, the festival's founders had

> a vision that would clearly lead away from [its reputation for] traditional culture and old-style heavy industries: [They] wanted to put the focus on upcoming new technologies—then summed up as "microelectronics"—and their cultural implications as well as their impact on societies [,] activities relating to the future shape of the new image of Linz: [As founder Hannes Leopoldseder puts it], "From the beginning, Ars Electronica has been open to signals from the future, open to experiments. This openness is based on the idea that in conjunction with the computer, the basic technology of microelectronics is changing our work, our economy, our thinking, and ultimately our culture, more than almost any other technology before."[4]

In terms of the nascent intellectual scene concerning media and technology specifically, the venue was significant precisely because it provided a space apart: on the one hand it was cordoned off intellectually from continental theory and its literary influences; and on the other it was geographically separated from the United States, which supplied the innovation wellspring for industrial hardware and software. Intellectually, Germany itself remained hardwired by Frankfurt School preoccupations and its occasionally luddite version of the culture industry that questioned whether or how new media inventions could act as potential loci for new forms of social and political domination. Although the United States had developed and deployed new technologies more readily, as Lev Manovich observes, its rapidity of assimilation rendered them largely theoretically and aesthetically invisible. In Europe, higher costs and slower general adoption meant more time for avant-garde experimentation, critical engagements such as those exemplified by Flusser's appearance at Ars Electronica.[5] With limited expenditure for public culture in the United States, museums were also neither equipped nor adequately funded for creating comparable exhibitions to those in Europe, Japan, or Australia.[6] This absence of potential commercialization in the United States consequently led to a gap in intellectual discourse that would only get backfilled in the mid-to-late 1990s cyberculture that did not require technically complex installations. But there is a stark difference in foci: whereas "cyberculture is focused on the social and networking; new media is focused on the cultural and computing."[7] Thus, it can be fruitful to glance at European art festivals in the 1980s as spaces of convergence and reflect on their engagement with media discourses. My particular interest here lies with Ars Electronica's encouraging dialogue between cybernetics, media philosophy, and the arts that offered interdisciplinary innovators like Flusser a receptive multifocal audience beyond the discipline-specific university lecture or museum crowd he would have encountered in the United States.

If these trends paved the way for Flusser's arrival in a general sense, what specifically brought Flusser to Linz at a time when he was shuttling between his home in Robion,

France, and various speaking opportunities? Here, I want to point to the likely influence of Peter Weibel, an artist-turned-researcher and curator long associated with the pioneering arts and media theory institute ZKM (Center for Art and Media) in Karlsruhe, Germany, which itself was founded the year after the symposium. Weibel first worked with Flusser in 1981.[8] Furthermore, Flusser and Weibel corresponded on a regular basis, and Weibel continues to be a prominent supporter of Flusser's work to this date. Described by Andreas Hirsch as "the embodiment of the typical Ars Electronica artist," Weibel was responsible for the organization of the 1988 Ars Electronica and the development of an explicit intellectual program. As Hirsch writes, "[Weibel] started [the practice of] giving the ... festival a special topic each year with the intention of identifying the coming trends before they reached the mainstream."[9] Flusser's presence may be thought of as part of a deliberate effort at self-reflexivity, and the symposium itself served as a critical discourse connector that marked his official inauguration into the avant-garde/media-theoretical-academic community per se. It also had a particular impact on the dissemination of his ideas through his encounter with Kittler whom he met at the symposium. Kittler ranks among Flusser's most influential supporters and later offered him his first and only lecturing position at the Ruhr-University, Bochum, Germany, in 1991 at the age of seventy-one.

Ars Electronica was set up not as an inert exhibition hall but was instead envisioned by its directors as a dialogically active space presenting "a challenge to artists, technicians, cultural critics, and ultimately to the public encountering new forms of expression in art."[10] Pitching itself in opposition to the usual academic formalities, Ars Electronica aimed for a more experimental ethos with topics shifting on a yearly basis. Covering cybernetics, the future of humanity and the arts, modern media, and the "interdependence of art, philosophy and science," as the *Ars Electronica Program* put it, 1988 was the first year the organizers added this aforementioned philosophical symposium. Known in Germany as postmodernism's publicist, Peter Gente's publishing outfit Merve-Verlag published the keynotes.[11] Merve-Verlag possessed a cutting-edge, avant-garde theory catalog, coming to prominence as one of the first outlets for translations of French theory for a German readership. In his invitation to this "Philosophies of the New Technologies" symposium, Gente notes that he was initially unhappy with the "sociologized academicism" indicated by the symposium topic.[12] The event's goal was to engage a transdisciplinary range of speakers on theorizing the future of arts, technics, and communication to come in the twenty-first century—in other words, an approach congenial to the form of the ideal telematic dialogue that Flusser had more or less conceptualized in *Into the Universe of Technical Images* as a negentropic form of knowledge sharing.[13]

Signals from the Future: The Cybernetic Turn

According to Jan Müggenburg, cybernetics became a particularly pressing concern for German academia in the early 1980s, since "the break with neo-Marxism and following the erosion of structuralism, the German humanities were on the lookout for new role models and propositions in theory" that were uncontaminated by the supposed destructive relativisms associated with French post-structuralism.[14] This is also one of the central reasons for the surprisingly warm reception of Flusser's 1983 publication *Für eine Philosophie der Fotografie* (*Towards a Philosophy of Photography*), which evoked an "old" European philosophical discourse associated with Husserl, Heidegger, Wittgenstein, and the Vienna Circle. In another sense, Flusser arrived on the scene fully modernized, conversant in the language and key concepts of cybernetics. First developed by Norbert Wiener in the 1948 *Cybernetics; or, Control and Communication in the Animal and the Machine*, cybernetics promised a meta-science of communication, and the Austrian-born physicist Heinz von Foerster was a critical exponent of cybernetics and he provides an essential piece of this puzzle. His research at the University of Illinois, Urbana-Champaign, shifted from engineering to systemic constructivism's reach into the social sphere and human cognition, leading him to develop a theory of "observing observers," or what he termed second-order cybernetics.[15] Due to the phenomenological focus of his approach and his philosophical bent, von Foerster's work sparked critical interest in media-theoretical circles in the 1970s and early 1980s. In particular, his influential *Observing Systems* (1981) stands out. Per Müggenburg, "[N]umerous influential authors made his texts popular in the German-speaking discourses during the first half of the decade," including "the Berlin postmodernists, who were thirsting for new theoretical trendsetters that could further their discourse on media arts and media sciences."[16] In addition to the "German postmodernists," von Foerster's work greatly informed systems theorist Niklas Luhmann, who "would adopt numerous concepts of [von Foerster's] for his sociological systems theory and . . . quote the cyberneticist in his main work, *Soziale Systeme*, multiple times and in prominent positions."[17]

These techno-scientific and military-adjacent discourses[18] would in turn end up informing Kittler and other younger scholars and artists in two important ways: on the one hand, indirectly through the scholarly discourse working with second-order cybernetics, and on the other, explicitly refashioning cybernetics as a theory of media.[19] Kittler ended up exploring these tendencies explicitly in his representative and pioneering magnum opus *Discourse Networks 1800/1900* (*Aufschreibesysteme*), which reads scientific military-industrial cybernetics alongside new philosophical hybrids from Lacanian, Derridian, and Foucauldian discourse analyses.

It is difficult to reconstruct the exact dialogical forces in motion at Ars Electronica 1988, but the edited collection *Philosophien der neuen Technologie*, published by Merve-Verlag and containing all six keynotes, provides some clues. In retrospect, we can assign an inflection point to the unconventional intersections of Flusser with von Foerster, Böhringer, Baudrillard, Weibel, and Kittler for the academic institutionalization of what we now call media studies or communications studies as a polymathic alternative to the attempted transdisciplinary reckonings promised prematurely by cybernetic systems theory and cybernetic media discourse in the humanities. Von Foerster and Baudrillard hover in the background of the Merve-Verlag collection, over the shoulders as it were, of the younger media thinkers Böhringer, Kittler, and Weibel, but Flusser provides a critical point where all the planes intersect. Above all, the respective contributions comprise a kind of multifaceted, dialogical sketchpad about anthropotechnics, media, and the arts at a particular historical juncture. The volume repeatedly de-emphasizes the newness of new technology, underscoring instead its procedural nature, by explaining varieties of media philosophy in ways deeply intertwined with cybernetics. Case in point is the first speaker in the symposium, Böhringer, who develops an etymological fable of the arts and technics via Greek antiquity: *Das hölzerne Pferd*, the Trojan horse. Considering the *Odyssey*, Böhringer reflects on the oscillating relationship between *techné* (art and science) and *mechané* (means, aids, power) to contrast them with *amechané* (impotence, helplessness) and *aporia* (hopelessness). Odysseus pursues agency by changing his environment, building a vehicle that serves both technical and mechanic ends.[20] We might think of Flusser as the Trojan horse of cybernetics.

Shifting approaches in topic and style away from Böhringer's classical references, von Foerster's keynote is simply called *Wahrnehmung* ("Perception"). It deals with early conceptualizations of perception rooted in psycho-physiology. Von Foerster opposes this kind of physicalism; perception remains a fundamentally metaphysical issue, a "logical-philosophical, a socio-cultural, sometimes even a political problem," in his formulation.[21] Borrowing from Kurt Gödel, Bertrand Russell, and Alfred North Whitehead, he suggests that we can only decide on questions that are undecidable in principle, thereby gaining freedom and responsibility through the deciding decision.[22] Von Foerster subsequently works through a number of perception theories, ranging from one-to-one mental projections to *anthropomorphia inversa* to *homuncla mysteriosa*, blending scientific theories with the poetics of "witty writers."[23] For von Foerster these theories all work within the sphere of non-understanding—or, otherwise formulated, fostering understanding through a communicative system that constructs personal ontology. We can also see a clear strand of modernist positivism in his thinking; building on Henri Poincaré, von Foerster's account of perception is linked to changes in perceived movements.[24] With perception, we may grasp and understand but generally—to connect to second-order cybernetics—"we do not understand understanding [which] eludes us, or slips away":

> For we do not notice the unbelievable, the mysterious, the monstrous, the amazing, the miraculous that goes on in everyday conversation and reflection. Only when this stream of matter-of-course is disturbed do we stand in amazement before this miracle.[25]

Von Foerster's procedural re-vision ultimately gives pride of place to communication itself: perception remains always in the flux of communication, language appears "monological, denotative, descriptive" while also presenting a radical constructivist understanding of perception in which knowledge and sensory perception are the result of subjective internal processing. To von Foerster, dialogue procedurally changes our perception and urges us to rethink the Cartesian cogito ergo sum as *sumus*.[26]

Pivoting from von Foerster's point about the radical uncertainty about physicalism of memories, Flusser's own lecture is called *Gedächtnisse* ("Memories"). Following his publishing practice, he worked this material over multiple times in different versions and translations, as detailed by Steffi Winkler and Rainer Guldin, arguably giving himself the opportunity to hyperlink its contents with the materials presented by the other speakers in Linz.[27] The Merve-Verlag version takes up the subject of memory in the context of entropy and information, noting that humans "pass on not only inherited but also acquired information to future generations;" for Flusser, both cultural and genetic memory carries forth a form of human dignity that makes humans into historical beings.[28] He is chiefly interested in the possibilities offered by electronic memory and its impact on cultural memory that he sees related to humans imprinting information into the biomass and into mnemonic, "hard" objects and tools like stones and bones to overcome the ephemeral nature of oral communication.[29] The shift to electronic memories partially simulates "an imitation in which some aspects of the limited are exaggerated and others are despised" to Flusser—brain functions, data processing, and retention are outsourced, freeing up our brain for other functions and causing an "explosion of creativity."[30] In this posthistorical moment, then, information becomes transcoded into gestures "imprinting information onto objects," whereas humans become programmers, shifting from workers to players with information.[31] For Flusser, information and memory are always procedural, constantly being rewritten—and it is for us to recognize that "all these objects (including our own bodies) [serve] as media of the information process," leading us to a new kind of intersubjective anthropology that considers "humans as knot, or curvature, of overlapping fields of relations" in which both arts and sciences study cognition and re-cognition, and in which we shift "from discourse to dialogue."[32] In contrast to the other speakers and in his typical idiosyncratic fashion, Flusser insisted on not including a bibliography as he considered such sourcing both distracting and irrelevant; in alignment with his reflections, his piece ought to be considered a "report from collected information ... just thought reflections, not a thesis."[33] In computer technology, Flusser thus ultimately recognized the chance for human fulfillment shaped by responsibility and respect, the *cogito sumus* highlighted by von Foerster.

If Flusser is the dialogical axis of Ars Electronica 1988, bridging cybernetics and the emergence of German Media Theory, Baudrillard represents the extreme limit case, who name-checks McLuhan but neglects cybernetics and basically goes against the Flusserian grain. As the final keynote of the symposium for good reason, Baudrillard was, following the publication of *Simulacra and Simulation* in 1981, one of the most influential and controversial European media theorists at the time. In his chapter titled *Videowelt und Fraktales Subjekt* ("Video World and Fractal Subject"), he takes on fractals, a somewhat trendy topic at the time. For Baudrillard, the ontology of fractals heralded something very different from Flusser's technical image. It was an object in which "all identifying information is included in the smallest individual detail, a condition homological with contemporaneous subjecthood in which the self is perpetually reproduced on screens as technical artificiality becomes our true desire shaped by frantic self-reference."[34] Despite some engagement with computers and circuit-boards, Baudrillard is stuck on TV screens and videos, noting provocatively that "[t]he video stage has replaced the mirror stage."[35] In the promiscuity of the screen, he writes, "communication becomes commutation," even when the interface suggests otherwise.[36] He concludes by pronouncing that desire—and, ultimately, zest for life—is what distinguishes humans from machinic beings—but wonders whether human intelligence resolves itself not via algorithmic art and culture but into a self-parodying fractal pathos of computer viruses.[37]

In a sense, Kittler's and Weibel's contributions propose Flusser-fueled or Flusser-inspired alternatives to the key concept Baudrillard locates in video virality: namely, simulation. With Kittler's lecture, *Fiktion und Simulation* ("Fiction and Simulation"), the symposium turns more directly to the arts in modernity and the contemporary moment. For Kittler, art is fundamentally shaped by technics and code from the manipulations of the phonetic alphabet to the codifying effects of rhyming dictionaries that quickly process the limits of the aesthetic realm. Per the essay's title, Kittler distinguishes between literary aesthetics and simulations-as-peak data processing.[38] "Fiction is an analog medium with no negation," he writes.[39] Simulations, he claims, have negations already built in: "While affirming only affirms what is, and negating only negates what is not, simulating means to affirm what is not, and dissimulating what is negatable."[40] A computer simulation, therefore, can mechanically affirm that which does not exist. For Kittler, media means processing and transmitting data. The medial shift from fictions to simulations means that humans are disappearing procedurally. Processing and transmitting calculations render the Lacanian Real as manipulable code, Kittler claims.[41] For its part, Weibel's lecture *Territorium und Technik* links modernity with the development of weaponry that made the study of movement necessary, stressing an interdependence between territory, sociality, and technology.[42] Taking a different approach to simulations, Weibel sees in tools perfect simulations of natural laws: "tools as technology also have a representation of nature in them."[43]

If technology "is always territorially reversed; sensory organs interpret nature, making tools products of this interpretation," then, he claims, the technical image can "simulate the presence of a territory."[44] Writing's "commutative nature cannot make absent what is currently present," he notes in a Flusserian moment.[45] Building on Flusser's ideas on the ex-territorialization of memory, Weibel goes even further and suggests that we can speak of a technology inducing a threefold ex-territorialization: de-realization, de-corporealization, and de-materialization in which one sees that the true power of technology is "the language of the one who is absent."[46] In contrast to skeptics—Foucault is mentioned specifically and in line with Flusser—Weibel leans positively toward technology and suggests that humans might only reach their full potential through telecommunication.[47]

Less than two years later, Flusser and Weibel headlined another international symposium in Budapest, Hungary called "The Media Are With Us!: The Role of Television in the Romanian Revolution," after the fall of Ceaușescu in Romania. It provides a similar episode, again published by Merve-Verlag and remediated in various forms, but also leading Flusser to his ironic observation that "the effect of the information revolution consists of the fact that we have to stay at home when we want to be informed."[48] In many ways, Linz was an equally fortuitous event for Flusserian

Figure 4.1 The panelists at the Philosophies of the New Technology symposium, Ars Electronica 1988. From the left: Peter Gente, Hannes Böhringer, Vilém Flusser, Peter Weibel, Jean Baudrillard, Friedrich Kittler, Heinz von Foerster.

thought and its reception; it signaled his arrival and also his complex, non-incidental influences in the emergent domains of (German) media theory and the (German) media art scene and his encounter and contact with the (French) postmodernist Jean Baudrillard, in particular. Flusser's contacts with the intellectual scenes in Germany and France are obvious: he was a voracious reader, fluent in French and German, of course, and living in France since his return to Europe. Just as the intellectual influences on Flusser are sometimes hard to trace due to his general ethos of autodidacticism and his idiosyncratic, sometimes deliberately beguiling, scholarly practices, so too is Flusser's direct impact on Kittler's ideas difficult to trace, and his presence in the genealogies of new media thinking can be often obscure. Evidence is there, but all too often the receipts are lost. Aside from putting Flusser, Baudrillard, Weibel, Kittler, among others, in the same room, literally on the same stage, a notable common denominator of the event is cybernetics. Flusser was a strong proponent—even a belated popularizer—of many cybernetic concepts, usefully delineated by Claus Pias in *Flusseriana: An Intellectual Toolbox*, and, with the notable exception of Baudrillard, the rest of the participants were clearly immersed in this discourse.[49]

In a sense, this chapter takes the photograph in the frontispiece photo of the Merve-Verlag and returns it back to the sender (or returns it back to the apparatus)—not as a technical image but as a reconstruction of a multilayered network of relationships, a hidden space full of potential discourses it both implies and invites, to borrow from Flusser's own discussion of these phenomena in *Kommunikologie*: amphitheaters, concert halls, classrooms, foyers, boxing matches, roundtables, parliaments, keynotes, question and answer times, chitchats, documentations, exhibitions, manuscripts, translations, interviews, letters, and, of course, essay collections.[50]

Notes

1. Geert Lovink, Rev. of *Philosophien der neuen Technologie*, *Mediamatic Magazine*, 4, no. 1–2 (January 1989), https://www.mediamatic.net/nl/page/83984/philosophien-der-neuen-technologie.
2. Andreas J. Hirsch, *Creating the Future: A Brief History of Ars Electronica 1979-2019*, ed. Gerfried Stocker and Diethard Schwarzmair (Berlin: Hatje-Cantz-Verlag, 2019): 54.
3. Timothy Druckrey, ed., *Ars Electronica: Facing the Future. A Survey of Two Decades, Electronic Culture—History, Theory, Practice* (Ars Electronica, Cambridge, MA: MIT Press, 1999), 18.
4. Hirsch, *Creating the Future: A Brief History of Ars Electronica 1979-2019*, 54. Leopoldseder also quoted in Druckrey, *Ars Electronica*, 7.
5. Lev Manovich, "New Media from Borges to HTML," in *The New Media Reader*, ed. Noah Wardrip-Fruin and Nick Montfort (Cambridge, MA: MIT Press, 2003), 13–25, 13.
6. Ibid.
7. Ibid., 16.
8. Martha Schwendener, "The Photographic Universe: Vilém Flusser's Theories of Photography, Media, and Digital Culture" (Proquest diss., New York: New York University, 2016), 290.
9. Hirsch, *Creating the Future: A Brief History of Ars Electronica 1979-2019*, 99.
10. Druckrey, *Ars Electronica*, 3.
11. *Ars Electronica Program 1988* (Linz: Linzer Veranstaltungsgesellschaft, 1988), 37.
12. Peter Gente and Adelheid Paris, "Invitation: Symposium 'Philosophies of the New Technology,'" 1988, 2. More on Gente: https://www.berliner-zeitung.de/kultur-vergnuegen/merve-verleger-peter-gente-gestorben-li.22130. https://zkm.de/en/merve-verlag.
13. Flusser, *Into the Universe of Technical Images* (Minneapolis: University of Minnesota Press, 2011), 93–4.
14. Jan Müggenburg, "Bats in the Belfry: On the Relationship of Cybernetics and German Media Theory," *Canadian Journal of Communication* 42, no. 3 (July 28, 2017): 477. https://doi.org/10.22230/cjc.2017v42n3a3214. For a classic example of German antipathy to French post-structuralism, see Klaus Laermann, "Lacancan Und Derridada: Frankolatrie: Gegen Die Neueste Mode, Den Neuesten Nonsens in Den Kulturwissenschaften," *Die Zeit* (May 30, 1986).
15. Müggenburg, "Bats in the Belfry," 476.
16. Ibid., 477.
17. Ibid.
18. See Peter Galison, "The Ontology of the Enemy: Norbert Wiener and the Cybernetic Vision," *Critical Inquiry* 21, no. 1 (Autumn 1994): 228–66.
19. Moritz Hiller, "Unter Aufschreibesystemen: Eine Adresse Im A̶d̶r̶e̶ß̶b̶u̶c̶h̶ IC Der Kultur," *Metaphora: Journal for Literary Theory and Media* 1 (2015), https://metaphora.univie.ac.at/volume1-hiller.pdf. quoted in Müggenburg, "Bats in the Belfry," 478.
20. Hannes Böhringer, "Das hölzerne Pferd," in *Philosophien der neuen Technologie*, ed. Peter Gente, Internationaler Merve-Diskurs 146 (Berlin: Merve, 1989), 7–26, 9. This

and all subsequent sections from *Philosophien der neuen Technologie* have also been translated by the author.
21 Heinz von Foerster, "Wahrnehmung," in *Philosophien der neuen Technologie*, ed. Peter Gente, Internationaler Merve-Diskurs 146 (Berlin: Merve, 1989), 27–40, 27.
22 Ibid.
23 Ibid., 33.
24 Ibid., 35–6.
25 Ibid., 37.
26 Ibid., 40.
27 For the complicated publication history of this matter, see Steffi Winkler and Rainer Guldin, "Introduction," *Flusser Studies* 24, http://www.flusserstudies.net/sites/www.flusserstudies.net/files/media/attachments/introduction24.pdf.
28 Flusser, "Gedächtnisse," in *Philosophien der neuen Technologie*, ed. Peter Gente, Internationaler Merve-Diskurs 146 (Berlin: Merve, 1989), 41–56, 41.
29 Ibid., 42–4.
30 Ibid., 49, 50.
31 Ibid., 50.
32 Ibid., 52–4.
33 Ibid., 55.
34 Jean Baudrillard, "Videowelt und fraktales Subjekt," in *Philosophien der neuen Technologie*, ed. Peter Gente, trans. Matthias Rüb, Internationaler Merve-Diskurs 146 (Berlin: Merve, 1989), 113–32, 113–14.
35 Ibid., 120.
36 Ibid., 129.
37 Ibid., 130–1.
38 Kittler, "Fiktion und Simulation," in *Philosophien der neuen Technologie*, ed. Peter Gente, Internationaler Merve-Diskurs 146 (Berlin: Merve, 1989), 57–80, 60.
39 Ibid., 61.
40 Ibid., 64.
41 Ibid., 70–1.
42 Peter Weibel, "Territorium und Technik," in *Philosophien der neuen Technologie*, ed. Peter Gente, Internationaler Merve-Diskurs 146 (Berlin: Merve, 1989), 81–112, 85.
43 Ibid., 99.
44 Ibid., 99–100.
45 Ibid., 103.
46 Ibid., 102–5.
47 Ibid., 107.
48 "The Media Are with Us," *Monoskop* (March 26, 2020), https://monoskop.org/The_Media_Are_With_Us.
49 Claus Pias, "Cybernetics," in *Flusseriana: An Intellectual Toolbox* (Minneapolis: University of Minnesota Press, 2015).
50 Vilém Flusser, *Kommunikologie* (Frankfurt: Fischer, 1998).

5

Flusser in the Light of Radiation

Clint Wilson III

In September of 1986, Vilém Flusser published his first essay for *Artforum*, the initial entry in a series that would come to be known as "Curie's Children." The essay was titled "On Science," and according to Martha Schwendener, its "seven paragraphs . . . packed a dense meditation on light, from Enlightenment reason and artificial intelligence to technology after Auschwitz, Hiroshima, and Chernobyl."[1] By singling out these three historical events, Flusser's maiden effort for *Artforum* tethers together catastrophic legacies facilitated by the ideologically fraught technologies of the rapidly modernizing twentieth century. However, "On Science" also introduces a distinctly Flusserian pun: "radiation," by which he means, paradoxically, both the emanation from the "light of reason" and the more familiar threat of contamination brought about by improperly secured nuclear materials. "Nuclear physics," his essay argues, has changed how we think about the very word "light," and by extension, "reason" more broadly. Flusser goes on, "Most of the modern metaphors that deal with light—clarification, enlightenment, reflection—mean the awareness projected by the human subject onto the objective world. But we are no longer moderns, and as postmoderns, we do not trust this beam either. We are after a different sort of radiation."[2] Associating exposure and knowledge by way of this "different sort of radiation," Flusser implies that "postmoderns" are no longer subjects controlling the "beam" of knowledge, but rather vulnerable objects exposed to the beam of radioactivity.

"On Science" entertains a wider reflection on knowledge formation in an age of new environmental media by addressing one of the most pressing ecological and political issues of its moment: nuclear power and its containment. "At present," writes Flusser, "when science no longer searches for truth but for falsification, and when technology results in Auschwitz, Hiroshima, and Chernobyl, in thermonuclear devices and in environmental pollution, we are in a position to taste the Luciferian flavour [sic] of the light of reason."[3] Human Enlightenment engenders environmental catastrophe; the "light of reason" makes possible a new, quite literal, and quite deadly radiation. While Flusser never directly mentions Marie Curie or her discoveries, the title of the *Artforum* series, "Curie's Children," codes the relevance of her ideological—and, one must add, toxic—legacies for media thinking. Flusser's work does not express the kind of anxiety that would indicate its participation in what Lawrence Buell calls "toxic discourse," but its canny yoking of human reason to "environmental pollution," as Flusser himself puts it, does express a larger interest in the subject of risk.[4]

Flusser's skepticism regarding the value of scientific advancements is contained most forcefully, but also most figuratively, in *The History of the Devil*. Here, in a section entitled "The Devil's Childhood," Flusser writes that "nuclear physics is a type of sin."[5] His insight conditions the analysis to follow, which, according to Schwendener, becomes "a teleology served up in 'layers' that builds an argument about history and the contemporary moment."[6] When Flusser expands on why "nuclear physics is a type of sin," he does so by offering up one such commentary on science in the contemporary moment:

> Let us now imagine a soul that has overcome the phenomenal world thanks to nuclear physics and has thus attained a vision of "pure Being" through the Wilson Chamber. Nuclear physics is a type of sin, therefore, how could one lose that soul?.... I believe that for the first time in the history of human thought the Devil has started to fulfill his promise that *eritis sicut Deus, scientes bonum et malum*.[7]

Citing the Vulgate translation of Genesis 3:5—"You shall be as God, knowing good and evil"—Flusser plays with the idea that knowledge can be our undoing (notably, these same lines are also inscribed by Mephistopheles, disguised as Faust, in Goethe's *Faust*).[8] For Flusser, "nuclear physics" represents an overextension of human ingenuity, a "Luciferian" effort to contradict the nature of human limitation and entropy. In Schwendener's reading, Flusser's examination of science's "sins" is an "argument that science has turned nature into technology," a move which "prefigures" his contributions to *Artforum*.[9]

It is precisely this myopic sense of "Enlightenment," this radiation of the mind, which Flusser fears and which his *Artforum* essays continue to investigate in their many, diverse installments. Throughout his years contributing to the journal, Flusser repeatedly emphasizes that a core problem for both knowledge and artistic creation is a fundamental misunderstanding of how media functions. "Our tools," he adds in an unpublished late essay, "are striking back at us in a way we can no longer tolerate, if we want to survive as human beings—not only the tools designed to destroy humans (like nuclear weapons), but tools that were designed to serve humans (like computers)."[10] The directionality of these tools—that is, whether these media harm or help humans—is much less concerning for Flusser than the fact that we do not understand how these tools work or why they continue to "strik[e] back." More importantly, this yoking together of technical and scientific media—computers and nuclear weapons—returns us once again to Flusser's dual meaning of "radiation." The computer, a metonym for the making and storing of knowledge, is tied to nuclear weapons, a metonym for the capacity of human knowledge to become self-destructive.

Flusser's *Into the Universe of Technical Images* extends his argument further, insisting that the danger of "nuclear physics" is related to the danger of technical images more broadly. Regarding the cultural proliferation of technical images, Flusser identifies a progressive homogenization, which threatens to erase all difference within communication. He laments the totalizing capacity of the technical image and its attendant platforms, claiming, "No catastrophe of any sort (e.g., nuclear) is necessary—technical images are themselves the end."[11] Given that Flusser is writing a year before Chernobyl and only months after Bhopal and six years after Three Mile Island, he is undoubtedly responding to the cultural purchase of those nuclear events that had altered public perception of risk in the twentieth century.

For Flusser, the risk posed by "nuclear physics" is twofold: first, it threatens to lay waste to our rightful epistemological relation to the world, and second, it threatens to undo the world we must enter in order to engage in critique. Risk theory grows out of the selfsame events that Flusser investigates throughout "Curie's Children": most notably, the Chernobyl disaster. Given that this moment serves as a touchstone for sociological work in the field of "risk studies," Flusser's essays' repeated invocation of both "nuclear physics" and Chernobyl invites countless parallels to the work of critical media studies. Writing of the timescales of risk instituted by "second modernity," the great risk theorist Ulrich Beck once wrote, "[T]o express it by reference to a single example: the injured of Chernobyl are today, years after the catastrophe, not even all *born* yet."[12] For her part, Ursula Heise argues that Chernobyl created "a truly transnational risk scenario" as both fallout and the "information flows" crossed national borders and boundaries.[13] Heise's reading uncannily echoes Flusser's concern for how "radiation" means both how we receive information and how we are exposed to evolving, hostile environments. Sites like Chernobyl and Hiroshima create what Aaron Jaffe might call "biopolitical junkyards," sites that are dangerous for not only their radiated aftermath but, perhaps more vitally, for the ways these nuclear events change perceptions of risk, reason, and technology.[14]

Hence, Flusser's example of nuclear catastrophe is no casual reference. With these tragic and image-circulating events in mind, one must not miss the implication of *Into the Universe of Technical Images*' analysis. According to Flusser,

> The current interaction between images and human beings will lead to a loss of historical consciousness in those who receive the images, and, as a result, also to a loss of any historical action that could result from the reception of the image. . . . For images are beginning to bore us, in spite of the contract we have with them.[15]

Major media events like nuclear disasters or atomic detonations, despite receiving widespread public attention and despite being recorded and disseminated as technical images themselves, become "boring" for those who have lost sight of what Flusser calls "historical consciousness." The real catastrophe, Flusser clarifies, is not Three Mile Island so much as humanity's inability to imagine the historical action demanded by those incidents.

What Flusser calls "posthistory" is brought about by the end of historical consciousness as well as an end to humanity's ability to tell narratives *about* history. Indeed, in one of his most compelling formulations of how one might identify the posthistorical era, he explains that the end of history is precipitated by the end of stories. When faced with the "unimaginable complexities" of the universe's size, Flusser says that humans have traditionally relied on a "short story" otherwise known as the second law of thermodynamics.[16] The second law of thermodynamics interests Flusser because of its emphasis upon the entropy of any system, which can never decrease and must only increase over time. The story that explains the world, for Flusser, is the realization that entropy is inevitable. In the age of posthistory, however, Flusser contends that people are no longer compelled to follow the logic of such a simple narrative, presumably because they believe the *decrease* of entropic function to be not only plausible but also achievable. (This irrational conviction is parodied in *The History of the Devil*, where he imagines that people will petition for entrance to heaven by citing their ability to achieve a so-called pure Being by way of the Wilson Chamber.) Hence, "If this one short story of the one large story can no longer be told," says Flusser, "then one can no longer tell stories in general."[17] Following this argument to its logical end, acknowledging the inexorable progress of entropy is critical to the creation of all stories and all histories. In effect, Flusser is proposing a theory of narrative where, in order to remain a narrative, the story's end must always remain in sight.[18] In *Artforum* and *The History of the Devil*, "nuclear physics" is likewise dismissed on the grounds of denying entropy, and thus the "posthistorical" is another way in which Flusser is fleshing out his thinking about the risks of the nuclear age.

When Flusser writes that "one can no longer tell stories in general," we must hear, I think, Theodor Adorno's famous claim that Auschwitz marked the end of our ability to write poetry. In *Prisms*, Adorno argues, "To write poetry after Auschwitz is barbaric. And this corrodes even the knowledge of why it has become impossible to write poetry today."[19] Adorno's thinking embodies a similar discomfort toward the progressive homogenization of discourse under the regime of advancing, totalizing media. In defending his claim that it is "impossible to write poetry," Adorno adds, "The more total society becomes, the greater the reification of the mind and the more paradoxical its effort to escape reification on its own. Even the most extreme consciousness of doom threatens to degenerate into idle chatter. Cultural criticism finds itself faced with the final stage of the dialectic of culture and barbarism."[20] If, for Adorno, the dialectic's progress lies on an axis balancing culture and barbarism, Flusser's model might be conceived as a dialectic between history and posthistory, between the natural progression of entropy and the unnatural techniques of so-called nuclear physics.

For Flusser, even communication operates in the dialectic of history and posthistory. He writes that communication can be thought of as shoring up information against the ruinous advancement of our individual entropic trajectories (but it does not deny entropy). In much the same way he dismisses nuclear physics' scientific solutions to the problematic "story" of our existence, he likewise doubts the natural sciences' ability to properly account for the intricacies conditioning human communication:

> Human engagement for the storage of information in opposition to death cannot be measured with the same scales used by the natural scientist. Carbon-dating tests measure the natural time according to the information loss of specific radioactive atoms. However, the artificial time of human freedom ("historical time") cannot be measured by simply turning carbon-dating formulas around, so that they now

measure the accumulation of information. The accumulation of information is not the measure of history, but rather, it is the dead waste of a human intention that motivates history in opposition to death. In other words, of freedom.[21]

Flusser here celebrates the potential wasteful expenditures of human communication, as he does throughout his work. "Philosophy," he writes, "has often been said to be a garbage disposal. Philosophy must not die, if we are to live."[22] Survival is somehow linked to waste; or, as he puts it in the same essay, "It may be that at present we are more determined by garbage than by nature."[23] Neither nuclear physics nor the natural sciences can save us if their salvation is linked to dismissing the "waste" that might, after all, hold the key to our future.

Flusser's interest in nuclear physics is consonant with his larger goal of interpreting the role technical media play in shaping our historical consciousness. The end of history brought about by the cultural triumph of technical images is commensurate with the end of history enacted by the scientific triumph of "nuclear physics." Speaking of particles and waves in a 1991 *Artforum* essay, "On Three Spaces," he once more articulates the necessity of understanding even the least visible realities of our world. "We may look for galaxies," Flusser admits,

> but if we look for particles like quarks we see only traces. But, we might ask, if we cannot even see these particles, why should we try to put ourselves in their place? The answer is, we must do so, not only because of nuclear power and Chernobyl, but because we are able to calculate it. Now let this be put more carefully: since we cannot say exactly where a particle is, we should better say of that space not what or how it is but what and how it might be.[24]

In the absence of empirical data, such that one must work only with the "traces" of particles, Flusser supplies a bold and perhaps "unscientific" suggestion: follow the imagination. We should instead imagine "what and how [the world] might be." To not do so is to invite disaster in the form of "nuclear power and Chernobyl." Nuclear catastrophe serves as a metonym for the large-scale risks associated with refusing to examine the inner workings of our media cultures.

If the end of history is marked by the end of storytelling, and if the end of storytelling is instituted by the seeming victory of the twentieth century's advanced sciences, then Flusser's recurring interest in "nuclear physics" is thus a primary extension of his posthistorical thinking. By the lights of this logic, events like Chernobyl and Three Mile Island—and, later, Goiânia, an incident which would no doubt hit closer to home for Flusser—indicate the end of "history" in the sense that they terminate that "short story" of entropy and traditional Enlightenment reason. From his first to his last *Artforum* contributions, Flusser's frequent references to "nuclear physics" operate as a signal of posthistory. In straining to deny entropy, "nuclear physics" ushers in the posthistorical: ushers in, that is, a time in which stories are not only impossible but also worthless. The *Artforum* essay that follows "On Three Spaces" is titled "On Books," and despite its clear departure from this nuclear line of thinking, one can see that Flusser is actually still thinking about history, entropy, and narrative. The essay begins with these words: "As material objects they are almost worthless. Their specific gravity is high, and to carry even a few of them can be an uncomfortable matter."[25] (The migrant philosopher Flusser, living in exile in Brazil, would of course know all too well about the cost and difficulty of transporting books.) The article soon becomes, as one might anticipate, a love letter to the power of these "almost worthless" objects and the imagination they inspire.

In an unexpected development, Flusser adds that books are objects that, like "nuclear physics," attempt to resist the second law of thermodynamics, with fleeting, miraculous success:

> According to the second law of thermodynamics, nature is a system that tends to lose information. A book, then, is an unnatural object. In fact a book, any book, is a miracle, and we should fall on our knees every time we pick one up.... The miracle is temporary: the attempt to defy nature, to defy death, is in the long run doomed to failure in everything we do, in books as in paintings, music, architecture, science, and technology. All these energies will in time be devoured by time, by entropy, and will be forgotten.[26]

The "miracle"—or, to use another favorite word of Flusser's, "magic"[27]—of books is that they will ultimately be "devoured" and "forgotten." Yet, recall here that Flusser elsewhere labels waste—"the dead waste of human intention"—the real "measure of history." The natural resistance to entropy is how history is "motivated." Unlike "nuclear physics," however, the failure of books does not result in that pervasively toxic form of "radiation" for which Flusser reserves so much anxiety. At the same time, the survival of books reveals that there are those who have not yet come to terms with the "communications revolution going on around us ... [where] the future goes as follows: an elite of scientists and technicians uses numbers (algorithms) to articulate and communicate information. The majority is informed (and manipulated) by images—TV and advertising, say—that tend to become ever more perfect."[28] Books counter the slow march toward posthistory, resisting the revolution within communications that would have us informed and manipulated by images rather than words.

While "On Books" is the last *Artforum* essay Flusser would see circulated in his lifetime, he would nevertheless have one more piece slated for publication prior to his death. "On the Term Design," printed in March of 1992, ends with a final reflection on posthistory—one which resonates with Flusser's diverse range of comments on "radiation" throughout the journal's pages. In the last sentence Flusser ever planned to publish in *Artforum*, he writes, "'Posthistory' may be that terrible period when designs no longer work, because, finally, we have learned too much about them."[29] With these words, one must hear Flusser's refrain throughout so much of his writing, including *Into the Universe of Technical Images*, *The History of the Devil*, and of course "Curie's Children." The overload of information that inaugurates the posthistorical era is that "different sort of radiation": a radiation that rewires and distorts the human attention span in the late twentieth century. This "different sort of radiation," one which denies the second law of thermodynamics, threatens to create a systemic apathy regarding both our ecological and cultural futures.

Flusser's "radiation" is both metaphor and material, and it highlights both the communicative "light of reason" and the ecological, human disasters brought forth by the entropy-denying advanced sciences. But when Flusser tells his readers that, now, "[w]e are after a different sort of radiation," they should be reminded that this radiation is the light of a posthistorical moment marked by the potential end of narrative itself. An event like Chernobyl reminds us that we still do not grasp how transformations within our communicative and technical media might spell the end of history, in more ways than one. Flusser's theory of radiation not only heralds his concern for the imprudent progress of so-called nuclear physics but also serves as a robust metaphor for the human proclivity to ignore the inevitable triumph of entropy and information loss. By these lights, or by this radiation, Flusser is the kind of provocative thinker who anticipated the inextricable link between ecology and media. Flusser's theory of radiation, in the final sum, renders the concept of media ecology more legible than ever before.

Notes

1. Schwendener, "Introduction," in *Artforum Essays* by Vilém Flusser (Metaflux, 2017), 11–31, 12.
2. Flusser, "On Science," in *Artforum Essays*, 45–51, 46.
3. Ibid., 47.
4. See Lawrence Buell, *Writing for an Endangered World: Literature, Culture, and Environment in the U.S. and Beyond* (Cambridge, MA: Belknap Press, 2001).
5. Flusser, *The History of the Devil*, trans. Rodrigo Maltez Novaes, ed. Siegfried Zielinski (Minneapolis: Univocal, 2014), 22.
6. Schwendener, "The Photographic Universe: Vilém Flusser's Theories of Photography, Media, and Digital Culture" (PhD diss., City University of New York), 53.
7. Flusser, *History of the Devil*, 22.
8. See "Eritis sicut Deus, scientes bonum et malum," *Oxford Reference*, accessed October 30, 2019, https://www.oxfordreference.com/view/10.1093/oi/authority.201 10803095756647.
9. Schwendener, "Photographic Universe," 54.
10. Flusser, "Backlash," in *Artforum Essays*, 283–90, 289.
11. Flusser, *Into the Universe of Technical Images*, trans. Nancy Ann Roth (Minneapolis: University of Minnesota Press, 2011), 59.
12. Ulrich Beck, *World Risk Society* (Cambridge, MA: Polity Press, 1999), 77.
13. Ursula K. Heise, *Sense of Place and Sense of Planet: The Environmental Imagination of the Global* (Oxford: Oxford University Press, 2008), 179.
14. See Aaron Jaffe, "Biopolitical Junkyards, Remediation, and Risk: Blood, Sex, and Soil" (conference paper, the 2015 Annual Meeting of the Society for the Study of Literature, Sciences, and the Arts, Houston, TX, November 12, 2015).
15. Flusser, *Into the Universe of Technical Images*, 60.

16 Flusser, "On the End of History," in *Writings*, trans. Erik Eisel, ed. Andreas Ströhl (Minneapolis: University of Minnesota Press, 2002), 143–9, 145.
17 Ibid.
18 See Peter Brooks, *Reading for the Plot: Design and Intention in Narrative* (Cambridge, MA: Harvard University Press, 1994); and Judith Roof, *Come As You Are: Sexuality and Narrative* (New York: Columbia University Press, 1996).
19 Theodor W. Adorno, *Prisms*, trans. Samuel and Shierry Weber (Cambridge, MA: The MIT Press, 1997), 33.
20 Ibid.
21 Flusser, "What Is Communication?," in *Writings*, ed. Ströhl, 3–7, 7.
22 Flusser, "Bottles," *ETC: A Review of General Semantics* (Summer 1988): 148–54, 154.
23 Ibid., 153.
24 Flusser, "On Three Spaces," in *Artforum Essays*, 205–15, 210.
25 Flusser, "On Books," in *Artforum Essays*, 217–23, 217.
26 Ibid., 217–18.
27 See Schwendener, "Photographic Universe," 13, 54–5.
28 Flusser, "On Books," 222.
29 Flusser, "On the Term Design," in *Artforum Essays*, 225–33, 232.

6

Games and Play

On Being Human in the Universe of Technical Images

Nancy Roth

To see the world as a set of games, and to see it as a player who knows he is playing, is to see aesthetically.

—Vilém Flusser, 1969

"This discovery was like a rupture of dams," Flusser wrote of his recognition of games as a means of synthesizing his diverse thoughts about communication. Writing in an autobiographical essay from 1969, he describes the experience as an event in the recent past that he expects to shape his thinking into the foreseeable future:

> Suddenly, I saw a whole new field of action extending before me: the field of critique and translation between games . . . in fact, critique as transcendence of games, that is, critique as metalanguage.[1] The problem thus stated made the odd pieces of my previous phases fall into a pattern that, with discipline and imagination, might form a whole in the future.[2]

A contemporary reader might well wonder how a potential unity among such apparently disparate concepts—games, critique, translation, "metalanguage"—could have appeared so abruptly, so clearly. The passage does not indicate any particular curiosity about the phenomenon "games" as such. Rather it speaks of games as a means to an end, a clearing away of obstructions to the accomplishment of a project already well underway. To put it differently, the passage suggests a turning point in the development of an artistic or architectural practice rather than a scientist's program of observation or experimentation. A reader is left wondering about the questions to which "games" offered such an exciting answer. At one level Flusser, having focused on language in all his previous work, makes this very clear: "I was looking for a way out into nonlanguage within the loops and tissue of language."[3] And yet the statement begs any number of additional questions: What had changed to make language seem unacceptably limited? What would the alternative do that language cannot? How do *games* provide an escape from language? What is so desirable about the eventual pattern being "whole?"

Among the "odd pieces of my previous phases" would certainly have been Wittgenstein's well-known characterization of language as a game and Johan Huizinga's study of play as a critical force in the development of human culture (more on this later). Flusser had studied formal logic with Leonidas Hegenberg, who was one of the most prominent professors of the discipline in Brazil; he had listened to—and often refuted—his friend Vincente Ferreira da Silva enthusiastically welcoming new technology, specifically communications technology. But it was his relatively recent encounter with decision theory and games theory[4] that seems to have produced the "rupture of dams." Created to model human economic behavior (and open prospects for controlling it), games theory generates mathematical models of decision-making among groups, human or not. Flusser's established sympathies with such thinkers as Wittgenstein and Huizinga would suddenly have come into view against the prospect that aspects of human cognition could soon be automated.

Perhaps not coincidentally, "In Search of Meaning" was first written in English, Flusser's third language.[5] Elsewhere, he describes being drawn to one of his four languages by the particular thought he wanted to express—although the reasons were not always clear even to him.[6] Perhaps the attraction of English in this case concerned the clear distinction that can be made between "games" and "play" (in German and French, the words for "game" and "play" are the same; in Portuguese, there are two words for play, but they divide along different lines). Or, if he had been familiar with recent research on play as an activity that cuts across logical levels (Russell) of communication, that is, with Gregory Bateson's work, he could have been drawn to the language in which it was published.[7] A more focused discussion of games and play followed the paper Bateson read at the Macy Group Processes Conference in 1955, "The Message 'This is Play.'"[8] The discussion hovered around an idea of "games" as comparatively stable structures and "play" as a means of subverting, reinventing, changing them. One of the participants, the anthropologist Ray Birtwhistell, offered a strong conclusion: "At this point, if we were trying to make a definition of play, I would almost be willing to eliminate games as such from play, and state that those things which are games are not play." But, the participants continued, can there be games without play or play without games?

Flusser invariably discussed *games* as objects, seen from the outside, a space for definitions and categorization. He usually described *play*, by contrast, from the inside—the position of the player. Loosely, over various appearances of the pair in various texts, it can seem that Flusser treats a "game" as a thing—a noun—and "play" as a verb, ordinarily used in its intransitive form. This is, however, one of at least two significantly different understandings of the relationship between games and play that appear in his writing. The first, more familiar, forms the background against which the new one, characteristic of telematic society, comes into view. There is a particularly memorable example in a chapter entitled "To Create," in *Into the Universe of Technical Images*:[9] two people are absorbed in a game of chess, following its time-honored rules in the expectation that it will conclude with one winner and one loser. In this case, however, "unpredictable, improbable, exciting situations (i.e., informative situations)" arise. Both players lose interest in winning or losing and begin to think, together, about the implications of the new situation. No longer opponents bound by the discursive structure of the game, they start to speak and listen to one another freely, dialogically, playfully. Both come away with something new.

By the time he was writing about "a rupture of dams" in 1969, Flusser had already published "Games,"[10] a very short essay outlining a new way of understanding communication itself as an infinity of games. It begins, significantly, not with a definition of the term—although there is one—but with a reflection on the best way to characterize human beings. Flusser offers a series of possibilities likely to be familiar to his reader—*Homo sapiens* or *Homo faber* or *animal laborans*—but he settles on *Homo ludens*. In sharing his reasons for the choice, he sets out the essay's main purpose: the other terms designate ways human beings differ from animals, but he intends to identify human beings "in comparison to their own apparatuses."[11] Since apparatuses, too, can be creative, reflective, or purposeful, he writes, the first three terms do not suit his purpose. *Homo ludens* may not be the only animal capable of playing. He is, however, the one who needs this capacity to distinguish himself from apparatuses.

The phrase *Homo ludens* inevitably acknowledges Johan Huizinga's groundbreaking study by that title from 1938.[12] Flusser clearly knew the work, having included it in a list of sources for a book manuscript from 1958 (never published).[13] Huizinga's book has since become a founding text in the new and rapidly expanding academic field of games studies. In this context it is widely used to furnish a definition of "play." Play is: "not serious; utterly absorbing; not associated with material interest or profit; takes place in its own boundaries of time and space; proceeds according to rules; and creates social groups that separate themselves from the outside world."[14] The authors of a prominent textbook in which the list appears go on to take issue with a few of the characteristics, notably the disassociation from profit, along with the absence of a clear statement about the relationship between "game" and "play." But as Peter McDonald has pointed out in a revealing study of *Homo Ludens*' reception, this use of Huizinga's work constitutes an "overly formalist misreading."[15] The sheer breadth of Huizinga's study, embracing as it does law, war, philosophy, poetry, myth, art, and more as forms of play, affected its many readers' thinking, despite the disagreements they may have had with the book's conjectures and conclusions, and Flusser is unlikely to have been any exception. More specifically, McDonald proposes that Huizinga practiced a *phenomenology* of play, and that an overemphasis on the formal definition obscures one of the book's key innovations, namely its insights into play from a player's point of view. One nice example is Huizinga's interest in play as *fun*, a judgment that can be made by players alone. *Homo Ludens* describes the "play-spirit" as crucial to the possibility of fiction—the conscious construction of a world. It recognizes the aesthetic dimension. All of these aspects of play appear in Flusser's work as well.

By contrast to Huizinga's carefully assembled evidence bearing on a *question* about the role of play, however, Flusser simply installed play at the beginning of "Games" as a premise: "I will take human beings' capacity for play to be their defining characteristic."[16] The statement could almost be a paraphrase of the most famous sentence in Friedrich

Schiller's *On the Aesthetic Education of Man*: "man only plays when he is in the fullest sense of the word a human being, and he is only fully a human being when he plays."[17] Schiller's book, written a few years after the shocking violence of the French Revolution, describes human beings as subject to two fundamentally opposing drives—one toward rationality and the other toward sensuality. In a healthy, happy person, these drives are in balance, each holding the other in check. With reference to his own contemporary society, in which he found excesses of both kinds much in evidence, Schiller identified aesthetic experience—at this point bound up with the arts and widely understood as an appreciation of beauty—as the way to achieve balance. Aesthetic education then emerges as the crucial element in the development of creative and responsible citizens. It seems most unlikely that Flusser would have been interested in innate drives or balanced personalities. But Schiller assigns *play* a function that may have resonated deeply with Flusser's own experience. With the instincts of a phenomenologist before there was any such identity available, Schiller describes play from the standpoint of the player, the way a player feels, what the experience is like. At such moments, he says, a player senses his own humanity.

From its opening reference to Homo ludens, in any case, the essay "Games" jumps to a formal description. A game, Flusser writes, is "a system of elements that regularly combine."[18] Elements may be words in a language, pieces on a chessboard, people bound together in any sort of system—the possibilities are unlimited. Then comes a set of concepts that govern the way elements combine to constitute games:

> The sum total of the elements is the game's "repertoire." The sum total of the rules is the game's "structure." The sum total of possible combinations from the repertoire within game's structure is the game's "competence." And the sum total of the combinations from the repertoire that have been realized is the game's "universe."[19]

The essay goes on to distinguish between open and closed games, that is, between games like chess that have a fixed repertoire and structure, and games that gain and lose elements and have no fixed ending, such as language. Open games are infinite, he writes, but not all-encompassing—each game has its specific competence and universe.

A reader gets a strong sense that this theory relies on particular sources, but there is no specific information about them. Tracing Flusser's sources is always difficult and never entirely certain. Rainer Guldin has provided a general description of the way Flusser used sources, taking the specific example of Anatol Rapoport as evidence.[20] Among the many instances of Flusser's borrowing, adapting, compressing, or omitting aspects of Rapoport's work, Guldin gives one particularly clear example. Rapoport is best known for his work in game theory, having developed the concept and term "zero-sum" game. This is a game in which the gain among players is exactly equal to other players' losses, resulting in zero. Rapoport also recognized "non-zero-sum" games, in which an overall gain or loss might be sustained. In "translating" Rapoport's English terms into German, Flusser also adapted them to his own theory, keeping "zero-sum game" and changing "non-zero-sum" to "plus-sum" game.[21] Eventually he added a "minus-sum-game" as well, in reference to entropy—a term from physics referring to the universe's overall gradual loss of energy. Almost as an aside, with no direct reference to Rapoport, Guldin remarks on the way Flusser's theory of games adapts terminology from linguistics—"structure" and "repertoire" resembling syntax and semantics, competence and universe constituting established linguistic terms.[22]

"Games" relies on just three examples—chess, language (he chose Portuguese), and the natural sciences—to extend the structure to virtually any kind of communication. A reader can hardly help but be startled by the sheer scope of the definition. If a system with the breadth and depth of a language or the highly abstract structures associated with natural science can be games, is there any kind of communication that is not? Flusser's answer is, in a word, no. And this "no" separates him from almost everyone else who has written about games in any capacity. For Flusser, there is no "outside" of games—playing or being played, we are always engaged in some game—probably many simultaneously. Without them there is no meaning at all.

As is often the case in Flusser's essays, "Games" ends by repeating and resolving the question or issue set out in the beginning. In this case, the conclusion quietly repeats the move from *Homo sapiens*, *Homo faber*, *animal laborans* to *Homo ludens*. Now the species is distinguished by its capacity to open games, expand or reduce repertoires, alter structures, criticize—in short, to play:

> A human being as "homo ludens" is set apart from animals by the absence of seriousness. Play is his answer to the stolid seriousness of life and death. As a player he resists this stolidity. And he becomes more of a rebel the more games he plays and the more he cheats. He sets himself apart from the apparatuses he deceives in the course of his playing by means of his ability to open games. In other words: he sets himself apart from computers, government regulations and other visible and invisible monsters by means of poetry, philosophy and translation. That is his hope. As a subject of history, he may be liberated by these apparatuses. But history itself is only a game, and he can find others.[23]

When the theoretical terms Flusser introduced in "Games" resurface in his subsequent writings, they refer broadly to the idea of infinitely many systems linking human beings meaningfully—if not always happily—together in some way. More specifically, they refer to the possibility of the aesthetic experience of playing with those systems or, conversely, to a failure to realize that possibility, a falling back into a position of "being played." The term "game," as it appears in *Towards a Philosophy of Photography*, for example, reminds the reader that the object in question has elements, a structure, a competence, and a universe. Most photographs and most photographers function in accordance with an established system—in the case of photography from design and marketing of cameras to education, exhibition, publishing, and more. But this same system may be criticized, expanded, or translated into other discourses in new ways. In his published criticism of particular photographs and photographers, it is expressly the photographers who have recognized photography as a game and played with it who earn Flusser's praise. In 1985, for example, he wrote an introduction to a catalog of Joan Fontcuberta's series "Herbarium," an elaborate, and by now celebrated document recording the findings of a fictional botanist. Flusser credits Fontcuberta with having been able to play with both photography and botanical illustration, providing himself and us with a new insight into both.[24]

In short, when Flusser identifies a communicative structure as a "game," and this is as likely to be a discipline, a technology, or a discourse as it is to be something like chess or football, he is calling attention to its status as given—fixed, right, "true"—and inviting a challenge to this status; when he speaks of "play," he is referring to the activity that follows the question "what if . . . " What if we changed the rules, say, added elements (e.g., inserted an elephant between the knight and rook in chess)[25], used one game to express information originally encoded for another?

* * *

Among the last essays Flusser wrote, "Digitaler Schein" ("Schein" sounds like the English "shine" and might be translated as "semblance," "appearance," or possibly "illusion") addresses the phenomenon of "alternative worlds" that were just beginning to appear on computer screens at the time of writing.[26] Anticipating that his readers would dismiss such worlds as empty and trivial simply because they were artificial, Flusser argues that since all meaning is constructed, alternative worlds are as "real" as any other and have just as much potential to generate meaning. All are made up of whirling particles, and although at present the distribution of those particles tends to be much denser in the world we have been given than they are in the alternative worlds, there is no technical reason the current imbalance should not gradually resolve into so many equally persuasive possibilities. "Digitaler Schein" does not mention videogames. He may have been thinking of something more like what we would call simulation software. In any case he sees such worlds as sites where elite practitioners of an unprecedented kind of communication are establishing themselves, learning to operate the controls.

The reason he did not identify alternative worlds as games in this essay, I think, is that the idea of a game was not of interest to Flusser if there was no possibility of playing—in the sense of experiencing one's own humanity, and he found the new worlds inaccessible. The essay casts both author and reader as onlookers, their noses pressed up against a glass through which they watch others "play" in, or with, the new alternative worlds. The "glass," clearly, marks a boundary between those who write computer codes and those who do not. In *Into the Universe of Technical Images*—and "universe" may now be understood as "the sum total of combinations" of technical images—Flusser further projected a future world in which reading and writing have become exotic skills and people lead their lives in synthesized environments, tapping keyboards with their fingertips, so engrossed in what they are doing that they forget to eat and sleep.[27] A contemporary reader will surely think of MMORPGs (Massively Multi-player Online Role-Playing Games) such as *World of Warcraft* or *Fortnite*.

At the end of *Does Writing Have a Future?*, first published in 1987, Flusser had already expressed such a sense of exclusion, of regretting that he was too old, too deeply and durably shaped by language and print to adapt to the new devices.[28] Later, in "Digitaler Schein," he reiterates his sense of exclusion, now with a more pointed effort to show us—readers of essays—that we are likely to be in the same position:

> just those few people who have left this [historical] consciousness behind, who no longer experience, recognize and value the world as a chain of events but as a toss of the dice, whose thinking is no longer progressive and enlightened, but futurological and system-analytical or "structural," are producing the models the majority of people follow. They program advertising, films and political programs according to structural criteria, and cannot be called to account by those who are manipulated.[29]

They also design digital games, we might add.

To the extent that Flusser's "alternative worlds" resemble contemporary videogames, we are obliged to respect his very clear and consistent distinction between "programmers" and "programmed," or, to stay with his language, between games and the possibility of actually *playing*. We are perhaps particularly constrained to respect his definition of the capacity for play as the feature that distinguishes human beings from their apparatuses. In light of the astonishing recent expansion of the sheer numbers, diversity, subtlety, and popularity of computer games, along with proliferating claims for their value in helping users learn new skills, resolve old problems, and adapt to changes in their circumstances and identities, it may seem almost perverse to ask, in the interests of representing Flusser's sense of games and play, who is really *playing*.

Some readers of this essay may agree that online video games seem alien, unapproachable: whatever they may be, they are not "fun." A few may further support Flusser's contention that "the alternative worlds that are now forming in computers must be understood as designs of the ruling elite." Flusser accepts—in fact welcomes—the radical artificiality of such games and sees no inherent limit to their potential for engaging people in persuasive, attractive, satisfying, meaningful realities. Only he can't play. Not only did he lack the technical skills to operate the game controls (he did not use a computer at all, not even a word processor. He wrote on a manual typewriter), he also resisted the kind of thinking that can calculate and compute imaginary worlds. He draws an analogy to the gradual implementation of writing into oral culture between 3500 BC and the early nineteenth century, those centuries in which a literate elite could "program" an illiterate majority.

In his book *Videogames, Identity and Digital Subjectivity*,[30] Rob Gallagher lends support to the contention that "gamers"—loosely, people who invest a significant proportion of their time and energy in mastering and critiquing digital games—constitute an elite. Drawing on Graeme Kirkpatrick's study of gaming culture in the United Kingdom,[31] Gallagher identifies *gameplay* as the key feature around which gamer culture coalesces:

> In order to forge an image of "gamers" as "young, male and cool," "subjects who appreciate gameplay and are good at it," early gaming culture began to define itself in opposition to those who did not meet these criteria. If this meant jokes at the

expense of women and older people, it also meant striving to differentiate gamers from enthusiasts next to whose truly nerdy hobbies (hobbies like trainspotting, stamp collecting or tabletop gaming) digital gaming could be considered exciting and subversive. More than that, though, it entailed mockery of insufficiently skilled would-be-gamers [who] . . . prize dazzling graphics or an absorbing plot over that ineffable but all-important criterion of compelling gameplay.[32]

To return to the criteria introduced in the example of the chess game earlier, gamers can and do play, in Flusser's sense, when they step outside the game, play with it. They may be critics—often outspoken, articulate, and enthusiastic critics—of particular games or of tendencies or companies or particular designers. Such criticism—invariably written—may feed back to the companies or designers in question and may have some impact on the digital world in question—or not. Some gamers meet outside the game as well. As in the earlier example of the chess game, their focus turns to one another. In this context, "gameplay" furnishes an aesthetic framework in which individuals perceive beauty, elegance, satisfaction—or above all, fun—in a given game differently. In differing, they act themselves out, align themselves with the aesthetic values that make them the specific human beings they are.

In his discovery, adaptation, and projection of games, Flusser was playing. That is to say, he was engaging in games of mathematics, linguistics, anthropology, history, quantum theory, music, visual arts, and more, translating among them, criticizing and changing them without losing awareness that they *are* games, that is, without surrendering his freedom to participate whenever and for whatever reasons he might choose and to abandon the game at will. He endorsed cheating, jumping between games, inventing new ones on the spot. He encouraged others to do the same. But, as he once put it, "without responsibility there is no freedom."[33] The jumps and transformations and inventions are constrained by the need for meaning and a desire for the various pieces to "form a whole," a constraint that can only be identified as aesthetic.

Flusser's play with games seems in many ways to model what he calls, in his last book, a "project." *Vom Subjekt zum Projekt* [*From Subject to Project*][34] begins with the question "Are we really postmodern?" It goes on to characterize the modern as a long shift in communicative codes—from alphabetic to numeric—a shift toward greater abstraction and precision, and from human subservience to God to a subservience to things—nature as the object of human knowledge. He marks the end of the modern as the point where there can be no further abstraction. Minds and mountains, planets and people, have all dissolved into whirling particles, and a subject is left without an object, with no sense of a relationship to the world. In the course of learning to calculate the world, however, human beings also learned to compute new ones. Surely drawing on his own encounter with despair, Flusser speaks of a point where human beings can turn away from subjectivity and walk into the future as designers or artists, drafting, projecting worlds as they go, conferring rather than exposing meaning. Flusser's play with games may be a modest example of a project, relying as it does on alphabetic text, leaving readers to fill in much of the dialogue with other thinkers for themselves, making hardly any technical demands at all. But he insists that when we have really accepted the absence of any accessible common "reality," grasped the urgent need to generate meaning, and begun to use technology to think and dream together, we will truly have become postmodern.

Notes

1. Unless otherwise noted, translations from German are mine.
   Flusser employs the prefix "meta" with regularity. One of Gregory Bateson's innovations, it would have been relatively new in 1969, and its appearance here suggests that Flusser was familiar with Bateson's work.
2. Flusser, "In Search of Meaning," in *Writings*, ed. Andreas Ströhl (Minneapolis: University of Minnesota Press, 2002), 197–207, 205.
3. Ibid., 205.
4. The book acknowledged to have founded game theory as a mathematical discipline is Johan von Neumann and Oskar Morgenstern's *Theory of Games and Economic Behavior* (Princeton: Princeton University Press, 1944).
5. Flusser wrote for publication, in descending order of frequency, in German, Portuguese, English, and French.
6. Flusser, "The Gesture of Writing," *New Writing: The International Journal for the Practice and Theory of Creative Writing* 9, no. 1 (March 2012): 25–41.
7. Gregory Bateson, "A Theory of Play and Fantasy," in *Steps to an Ecology of Mind* (New York: Ballantine, 1972 [1955]), 177–93.
8. Bateson, "The Message 'This Is Play,'" in *Transactions of the Second Conference on Group Processes*, ed. Bertram Schaffner (Princeton: Josiah Macey Foundation, 1955), 145–241.
9. Flusser, *Into the Universe of Technical Images* (Minneapolis: University of Minnesota Press, 2011), 100.
10. Flusser, "Jogos," *O Estado de São Paulo*, 1967, and "Die Welt als Spiel," *Frankfurter Allgemeine*, 1968. The German text was reprinted as "Spiele" [Games] in Florian Rötzer, *Ist das Leben ein Spiel?* (Berlin: Wilhelm Fink Verlag) and the Vilém Flusser Archive, Universität der Künste, Berlin, 2013.
11. Ibid., n.p.
12. Johann Huizinga, *Homo Ludens: A Study of the Play Element in Culture* (London: Routledge & Kegan Paul, 1949 [1938]).
13. Flusser, *Das Zwanzigste Jahrhundert. Versuch einer subjektiven Synthese* [*The Twentieth Century. Attempt at a Subjective Synthesis*] (unpublished typescript, Vilém Flusser Archive, Berlin).
14. Katie Salen and Eric Zimmerman, *Rules of Play: Game Design Fundamentals* (Cambridge, MA and London: The MIT Press, 2004), 75.
15. Peter McDonald, "Homo Ludens: A Renewed Reading," *The American Journal of Play* 11, no. 2 (Winter 2019): 247–67.
16. Flusser, "Spiele" [Games], n.p.
17. Friedrich Schiller, *On the Aesthetic Education of Man in a Series of Letters*, trans. and ed. Elizabeth M. Wilkinson and L. A. Willoughby (Oxford: Clarendon Press, 2005 [1795]), 107.
18. Flusser, "Spiele" [Games], n.p.

19 Ibid., n.p.
20 Rainer Guldin, "Vom Nullsummen-zum Plussummenspiel: Zur Bedeutung Anatol Rapoports in Vilém Flusser's Spieltheorie," in *Play It Again, Vilém! Medien und Spiel im Anschluß an Vilém Flusser*, ed. Hermann Haarmann, Michael Hanke, and Steffi Winkler (Marburg: Tectum Verlag, 2015), 87–111.
21 Ibid., 104–6, 108–9.
22 Ibid., 101.
23 Flusser, "Spiele" [Games], n.p.
24 Flusser, "Einführung," in *Standpunkte: Texte zur Fotografie*, ed. Andreas Müller-Pohle (Göttingen: European Photography, 1998 [1985]), 113–16.
25 Flusser, "Spiele" [Games], n.p.
26 Flusser, "Digitaler Schein," in *Medienkultur*, 3rd ed. (Frankfurt am Main: Fischer, 2002 [1991]), 202–15.
27 Flusser, *Into the Universe of Technical Images*, 104.
28 Flusser, *Does Writing Have a Future?* (Minneapolis: University of Minnesota Press, 2011 [1987]), 157–61.
29 Flusser, "Digitaler Schein," 207.
30 Rob Gallagher, *Videogames, Identity and Digital Subjectivity* (London: Routledge, 2017).
31 Graeme Kirkpatrick, "Constitutive Tensions of Gaming's Field: UK Gaming Magazines and the Formation of Gaming Culture 1981-1995," *Game Studies* 12, no. 1 (2012): n.p. http://gamestudies.org/1201/articles/kirkpatrick.
32 Gallagher, *Videogames*, 9.
33 Flusser, *Gestures* (Minneapolis: University of Minnesota Press, 2011 [1991]), 136.
34 Flusser, *Vom Subjekt zum Projekt* [*From Subject to Project*] (Bensheim and Düsseldorf: Bollmann Verlag, 1994).

7

Flusser's Philosophical Backgrounds

Martha Schwendener

Wittgenstein, Husserl, and Heidegger

This chapter will discuss Flusser as a twentieth-century thinker: his European—and particularly Central European—upbringing and enduring interest in the philosophy of that region. Writers such as Andreas Ströhl have argued that Flusser saw himself as an Old European, and I want to examine this first by looking at the philosophers Flusser referenced most frequently. For instance, Flusser wrote that when he read the first sentence of Wittgenstein's *Tractatus Logico-Philosophicus* (1921) it resulted in a "moment of transformation." But Wittgenstein's influence continued to the end of Flusser's life: his first and second books, *Language and Reality* and *The History of the Devil*, were structured in what Flusser called a "caricature of the Wittgensteinian method," mimicking the numbered, philosophical propositions in the *Tractatus*;[1] Flusser reviewed a new German edition of Wittgenstein's *Philosophical Investigations* for the *Revista Brasileira de Filosofia* in 1966, in which he called Wittgenstein a "gigantic figure" and "one of the major thinkers";[2] and Flusser was still quoting Wittgenstein in texts like *Gestures*, a German version of which he was preparing shortly before he died in 1991.[3]

For Wittgenstein, the primary problems of philosophy rested on "the misunderstanding of the logic of the language."[4] This included cleaning up philosophical language, since he felt that most philosophers do not understand the logic of language and thus fall into making nonsensical propositions. For Flusser, the importance of Wittgenstein can be felt most obviously in *Language and Reality*, although some writers have argued that he was reading Wittgenstein against the grain in this text.[5] Wittgenstein provided a grounding in language, and *Language and Reality* reflected this insistence that not only does language create reality, but thinking itself is limited by language. Flusser would later borrow from Wittgenstein the idea of *Sprachspiele* or language games as laid out in the *Philosophical Investigations*, in which different forms of language function differently (Wittgenstein provided an exhaustive list, from reporting an event to making up a story, asking, thanking, translating, or telling a joke.).[6] The Wittgenstein of *Tractatus* argued that "the object of philosophy is the logical clarification of thoughts. Philosophy is not a theory but an activity."[7] Similarly, Flusser would often set aside the word "theory" in quotation marks (as he did many terms) and push this further to indicate that theory and philosophy were a kind of game: "everything is art, language, including that utmost game: *ars moriendi*. It must be translated between games, including the game of death."[8] But if language itself was a "game," it could be simplified rather than complicated: the late Wittgenstein emphasized ordinary language over formal logic, and this reliance on simple language can be felt throughout Flusser's *oeuvre*. Moreover, Wittgenstein's idea that the "picture is the model of reality" could be seen as an early seed for Flusser's thinking, not only because it reveals Wittgenstein's attitude that language is un-representable, but because it suggests the importance of technical images within a new posthistorical reality in which writing is eclipsed.[9]

In terms of important European philosophers, Flusser also cites members of the Vienna Circle, who were influenced by the *Tractatus*—particularly Rudolf Carnap, whose logical positivism concerned the distinction between philosophy and science, as well as Ernst Cassirer. Michael Hanke extends the list to include Otto Jespersen, Fritz Mauthner, Max Black, A. Waag, Nicolai Hartmann, Russell, Whitehead, and Wilhelm Dilthey—along with Husserl and Heidegger.[10] Flusser's essay "On Edmund Husserl" went through several iterations and serves as a testament to his enduring debt to Husserl, the principal founder of phenomenology.[11] With Husserl, knowledge takes precedence over the subject and the object, creating what Flusser calls a "dynamic net" of "concrete intentionalities" in which experience is concrete and subject and object are abstract. Nothing is known without being experienced and evaluated and the world becomes a "pure and concrete field of relations."[12] One can discern in this premise the idea of the "photographic universe," which is "to know and to evaluate the world as a function of photographs."[13] But one can also see the overlap with Buber, who was more interested in human relations—intersubjectivity—than in knowledge, per se. Flusser writes that "under phenomenological vision, society will be seen as a net composed of intersubjective intentional relations. The knots in the net are what used to be called 'individuals.' . . . Since Husserl, there can be no such thing as an 'I' that is unrelated. In fact, I am the sum of my relations."[14] Furthermore, "there is no such thing as 'a society.' If the knots are unknotted, the net will collapse and disappear: it comprises the knots. 'I' and 'society' are abstract extrapolations from concrete intersubjective relations."[15]

The concept of the photographic universe can be linked even more strongly to Heidegger. Flusser's friend Vicente Ferreira da Silva was credited with bringing Heidegger to Brazil and Dora Ferreira da Silva, the poet and wife of Vicente, dedicated an issue of the literary journal *Cavalo Azul*, to which Flusser was a frequent contributor, to Heidegger in 1968.[16] Flusser dedicated "Our Inebriation" in *Post-History* to Heidegger, whom he claimed had "changed my vision of things."[17] One can discern in Flusser's concept of the photographic universe Heidegger's *Dasein* or "being-in-the-world," as laid out in *Being and Time*, in which we're immersed in a situation—time, history, context—of which we are not fully conscious.[18] *Dasein* is always rooted in time, but also vaguely aware that the world is *ungrounded* (the familiar word is *Bodenlos*; Flusser also used the term "*Dasein*," untranslated). Flusser follows Heidegger in attempting to create a language appropriate to this state of affairs. If Heidegger felt like philosophical language was unsuited to describing *Dasein*, Flusser set about fashioning philosophy that would reflect shifts in translation, but also *Dasein* in a world in which technology determines the human condition. (Flusser's writings on the technical image as well as his use of etymology to explain terms like "apparatus" and "technology owe much to Heidegger's essays 'The Age of the World Picture' (1938), 'The Turning' (1949), and 'The Question Concerning Technology' (1955) in particular.")

Heidegger is also important for Flusser in considering history. For Heidegger, historical epochs represent different ways of being in the world: Greeks, Christians, and modern humans each had their own *Dasein*. For Flusser, the formulation of "hands, tools, machines, robots" addresses a similar situation in which there are no universal structures and our *Dasein* is mediated through technology.[19] Heidegger's philosophical presupposition that technology determines our human condition is central to *Towards a Philosophy of Photography*—but *Into the Universe of Technical Images* takes this even further.[22] For Heidegger, history has changed from antiquity to the present, culminating in a technological state of being that dominates the planet. For Flusser, we have entered *posthistory*, an epoch of technological images in which writing, which created history, doesn't have a future. Heidegger saw our version of being at a dead end: nihilism. But in technology Flusser sees optimism and a way of creating a telematic society. Following the later work of Heidegger, thinkers such as Foucault and Derrida attempted to deconstruct the definition of being or the subject, deploying a genealogical analysis of the trajectory through which "the subject" was constructed and legitimized, not just in philosophy (by Descartes, for instance) but in the political, juridical, educational, and ethical realms—and adapted idiomatically in various languages. For Flusser, writing near the end of his life in *From Subject to Project: On Becoming Human*, the human subject becomes "project": a projector of possible lives and alternative worlds.[20]

Invoking Derrida also helps in thinking about Heidegger and nationalism. In a 1992 interview at Oxford University, Derrida discussed how we think of philosophy as a universal discourse while it has always been linked to specific cities and languages—particularly in the nineteenth century, when European nations were being formed.[21] For Derrida, deconstruction was a project aimed at reaffirming "singularity" without giving rise to violent forms of nationalism, an attempt to reaffirm difference while respecting the Other's difference. Heidegger, of course, represents the "bad" sort of nationalism: the recent publication of his "Black Notebooks," journals he kept between 1931 and 1941, confirms his anti-Semitism and unmistakable rather than naïve allegiance to Nazism.[22] However, many Jewish philosophers have been influenced by Heidegger; Derrida, like Flusser, was Jewish—and heavily indebted to Heidegger. As with Derrida's approach to philosophy and nationalism, one might say that Flusser found his strongest weapon in writing texts like *The Freedom of the Migrant: Objections to Nationalism*, which both "uses" Heidegger and critiques nationalism.[23]

Martin Buber, Franz Kafka, and José Ortega y Gasset

When Flusser left Europe in 1939, the only books he had with him were Goethe's *Faust* and a small Jewish prayer book his mother gave to him at the last moment.[24] After seeing Martin Buber give a lecture in Prague, Flusser began to formulate his ideas about how the circulation of technical images in a "dialogic" society might be seen as a secular version of Buber's "I" and "thou" relationship. For Flusser, however, "dialogical life" transformed into "dialogical programming" in which each image-maker sitting before her computer can program her own apparatus, rather than being programmed. The "I" becomes a knot in a dialogical web of networked society.[25] In other places, Flusser synthesizes Husserl's notion of the lifeworld as a network of concrete intentionalities with Buber's transcendental, existential version of dialogue:[26]

> A telematized society will be exactly that network of pure relationships that Husserl defines as the concrete structure of the social phenomenon. . . . Instead of the individual man being the supreme value, it is now the dialogue between men that becomes the supreme value, or what Martin Buber, whose thought was profoundly influenced by Husserl, called the "dialogical life" (*das dialogische Leben*).[27]

For Flusser, Buber's dialogical life spoke not "of" God but "to" God, with "the Judeo-Christian tradition breaking through the technological surface."[28]

If Buber served as a beneficent link between Flusser and Prague, Andreas Ströhl calls Franz Kafka Flusser's "threatening older brother": the one whose God stranded him absurdly at the edge of nothingness.[29] Like Flusser, Kafka (1883–1924) was from the German-speaking Jewish minority in Prague. In "Waiting for Kafka," an essay written in the sixties and published in Portuguese and German, Flusser addresses this:[30] "Kafka's thoughts are determined by the structure of German grammar. Kafka had German thoughts, and everything he thought was structured *a priori* by the grammar of this language. When [his writings] are translated into other languages, Kafka's thoughts are structurally distorted. Thus, any alleged sympathy with these translated thoughts may actually be based on errors."[31] Flusser was freed from the "sterile" High German of Kafka, which originated as an artificial literary language in the chancellery offices of Emperor Charles IV of Prague.[32] But his tone and approach became part of Flusser's thinking and writing—particularly with regard to irony:

> Because of this idiom, Kafka's message possesses the aura of ridiculously absurd pedantry so characteristic of him. The language of Prague oscillates between the poles of pedantic artificiality (historically embodied by the Austro-Hungarian bureaucracy) and ridiculous language mixes (for example, historically embodied in the Czech, semi-German Officer Schweik). Because this language structures Kafka's thoughts *a priori*, they automatically oscillate within this dialectical tension. The overcoming of this tension leads directly to a malicious irony, which we usually call Kafka's irony.[33]

Flusser argues that Kafka used this "climate of inauthenticity" to create an ironic authenticity.[34] Kafka's search is like that of the mystics: a search for God. But what Kafka ultimately accomplishes is the "existentialization of Nietzsche" in which God is a "pedantic, over-organized, ridiculously incompetent God" who is "sick and tired of himself."[35] The result of this is that human progress is progress in the direction of nothingness, leading through various hierarchies that illustrate "experiences of nothingness."[36] Amplifying this even further is the way Kafka's "message"—the language of information theory pervades the essay—was ultimately delivered: through his protégé, Max Brod, who disobeyed Kafka's orders to destroy his writings and published them anyway. This historical fact contributes to the reception of Kafka's message, heightening our doubt concerning its authenticity and leaving Flusser himself in limbo: waiting for Kafka—or, more precisely, "an authentic answer to Kafka"[37]—while looking for a way to escape the "incompetent bureaucratic apparatus" by confronting other forms of apparatus.[38]

I have focused so far on German-language thinkers, but the last European I want to mention is Spanish: José Ortega y Gasset. One might imagine that since Flusser formulated an idea of posthistory, he might be drawn to Ortega's "History as a System," in which the Spanish writer challenged Cartesian rationality, faith in science, the Western concept of "nature," and history as a "science of the present" in need of a contemporary reassessment.[39] Ortega also questioned concepts like liberalism and nationalism, which would be important for Flusser. Near the beginning of "In Search of Meaning," however, Flusser writes that Ortega's *Revolt of the Masses*, which he read during his formative years in Prague, helped him discover "that vast world vaguely called 'Existentialism,'" and led him back to Nietzsche.[40] Ortega's "mass-man" is a bourgeois-educated figure who is incapable of leadership, leading to a rudderless existence that foreshadows the existentialists. (Albert Camus called him, "after Nietzsche, perhaps the greatest European writer.")[41] One could also imagine Ortega's idea of a historical rupture having a lasting effect on Flusser's thinking. In the last essay of *Revolt of the Masses* Ortega wrote that "Europe is now reaping the painful results of her spiritual conduct. She has adopted blindly a culture which is magnificent, but has no roots."[42] Like Kafka the "prophet," as Flusser called him, Ortega was a prognosticator. Flusser himself grew famous in certain realms for predicting a society glued to and communicating through its computer screens. Per Ortega's predictions, Europe's character defects would shortly be exposed, and Flusser himself would be profoundly affected.

* * *

Flusser's philosophies of language, phenomenology, history, and technology drew upon sustained, identifiable encounters with earlier European thinkers like Husserl, Heidegger, Wittgenstein, Buber, Kafka, and Ortega y Gasset. These influences are part of the fabric of Flusserian thought. In an important sense, Flusser's subsequent encounters with concepts from midcentury US information theory and thinkers such as Norbert Wiener and Claude Shannon might be understood in terms of a cybernetic remediation of the modernist ideas that affected his thinking and which I outlined earlier. Connecting modernist philosophers and midcentury theories of information, Flusser casts them both in a radically different hue from contemporaries such as Hans Magnus Enzensberger, Jean Baudrillard, Paul Virilio, and Gilles Deleuze with whom he is so often compared.

Notes

1. Flusser quoted in Rodrigo Maltez Novaes, "Introduction," in *The History of the Devil* (Minneapolis: Univocal, 2014), xvii.
2. Vilém Flusser, "Ludwig Wittgenstein: *Philosophische bemerkungen*," *Revista Brasileira de filosofia* 16 (1966): 129–32. Also see Matthias Kross, "Zwischen Logik und Existenzialismus. Flussers Wittgenstein," *The Third Shore*, 81–98.
3. See Flusser, "The Gesture of Speaking," in *Gestures*, trans. Nancy Ann Roth (Minneapolis and London: University of Minnesota Press, 2014), 31. Also see Karlheinz Ludeking, "Pictures and Gestures," *British Journal of Aesthetics* 30, no. 3 (July 1990): 218–32.
4. Ludwig Wittgenstein, *Tractatus Logico-Philosophicus* (London: Kegan Paul, Trench, Trubner & Co.; New York: Harcourt, Brace & Company, 1922), 23. Project Gutenberg eBook, released October 10, 2010, accessed November 8, 2014, http://www.gutenberg.org/files/5740/5740-pdf.pdf?session_id=a869dbc014e06717ee34be1481a6de0ec5d11611.
5. Matthias Kross, "Medienphilosophie als ethisches Projekt? Vilém Flussers Wittgenstein," *Publications of the Austrian Ludwig Wittgenstein Society* 6 (2006), accessed November 8, 2014, http://wittgensteinrepository.org/agora-ontos/article/view/2070.
6. Ludwig Wittgenstein, *Philosophical Investigations*, trans. G. E. M. Anscombe (Oxford: Blackwell, 1953). For a discussion of *Sprachspiele* with regard to literary interpretation, see G. L. Hagberg, *Meaning and Interpretation: Wittgenstein, Henry James, and Literary Knowledge* (Ithaca, NY: Cornell University Press, 1994), 9–44.
7. Wittgenstein, *Tractatus Logico-Philosophicus*, 52.
8. Flusser quoted in Anke Finger, Rainer Guldin, and Gustavo Bernardo, eds., *Vilém Flusser: An Introduction*, (Minneapolis: University of Minnesota Press, 2011), 59–60.
9. Wittgenstein, *Tractatus Logico-Philosophicus*, 28. Also see Eugen Fischer, "Philosophical Pictures," *Synthese* 148 (2006): 469–501.
10. Michael Hanke, "Vilém Flussers Sprache und Wirklichkeit von 1963 im Kontext seiner Medienphilosophie," *Flusser Studies* 02 (2006): 5.
11. Flusser, "On Edmund Husserl," *Philosophy of Photography* 2, no. 2 (2011): 234–8. This version is from an unpublished manuscript, written in English, in the Vilém Flusser Archive, document No. 723.
12. Flusser, "On Edmund Husserl," 236–7.
13. Vilém Flusser, *Towards a Philosophy of Photography* (Göttingen, Germany: European Photography), 51.
14. Ibid., 237.
15. Ibid.

16 Dora Marianna Ferreira da Silva, ed., *Cavalo Azul* 6 (São Paulo, 1968). See Flusser, "A Alma Vendida," *Cavalo Azul* 6 (São Paulo, 1968): 88–93.
17 See Vilém Flusser, "Heidegger et le Nazisme: 'Nous sommes face à l'expression la plus importante de la pensée de notre siècle' (Heidegger and Nazism: 'We are facing the most important expression of thought of our century')", *Calades* 86 (February 1988). Quoted in Sjouke van der Muelen, "Between Benjamin and McLuhan," 198.
18 Heidegger, *Being and Time*, trans. John MacQuarrie and Edward Robinson (New York: Harper Perennial, 2008).
19 Gabriela Freitas, "Um diálogo entre Flusser e Heidegger: o ser no universe das imagens técnicas," *Flusser Studies* 17 (June 2014), accessed November 24, 2014, www.flusserstudies.net. In her article, Freitas argues that Flusser inverts Heidegger's "being-in-the-world" into "being-face-to-face-with-the-image," so that only the image is concrete and we end up back in the objective world, in a state of being -in-the-universe-of-technical-images. Also see Matthias Kross's "Arbeit am Archiv: Flussers Heidegger," in *Technobilder und Kommunikologie: Die Medientheorie Vilém Flusser*, eds. Oliver Fahle, Michael Hanke, and Andreas Ziemann (Berlin: Parega, 2009), 73–91.
20 Flusser, *Vom Subjekt zum Projekt. Menschwerdung* (Bensheim and Düsseldorf: Bollmann, 1994).
21 Jacques Derrida interview with Alan Montefiore, February 13, 1992, Oxford University, accessed July 15, 2015, https://www.youtube.com/watch?v=7s8SSilNSXw.
22 Martin Heidegger, *Überlegungen II–VI (Schwarze Hefte 1931–1938)* [Reflections II–VI (Black Notebooks 1931–1938)], ed. Peter Trawny (Frankfurt: Klostermann, 2014); *Überlegungen VII–XI (Schwarze Hefte 1938/39)* [Reflections VII–XI (Black Notebooks 1938/39)], ed. Peter Trawny (Frankfurt, Klostermann, 2014); *Überlegungen XII–XV (Schwarze Hefte 1939–1941)* [Reflections XII–XV (Black Notebooks 1939–1941)], ed. Peter Trawny (Frankfurt: Klostermann, 2014). Hannah Arendt, Heidegger's former student and lover, also served as an apologist. See Hannah Arendt's "Heidegger at Eighty," *The New York Review* (October 21, 1971): 51. For a less sympathetic account written by another Heidegger student, see Victor Farias, *Heidegger and Nazism* (Philadelphia: Temple University Press, 1989).
23 Also see Flusser, "Heidegger et le Nazisme."
24 Novaes, "Introduction," xi.
25 Flusser, *Into the Universe of Technical Images* (Minneapolis: University of Minnesota Press, 2011), 92.
26 Ströhl, "Introduction," in *Writings*, ed. Andreas Ströhl (Minneapolis: University of Minnesota Press, 2002), xiv.
27 Flusser, "On Edmund Husserl," quoted in *Writings*, ed. Ströhl, xiv.
28 Flusser, from "Dialogische Medien," in *Kommunikologie* (295), quoted in *Writings*, ed. Ströhl, xv.
29 Ströhl, "Introduction," xvi.
30 Flusser, "Waiting for Kafka" (1967), in *Writings*, ed. Ströhl, 150–9.
31 Ibid., 151.
32 Ibid.
33 Ibid., 152.
34 Ibid.
35 Ibid., 158.

36 Ibid.
37 Ibid., 159.
38 Ibid., 154.
39 José Ortega y Gasset, *History as a System and Other Essays Toward a Philosophy of History*, trans. Helen Weyl (New York: W.W. Norton, 1961).
40 Flusser, *Writings*, 199.
41 Quoted in Pedro Blas Gonzalez, *Ortega's* Revolt of the Masses *and the Triumph of the New Man* (New York: Algora, 2007), 8.
42 José Ortega y Gasset, *The Revolt of the Masses* (New York: W.W. Norton, 1932), 189–90.

8

Vilém Flusser's Quasi-Phenomenology

Andreas Max Ströhl

Flusser was mainly perceived as a media theorist. There is a lot of truth to that, but it is only half the truth. *More than anything else, Flusser was a cultural theorist, and his methodological instruments were taken from phenomenology.* But was he a phenomenologist in the true sense?

My argument in this chapter will roughly proceed as follows: Flusser believed that politics was an aspect of the historical paradigm and that with the paradigm shift away from linearity toward the universe of zero-dimensionality, the respective codes and ways of being in the world would change accordingly. Instead of reading and writing, the dominant cultural techniques would become the reception and computation of technical images from calculated, zero-dimensional dots and bits. And our way of being in the world and our corresponding lifeworld would develop from a historical culture, ideology, and society to a posthistorical one. Along with the historical paradigm, the concept and notion of politics would disappear. And that would be a loss Flusser mostly welcomed—bearing in mind what incredible disasters the political paradigm had already caused.

I will then briefly explain how the concept of *development* on the basis of continuously produced new information from dialogues keeps the posthistorical society from being truly posthistorical. History in the sense of dialectics, of a further development, will still take place there and along with it *politics*.

* * *

Vilém Flusser was eager to welcome the *end of the linear paradigm* (often referred to as the "end of history") and, with it, the end of the paradigm of progress and politics. In a posthistorical society, a net dialogue, a dialogue that permits simultaneous dialogical communication among all participants, would connect human beings who playfully create new information in free relationships of appreciation (*freie Anerkennungsverhältnisse*).

Politics, however, like *work*, is not part of this utopian dialogical lifeworld. The political paradigm belongs to the preceding historical world based on linear, progressive codes like writing. The dangers of linear, historical thinking based on writing come from a source that is deeper than the phenomena caused by it (like nationalism or patriotism). The *code of writing* itself, the *principle of history* as a program that successively realizes all its inherent potentialities, already foreshadows the catastrophe in Flusser's eyes. To him, Auschwitz was the result of humanism, the necessarily accidental product of the entire Western complex of history, politics, science, and technology. Under no circumstances, Flusser argues, must Auschwitz be misunderstood as an operational accident of modernity. According to Flusser, we are unable to cope with the Holocaust, because we are unable to admit that Auschwitz was not a violation of the historical, scientific paradigm but rather a possibility within the program of history and politics itself, a product of the rules of our own culture: "What is so monstrous about Auschwitz is that it was not an 'accident' never to be repeated but rather the first realization of a predisposition within the program of the West,"[1] "a result of our culture [. . .] that has become inevitable."[2] Like all virtualities within a closed program, it had—of necessity—to become real at one point.

After Auschwitz, Flusser argues, there is no choice left but to discard the present condition of humanity and to project ways of *becoming human*, of a *humanization* (*Menschwerdung*). The despair in the face of humanity and humanism as well as the paradigm shifts from writing to techno-images, from the dominance of discourse to an equilibrium with dialogue, and from a historical to a posthistorical attitude culminate in Flusser's attempt at *overtaking politics for political reasons*. In his utopia of a posthistorical society, human beings will be responsibly connected through leisurely dialogue, and the linear, historical, political paradigm will be a thing of the past.

However, there is a contradiction I find in his sketch of an apolitical, dialogical, posthistorical society: discourse, Flusser argues, is a necessity, because without it society would sink into poverty of information, because the information created in dialogues could no longer be passed on. Therefore, like dialogue, discourse is a cultural requirement. What this implies is the ideal of a culture and a society in continuous advancement. Thus, a progressive element remains inscribed even into the ideal type of a posthistorical society. This, however, contradicts the polarizing distinction Flusser makes between historical and posthistorical societies, because, as a consequence, the dynamics of historical development would remain intact even in posthistorical societies. This results in an irreconcilable contradiction. Such a dynamic, negentropic society, propelled by discourses (which in turn are fed by dialogues), would have to be called *historical* and *linear* at its core according to Flusser's own criteria.

Any way we look at it, it is easy to see that even in Flusser's most resolute rejection of the paradigms of history and politics *he cannot but reinscribe the paradigm of progression into his antipolitical utopia*. Like the alien in Ridley Scott's film *Alien* (1979), the ugly, unwanted, and repressed thing breeds within us and finally hatches and breaks free. In Flusser's case, the evil alien is the eternal return of repressed dialectics, the political paradigm itself.

* * *

Among the most obvious influences on Flusser's thinking was Edmund Husserl's phenomenology. Husserl, originally a mathematician and like Flusser a German-speaking Jew from what later became Czechoslovakia, is generally considered the founding father of phenomenology. He argued both against the tendency of his time to consider logic a product of psychology and against naïve naturalism that does not take its own epistemological prerequisites into account. As we know everything we know only through our consciousness, we need to understand what all acts of consciousness in general have in common. Those acts are always intentional; they are directed toward something, some object.

When I interviewed Edith Flusser, Vilém's late widow, a few years after Vilém had passed away, I asked her how he had thought of himself, how he would have defined himself. Without hesitation, Edith Flusser replied that Vilém had always considered himself a phenomenologist more than anything else.

However, due to the publishing policy of Bollmann Publishers in Germany, Flusser was widely perceived as a speculative media theorist. His philosophical qualities were disregarded and so were his achievements as a phenomenologist. Labeling and marketing Flusser as a prophet of the coming media society granted him more attention—and better book sales. Phenomenological philosophers of communication are much harder to sell. But in my opinion that is exactly what Flusser is. Only slowly have Flusser's reputation and general classification changed. But until this day Flusser is not always valued as a phenomenologist whose perhaps greatest achievement was the application of Husserl's method of eidetic reduction to a lifeworld increasingly shaped by mass media. I have tried to do my share to change that, and I did manage to get some phenomenologists interested in Flusser. Actually, I was invited to give the keynote speech at the sixteenth Annual Conference of the Society for Phenomenology and Media at the Husserl Archives in Freiburg in 2014, and this chapter is loosely based on my Freiburg keynote.

It is amazing how freely and yet true to its essence Flusser used Husserl's phenomenology as a tool. He adopted Husserl's method of *phenomenological reduction*, the *bracketing of prejudice*, as his own analytical technique of examining things in their essence:

> Looking at things as if for the first time is a method to discover aspects previously unnoticed. It is a powerful and fruitful method, but it requires strict discipline and that is why it can easily fail. At its heart, the discipline consists of forgetting, of excluding habituation, experience and knowledge. This is difficult, because as is well known, it is easier to learn than to forget. But even in cases where this method of purposefully forgetting does not succeed, its application will still bring about surprising results. And it achieves this precisely because of our inability to apply it in a disciplined way.[3]

Flusser's intellectual background in phenomenology permitted him views and insights that set him apart from the popular media theorists of the 1970s and 1980s, whose origins were mostly in either Marxism or post-structuralism. Using the phenomenological method, however, Flusser managed to diagnose an apparatus-operator complex as the *movens* behind contemporary social and technological developments, an "indistinguishable unity,"[4] considered by Flusser as a black box.

Flusser's relation to Husserlian phenomenology becomes most obvious in his book *Gesten: Versuch einer Phänomenologie* [*Gestures: Attempt at a Phenomenology* (1991)]. In *Gestures*, Flusser reflects on cultural attitudes the way they manifest themselves in gestures like writing or smoking. Flusser uses concrete exercises to demonstrate the kind of results the phenomenological glance can achieve if it is oriented toward unbiased findings of relations and actual situations.

The very titles of several of Flusser's books clearly reflect their reference to phenomenology: *Dinge und Undinge. Phänomenologische Skizzen*/*Things and Non-Things. Phenomenological Sketches* (1993, partly published in English as *The Shape of Things*), *Brasilien oder die Suche nach dem neuen Menschen. Für eine Phänomenologie der Unterentwicklung*/*Brazil, or the Search for the New Man. Towards a Phenomenology of Underdevelopment* (1994), or *Lob der Oberflächlichkeit. Für eine Phänomenologie der Medien*/*In Praise of Superficiality. Towards a Phenomenology of the Media* (1993), containing, among others, the 1974 essay *Für eine Phänomenologie des Fernsehens*/*Towards a Phenomenology of Television*.

* * *

Let us now take a look at Flusser's approach to photography, an example for the way he practically applied his media phenomenology. Flusser draws a clear distinction between the gesture of taking a photograph and the gesture of filming. In his analysis, Flusser argues that the photo camera is a *categorical* apparatus. The photographer leaps from one point of view to the other, from one world outlook to several disconnected other ones:

> This is what completely separates the photographic gesture from the cinematographic gesture; the camera does not "travel." This gesture is composed of a series of leaps across invisible obstacles, and of decisions. The photographer's quest is a series of abrupt acts of decision-making. The photographer pervades time-space which consists of different areas of vision (of different "Weltanschauungen") and of obstacles separating these visual fields. The structure of photography as a philosophical gesture is due to its quantum quality, the fact that it is about a "clara et distincta perceptio." The gesture of filming, however, dissolves this structure.
>
> The reason for this difference is obviously of technological nature: like the philosopher, the photographer looks through a "categorial" apparatus and pursues the goal of capturing the world as a series of distinct images or definable terms. The filmmaker looks through a "process-related" apparatus. His goal is to capture the world as a stream of undistinguishable images or indeterminable terms. This "technological" difference between the two apparatuses accounts for the difference in structure of the two gestures.[5]

The distinction Flusser draws between the two cultural techniques, the gestures of taking photos or of shooting a film, is of double interest to us. First, because Flusser actually follows through with what other media theorists usually claim but never exemplify or prove: how the use of different media technologies (of different environments, as McLuhan would have put it) actually leads to different perceptions of the world.

Second, Flusser argues that photography is a *philosophical* gesture. To him, it is *applied phenomenology*, the act of phenomenological epochē as physical action, as an observable gesture that, in turn, lends itself to phenomenological observation and analysis. And that is exactly what Flusser does. His analyses take place on two different levels. One is the level of objects: Flusser analyzes everyday objects and gestures. The object level also includes his phenomenology of cultural techniques, of codes and channels of communication, as he develops it in his *communicology*. We will take a closer look at this later. On the other level, however, the meta-level, Flusser analyzes the act of photographing. And as we have seen, to him that is the philosophical gesture per se, the way relational and phenomenological thinking manifests itself in practice.

But can Flusser's exercises really be called "phenomenological"?

At this point, I would like to introduce Lambert Wiesing, a renowned and distinguished German philosopher who focuses on phenomenology, perception theory, and esthetics. Wiesing, who is currently professor of *Comparative Image Theory* at Friedrich-Schiller-University Jena and President of the German Society for Phenomenological Research, argues that no, you cannot consider Flusser a phenomenologist. And I agree with him on this—but only to some extent. In the following paragraphs, I will follow Wiesing's arguments, but also add mine, and then further on will basically disagree with Wiesing.

"We get to the point of the difference between Flusser's and Husserl's understanding of phenomenology," Wiesing writes, "if we work with the term 'phenomenography'. Then the difference becomes clear: Flusser does not, like Husserl, understand phenomenology as the logic of phenomena, but as a phenomenography, that is, as the *description* of phenomena."[6] Flusser does indeed use the instrument of epochē, but he does not move on from there.

The principle of a *description free of theory* is without a doubt crucial to the entire process of phenomenological analysis, but as important as it may be, it is only the first step. To Husserl, this first step is but a necessary foundation for the second, equally important step that follows it: the *Wesensschau*, the eidetic variation. Flusser does not take this second step—and in a moment I will talk about the one exception I can see; he *does not generalize*. He shows no interest in comparing objects and actions after analyzing them. He does not construct groups or clusters, and he does not marshal the reduced observations of phenomena into *sets*. Instead, he seems quite satisfied with his indeed brilliant, descriptive analyses of objects and gestures and their functionality and relationality, with the way he manages to expose their essential features. This is not a mistake. Flusser simply acts based on a different range of interests, a different cognitive interest. "In this respect," Wiesing writes,

> Flusser's oeuvre is supported by a different basic concept, one that is without doubt more common today. It tends more towards the view of the cultural sciences, perhaps even a post-modern view that does not see the description of the phenomena as a

primary stage of the identification of principles. Instead, it considers this description the only possible alternative to an antiquated and mistaken philosophical quest for timeless and culturally invariant principles. And this is exactly why to Flusser photography can be philosophy: both share reflexive and self-conscious qualities. And taken merely as a cultural phenomenon, this is all philosophy really is.[7]

Despite Wiesing's rush to defend Flusser as a true phenomenologist (albeit on different grounds and with different goals), I think it does make sense to bear in mind that Flusser should really be called a "phenomenographer" instead.

Flusser's method is thoroughly descriptive; there is no generalization or abstraction, no logical causation to it. And indeed, Flusser does not tire of pointing out how much he is in favor of surfaces, of the *phainomena*, of appearances. Flusser did not believe in a kind of thinking "behind" surfaces, or behind the words. Instead, he made a case for taking surfaces, as such, more seriously. "We no longer attempt to explain away the images. On the contrary, we try to produce images from dots, like mosaics. We no longer try to overcome superficiality but to enter it from the yawning gap. We try to stretch this surface artificially across the abyss"[8]

Flusser developed a broad and comprehensive phenomenography of things and gestures. After decades of writing, including years of daily phenomenographical sketches for a Brazilian newspaper, the *Folha de São Paulo*, these phenomenographical writings amount to a catalog of sheer baroque diversity, reflecting all kinds of formerly unnoticed aspects of everyday life. And I would like to emphasize again: this body of work should be considered a phenomenography of things and gestures.

But then, on the other hand, there is also another side to Flusser. A less playful, more systematic—and perhaps even slightly academic—side. Flusser did develop a systematic approach to what he called the "wiring of the channels" (die "Schaltung der Kanäle") of communication. This complex system, beginning with the distinction between discourse and dialogue, and then differentiated into detail, adds up to what Flusser called his *communicology* (*Kommunikologie*). Flusser worked decades on this systematization of the structures of communication. And yet, it seems to have been there from the very beginning. If you compare his Bochum Lectures of 1991 with the *Kommunikologie* as a series of lectures he held at the University of Marseille-Luminy in 1977, the most striking thing is how similar his wording is after a distance of fourteen years. From the early 1970s until Flusser's death in 1991, his concepts and views changed almost not at all.

First, Flusser analyzes phenomena of communicative situations (like television or the circus, etc.). And then he systematizes the structures he abstracted from them. In this way he arrives at a whole system of structures of communication.

At this point, I would like to remind you of Lambert Wiesing's remark that Flusser, in his phenomenographical studies, does analyze phenomena in what can correctly be called an *eidetic reduction* but that Flusser refrains from the next step, the *Wesensschau*. In a different essay, Wiesing explains:

> The phenomenologist's goal is to vary the phenomena described and to thus discover, as the next step, logical principles without which these phenomena could

not be the ones they are. This attempt at defining out of one's own experience what is necessary for them is made by means of the so-called eidetic variation—that is, not through induction. That is why phenomenology perceives itself not as an empirical science like psychology. On the contrary, the concern is to make evident the unchangeable core of the phenomena by varying them in our imagination. This is what Husserl calls "Wesensschau" (the intuition of essences).[9]

This is exactly how Flusser proceeds and what he achieves with his *communicology*. It is nothing short of a phenomenology of (mostly technically implemented) relations, the *wirings of the channels*, "Schaltungen der Kanäle"—all derived from the departure point of the opposition of *dialogue versus discourse*. Flusser also created another closely related phenomenology: the phenomenology of codes (images, writing, technical images) and of the different repercussions they cause to our lifeworld, to our being.

So, in the end Flusser's *phenomenography of things and gestures* is put into perspective and superseded in a meta-phenomenology, whose objects are the means of communication, the *codes and channels*, the *repertoire and structure*, the *words and grammar* of how we perceive phenomena, how we give meaning to them, and how we try to convey that meaning to others. What Vilém Flusser called his *phenomenology of things and gestures* was really but a phenomenography. But Flusser's most important achievement is his *phenomenology of communication*.

If it is true that Flusser sublates his comprehensive phenomenography of things and gestures as an antithesis and lifts it into a *synthetic phenomenology of communication*, into a phenomenology of communication that claims a more encompassing validity, *he actually re-inscribes dialectics* into his thinking. *Dialectics*, the political paradigm, remains inherent to Flusser's work and thought.

> Like Moses, we ourselves will most likely not walk the New Land, because we are entangled in the categories we are programmed for, even if we do not believe in them. [. . .]. [W]e ourselves, we are like the mythical inventors of linear writing: we have lost the faith that carries us, but we ourselves cannot perform the step into the new existence. We are a first and a last generation, the faithless founders of a faith. This is our tragedy and our grandeur at the same time.[10]

* * *

In this chapter, I have tried to point out why I agree with Lambert Wiesing that Flusser was not a phenomenologist but, instead, a phenomenographer. And finally, I disagreed with Wiesing after all: on the level of a phenomenographical description of phenomena, Flusser was indeed no more than a phenomenographer for want of any *eidetic variation*, *Wesensschau*, one would expect to follow the *eidetic reduction*, the *epochē*. But on another level, Flusser does compare the essence of patterns of communication, and he does gather these reduced phenomena in groups or shadowings.

So, one could say that Flusser's phenomenological method gets stuck at the level of thesis and antithesis and does not succeed in surpassing the phase of phenomenography.

But on a meta-level—and one can call that the "synthetic level"—Flusser reunites and reconciles this contradiction. Is this not the very dialectical method Flusser was so ostentatiously happy and impatient to see go?

There is a lot left of the young Marxist Flusser used to be before his world was shattered and torn into *bottomlessness*, into the ungrounded abyss. The old, world-wise media-phenomenologist Flusser did not shake off his roots altogether, roots that were deeply grounded in dialectical materialism, where there really should be *no ground* at all—according to everything Flusser himself wrote and said.

Flusser never quite freed himself from the dialectical method. And in spite of this, his work is phenomenological at its core. He may have been a mere *phenomenographer of things and gestures*, but without a doubt he was a *phenomenologist of communication*—and certainly a very inspiring one at that, abundant with intriguing new insight.

Notes

1. Translations by the author. Flusser, *Nachgeschichte: Eine korrigierte Geschichtsschreibung* (Bensheim and Düsseldorf: Bollmann, 1993), 14.
2. Ibid., 12.
3. Flusser, *Dinge und Undinge: Phänomenologische Skizzen* (München: Hanser, 1993 [1972]), 154.
4. Flusser, *Kommunikologie* (Mannheim: Bollmann, 1996), 150.
5. Flusser, *Gesten. Versuch einer Phänomenologie* (Düsseldorf and Bensheim: Bollmann, 1991), 140 f.
6. Lambert Wiesing, "Fotografieren als phänomenologische Tätigkeit," in: Flusser Studies 10, 2010, 7.
7. Ibid., 8 f.
8. Flusser, *Lob der Oberflächlichkeit. Für eine Phänomenologie der Medien* (Bensheim and Düsseldorf: Bollmann, 1993), 46.
9. Lambert Wiesing, "Edmund Husserl in der Medienphilosophie," in *Philosophie in der Medientheorie: Von Adorno bis Žižek*, ed. Alexander Roesler and Bernd Stiegler (Wilhelm Fink: Paderborn, 2008),152 f.
10. Flusser, *Lob der Oberflächlichkeit*, 82.

9

Migrants, Flâneurs, Critics

Flusserian Irony and the Genealogy of Modern Cynicism

Alexander B. Adkins

Vilém Flusser connects the rise of "enlightened false consciousness" diagnosed by Peter Sloterdijk as post-ideological cynicism with a more explicitly media theoretical development: the onset of the "photographic universe" described in *Towards a Philosophy of Photography* (1983).[1,2] This universe coincides with the seismic escalation of humanity's subjection to inhuman media apparatuses that not only manipulate media subjects but also transform us into functional addicts to cynicism:

> Our magical-ritual acts are nevertheless not those of Native Americans, but those of functionaries in a postindustrial society. Both Native Americans and functionaries believe in the reality of images, but functionaries do this out of bad faith. After all, they have learned to write at school and consequently should know better. Functionaries have a historical consciousness and critical awareness but they suppress these. They know that the war in Lebanon is not a clash between good and evil but that specific causes have specific consequences there. They know that the toothbrush [for example] is not a sacred object but a product of Western history. But they have to suppress their superior knowledge of this. How else would they buy toothbrushes, have opinions about the war in Lebanon, file reports, fill in forms, go on holiday, take retirement—in short, how would they function?[3]

Directed against the Marxist mainstay that media obscure the social reality of the sincere and naive ("Native Americans"), the passage describes a subject with "superior knowledge" of their capture by technical images. The media cynicism of this subject ("They know that the war in Lebanon is not a clash between good and evil") is that of an enlightened false consciousness that, in its strategic resignation to the status quo, "suppresses" the fact of its collaboration with a less-than-ideal reality. "To act against better knowledge," says Sloterdijk, "is today the global situation in the superstructure; it knows itself to be without illusions and yet to have been dragged down by the 'power of things.'"[4]

This conceptual overlap between Flusser and Sloterdijk is not coincidental. The publication of Sloterdijk's *Critique of Cynical Reason* (1983) in the same year as Flusser's opus on photography suggests German Media Theory's late-century attempt to rescue and update the Enlightenment ideal of progress in a postmodernity synonymous with the pacification and splitting of the subject. Exemplary in this regard is Sloterdijk's positioning of modern cynicism as evidence against the Marxist Enlightenment humanism that conflates ideology critique with autonomous action and social change:

> Cynicism is enlightened false consciousness. It is that modernized, unhappy consciousness, on which enlightenment has labored both successfully and in vain. It has learned its lessons in enlightenment, but it has not, and probably was not able, to put them into practice. Well-off and miserable at the same time, this consciousness no longer feels affected by any critique of ideology; its falseness is already reflexively buffered.[5]

The passage is perhaps most famous as the source for Slavoj Žižek's skeleton key concept that cynicism structures the arch-ideological fantasy that we, the modern and disillusioned, are beyond ideology altogether.[6] Such, at least, is one legacy of Sloterdijk's early work on cynicism. Still, Sloterdijk's oblique reference to Hegel's concept of the "unhappy consciousness" charts an alternative genealogy of cynicism, one that Flusser himself uses to plot the meta-reflexive styles of critical distance, irony, and abstraction that populate his descriptions of modernity. At stake in the literary-philosophical figure of the unhappy consciousness is a revision of Enlightenment humanism that might satisfy both Sloterdijk's search for a new optimism and Flusser's alternative to the "kitschy, stupid murder" that he ascribes to Enlightenment.[7]

This chapter examines Flusser's contribution to the genealogy of modern cynicism. It does so by returning to the concept of the unhappy consciousness, Hegel's epithet for Romanticism's mode of ironic distance that continues today in the hypocritical demands for purity that define so much of modern media discourse. Flusser is no dialectician, teleologist, or parochial partisan of what he called Hegel's "pallid notion of nationalism," but he shares the latter's concern with the denial of human intersubjectivity and mutual implication, philosophical commitments he ties most explicitly to Martin Buber's "Man becomes I through Thou."[8] The resurgence of critical interest in the unhappy consciousness appears most clearly in Timothy Morton's repackaging of the concept as "beautiful soul syndrome," a condition that describes the reflexive styles of environmental activism that hypocritically deny their own complicity in the world. In this way, Flusser's scattered explorations of cynicism speak to our own era's struggle to define the purchase and value of critique in a posthistorical era defined by mutual implication and the loss of an Enlightenment hope for a better future.

Migrant versus Unhappy Consciousness

For Flusser, critical distance is baked into humanity's technical interface with a natural world that it is always battling against for survival. The distinguishing feature of Flusser's fully realized subject, then, is its ability to reconcile its primordial alienation from the world in the pursuit of intentional forms of communication and worldmaking. Throughout Flusser's corpus appear figures that either fail to resolve the primordial split between self and world or manage to leverage this ontological gap into a philosophy of action in the face of our absurd, entropic existence.

In "Taking up Residence in Homelessness" (1987), Flusser transvalues the suffering of exile into a creative philosophy of migrancy, one where the displaced overcome the desolate and desolating nature of existence through self-realizing forms of action.[9] Flusser's celebration of the migrant thus begins with the alienation of a posthistorical, post-national subject, the seat of his brand of existentialism. This is an existentialism where we all—exiles of one kind or another—might achieve freedom by rejecting the nostalgic satisfactions of *Heimat*, the German word for the embedded, historical experience of belonging that reaches "beyond the consciousness of our adult life into regions that are at once childish, infantile, and perhaps even fetal and transindividual."[10]

Flusser's migrant is an avant-gardist of experience who learns to overcome the unconscious sacralization of our immediate environment.[11] Such overcoming entails a normative dyad—"home" versus "world"—we experience aesthetically: the former appears "beautiful" (familiar and favorable), the latter "ugly" (strange and menacing). The migrant's "hard-won freedom of homelessness" is synonymous with a modernist brand of alienation-as-freedom, a technique of aesthetic abstraction from the patriotism that, by conflating the strange with the ugly, is "a symptom of an aesthetic disease."[12]

Opposite the beautiful native stands the ugly migrant, a figure that embodies the modernist exchange of native cultures and identities for the transculturation and hybridity that unravel the allure of fascism, "the perniciousness of a mysterious attachment to things."[13] Flusser's phenomenology of abstraction borrows from the stage of Hegel's dialectic where consciousness has yet to reconcile itself to the tragic split between self and world, private and public:

> According to Hegelian analysis, the dialectic between a home and the unusual, between redundancy and noise, is the dynamic of unhappy consciousness, which is consciousness in general. Consciousness is the back-and-forth between a home and the unusual, between private and public. According to Hegel, if I find the world, then I lose myself; if I find myself, then I lose the world. Without a home, I would be unconscious; that is, without a home, I would not actually exist. A home is how I find myself in the world—if at all. It is primary.[14]

Here we see not only the ouroboric structure of home (and subjectivity) in general but also the split subjectivity of the native who denies its primordial entanglement with the outside world ("if I find the world, then I lose myself"). Framed within Flusser's thermodynamic theory of information, the unhappy consciousness is an entropic mode of relationality, one tied to the nativist fantasy of preindustrial life celebrated in the concept of *Heimat*. Internally divided, the unhappy consciousness is an unreconciled form of nostalgia that laments a bygone era. Unlike the migrant who projects themselves into an unknown future, this melancholic figure fails to mourn the "painful departure from agriculture and its industrial legacy for the uncharted lands of postindustrial society and posthistory."[15]

Hegel models the unhappy consciousness after German Romanticism's literary authors and archetypes, figures who aestheticize the division between self and world by opposing an inward delicacy of moral insight against a corrupt and corrupting humanity. The unhappy consciousness is the Romantic poet-figure of divine solipsism against which Flusser measures the heroism of the implicated and implicating migrant:

> Is the freedom of the migrant, this "spirit" who belongs nowhere, a solipsistic freedom devoid of responsibility? Has he attained his freedom at the cost of being with others? Or is solitude devoid of responsibility not, rather, the migrant's fate (as the Romantic poets described it)? As I described earlier, the transition from expulsion into freedom negates this question.[16]

Here Flusser sketches competing models of reaction to the "expulsion" that defines humanity as an exiled species that is *bodenlos*. Opposite the migrant's humanizing enmeshment in the world stands an unhappy consciousness awash in the negative freedom that views otherness as a threat. In its "transition from expulsion into freedom," by contrast, the migrant offers the form of alienation that externalizes its self-division into action, modeling an existentialism that fuses human transcendence and "responsibility" for the other.[17]

Understood within a longer account of modernism, Flusser's migrant ferries the projects of Enlightenment humanism and progress across the centuries, rejecting the reactionary, nineteenth-century antimodernism that persisted, with disastrous consequences, into the twentieth century. The unhappy consciousness, by contrast, names the reactionary yearning for experiential unity that followed Enlightenment, Romantic, and modernist upheavals of social ontology. For Hegel, such yearning is an immature form of religious alienation that cannot reconcile its separation from the transcendental:

> The "beautiful soul," lacking an actual existence, entangled in the contradiction between its pure self and the necessity of that self to externalize itself and change itself into an actual existence, and dwelling in the immediacy of this firmly held antithesis—an immediacy which alone is the middle term reconciling the antithesis, which has been intensified to its pure abstraction, and is pure being or empty nothingness—this "beautiful soul," then, being conscious of this contradiction in its unreconciled immediacy, is disordered to the point of madness, wastes itself in yearning and pines away in consumption.[18]

The passage dismisses the literary irony associated with German Romanticism—especially that of the consumptive Novalis who aspired to bridge the gap between God and humanity through intermediary concepts. What Hegel hated most, it seems, were Romantics who ascribed to themselves and their literary protagonists the Christ-like inner voice that reconciles humanity with the divine. Thus, the beautiful soul's ascription of evil to the world outside the self is in fact a projection of its own internal strife, rendering the beautiful soul incapable of action, a willing victim of the ethical paralysis that instantiates the evil it abhors.

Scholars recognize in this backward-looking Romantic sensibility a mode of totalitarian virtue signaling rooted in the Enlightenment concept of *Bildung*. The ironic example of Hitler's commitment to vegetarianism and antivivisectionism thus confirms H. S. Harris's reminder that "Hitler saw himself, and was seen by some of his admirers, as a 'Beautiful Soul.'"[19] The concept therefore allows for a sweeping historical and cultural analysis of the corrosive persistence of a post-Enlightenment longing for reconciliation that formalizes itself in ironically righteous—and potentially violent and nativist—demands for purity. Writing in this vein, Timothy Morton constructs a genealogy of hypocrisy he calls "beautiful soul syndrome," a condition he traces to the eighteenth-century English practice of boycotting sugar (an agricultural by-product of colonialism and slavery). Synonymous with the activism of Percy and Mary Shelley, boycotting is the form of anti-consumerism that, ironically, achieves the pinnacle of consumerism in its reliance on the practice of "window shopping"—of aesthetically measuring, calculating, and distancing the world outside the self.[20] Of chief concern to this genealogy of cynicism is the corrosive influence of Romantic irony on a present we can no longer afford to distance from ourselves. This is a brand of irony that denies the existential interdependence and mutual implication that are the bedrocks of Flusser's ontology.

Irony and Flânerie

Despite its alignment with the unhappy consciousness, irony is appealing to Flusser because its expression de-essentializes and multiplies meaning. In "We Need a Philosophy of Emigration," for instance, irony operates as a double concept, both a pathway and impediment to existential freedom:

> The movement into irony is an act of outrage. And with this motion a person rises above contingence. Movement away from irony is a form of engagement. With this motion the person returns to his state of contingence to change it. These two movements taken together are called freedom. Human beings are free because with this inexplicable and unpredictable movement they are able to become outraged about their contingence and to change it. Because of this potential we are virtually free, and when we complete this action we are free in fact.[21]

Here irony is a proxy for the critical distance required to alter contingent social realities that, as in the concept of *Heimat*, remain opaque until the denaturalizing work of alienation. Opposite this critical irony stands the sincerity ("movement away from irony") that balances "outrage" with "engagement," leading to the "dignity" inherent in the ability to consciously choose the new and old contingencies that delimit our lifeworlds.[22]

Flusser's irony, then, is no mere Sartrean differentiation of human autonomy from the physically determined world. For although "the potential for moving into and out of irony is what differentiates human beings from the things in their surroundings," it is still, says Flusser, "more promising to . . . become outraged at middleclassness than my mammalianism, because I have a better chance of changing the former."[23] By framing outrage as a necessary but insufficient condition for political change, Flusser repurposes an activist idiom with which we are undoubtedly familiar into a form of critical distance applied to social injustice rather than individual purity ("middleclassness"). But as with so many of his double concepts, Flusser's irony is also one vector of the totalitarian impulse that suffuses posthistorical society.

Before leaving Brazil in the midst of military dictatorship and anti-intellectual sentiment, Flusser wrote a series of think pieces in the *Folha de São Paulo* newspaper that describe the self-sabotaging nature of Romantic irony: "a double-edged sword, which, though drawn by romantics and romantically brandished, cuts romanticism into pieces—the death of romanticism."[24] Unsurprisingly, Flusser's take on Romantic irony is polyvalent, for however self-defeating it might be, "[s]elf-irony" is also "weapon of the weak" when it takes the form of the self-deprecating gallows humor that aided Jewish survival in the camps.[25] But in an earlier issue of *Folha de São Paulo* we encounter the irony of being-with-others in public space, one that channels the calm detachment of Nazi violence:

> But the park gaze is still different. It annihilates the other without resorting to annihilation fields. Those sitting in the park do not admit that the other exists, not even as a thing. The sitter contemplates the void. He is seated beyond history, beyond humanism; perhaps within the "fullness of time." The parks of European cities are, in this curious sense, heavens. Those seated in them are sitting in the stillness of time, in eternity; each inside their individual bubble, emanating an inhuman coldness. This is "post-history," the goal of development as a whole.[26]

This is a Flusserian technofuture where discourse has so thoroughly suffused crowd culture that only solipsism and abstraction remain. Flusser's park gaze aphorism pictures the flâneur as the primary social type of posthistory, a time where detached contemplation characterizes the "bubbles" that make up radically atomized social life. The passage likewise draws on the language of purity ("seated beyond history") and religion ("heavens," "in eternity"), suggesting a form of ironic distance that employs the divine cruelty of the unhappy consciousness ("it annihilates the other").

These descriptions of the latent violence in flânerie also apply to Flusser's photographer, a figure of physical, cultural, and critical distance who, as in a "hunt," lies in wait to shoot its prey: "[s]talking their way through these objects, avoiding the intention concealed within them, photographers wish to liberate themselves from their cultural condition and to snap their prey unconditionally."[27] At work here is Benjamin's concept of the flâneur, a modernist mode of nineteenth-century

European spectatorship, perambulation, and leisure that marks the expansion of mass consumerism and spectacle as features of urban landscape and subjectivity. As recent media theorists have observed, the strolling observers of nineteenth-century Paris have been updated and replaced by the screen-scrollers of the twenty-first century. Miriam Paeslack, for example, argues that "flânerie is now everywhere" in the sense that the "media savvy" today have worked to radicalize "the classical flâneur's openness and even passivity in the face of overwhelming stimuli."[28]

That passivity is the feature augmented most by the development of flânerie across the centuries is ironic given Benjamin's positioning of the figure of the flâneur as a critical reproof of capitalism ("The idleness of the flâneur is a demonstration against the division of labour").[29] Indeed, the concept now serves the purposes of expressing angst about the status of modern criticism—about, that is, the moral and ethical limits of disengaged spectatorship in a time of increasing mutual implication. Lauren Rabinovitz reminds us that Benjamin's flâneur "was a dialectical figure who presented himself as open to everything but who actually saved himself from the chaos of randomness through his pretensions to epistemological control."[30] In the flâneur, then, we again encounter the internally divided subject of Romanticism, the modern beautiful soul whose failure to dialectically develop with the outside world is obscured by a claim to receptivity ("who presented himself as open to everything") that cocoons a pristine inner autonomy.

Flusser's photographer thus bears the commitment—and failure—of the flâneur's attempt to establish aesthetic distance from its object: "[i]n choosing their categories," Flusser tells us, "photographers may think they are bringing their own aesthetic, epistemological or political criteria to bear. They may set out to take artistic, scientific or political images for which the camera is only a means to an end. But what appear to be their criteria for going beyond the camera nevertheless remain subordinate to the camera's program."[31] Here the dissipation of humanist autonomy under the regime of the photographic apparatus doubles as a gesture toward the illusion of critical distance—the illusion of human freedom in general. In Flusser's analysis of photography the technological conditioning of the subject puts into question the possibility of unprogrammed freedom. It may very well be, as Flusser tells us, that in the photographic universe of modernity "[w]e are not dealing with the classical problem of alienation, but with an existential revolution of which there is no example available to us"; yet the models of unfreedom that Flusser cites throughout his corpus are rooted in the alienation of an unhappy consciousness that has become a primary social type, category of thinking, and form of criticism today.[32]

Postcritique and the Saboteur

Writing in the midst of a cold war that for many marked the final failure of Critical Theory, Flusser and Sloterdijk seek to salvage the emancipatory project of Enlightenment, proposing alternatives to the varieties of paralyzing cynicism that appeared in the wake of world-shattering events that have come to define the modern

West: the Holocaust, the failed student movements, and the 1980s collapse of actually existing alternatives to neoliberalism. However divergent they might be in their diagnoses of the modern West—Flusser highlights the technological programming and pacification of the subject, Sloterdijk the militarization of masculine ego and dialogue—both doubt the purchase of critique in posthistorical worlds bereft of grand narratives.

Calling out the failure of ideology critique to effect change in the world, Sloterdijk and Flusser speak on behalf of a generation of world-weary intellectuals. Indeed, the early Sloterdijk has become something of a poster child for "postcritique," a recent call by politically disillusioned critics to exchange the suspicious, aggressive, and ineffective modes of critique associated with Marx, Freud, and Nietzsche for the enchantment, sympathy, and Kantian nonpurposiveness that structure one's initial encounter with and love for aesthetic objects. This tradition of thinking sees in critique the same evils Hegel applied to Romantic irony and which Jedidiah Purdy describes as an illness particular to modernity:

> We practice a form of irony insistently doubtful of the qualities that would make us take another person seriously; the integrity of personality, sincere motivation, the idea that opinions are more than symptoms of fear or desire. We are wary of hope, because we see little that can support it. Believing in nothing much, especially not in people, is a point of vague pride, and conviction can seem embarrassingly naïve.[33]

Here Purdy's diagnosis of modern cynicism mirrors that of Sloterdijk's, framing failed idealism as a generalized social condition and a source of the "vague pride" that compensates for a lack of empowerment, purpose, and vision. Sloterdijk goes one step further to insist that cynicism is a primary feature of critique itself, for it is a methodology that projects onto "the minds of human beings precisely those errors that have to be in them so that the system can function—toward its collapse. In the gaze of the Marxist system-critic, there glitters an irony that is a priori condemned to cynicism."[34] More recently, Bruno Latour cites precisely this distasteful feature of critique when he characterizes its appeal to the self-righteous:

> You are always right! When naive believers are clinging forcefully to their objects, claiming that they are made to do things because of their gods, their poetry, their cherished objects, you can turn all of those attachments into so many fetishes and humiliate all the believers by showing that it is nothing but their own projection, that you, yes you alone, can see.[35]

A founding figure of postcritique, Latour claims that the inability to think outside the paradigm of critique has led to a crisis of knowledge, one that has stripped the humanities of their authority and purpose. This iteration of the postmodern crisis of knowledge is part and parcel of the futility of humanities graduate programs in which the exposure of ideological interest is tantamount to action and progress:

> While we spent years trying to detect the real prejudices hidden behind the appearance of objective statements, do we now have to reveal the real objective and incontrovertible facts hidden behind the illusion of prejudices? And yet entire Ph.D. programs are still running to make sure that good American kids are learning the hard way that facts are made up, that there is no such thing as natural, unmediated, unbiased access to truth, that we are always prisoners of language, that we always speak from a particular standpoint, and so on, while dangerous extremists are using the very same argument of social construction to destroy hard-won evidence that could save our lives.[36]

Latour's Enlightenment project of ideological unmasking leads to a dead end, a capitulation to reactionary forces that have, to our horror, also learned the lessons of social construction from Marx, Freud, and Nietzsche. This, he says, is why "the humanities have lost the hearts of their fellow citizens."[37] But as with all postcritical characterizations of critique's bad days, Latour's recourse to the wonder and enchantment of a Heideggerian revaluation of objects ("What would critique do if it could be associated with *more*, not with *less*, with *multiplication*, not *subtraction*?") replaces the crisis of critique with a consoling metaphysics, a disillusionment with disillusionment that accomplishes little more than a blithe resignation to the little things in life.[38]

Here at the impasse between the collapse of critique and its arid alternatives is where Flusser's own encounter with the early days of posthistory might prove useful to our cynical time. "We are," Flusser says,

> counter-revolutionaries in both senses: we dread romantic anti-rationalism as much as enlightened rationalism. We know that they are both within the program and we know their realizations: fascism and the apparatus society. In other words: we know that intelligence has stupidity, which the stupidity of the heart ignores. This makes our counter-revolutionary zeal ambivalent. We are counter-everything. Our engagement with freedom is totally negative."[39]

Flusser's is no facile rejoinder to the impasse of postcritique, but rather a recognition that we are, as posthistorical subjects, caught between the legacy of Romantic idealism ("romantic anti-rationalism"), on the one hand, and the totalitarian impulse that continues to inform our time, on the other ("enlightened rationalism"). Hanging in the balance is a vision of human freedom that can do without the fantasies of total revolution Flusser implores us to abandon ("We can no longer be revolutionaries.").[40]

In Flusser's posthistorical future the unhappy consciousness has resigned itself to its compensatory brand of failed idealism by abandoning the search for a new freedom:

> Apparatus have codified the world in order to entertain us. They have turned the world "spectacular." They are now seeking to sensationalize our own death. They have already sensationalized the deaths of others. They have overcome mourning. They have turned the death of others into kitsch. They will turn our own death

into kitsch. Once this has been reached, we will have been reprogrammed. Our unhappy consciousness will finally rest. Programmed life shall be totally entertaining.[41]

The "stupidity of progress" described earlier sets the stage for Flusser's figure of posthistorical resistance: the "saboteur." This futuristic subject's subversion of the world of apparatus is "strategic," "intelligent," and "dignified," a form of contingent mischief that dispenses with the fantasies of total revolution that Wendy Brown, following Benjamin, calls "left melancholy."[42] Flusser's saboteur is, admittedly, no glamourous revolutionary in its humble throwing of "sand on the apparatus' wheels."[43] Neither is this figure a capitulation to the postcritical call for modesty. The saboteur is a collective call toward a freedom that would, in its strategic plumbing of technical programming, overcome the Romantic yearning for a pre-technological mode of being that never was.

Notes

1 Peter Sloterdijk, *Critique of Cynical Reason*, trans. Andreas Huyssen (Minneapolis: University of Minnesota Press, 1987).
2 Flusser, *Towards a Philosophy of Photography* (London: Reaktion Books, 1983).
3 Ibid., 63.
4 Sloterdijk, *Critique*, 5.
5 Ibid.
6 See Slavoj Žižek, *The Sublime Object of Ideology* (UK: Verso, 2009).
7 Flusser, "Betrayal," in *Writings*, ed. Andreas Ströhl (Minneapolis and London: University of Minnesota Press, 2002), 60.
8 Flusser, *History of the Devil* (Minneapolis: Univocal, 2014), 80.
9 Flusser, "Taking Up Residence in Homelessness," in *Writings*, ed. Ströhl, 91–103.
10 Ibid., 93.
11 Ibid., 99.
12 Ibid., 101.
13 Ibid., 94.
14 Ibid., 100.
15 Ibid., 92.
16 Flusser, "Homelessness," 94–5.
17 Ibid., 95.
18 Hegel, *Phenomenology of Spirit* (Oxford: Oxford University Press, 1997), 406–7.
19 H. S. Harris, *Hegel's Ladder* (Indianapolis: Hackett, 1997), 483.
20 Timothy Morton, "Thinking Ecology: The Mesh, the Strange Stranger, and the Beautiful Soul," in *Collapse IV*, ed. Robin Mackey (Falmouth: Urbanomic, 2010), 265–93.
21 Flusser, "We Need a Philosophy of Emigration," in *The Freedom of the Migrant*, ed. Anke K. Finger (Champaign: University of Illinois Press, 2003), 21–2.
22 Ibid., 21.
23 Ibid., 22.

24 Flusser, "Ground Zero," trans. Rodrigo Maltez Novaes, http://www.slug.directory/18-ground-zero-by-Vilém-flusser-excerpt-translated-by-rodrigo-maltez-novaes/.
25 Ibid.
26 Ibid.
27 Flusser, *Towards a Philosophy*, 39, 33.
28 Miriam Paeslack, "Subjective Topographies: Berlin in Post-Wall Photography," in *Spatial Turns: Space, Place and Mobility in German Literary and Visual Culture*, ed. Jaimey Fisher and Barbara Mennel (New York: Rodopi, 2010), 400.
29 Walter Benjamin, *The Arcades Project* (Cambridge, MA: Belknap Press, 1999), 7.
30 Lauren Rabinovitz, *For the Love of Pleasure: Women, Movies, and Culture in Turn-of-the-Century Chicago* (Rutgers: Rutgers University Press, 1998), 7.
31 Flusser, *Towards a Philosophy*, 36.
32 Ibid., 79.
33 Jedidiah Purdy, *For Common Things: Irony, Trust, and Commitment in America Today* (New York: Vintage, 1999), 6.
34 Sloterdijk, *Critique*, 20.
35 Latour, "Why Has Critique Run Out of Steam?" *Critical Inquiry* 30, no. 2 (Winter 2004): 225–48, 239.
36 Ibid., 227.
37 Ibid.
38 Ibid., 248.
39 Flusser, *Post-History* (Minneapolis: Univocal, 2013), 129.
40 Ibid., 128.
41 Ibid., 114.
42 Wendy Brown, "Resisting Left Melancholy," *Boundary* 26, no. 3 (Fall 1999): 19–27.
43 Flusser, *Post-History*, 127.

10

Vampyroteuthis Infernalis as Media Theory

Geoffrey Winthrop-Young

Disciplines become interesting once they start to question themselves. Media studies is a prime example. At one point it aspired to be a master discourse, but now it has become a fractious enterprise at odds with its alpha term. The proliferation of social media and the collapse of formerly distinct transmission, processing and storage technologies into the digital supermedium on the one hand and the conceptual extension of media into environments, elements, and earth itself on the other, have turned *media* into an increasingly unreliable point of departure for analysis. Not surprisingly, a growing number of practitioners insist that they focus on communication, information, infrastructures, operations, or networks but not on media.

Vilém Flusser was ahead of the curve. He contributed to the construction of the media-theoretical bandwagon, but he snuck off while others were still climbing aboard. He refused to refer to himself as a media theorist, preferring safer, woollier epithets like communications theorist or communicologist. He was precise enough a thinker to recognize his own imprecisions. "Medium" and "media" tend to be promiscuous terms in his texts, referring either to entire communications structures, the ongoing mediation between organisms and environment, or simply *mass* media. Part of Flusser's dislike of the term "media" was rooted in his dislike of mass media, especially of star-shaped media infrastructures that enable a center to send a bundle of messages to many isolated points with no mechanism for response. The Latin word for bundle is *fascis*. Such unidirectional one-to-many mass media, Flusser claimed, are intrinsically fascist.

On a more conceptual level Flusser's reservations are based on the premise that to speak of medium or media only makes sense if you posit something not mediated or *immediate*. But the immediate, whatever that may be, is as suspicious a concept as the pure. It conjures up something removed from the ongoing cycles of storage, processing, and transmission that in Flusser's eyes underlie, enable, and maintain life itself. After all, a human being "is a sort of feedback loop through which data, gathered from out of the world, can re-enter into the world,"[1] so is there anything at all in humans that escapes mediation? But rather than calling it quits and jettisoning the inflated term, Flusser suggested an alternate approach. When we distrust politicians, we turn to comedians; when we lose confidence in analysis, we turn to philosophical fables. Analysis is replaced by a sophisticated form of ludic defamiliarization capable of putting a new spin on phenomena in order to prepare the grounds for a rejuvenated analysis.

An old hymn first recorded in the 1930s begins with the line *I wonder as I wander out under the sky*. For Flusser, whose life story reads like the concentrated essence of a century that specialized in expulsions, migrations, and exile, wandering and wondering were inseparable. Movement that does not induce mental activity is wasted mechanical motion; mental activity not spurred by movement is stale intellectual routine. At its core Flusser's oeuvre is powered by an ongoing transfer of kinetic energy from world to mind. He came to think the way he had to live; and for him to live was to move. Politically enforced deracination returns as cognitively beneficial defamiliarization: the adaptive skills required to remain afloat in the bottomless waters of an unmoored existence between nations, continents, and languages were converted into the mental exertions required to escape confining groundedness. This does not imply that he legitimized the forces he fled from, quite on the contrary. Ultimately, Flusser's goal was to create a mobile philosophy incompatible with the conditions from which it emerged. The ongoing practice of conceptual release will preclude mental and political confinement.

Or, to quote the greatest ambulatory thinker: "Only thoughts that come by *walking* have any value."[2] But Flusser, with his knack for squeezing metaphors to extract every last analogical drop, responded by going into detail: Can you walk *away*? Can your feet and thoughts move beyond their native ground and end up under a different sky? In fact, how do you walk? With your legs? How many do you have? What are their principles of locomotion? What if you were to change the number or shape of your legs? And what if you did not walk but flew or swam? What kind of an information-processing entity would you be if you exchanged your arms and legs for wings, fins, or tentacles? Not surprisingly, some of Flusser's most intriguing media-focused texts deal with animals—more precisely, with animals *as* media and the alternate mediality of animal bodies.[3] Take, for instance, his short essay on cows.[4] It starts with the well-known feedback circuit connecting organ projection to projection amnesia. We create products that are projections of our body and nervous system, but then we forget that we were the model for our creations, at which point the latter start modeling us. "The model is realized as a product. Subsequently, the human model behind the product is forgotten and the product establishes itself, in its turn, as a model."[5] The telegraph, so the story goes, is modeled on our nervous system, but the more the initial act of modeling is forgotten (if it was not an unconscious operation to begin with), the more we come to model our nervous system on the telegraph. This blurring of nerves and wires, in turn, will be the point of departure for the next projection iteration. In Flusser's words it amounts to a "tragic feedback."[6] Those who forget their creations are condemned to resemble them.

At first glance Flusser is parroting organ projection theorists from Ernst Kapp to Marshall McLuhan, but not even McLuhan, the prairie boy from the Canadian beef province of Alberta, applied it to cattle. Flusser, by contrast, merges cows with computers. Cows are cheap and functionally simple yet structurally complex technologies "for the transformation of grass into milk."[7] They may require the occasional "intervention of expensive university specialists,"[8] yet on the whole they are docile, agreeably multifunctional, and blessed with great plasticity. To top it off, once they cease to function their "'hardware' can be used in the form of meat, leather and other consumable products."[9] Cows are a technological triumph; they are nothing less than "prototypes of future machines that will be designed by advanced technology."[10] And with that, cows have morphed into bovine universal machines. But if machines are multipurpose prosthetic extensions of mind and body, and if domesticated animals, in turn, are similar technological products, the prospect arises that we information-grazing humans will assimilate to our cows as we do to our computers.

But if the fate of species through time is always already a matter of con-specific and con-machinic evolution, was there ever a point in evolution when "pure" humans were *not* shaped by this recursion of internalized externalizations? Flusser's response is a clear no. *Homo sapiens* is *bodenlos*. We are a groundless species; we have no fixed point of reference to determine where we are in the great chain of being, where we came from, and where we are headed to (and which direction we should avoid). We are not of Isaac Newton's world, for we cannot orientate ourselves by referring to absolute frames. We can only, as in the relativistic thought experiments of the young Albert Einstein, observe other observers in order to deduce different frames of reference and work from there. But these heuristic defamiliarizations require that we select a being that is both like *and* unlike us, otherwise there is no possibility for productive comparisons. We need an uncanny monster both eerily similar and repulsively different. We need *Vampyroteuthis infernalis*.

Flusser's vampire squid is a creature of mixed origins. Its grand guignol name and some of its physiological features are derived from the real animal, the "Vampire Squid from Hell," discovered and described by Carl Chun, leader of the 1898/9 German *Valdivia* deep-sea expedition.[11] Flusser's genealogical excursions recapitulate many evolutionary and cephalopodic details but then depart from biological facts by expanding on early classificatory difficulties.[12] Initially it was not quite clear whether *V. infernalis* is a squid or an octopus; and it was first classified as part of the Cirroteuthidae family before receiving its own, exclusive family, the Vampyroteuthidae. Then follow the more obvious deviations, beginning with a change of size. Equipped with the sinister, cloak-like interbrachial web from which Chun derived its acherontic name, the real *V. infernalis* has a maximum length of around 30 centimeters. To guarantee a sufficient degree of scariness, Flusser blows it up to kraken proportions. This is both a magnifying and a magnetizing operation. A lot of biological, philosophical, literary, and mythological material is attracted and deployed. Like Chun, Flusser lowered his nets into various depths.

Flusser's originality is a touchy topic. At times, it is the effect of missing footnotes. Or, to apply Flusser's dialogical model to his own writings, once certain material has been incorporated, processed, and modified for the purpose of further communicative exchange, it is no longer necessary to point out where said material came from in the first place. Flusser's vampire squid is indebted to a sequence of well-known cephalopod suspects that first appeared in nineteenth-century literature:

Alfred Tennyson's slumbering kraken, the giant *poulpes* that attack Captain Nemo's *Nautilus* in *Twenty Thousand Leagues under the Sea*, and the infernal *pieuvre* that haunts Victor Hugo's *Toilers of the Sea*. Alongside these literary antecedents there are nonfictional texts that anticipate the hybrid nature of Flusser's philosophical animal fable, including the chapter on cuttlefish and calamari in Jules Michelet's *The Sea* and the description of the airborne equivalent, as it were, of Flusser's deep-sea squid, the sinister bat in Alphonse de Toussenel's allegorical bestiary *Passional Zoology*. Arguably the most intriguing unmentioned influence is the work of Roger Caillois, especially his kraken study *La pieuvre: essai sur la logique de l'imaginaire*. Much like Thomas Nagel's bat, Humberto Maturana's frog, and Jakob von Uexküll's tick, Flusser's vampire squid is an epistemic creature designed to represent how its own representations emerge from the cycle that links embodiment, perception, and environment. The underlying media-theoretical thrust of Flusser's fable, then, is to confront human readers with an antihuman creature that will compel the former not to confuse the net result of their cognitive contingencies with any kind of objective reality.

Flusser introduces a sequence of recursive binaries that move from simple to complex. First example: humans live above, the squid resides below; we have adapted to a dry airy surface, it thrives in watery depths; we are surrounded by reflected sunlight that conveys information to us, it illuminates the surrounding darkness by means of its bioluminescent organs. Our human point of departure, therefore, is to assume that we register things as they are, whereas the squid initially assumes that it projects its perceptions straight onto the world. Philosophically speaking, "we are born Platonists who can contrive of our Kant only after great deal of critical thinking."[13] *V. infernalis*, by contrast, "is a born Kantian whose Plato comes later."[14] A second, related sequence: we have arms with hands extending from our upper body, the squid has tentacles surrounding its mouth. We approach, reach out, and grasp, it takes in from a world rushing by. "We comprehend what we happen upon, and it comprehends what happens to it."[15] As a result, we are a creature of "problems" while it is one of "impressions."[16]

Opposing habitats, then, correspond to contrasting physiological and perceptual structures, which in turn give rise to opposing epistemologies. To unpack the media-theoretical implications it is necessary to note that Flusser refuses to separate organism and environment. This may sound trite, yet it involves more than a Darwinian emphasis on selective pressures exerted by the environment on organisms. Flusser is aligned with Uexküll's notion of *umwelt* as the circumscribed portion of the environment that is meaningful and effective for a given organism. There is no neutral or absolute environment against which all life on earth plays out. Thus Flusser concedes that "humans and vampyroteuthes inhabit planet Earth," yet it is nonsense to assert that both of us "occupy the same earth."[17] The glaring difference between the squid's benthic depths and our arid heights serves to illustrate that we are creatures in and of very different worlds. But Flusser goes a step further by arguing that organisms and environments are emergent properties of mutually constitutive entanglements:

> In succinct and concrete terms, the environment is that which we experience, and we, in turn, are that in which the environment is experienced. Reality is a web of concrete relations. The entities of the environment are nothing but knots in this web, and we ourselves are knots of the same sort. We are linked to the entities; they are there for us. And the entities are linked to us; we are there for them. Both the environment and the organisms are abstract extrapolations from the actualities of their entwined relations.[18]

All ambitious media theories are forced to confront their inner Hegel. At one point the temptation arises to view history as the playground of an overarching entity, a kind of absolute media spirit, that in the course of its quest to understand itself in nature employs the human mind. The self-understanding of nature is temporarily contracted out to our cognitive apparatus. While many theorists refuse to engage this conceptual specter, Flusser barges ahead in an attempt to update and outdo Hegel. The notion that different minds are entangled platforms for different representations through time is said to be based on the changing tools of cognition. In other words, the ways in which organisms emerge as mediating entities capable of internally processing and then projecting representations of an emerging external surrounding are subject to the development of media technologies. Media determine our social, cognitive, and biological situation.

It is here that the human/squid encounter takes on an additional edge. To hammer home the point, Flusser inserts a passage that lets the squid speak. At the end of its antihuman diatribe it offers a highly critical take on the way humans use media technology—or rather, it derides the fact that humans resort to these tools at all. It is one of the supreme provocations in a text that aims to provoke and deserves a longer quote:

> Humans are surrounded by a mixture of gases called "air." Most inhabitants of the air possess an organ that can cause this gas to resonate. Among humans, these resonances are codified and used, like our chromophoric emissions, to transmit intraspecific information. Human memory is consequently designed to store information that is transmitted in this way. Compared to ours, however, its memory seems rudimentary, for the human is continuously reaching out for mnemonic crutches. It channels the majority of what it wants to communicate onto inanimate objects (. . .) A peculiar consequence of this blunder is that human history, in contrast to a genuine history such as ours, can be ascertained objectively—it can be established on the basis of these "(in)formed" objects. Not only we vampyroteuthes but even a visitor from Mars could reconstruct human history from these entities. Since it is soaked up by objective matter, human history is not properly intersubjective. It is an utter failure.[19]

The recommended procedure when dealing with Flusser's provocations is not to approach them head-on but to ask two questions. First, from whose point of view does the provocation make sense? And second, how relevant is that point of view to the provoked—in this case, to us humans?

Powered by its glands, *V. infernalis* uses self-generated light and sepia clouds to communicate with members of its species. It needs no storage media that syphon off and sabotage the communicative content. Chromatophores light up and coded patterns directly imprint themselves on the memory of other specimens. While inferior human history is a corollary effect of friction and residues, "real" vampyroteuthic history emerges from an "ongoing dialogue between vampyroteuthes" based on constant mutual imprinting.[20] At this point Flusser's fable takes on a noticeably allegorical character, for vampyroteuthic communication comes to represent human dreams of communicative immediacy, that is, of a direct *interbody* exchange (as opposed to mere interface) freed from all medial transformations and material recalcitrance. It is the well-known specter of media history, the lingering paradox of mediated immediacy in which every act of communication instantaneously (and orgiastically) consumes all information. The great irony, however, is that vampyroteuthes are always lying. Lights and clouds are used for purposes of camouflage, seduction, and above all predation: "The underlying purpose of all vampyroteuthic communication is to deceive the other in order to devour it. It is a culture of deceit, pretence, and falsehood."[21] Jürgen Habermas would be out of place among the squids; vampyroteuthic intercourse is not rational communication in the interest of objectivity but a frenzied communion of deceit carried out in "the spirit of orgasm."[22]

Compared to this orgiastic communion (occasionally described in the text as a form of rape), our technology-dependent human communication practices with their delays, residues, and transmission costs may indeed appear inferior. Yet how close or relevant is this jaundiced view to us? Flusser's troubling answer is that we are closing in on the squid. We humans "are becoming increasingly vampyroteuthic" because of the media-technological shift from analog to digital media.[23] Just as the soft, molluscan cephalopods adopted "a vertebrate strategy" by developing a skull to protect their complex brains, we hard vertebrates are adopting "an evolutionary strategy of molluscs" by going soft:[24]

> From now on, humans can realize their creative potential only by processing new and immaterial information, that is, by participating in the activity that has come to be called "software processing." In this context, there can be no doubt that "soft" alludes to molluscs ("soft animals").[25]

"No doubt"? This, no doubt, is a weak pun that elides the extensive hardware structure indispensable for software processing. But to pursue the argument to its radical conclusion, by discarding material objects and inscription surfaces (from papyrus and paper to vinyl and plastic) in favor of immaterial alternatives, we will graduate from merely "objective" to truly "intersubjective" communication. As we adapt to and internalize "soft" digital technologies, we will be capable of the majestic or diabolical vampyroteuthic instancy that haunts our media dreams. Once again, as in the case of cows, an animal body morphs into a computer.

Erick Felinto rightly notes that Flusser "was an important witness to and participant in a very specific moment in the development of digital culture."[26]

Flusser's fable, which should be read alongside contemporaneous cyberpunk narratives, is haunted by digital visions that accompanied the early PC revolution, when digital technologies expanded from the center into the many tiny capillaries of society. Yet to return to Flusser's unease over immediacy, as dangerous as this vampyroteuthic shift may be, it is not the greatest threat. Readers tend to overlook that Flusser does not restrict himself to the confrontation between humans and vampyroteuthes. A third, even more nefarious group or evolutionary option keeps intruding: eusocial hymenoptera, that is, social insects like ants and bees that have evolved into superorganisms. They "will one day come to dominate all life on earth" and may "provide a model for the future of human interaction."[27] Of course, to conjure up insect societies to represent totalitarian tendencies is anything but original. However, Flusser is not peddling the usual facile analogy. His take is both more dangerous and more grounded. Since he has enlarged the realm of media to also encompass the domain of embodiments, environments, and entanglements, the dynamics of media history are now caught in the gravitational field of biological evolution. The human word "politics" may apply to the relationship between anthills, but the relationship between the deindividualized components of each anthill is biologized. From a threatened human point of view, insect superorganisms amount to biologically grounded superfacism.

What is to be done? Flusser, whose own life was uprooted by a fascist regime espousing a pseudo-biological ideology, appears to advocate a variant of anti-biological decelerationism. Essentially, many of the human media-technological performances dismissed as "utter failure" by the haughty squid are viewed positively because they serve to delay our "progress" into vampyroteuthic immediacy or hymenopteran supersociality. An ineffective medium acts as a *katechon*, a delayer that defers the arrival of the apocalyptic end. "Freedom," a word of such innate fragility in Flusser's texts that it often needs the protective cover of inverted commas, emerges from the transitory uncoupling of human communication practices from evolution: It "is a provisional stage in the tendency of evolution toward socialization and death."[28] The human focus on the recalcitrant and intruding materiality of media gives rise to the maligned "objective" historical consciousness, while the focus on material resistance and the way in which material media usurp messages gives rise to art, for at bottom art is the recursive elaboration of the message that the medium is the message. The imperfection of pre-digital media technology temporarily relieves us from an evolution aiming for total perfection, immediacy, and coordination.

Indeed, the very worst would be the combination of the "soft" and instantaneous, friction- and residue-free communication of *V. infernalis* and the total coordination of an anthill that has moved "freedom" and "individuality" (another endangered concept) from the level of the constituent components up to the level of the collective. Think of a super-squid that makes even the most terrifying nineteenth-century kraken look like a quaint pet: a tightly coordinated swarm of murderous vampire squids all in immediate touch with each other. Faced with such an octopoid apocalypse, Flusser (in one of his most memorable slaps) turns what it means to be "progressive" and "reactionary" on its head:

Those who explain human life as a function of biology (...) are "progressive": They are wallowing in the evolutionary tendency toward socialization and death and are thereby contributing to the abolishment of freedom. Those who champion freedom, on the other hand, are "reactionary": they are attempting to resist the biological tendency toward socialization and death in order to conserve space for a fleeting, provisional condition.[29]

To repeat, the price you pay for an imperial notion of media that colonizes domains hitherto removed from a conventional understanding of technology is the blurring of the boundary between media "progress" and biological evolution. This becomes especially volatile if you—as Flusser does with great aplomb—assert that evolution goes beyond the Darwinian two-step of mutation and selection to include internal orthogenetic drives toward greater coordination and efficiency . What are the politics of nature and the nature of politics under such circumstances? Can we be reactionaries with regard to the former and progressive with regard to the latter? Where do we go from here if we are headed into something far worse than what we strove to avoid? The old fascism was one in which unidirectional one-to-many media ruled out the possibility of reflection and critical response; the new media superfascism of immediacy and synchronization will be one in which the very notions of reflection and response will be as obsolete as an extinct species.

Notes

1. Vilém Flusser and Louis Bec, *Vampyroteuthis Infernalis* (Minneapolis: University of Minnesota Press, 2012), 49.
2. Friedrich Nietzsche, *Twilight of the Idols* (Indianapolis: Hackett, 1997), 10.
3. See Richard Cavell, *Remediating McLuhan* (Amsterdam: Amsterdam University Press, 2016), 57–64.
4. Flusser, *Natural:Mind*, trans. Rodrigo Maltez Novaes (Minneapolis: Univocal, 2013), 43–8.
5. Ibid., 46.
6. Ibid., 47.
7. Ibid., 43.
8. Ibid., 44.
9. Ibid., 43.
10. Ibid., 44.
11. Carl Chun, *The Cephalopoda. Part I: Oegopsida. Part II: Myopsida, Octopoda* (Jerusalem: Israel Program for Scientific Translations, 1975), 419.
12. Flusser and Bec, *Vampyroteuthis Infernalis*, 5–26.
13. Ibid., 39.
14. Ibid., 40.
15. Ibid., 39.
16. Ibid.
17. Ibid., 43.

18 Ibid., 31.
19 Ibid., 50.
20 Ibid., 52.
21 Ibid., 52–3.
22 Ibid., 65.
23 Ibid., 67.
24 Ibid., 15, 67.
25 Ibid., 67.
26 Erick Felinto, "*Mare nostrum. Mare alienun*: Identity, Epistemology and the Flusserian Imagination of Flows," *Matrizes* 12, no. 3 (2018): 45–58, 50.
27 Flusser and Bec, *Vampyroteuthis Infernalis*, 9, 55.
28 Ibid., 56.
29 Ibid.

11

Posthistory Today

Historical Time and Virality after Flusser

Charles M. Tung

In 1969 Vilém Flusser wrote in "The Vanity of History" that the study of history was ineffectual and out of joint; and historicity, as he put it, "is an anachronism."[1] What was responsible for the shift in historical consciousness—from, say, Dilthey's "I am an historical being" in 1910 to Flusser's contention in the 1970s and 1980s that humans had entered a new *posthistorical* condition?[2] For Flusser it was a kind of change in operating system from the medium of writing: as he put it, writing "impose[s] a specific structure on thought, in that [lines of writing] represent the world by means of a point sequence," thereby generating a historical consciousness that perceives events in a causal, progressive, linear series.[3] Prior to the advent of writing, the medium of the static picture or image produced an *unhistorical* being characterized by mythic occurrences and repetitions rather than sequences of events. But now, *after* writing, the world of amphitheatrical mass media was marked by a "posthistorical" historicity, not to be confused with Francis Fukuyama's version of the end of history, in which writing and narrative, as our fundamental modes of grasping history, have reached their expiration date.[4] Although Flusser was not writing in the age of Facebook, Twitter, and Cambridge Analytica, he thought forward to a moment of technological development in which the previous order of alphabetic code, and the masters of linear historical thinking, "would then have swallowed and digested the mathematician and image-maker" and inaugurated a new way of conceptualizing history.[5] Today, to think about history *after* Flusser—both in the wake of his influence and in a period of intensified *post-script* conditions—is to consider the way the "age" of the technical image brings about new alterations to the concept of posthistory, the way historicity must be reconfigured in relation to networks, technological protocols, and technical mediations that operate on scales beyond the reach of the human, beyond the narrative interface or even the graphical one. That is, posthistorical historicity today entails a consideration of scalar communicability, viral transmission, and meme culture.

At a moment in which we are living through both a biological and informational-cultural pandemic, Flusser's meditations on times, spaces, and media are crucial for thinking about history from the point of view of the cultural epidemiologist. In "On

Three Times," Flusser describes his three major conceptions of time and history not by way of his more famous reference to modalities of signification but in relation to tropes for imagining temporal process: the wheel stands for the world of mythic repetitions and cyclical modes of ethical being; the stream is the metaphor for linear historical sequences and "epistemological values"; and the sand heap is the figure for grains of history clustering improbably against an entropic backdrop in which particles tend to disperse uniformly.[6] If "magic time is ordered by the sage, historical time by the scientist, [and] post-Modern time by the artist," then an updated version of posthistorical time might call for a different figure for understanding circumstances beyond the negentropic aesthetics of convergences. I would suggest that this figure is the critical epidemiologist who tracks the movement and clustering of particles in terms of their speed, direction, and scale. As Benjamin Bratton has written, a world of viral contagion requires "an epidemiological view of society" that shifts our thinking "away from private individuation and toward public transmissibility."[7] The epidemiologist reconfigures historicity by rethinking circles, lines, and heaps as a mixture of Rube Goldberg machines and trophic cascades.[8]

In addition to enduring the lockdowns of SARS-CoV-2 and violent anti-Black racism, many parts of the world are now living under the conditions of "platform capitalism"—a situation in which the intermediary of digital infrastructure functions simultaneously as a data capture, storage, and extraction apparatus. In these circumstances, virality stands for (and *is*) the process of "transversal infections and parasitical relationships," to use Jussi Parikka's terms—the process of self-reproduction and transmission of complex, nonlinear phenomena.[9] Nonlinearity in this context is not just about the writerly or narrative format but also about mathematical descriptions of rates of change—for example, linear versus exponential growth. Linear modes of contact in Flusser's vocabulary would be theatrical and intersubjective, a way of connecting analogous to early "point-to-point" networks in the history of internet protocols. However, our new modes of mass media communication require thinking about multiple trajectories, transversal linkages among different amphitheaters, and scalar virality.[10] For Parikka, the virus is the figure for contemporary techno-capitalist culture, just as in Susan Sontag's work tubercular wastage is the negative outline of earlier capitalist emphases on savings and limitations of desire, and cancerous growth is the figure for capitalism's next phase, marked by speculation and the creation of new needs.[11] As Miriam Felton-Dansky puts it, the virus and its mode of transmission are "primary metaphors of the contemporary imagination," because "they describe the workings of digital-age capitalism, the strategies fueling new modes of political action, and the affective properties of emerging media forms."[12] In a more explicitly negative register, we can see that the petri dish or culture of viral technical images expands from individuals "together-alone" to a zone in which they become manipulable and policeable information patterns marked by what Dominic Pettman calls "the will to synchronize," and then to an atmospheric situation that Pettman similarly calls "posthistorical," which he defines as a general climate marked by disorientation, the loss of chronology, and the weakening of spatiotemporal coordinates.[13]

What both descriptive and critical readings of virality suggest is that viral culture is characterized by the speed, multidirectional spread, and scale jumps of these information patterns and the smaller packets they comprise, in addition to the communication and transportation networks that are their material conditions of possibility and the conduits for what one might call the *pathologos*. "Meme" is one of the common names for a packet of pathologos: it comes from the 1976 book *The Selfish Gene*, in which Richard Dawkins coined the terms "mimeme" and "meme" to signify "a unit of cultural transmission" that replicates analogously to genetic material. Memes, wrote Dawkins, "propagate themselves in the meme pool by leaping from brain to brain via a process which ... can be called imitation."[14] Newer research in the memetics laboratory can be said to have taken Dawkins's packet-centered evolutionary gradualism and emphasized informational and infrastructural communicability. These more contemporary emphases locate the potential for scalability and spread in both content and platform. In medical science and public-health administration, the idea of scalar virality is often traced back to the 1989 conference "Emerging Viruses: The Evolution of Viruses and Viral Disease," chaired by Columbia University epidemiologist Stephen Morse.[15] In both the conference and the collection of essays that followed, Morse and others called attention, in Dahlia Schweitzer's words, to "the ways large-scale events like urbanization, globalization, environmental destruction, and war would have a direct impact on the microbial level."[16] As Nicholas King points out in his essay "The Scale Politics of Emerging Diseases," Morse's work was the first to establish "direct causal links between the largest and smallest scalar extremes."[17] In response to the HIV/AIDS epidemic and the spread of BSE/"mad cow" disease, Morse called for an interdisciplinary study of "the rules of viral traffic" that would explain and track the exchanges and transfers of pathogens at different scales, from bodies to species, from migration to molecular genetics, from deforestation to microbiology, from tiny packets to worldwide disease outbreaks.[18]

Likewise, in the realm of culture, communicability requires an attention to the two-way streets among the machines and mechanisms of small memetic units, medium platforms, and large-scale biopolitical objects and planetary environments. In Priscilla Wald's work on *Cultures, Carriers, and the Outbreak Narrative*, the narrative content about virality itself plays a crucial role in the formation of collective identity: riffing on Benedict Anderson, Wald argues that a nation's or a population's "imagined immunities" in various kinds of epidemiological fictions are, "like the microscope[,] a technology ... that delineates the membership and scale of a population."[19] However, while a plotline may be the contagious patient zero, it cannot function as a superspreader without infrastructure and a network of transmission. Viral communicability comprises memetic information but also the real and virtual pathways of hyper-infection on which the scale of biopolitical control, public hygiene, and cyber-warfare depends. As Parikka argues, virality is defined by "transversal movements across institutions, contexts, and scales" (290)—large, medium, *and* small. In a version of the "program era" *after* Flusser, memetic entities are inscribed with instructions and functions to propagate and increase exponentially, diagrammed to move in all directions according to larger institutional and contextual protocols, thereby generating different scales and layers through which the viral is able to jump crosswise. Here, programs are not just the institutional curricula and practices that Mark McGurl analyzes but also nonlinear media-technological inscriptions.[20] As Parikka argues, history as "a programmable object"—"posthistory as 'programmed history'"—reconfigures historical time not so much as "postmodern collage but . . . the various applications and platforms of computation, in which time is bent and twisted in a variety of ways that resurface as distinct alternatives to history-writing."[21]

Consider the terrorist attack on a mosque and Islamic center on March 15, 2019, in Christchurch, New Zealand, where a radicalized white supremacist killed fifty people. The gunman was described by Abby Ohlheiser in *The Washington Post* as belonging to a new world of "extremely online" murderers: "we know that mass murderers want to go viral and that social media is making it easier for that to happen."[22] In this horrific attack, the expression of hatred was subordinate to the act of live-streaming the murders, which the terrorist intended to be saved, copied, and mirrored endlessly, with minor alterations to the video bypassing social-media companies' moderation algorithms and their search-and-discover algorithms. In other words, the central aim of the shooting seemed to be a promotional video for a hatred engineered for amplification and replication, a video filled with memes, content-tags, and cultural references designed to go viral: "Subscribe to PewDiePie," "Remove Kebab," "Copypasta," for example.[23] This is different from the simple desire for fame in the theater of culture: to paraphrase a line from Aaron Jaffe, the implied reader is today a search field or an algorithm. Where the society of the spectacle faced the danger of the passivity of sleep and the decommissioned consciousness, the posthistorical society confronts digital contagion. Posthistorical culture after Flusser is one in which affect doesn't transfer via specular mirrors but spreads via contagion pathways in scalar cathexis networks. In this case, the myth of a Meme Zero's ability to redpill its audience into a zone of waking reality in fact tunnels directly into the illusions about reverse racism, gynocentrism, and globalist oppression that line the far-right's rabbit holes. Our narrative of history, and history as such, has already been operating for a long time under the sign of the program era, and the violence of that history was always designed to infect every aspect of US social life.

Calls for racial justice today, at the moment of the Black Lives Matter movement, thus face a new dimension of systematicity in analyses of systemic oppression, which has given rise to organizations such as the Network Contagion Research Institute (NCRI). The right-wing extremist group "boogaloo bois," dressed in Hawaiian shirts and armed with assault rifles and ambitions to spark a new civil war, has exploited and undermined BLM protests in ways that confirm the posthistorical and viral nature of systemic racism. The NCRI has been tracking boogaloo activity across social-media platforms and warning law enforcement of its tipping points. Founded by three professors, Joel Finkelstein, Jeremy Blackburn, and Barry Bradlyn, NCRI has built "the largest meme-classification pipeline that we know of in the world," in which their AI, named Contextus, analyzes "billions of posts and millions of images from fringe and mainstream websites" in order to "track and expose the epidemic of virtual deception, manipulation, and hate, as it spreads between social media communities and into the real world."[24] While "the extremism and the radicalism and the recruitment are nothing new," as Paul Goldenberg points out, "the methodology is new—that you can reach tens of millions of people with a click of a finger," and accordingly our ability to understand the incubation and spread that follows the click requires a posthistorical digitality of nonnarrative and nonlinear instruments and operations.[25] What is historicity, then, in posthistory? In Joris Vlieghe's summary, "time will no longer be experienced in terms of eras," and "the very idea of history will not make any sense for those who live it."[26] This is because, in the posthistorical condition, narrativity gives way to a mode of sense-making beyond sense: stories fail as time-telling devices; units of time that organize the social world reveal their irregular and multiple foundations; and historical temporality (as we typically understand it: singular, straight, uniform) begins to interpenetrate with what Wolfgang Ernst describes as the micro "tempor(e) alities" produced by "time-critical" machines that, like very large-scale rhythms, don't register on the human sensorium and are intractable to hermeneutics, unreadable as story. But in contrast to the anti-historical Ernst, sensibilizable information in the regime of the technical image surges across a network as commoditized packets, but its movement also tracks and opens onto ill-aligned "topological layerings" of technical infrastructure, social swarms, political contexts, and slow zones of weakened ecological immunity.[27] The problem in posthistory, as Flusser puts it, is not that we are "no longer interested in history as such," but that any concept of history requires engaging "the possibility of combining various histories," for example, the histories that cannot be told (such as those the poet M. NourbeSe Philip tells about the massacre of enslaved African people thrown overboard from the slave ship *Zong*), but also the ones that are not tellable without reference to the rules of programs, the mathematics of tipping points, and the modelling of transversal level-jumps.[28] Posthistorical historicity seems to belong to a science-fictional universe, a world of bad genres, scale-mixing, and unsatisfying aesthetic experiences. This reconfiguration of historicity can be outlined by tracing the blips on the radar of representational scale that have begun to flash more frequently in the twenty-first century—for instance, by tracking moments of alien narration in Kate Marshall's work, figures of swarms, increasing shifts in the arts to the expository mode, and certain kinds of metafictional exit strategies such as escapes to more encompassing alternate realities.[29]

In his final line of "History of Communication Technologies," Kittler traces the transition from orality to written word to mathematical code, as a scale-shift from persons and communities, to nations and populations, to exanthropic organizations/forms and the futures they bring with them. Technologies of communication, he writes, "will have overhauled each other until finally an artificial intelligence proceeds to the interception of possible intelligences in space."[30] Each moment in the advance of communication media for Kittler represents a shift in the scope of control signals that expand the system or coordinate new scales of command. If paper was "central to the rise of the universities which, with their incorporated book-copying departments and postal networks, broke the storage monopoly of the monasteries," the tangle of viral technical media invites us to consider the connection between communication technologies, culture, and a diagnostic memetics capable of tracking infection trajectories across different domains and layers of history. Read not as an historiographical account, Kittler's history suggests a need to reassemble the historical as a set of associations (some of them virulent) among futures and pasts, media-technological contexts and social history, the inhuman and the human. As Parikka writes, "the concept of the posthistorical refracts into multiple historical and temporal directionalities."[31] The medium historicity, or the media historicities it refracts, connects heterogeneously a variety of platforms, infection scales, and historical strata.

Notes

1. Flusser, "The Vanity of History," in *Writings*, ed. Andreas Ströhl (Minneapolis: University of Minnesota Press, 2002), 139.
2. Wilhelm Dilthey, "The Formation of the Historical World in the Human Sciences," in *Gesammelte Schriften*, ed. Bernhard Groethuysen, Helmut Johach, and Martin Redeker, vol. 7 (1910; repr., Leipzig: Teubner, 1927), 278.
3. Flusser, "Line and Surface," in *Writings*, ed. Ströhl, 25.
4. Francis Fukuyama, *The End of History and the Last Man* (New York: Avon Books, 1992). Fukuyama's thesis argues that liberal democracy is the culmination of history and human governance and forecloses the possibility of any progress toward alternative systems.
5. Flusser, "Afterword to the Second Edition," in *Does Writing Have a Future?*, trans. Nancy Ann Roth (Minneapolis: University of Minnesota Press, 2011), 163–4.
6. Flusser, "On Three Times," in *Artforum // Essays* (São Paulo: Metaflux, 2017), 202, previously published in *Artforum* 29, no. 6 (February 1991): 25–6.
7. Benjamin Bratton, "18 Lessons of Quarantine Urbanism," *Strelka Mag*, March 4, 2020, https://strelkamag.com/en/article/18-lessons-from-quarantine-urbanism.
8. See Jaffe, *The Way Things Go: An Essay on the Matter of Second Modernism* (Minneapolis: University of Minnesota Press, 2014), 13–16, 48–9, 127.
9. See Nick Srnicek, *Platform Capitalism* (Cambridge: Polity, 2018); Jussi Parikka, "Contagion and Repetition: On the Viral Logic of Network Culture," *Ephemera: Theory and Politics in Organization* 7, no. 2 (2007): 288.
10. Christian Sandvig, "The Internet as the Anti-Television: Distribution Infrastructure as Culture and Power," in *Signal Traffic: Critical Studies of Media Infrastructures*, eds. Lisa Parks and Nicole Starosielski (Urbana: University of Illinois Press, 2015), 225–45.
11. Parikka, "Contagion and Repetition: On the Viral Logic of Network Culture"; Susan Sontag, *Illness as Metaphor and AIDS and Its Metaphors* (New York: Picador, 2001).
12. Miriam Felton-Dansky, *Viral Performance: Contagious Theaters from Modernism to the Digital Age* (Evanston: Northwestern University Press, 2018), 7.
13. Pettman, *Infinite Distraction: Paying Attention to Social Media* (Cambridge: Polity, 2016), 53; 56–7.
14. Richard Dawkins, *The Selfish Gene* (1976; Oxford: Oxford University Press, 2006), 192.
15. See the volume that Morse published several years later, Stephen S. Morse, *Emerging Viruses* (New York: Oxford University Press, 1993).

16 Dahlia Schweitzer, *Going Viral: Zombies, Viruses, and the End of the World* (New Brunswick: Rutgers University Press, 2018), 5.
17 Nicholas B. King, "The Scale Politics of Emerging Diseases," *Osiris* 19 (2004): 65.
18 Ibid.
19 Priscilla Wald, *Contagious: Cultures, Carriers, and the Outbreak Narrative* (Durham: Duke University Press, 2008), 19.
20 Mark McGurl, *The Program Era: Postwar Fiction and the Rise of Creative Writing* (Cambridge, MA: Harvard University Press, 2011).
21 Jussi Parikka, "Planetary Memories: After Extinction, the Imagined Future," in *After Extinction*, ed. Richard Grusin (Minneapolis: University of Minnesota Press, 2018), 29–30, 42.
22 Abby Ohlheiser, "The Christchurch Mosque Shooter, Steeped in Online Culture, Knew How to Make His Massacre Go Viral," *Washington Post*, March 15, 2019, https://www.washingtonpost.com/technology/2019/03/15/christchurch-mosque-shooter-steeped-online-culture-knew-how-make-his-massacre-go-viral/.
23 See Talia Lavin, "The Death of Fascist Irony," *The New Republic*, March 19, 2019.
24 "Network Contagion Research Institute," *Network Contagion Research Institute*, accessed June 24, 2020, https://ncri.io/.
25 Craig Timberg, "As Trump Warns of Leftist Violence, a Dangerous Threat Emerges from the Right-Wing Boogaloo Movement," *Washington Post*, June 17, 2020, https://www.washingtonpost.com/technology/2020/06/17/trump-warns-leftist-violence-dangerous-threat-emerges-right-wing-boogaloo-movement/.
26 Joris Vlieghe, "Education in an Age of Digital Technologies," *Philosophy & Technology* 27, no. 4 (December 1, 2014): 527.
27 Parikka, "Contagion and Repetition: On the Viral Logic of Network Culture," 294. Also See Eugene Thacker, "Networks, Swarms, Multitudes," *CTheory* (May 18, 2004).
28 Flusser, "Line and Surface," 33. On histories that "cannot be told, yet must be told," see M. NourbeSe Philip, *Zong!* (Middletown: Wesleyan University Press, 2008), 198–9, 206–7.
29 On alien narration, see Kate Marshall's recent book project on the nonhuman turn in American literature and for an extreme example of the expository, see Stephen Emmott's *Ten Billion* (New York: Vintage, 2013), a play that is essentially a PowerPoint. Figures of swarms in both ecological and network fiction, and instances of alternate realities in science fiction, are too numerous to list but easily understood as generic explorations of scale jumps.
30 Kittler, "The History of Communication Media," *CTheory* (July 30, 1996).
31 Parikka, "Planetary Goodbyes: Post-History and Future Memories of an Ecological Past," in *Memory in Motion: Archives, Technology and the Social*, ed. Ina Blom, Trond Lundemo, and Eivind Røssaak (Amsterdam: Amsterdam University Press, 2017), 140.

Part II

Flusser's Expanded Modernism

12

Demonologies[1]

Laurence A. Rickels

Part One

In *The Devil Notebooks*,[2] I offered close commentary on Vilém Flusser's reading of our infernal relation in terms of a metabolic cycle for which the mortal sins serve as stations, and which I applied to the momentum of hesitation guiding Freud's speculations on the death drive in *Beyond the Pleasure Principle*. An error in Rodrigo Maltez Novaes's translation of Flusser's study, *History of the Devil*, enters into this performance and inscribes the death-wish increments of Freud's larger hesitation. A brain-twister in English, the fragile hierarchy of "substitution" depends entirely on either "for" or "by"—a distinction as muddled and bypassed in the meantime as the split-infinitive rule. When we read that "magic formulas are being substituted for more mathematical formulas" in the context of an argument about the "progressive scientification of the world" we must hesitate over an undertow of reversal of the intended meaning.[3] Successful mourning would shore up the limping distinction and make the decision for living on via the upgrade of substitution. But the shaky foundation for this decision-making reflects the greater likelihood of what we might term "unmourning," the ultimate inhibition that must be abandoned by those who sign up with the Devil and his Christian frame of reference.

The 2010 staging at the Berlin State Opera of Igor Stravinsky's *The Rake's Progress* (1951) under the direction of Krzysztof Warlikowski was another wrap of Flusser's reading of the Devil. Inspired by Hogarth's cycle of paintings, Stravinsky commissioned W. H. Auden to write the libretto for the opera he had in mind (Auden brought along Chester Kallman as his collaborator). It is immediately quite an intervention to add the Devil to Hogarth's resolutely secular tableaux, which represented, like storyboards before their time, complete scenes in the narrative of a spendthrift's decline unto madness. Shadowed all the while by his abandoned but steadfast true love, he is installed at Bedlam and doesn't go to Hell. At the end of the Auden/Stravinsky version, the Devil, Nick Shadow, can't convince protagonist Tom Rakewell to kill himself. So, he makes a bet, which is how Goethe's Mephistopheles bound his Faust to the terms of a compact. Tom is able to guess the cards Nick draws and the Devil withdraws directly to Hell without collecting a soul. When the departing sponsor of Tom's rise and fall just the same places the curse of madness upon him, the delusional system that results—in which Tom is Adonis and his abandoned beloved Anne Trulove his Venus—preserves the love relation he denied but which, like the Eternal Feminine in *Faust II*, saves him.

When the job that his prospective father-in-law Mr. Trulove offers him isn't good enough, since he aims to be rich not busy (and honest), Tom wishes for money, and Nick Shadow arrives to fulfill this wish. In *The Interpretation of Dreams*, Freud stages an allegory of the wish in fantasying, which then returns in the case study of Dora (*Fragment of an Analysis of a Case of Hysteria*) as follows:

> A daytime thought may very well play the part of *entrepreneur* for a dream; but the *entrepreneur*, who, as people say, has the idea and the initiative to carry it out, can do nothing without capital; he needs a capitalist who can afford the outlay, and the capitalist who provides the psychical outlay for the dream is invariably and indisputably, whatever may be the thoughts of the previous day, a wish from the unconscious.[4]

What underlies the wish for free money is masked by the free-floating fulfilment that Nick offers: Tom has inherited a fortune from an unknown uncle. The money he comes into, inherited from an unidentified dying object, implies and denies a relationship to the dead and Dad. Freud speculates that an infantile relationship to the father inscribed in the unconscious through prohibition and repression of masturbation backs the fantasying that determines Dora's symptomatic relations.

This fragment of a case is famous for the import it first won for the transference in Freud's assessment of what went wrong and right in the sessions with Dora. What went wrong with Herr K. went wrong with Dora's father and so on. Freud came to an appreciation of the transference in his effort to render intelligible the benefits the analysis did bestow on the patient after all and despite the botched termination. The transference that was left implicit and anticipated in the sessions with Freud caught up with the plotting of her symptoms, putting it all to rest. That it was a wrap became clear when she visited the K. couple to offer her condolences on the not unanticipated death of one of their children. It was as though nothing had happened and Herr and Frau K. spoke plain text. It was really over.

A transference interpretation that happens in session, Freud decided, was more cost-effective than the construction of such an auto-analytical roundabout. It was easier said and done that their relationship in the setting of the sessions was the current funding opportunity for the unconscious capitalist otherwise backing her double-dealing relations with Herr K. and with her father in prehistory. The only parent on the stage of *The Rake's Progress* is Mr. Trulove. His daughter Anne seems, like Dora, to be just one step ahead of old incest fantasies, which the father's proximity, at least in Warlikowski's staging, brings home. When toward the end of the Berlin production she arrives on stage with a baby, an accessory imported from the Hogarth paintings, one must wonder if Tom or her father sired the offspring. Her loyalty to Tom would be, then, her adaptation to reality—a prospect as pressing and remote as Dora's attachment to Herr K.

Tom's laziness, which is how Mr. Trulove faults the unwillingness to look for a job, gives rise to the wish for narcissistic supplies. The infernal impresario of wish fulfillment who arrives to initiate Tom into Lust wears an Andy Warhol wig throughout Warlikowski's interpretation of the opera. The alignment is made evident when Nick, seated at the table in front of the screening of the film in which Andy demonstrates how he eats a hamburger, follows suit. Flusser sets up Lust and Sloth as the framing supports of our relationship to the world through or according to the Devil. All the sins between could be seen as aspects of Lust, to which sin Flusser dedicates the longest chapter by far. His exegesis of Lust ranges widely but subtly and extends to the attachment to the mother tongue and the paroxysms of nationalism.

The Warhol identification applies a touch of perversion to Tom's initiation. Flusser, like Freud, emphasizes that the human sex drive is constitutively nonreproductive, technically perverse, still in thrall to the replicational sex of cells. In *The Rake's Progress*, the first stopover in Tom's full entry into Lust is a house of prostitution named (in keeping with the ancestry of the fantasy genre) Mother Goose. To obviate the introspection of dissipation, Nick proposes Tom's marriage to Baba the Turk, a Medusoid sideshow attraction that everyone loves to dread. In Flusser's metabolic cycle, Lust, doubled by infantile Wrath and Gluttony, is conjugated with power via the more Oedipal sins of Greed, Envy, and, ultimately, Pride. Nick reroutes the sense or direction of matrimony by brokering this alliance, which is Tom's shortcut to prestige. As the bearded lady's consort, Tom would proudly stand above the two defining limits of Everyman, mere desire for the sexy and adaptive *mores* (in other words: adolescence and its midlife criticism).[5]

Sloth (or "sorrow of the heart") is Tom's intermittent condition, which he escapes through wish fantasy. What the Devil must circumvent, according to Flusser, is contrition. To this end the Devil bestows on Tom a machine that purportedly turns stones into loaves of bread. By turning the backlot of mankind into a utopia, Tom hopes to make reparation. The singular machine, multiplied down the assembly line into gadgets for sale, will ensure free bread for all. But since the machine is but a magician's trick everyone who invests, backers and consumers alike, is soon out of money. In the Berlin production, it is the fantasy genre that folds out of the Devil's technology. At the auction following the bankruptcy of Tom's breadwinning scheme, Minnie Mouse, Darth Vader, and two superheroes are among the properties for sale.

What Freud in his 1907 article on the poetics of daydreaming calls a *Zeitmarke*, date-mark or time-stamp,[6] introduces the half-life of every fantasy-escape, which takes a running start in a happy past, on which the wish is based, and makes a leap into the future of wish fulfillment, outflying the incident in the present that prompted the wish and tags it. When Freud explores the daydream, the everyday model for the mighty aspirations and resolutions of *Dichtung*, he argues that the circumvention of present tension cannot elide its triggering in real time, its history. The indelible date-mark stamped upon the trigger-unhappy moment in the circumvented present openly lies waiting for historicization, the backfire of fantasy, its mortal recoil. The fantasy genre, therefore, is historicization waiting to happen. Like the transference happening in session the date-mark gives a rest to wish fantasy's speed-denial within the once-and-future.

The footnotes to Dora's second dream are addenda that came up in the course of free association in session. The second addendum in the footnote underworld concerns the out-of-placement of a question mark. In Dora's telling of her dream what follows the news imparted by her mother in a letter, "Now he is dead," is the fragment-phrase, "and if you like you can come." A question mark cut short the phrase and gave emphasis to "like."[7] Every increment in the lexicon of what the English and French reception of psychoanalysis might call "desire" is marked in the original language by willing and wishing: "Und wenn Du willst?" She recalls the question mark upon recognizing that her mother's dream sentence cites a note she received from Frau K.: "If you would like to come?" This was the note she followed to the lakeside setting where the breakdown of her relations with the K. couple led to her sessions with Freud. As Freud notes, the analysis was subsequently broken off in connection with the content of this dream,[8] which, aggravated by his own inattention to the transference, triggered his patient's acting out.

The death wish can be devastating prep work for the other's death. His analysis of Dora's second dream leads Freud to recognize in the somatic symptoms he earlier dismissed as history his patient's susceptibility to melancholic identification. The death of Dora's aunt triggered a series of identifications (notably with two cousins), which by the light of her second dream revealed the foundation of her subsequent hysterical symptom picture. In Dora's second dream, her father is gone, though not yet in her waking lifetime. The dream goner goes back to her earliest wish that he should get lost, out of the way of her infantile sex. A multilayered topography of wishing opens up around the dream news of the father's death. A dream, as Freud advises, circumvents repression to give a measure of representation to wishes that, in Dora's case, the dreamer in her waking state must actively unfulfill. Freud admits that Dora walked out on the analysis because he had not recognized that he was transferentially synonymous with Herr K. and therefore bound to receive the rebound of her revenge against them both.[9] Freud wagered that the negative transferential aspect that Herr K. triggered, also in Dora's relationship to him and to the analysis, most likely turned on money.[10]

Nick Shadow's granting of Tom's wish for free money in the form of inheritance from the unidentified dead steps closer to what is at the same time manically denied. It is the other's death that splits into shares the omnipotence of wishing (or the equation Flusser draws between the will and Pride). Because the other goes first, a departure we inevitably wished upon, there is a ghostly remainder or return, the goner's share in the omnipotence that the death wish flexed, on which we speculate.

In the final analysis, Flusser gives a powerful reading of the very span of hesitation Freud applied to his formulation of the death drive. Freud is surely able, as he writes in *Beyond the Pleasure Principle*, to throw himself "into a line of thought and to follow it wherever it leads out of simple scientific curiosity, or, if the reader prefers, as an *advocatus diaboli*, who is not on that account himself sold to the devil."[11] When Freud earlier formulated the hypothesis that the goal of life is death he still had to account for the instincts of self-preservation. In this speculative setting, however, they can be seen as issuing the guarantee that the organism will follow its own path to its proper death and not die in a random way. This is the Devil's best offer: an uninterrupted span of quality time that concludes on schedule at the certain deadline. But Freud interrupts himself ("let us pause for a moment and reflect") and counters that the sexual instincts reintroduce "potential immortality" after all.[12] In performing a deferral at close quarters of the deadline, Freud's hesitation leaves room for mourning and melancholia. Flusser follows Freud in disbanding a fantasy scenario but in lieu of mourning constructs a loop. In 1987 he publishes an alternate history that resituates the ends of fantasy within a dystopic science fiction.

Part Two

Before Donna Haraway's active affirmative reading of tentacular thought as a late cyborg manifestation, Vilém Flusser peeled and pealed the layers of analogy between an infernally named unique incarnation among the octopoda and the human condition.[13] He returned to the brand of psychohistory styling with Freud that went into *The History of the Devil* but sent the human conditioning out on an update for the late 1980s. Flusser had gone the distance that Walter Benjamin's oeuvre marked in the concluding work on media politics. The parallel course Flusser ran was, however, post-traumatic. While two decades earlier the traumatic recent past that brought him to his scene of writing in Brazil was subsumed within a pageant of mortal sins that allegorized the history of the Devil as our history, this second round of demonology placed the Nazi symptom in the foreground of his warning shout about the ahistoricizing push and pull of the digital relation.

It's getting late in his monograph when Flusser checks in with a contemporary expedition in the China Sea that has brought up more exemplars of the remarkable squid. Flusser's conceit throughout is that we stand in a relationship of specular reversal to the "vampire squid from hell." Before a renewed prospect of raising the squid up to the human level, Flusser warns against merging the mirrors. The result won't be a perfect spheric ensemble à la Plato "but rather a self-lacerating hermaphrodite: a cybernetic Naziism."[14] It is a hybrid model that had all its test runs within greater psychoanalysis.[15]

After pages of classification of the unique squid in its dialectical relationship to humankind—he argues that both species succeeded in overcoming their animal nature—Flusser summons Wilhelm Reich and his notion of the orgon to locate an alternative to the "spongy" concept of spirit.[16] Reich argued that an organism is an accumulator of repressed impulses, which are forwarded into its protective layer of armoring, in effect the body memory or repression of outer and inner influences.[17] The Reichian organism packs away energy until the cramping gives way and lets go in an explosive outburst, which Reich calls orgasm.[18] Every organism is in three segments, head, chest, and abdomen, and the alignment is either chest out or the core pushed forward, like in coitus. Reich's orgon explodes, then, in two directions. There is the insect-like military formation, the armored body marching as to death. But then there's the softness in the enfolding of abdomen and head, in the proximity of mouth and anus, which drifts toward love.[19]

The insect model doesn't really fit the human psyche, Flusser points out, if only because it overlooks the human's inner skeleton. But it throws a perfect fit with the vampire squid from hell, which is drawn to the model of its distant relation, the insect species. We at times are drawn with or through it.

Flusser takes us by surprise in anticipation of the dire straits of the Nazi symptom through which he navigates on the China Sea: the vampire squid eats its own anus and "makes love in order to make war."[20] With three penises, the vampire squid attains permanent orgasm. But its sexualized mouth and cerebralized genitalia abet cannibalism and suicide. From the vantage of the Reichian model, "the vampire squid becomes an ultimate move in the love game, the 'end game' of total love, and one of the opening moves in the meta-game of death."[21] The squid plays at love (consummately, like no other being) in order to kill and to kill itself.[22]

Human reflection (*Nachdenken*), which cuts into phenomena to supply models for thought, amounts to, in Flusser's cybernetic sci-fi formulation, "control of the feedback between model and appearance."[23] The vampire squid doesn't require the knife of reason. Its tentacles grasp what our illuminating reason has already rationalized. The tentacles, embedded with sex organs, bring back concepts that are sexually loaded: masculine and feminine concepts. Copulation synthesizes the gender difference and the resulting concepts serve as models for phenomena, like the lit stones on the ocean floor.[24] The concepts of pure gender drive the squid to orgasm.[25] What corresponds to human reflection, the cutting and measuring of reason, is the squid's comprehending coitus and climax.

Flusser goes many rounds of comparison between the squid and the human before he arrives at the harrowing valuation concluding his study. A telling contrast he turns up, given the prospect of our condition coming soon, concerns the human relationship to objects. Human history can be objectively realized by reading those objects of the world that humans have formed and "informed." At this juncture there is in addition to the human and the squid a hybrid preliminary to their fateful merger. It is occasioned by a visitation of judgment from outer space. "Not only we vampyroteuthis but also a visitor from Mars can reconstruct human history out of these objects. It follows that human history isn't really intersubjective but is absorbed by objective objects. A mistake."[26]

"Our" vampire-squid critique allows us to reconstruct a historical concept that rises up from the depths. The vampire squid is engaged in a process of recording intersubjectively communicated information. Of import, then, are the squid's intersubjective media of information transfer, which are glandular: vampire-squid history is a history of secretions. What might be summarized as a culture of art looks more like the conspiracy and agency of secrecy. The individual vampire squid lies to every other species and every other squid of its own kind. The aim is to take the other in, in both senses. But if we apply the checklist of evolution one might also judge the culture of the vampire squid in light of the "highest strategy" imaginable. Is this Darwinian conclusion in concert with the orgiastic, orphic, artistic character of squid culture? Flusser brings in Schopenhauer. The culture of the vampire squid is a light and color show, a presentation or concept (*Vorstellung*) that masks this raving predator's "will to power."[27] We observers are seized by the vertigo (*Schwindel*) of beauty, but *Schwindel* in the double sense of the word, which in German also means "deception." We stand before "a seductive culture of colors, lights, forms, caresses, all leading on every level of existence to orgasm, even to philosophical climax. It veils the will to kill."[28]

The multicellular community, which is the socialization goal of evolution, cannot, like the individual cell that divides and doubles itself, split without losing information, a loss that is "death."[29] The insect population gets around such loss by sacrificing individuality to specialized service to and within a superorganism.[30] Insects suffer their armoring as an error in their construction. They must disarm periodically to allow growth and are then utterly unprotected. That's why they have to be so tiny. The superorganism of biological (not social) relations overcomes the basic error. Freedom lies in the biologization of the preliminary sacrifice of freedom.[31]

Unlike ants, vampire squids and humans abide in poorly organized societies, which yet periodically pose the threat of turning into something modelled on the armor ideal.[32] The vampire squid developed from the same basic species as did the ants, and the pull of ant society is inscribed in its "collective unconscious:" it strikes out against this tendency antisocially.[33] On both sides of our specular relationship political engagement addresses the contradiction between equality and brotherhood.[34] Anarchic sibling war is the political ideal of the vampire squid.

To view the contradiction from the vantage of the squid Flusser turns again to science fiction. Not only does Flusser repeatedly identify the deep sea as the other outer space, but he relies on a sci-fi reference to motivate a political turn toward equality away from brotherhood: "Since Freud gave us instruction in the matter of sibling hatred and since we've known Big Brothers, the notion of brotherhood has for us too been somewhat tarnished."[35] Close, but go no further. It's a given that the squid decided long ago for equality since it eats its twin brethren, bundled together like grapes for the picking.

For humans, all biological conditions are culturally loaded.[36] We combat culture and imagine utopias in which all biological conditions have been overcome. For the squid, the political engagement goes against its own nature. It does violence to itself.[37] For us, too, freedom lies in the always available possibility of suicide.[38] "But isn't in the final analysis every human engagement pitched against nature, and are not all defenders of natural givens (of race, masculine rule, even of ecological balance) traitors against the human spirit?"[39]

The vampire squid overcomes its animal nature through hate. We do the same through love.[40] While even animals inherit and pass on information, super-animals place historical evolution above, over, on top of genetic evolution by transmitting acquired information via conventional codes.[41] The basic problem is memory. Animal memory lasts longer than the super-animal memory recorded in the works of man. But the super version is how, just the same, humans wanted to be remembered. Art is a method for supplying an artificial memory that is lasting. Transience is obvious on the ocean floor, but on the earth's surface the endurance for centuries of bones and ruins gives the illusion of a future to be remembered in objects.[42] The essence of the human artwork, however, is that it can be recognized. New information can be grasped and retained in its artificial memory. "Thus there arises an escalating feedback between object and human, in other words, 'art history.'"[43] When the object absorbs the existential interest of the human who lives in function of his or her object, there is a real danger that the purpose of art has been forgotten, namely the transformation of objects into memories from which other humans can extract information.

We struggle against the resistance of objects, while the vampire squid struggles against the other squid. The way we carve in stone, the vampire squid carves in the brains of the receivers. The art of the squid isn't objective but intersubjective, aiming for immortality in the memory of others. The intersubjectivity is carried forward through copulation with the squid receiver faked out and seduced by the sender body's light and color shows. Flusser brings the artistic process of the squid to a point: "It is rape of the other in order to become immortal in the other: art as strategy of rape, of hate."[44]

But our own update from hell now follows. Although our new electromagnetic media aren't organs of light on our skin, we are able to recognize in the vampire squid an art of our own increasingly not stuck on objective resistances but instead intersubjective and immaterial, no longer constructing artificial memories but passing information directly into the brains of the receivers. "The human achieves self-realization from now on in working out new immaterial information, that is, in the activity of processing that uses software. In this context, 'soft' unquestionably refers to molluscs" (the German word for molluscs is *Weichtiere*, "soft animals").[45] Our molluscular strategy is to make not objects but media through which we rape human brains and force them to store immaterial information. We, too, project chromatophora through our media and deceive and seduce the receiver. Art now lies in this strategy, unless, Flusser allows, we are ready to give up the concept of art and consign it to the underworld of missing links.

Since the Enlightenment and through Freud we have repeatedly attempted to stem the tide of the vampire squid's emergence. The ongoing failure lies in the mirror character of our relationship. The squid "indwells our depths and we its depths."[46]

> If theologians accordingly raise the infernal toward the divine, the cyberneticists automatic feedback toward the clarity of decision, the logicians the mechanical play of symbols toward true tabulation, the Freudians the repressed toward conscious thought, then that is because the vampire squid in turn attempts, through the deeds of the Nazis or through the thermonuclear apparatus, to sink us down into its depths.[47]

The care with which artificial intelligence is constructed in science fiction—not so as to be human but to protect humanity from itself—can be overheard in Flusser's characterization of the objective spirit of scientific inquiry that seeks knowledge "without inclusion of human being in its entirety, besmirched by experiences, wishes, and dreams."[48] That's why he has opted for the form of the animal fable in his study, which places his inquiry in this form, together with its moral lesson, squarely between science fiction and high fantasy.

Notes

1 Part One of this chapter is a modified version of a review article I wrote on Flusser's *The History of the Devil* (the 2014 translation). The article appeared in *Cultural Critique*, no. 97 (Fall 2017): 169–75. This version is part of the second volume of my *Critique of Fantasy*, subtitled *The Contest between B-Genres*. Part Two of this chapter adapts a section in the third volume of *Critique of Fantasy*, which is subtitled *The Block of Fame*. See Laurence A. Rickels, *Critique of Fantasy*, 3 vols. (Santa Barbara: punctum books, 2020).
2 See Notebooks Five and Six, in Laurence A. Rickels, *The Devil Notebooks* (Minneapolis: University of Minnesota Press, 2008).
3 *The History of the Devil*, ed. Siegfried Zielinski (Minneapolis: University of Minnesota Press, 2014), 103. Novaes translated the second version of the study, which Flusser wrote or rewrote in Portuguese.
4 Sigmund Freud, *Fragment of an Analysis of a Case of Hysteria*, *The Standard Edition of the Complete Psychological Works of Sigmund Freud*, ed. and trans. James Strachey, vol. 7 (London: Hogarth Press, 1953), 87.
5 We recall that Hannah Arendt, the author of "the banality of evil," turned down Auden's marriage proposal.
6 Freud, "Creative Writers and Daydreaming," in *The Standard Edition of the Complete Psychological Works of Sigmund Freud*, ed. and trans. James Strachey, vol. 9 (London: The Hogarth Press, 1959), 147.
7 Freud, *Fragment of an Analysis of a Case of Hysteria*, 95.
8 Ibid.
9 Ibid., 117–18.
10 Ibid., 119.
11 *Beyond the Pleasure Principle* (London: Hogarth Press, 1955), 59.
12 Ibid., 39–40.
13 Flusser, *Vampyroteuthis Infernalis* (Göttingen: European Photography, 1987). While Haraway's affirmation of tentacular thinking at the limit is allied with a sci-fi movie like *Arrival* (2016), it falls short of early science fiction, which, for example in A. E. van Vogt's early short stories and first fix-it novels built on them, saw the octopoda from outer space as evil along the lines of Ridley Scott's *Alien* (1979), which ultimately adapted this legacy without declaring the import.
14 Flusser, *Vampyroteuthis Infernalis*, 68.
15 Modeled on the term "Großdeutschland" used during the Third Reich to designate Germany together with the annexed "Germanic" territories, this expression, which I introduced in *Nazi Psychoanalysis*, performs the counterintuitive claim, which my trilogy put forward, that the establishment at the central institute in Nazi Berlin of an eclectic psychotherapy based on all the treatment modalities taking their departure from Freud's science and departing from it amounted to a reunification aggrandizing psychoanalysis. Laurence A. Rickels, *Nazi Psychoanalysis*, 3 vols. (Minneapolis: University of Minnesota Press, 2002).
16 Flusser, *Vampyroteuthis Infernalis*, 29.
17 Ibid.
18 Ibid., 30.
19 Ibid.

20　Ibid., 31.
21　Ibid.
22　Ibid.
23　Ibid., 46.
24　Ibid.
25　Ibid., 47.
26　Ibid., 49.
27　Ibid., 52.
28　Ibid.
29　Ibid., 52–3.
30　Ibid., 54.
31　Ibid., 55.
32　Ibid.
33　Ibid., 57.
34　Ibid., 55.
35　Ibid., 56.
36　Ibid.
37　Ibid.
38　Ibid., 58.
39　Ibid., 57.
40　Ibid.
41　Ibid., 59.
42　Ibid., 60.
43　Ibid., 61.
44　Ibid., 62.
45　Ibid., 64.
46　Ibid., 68.
47　Ibid.
48　Ibid., 69.

13

An Intersubjective Style

Frances McDonald

In the final chapter of *Gestures* (1991), Vilém Flusser reflects on our eroding faith in objective knowledge. Since Descartes, we have dreamed a dream of radical separability in which we, as thinking subjects, are able to occupy a transcendent position far above and outside the object world. By the midpoint of the twentieth century, though, this neat bifurcation of subject and object no longer held; as Flusser notes, "the foundation of the gesture of searching was the difference between the subject and object, human being and world, I and it. We are about to abandon this foundation."[1] It's hard to know what, precisely, broke the Archimedean point's back. Flusser gestures toward the usual suspects—here, Nietzsche and Freud, elsewhere, Heisenberg and Margaret Mead, but his eye is trained not on the agitators but on the aftermath of this "crisis in knowledge."[2] Impure times call for impure epistemologies. What we need, he argues, are neither subjective nor objective modes of engaging in the world—"subjectivity," after all, is just one more bid for transcendence, the gesture of a "solipsistic subject wanting to rise above the world."[3] Instead, we must develop intersubjective models that are based not in our separability and opposition to, but our constitutive entanglement with, the object world and each other.

Flusser understood intersubjectivity to be both the substrate and goal of Edmund Husserl's phenomenology, which begins with the recommendation that the researcher "abandon the futile search for an objective knowledge in favor of a concrete, intersubjective knowledge."[4] Although Husserl coined the term "intersubjectivity," he never offered a full and final definition of the term, and scholars tend to set it loosely among a constellation of proximate terms like "mutual understanding," "empathy," and "we-relationship."[5] Flusser's flatfooted approach to the concept is therefore particularly useful. In "The Gesture of Searching," he spins Husserl's intersubjectivity into a practical method of knowledge production:

> The researcher is located at the center of his environment. . . . Many things are happening around him, some of them are of great concern to him. They *press* themselves on him, and he throws himself toward them, *projects* himself against them. Toward the horizon, the mass of events becomes sparser and less interesting. Nevertheless, the mass comes nearer, and the researcher moves toward the horizon. The dimension of *proximity* is therefore dynamic.[6]

To press, to project, and to become proximate—these are the three movements that together comprise the intersubjective gesture of searching. Crucially, this dense, dynamic field of forces is an open system, and so research is necessarily dialogic. "Proximity is an intersubjective dimension," Flusser writes, "It measures the being I share with others in the world."[7]

Although this "intersubjective dimension" has always been our ontology, Flusser believed that it was only now, in the burgeoning age of new media technology, that we are able to access it as an epistemological mode. To do so, we must unhitch our patterns of thought from the grammatical and orthographic forms of linear writing, and instead learn to "think in video, in analog and digital models, and programs, in multidimensional codes."[8] In "On the Crisis of Our Models," an essay from the 1980s that was first published in 2002, Flusser offers a reprise of his model of intersubjective research. This time, though, he "thinks in video" to imagine the erstwhile researcher and his teeming lifeworld as a series of abstract shapes that pass through and mold themselves around each other:

> A hollow, translucid sphere appears on the screen swimming within a context. The context is composed of elements of various shapes that are dense around the sphere and spare toward the horizon of the screen. Some of the elements penetrate the sphere more or less deeply. The sphere sometimes secretes liquids that condense to form elements of the context. The sphere changes constantly its shape and color, and so do the elements of the context. At times the sphere breaks open and closes again. At times other similar spheres appear on the screen and make contact with the original one either directly or through elements of the context. The vacuum within the sphere and the horizon of the screen remain always black. This action is accompanied by sound. It should cause a dramatic impression.[9]

Like a circular slit fitted with seeded glass, Flusser's "translucid sphere" lets phenomena pass through but diffractively.[10] Over the course of three pages, Flusser describes how the researcher-shape (sometimes a sphere bristling with tentacular fingers, other times a "pointed cone") converges with and is mutually transformed by a stream of elements. One input turns the sphere into a pulsing red light, another into a sucking green channel. If it wasn't for the cold geometry of the piece, these scenes of secretion, submersion, diffraction, and diffusion would register as body horror: it's Mondrian meets *Naked Lunch*.

Having detailed these diffractive processes through fanciful adjustments of color, sound, and light, Flusser goes on to discard his model as "primitive." What we need, he says, is not this, per say, but something *like* this that has been rendered by experts in new media; the essay is nothing more than an invitation for others to take up this important work. Both here and in *Gestures*, Flusser speaks about the intersubjective model in the future tense: others must develop it now, he says, before it's too late. And yet, Flusser's own writings are and always have been intersubjective in the way he describes it here, which is to say they operate through tactics of pressing, proximity, and projection.[11] Consider, for example, the strange media ecology of the cybernetic fever-dream printed above, in which Husserl's notes on intersubjectivity are pressed first through the "space-time medium" of television and then again through alphabetical code.[12] This is Husserl on TV, in writing. Flusser uses these methods of submersion and diffraction repeatedly in his work, and perhaps most dramatically in the deep-sea dive of *Vampyroteuthis Infernalis*, in which he invites us to play a "game ... built out of distorting mirrors" that confounds the "objective position" of the sciences by pressing the human being through the hadal perspective of the vampire squid.[13] To do this work, Flusser presses disciplines and discourses through one another—here, phenomenology, zoology, and fiction thread together to create an idiosyncratic style of writing that Abraham Moles categorized as "philosophical fiction."[14]

In this chapter, I'm interested in how Flusser enacts intersubjectivity in his writing through various stylistic techniques of which his generic hybridity is just one. My impetus in doing so is an unpublished letter that Flusser wrote to Mira Schendel in September 1974 in which he meditates precisely on his long-standing attempt to cultivate an "intersubjective style:"

> I currently have three styles: (a) the objective, in which I float over language, (b) the subjective, in which I feel possessed by language, and (c) the intersubjective, in which, for example, I write this one letter ... it is the case (c) that interests me the most, because this is my "true" style.[15]

Here, as in "The Gesture of Searching," Flusser offers three modes of engaging with the world: the humanistic gesture of a transcendent intellect, the solipsistic gesture of the intellect turned inward, and the intersubjective gesture that responds to "the moment of being dialogically with others." The question that animates the letter in particular, though, is this: How can language be made to testify to this dialogical moment? Flusser doesn't offer a clear answer to this question, but he does suggest two possible lines of flight toward an intersubjective style—first, his unique method of translation and retranslation; and relatedly, the development of a writerly form that no longer heeds the separation of subject and object, which I see articulated formally by Flusser in his unorthodox citational praxis. Both of these techniques, I argue, resonate deeply with a quantum worldview, which understands radical entanglement, rather than radical separability, as the foundational state of the universe.

Because the goal of this chapter is to think about Flusser's intersubjective style as a creative response to developments in quantum physics, it's worth pausing here to outline what precisely those developments were. In 1913, the Danish physicist Niels Bohr proposed the first quantum model of the atom, which would prepare the ground for a series of advances in complexity theory, chaos theory, particle physics, and quantum field theory. Bohr's experiments showed that at the bottom of everything there are not pre-formed and discrete things but dynamic processes of entanglement. In her book *Meeting the Universe Halfway*, Karen Barad explains the challenge quantum indeterminacy posed to a Cartesian worldview:

In a stunning reversal of his forefather's schema, Bohr rejects the atomistic metaphysics that takes "things" as ontologically basic entities. For Bohr, things do not have inherently determinate boundaries or properties, and words do not have inherently determinate meanings. Bohr also calls into question the related Cartesian belief in the inherent distinction between subject and object, and knower and known.[16]

The epistemological implications of Bohr's discoveries are profound: when scientists believed themselves to be measuring and manipulating a determinate "thing," they were actually recording their own constitutive entanglement with the material world. Flusser subscribed wholeheartedly to quantum physics' dismantling of Cartesian criteria of measurement, as he explains in this 1990 interview:

> There are no two phenomena in the world that could be divided by a boundary. It would always be a bad and artificial separation. Phenomena cannot be separated in this way. They also cannot be organized according to straight lines. Phenomena overlap, they happen in layers. . . . Every systematic thinking is wrong, every system is a violation. Reality is tangled and therefore interesting. Every Cartesian thinking that creates order is fascist.[17]

As Flusser's boundary talk suggests, Bohr's discovery that reality is fundamentally "tangled" has ontological, as well as epistemological, implications. If "what we observe in any experiment is a *phenomenon* or entanglement or the inseparability of the apparatus and the observed object," then phenomena precede subject–object relations and not the other way around.[18] In a 1989 essay for *Art Forum*, Flusser states this idea explicitly. In a world composed of dynamic clusters of particle fields, he says, we must recognize that "we ourselves are such clusters where several fields overlap, mingle, and bundle."[19]

Flusser's self-translation practice is powered by his commitment to both a quantum epistemology and a quantum ontology. In his letter to Schendel, he describes a multistep process by which he presses a piece of writing first through German, then through Portuguese, then through English, before finally translating "into the language in which I would like to publish the text." Like a game of telephone, the gesture of translating produces interference patterns that expand and reshape the input in unpredictable ways. Scholars mostly understand the endgame of Flusser's translation experiments to be the infinite multiplication of meaning; Rainer Guldin, for example, understands it to be an "endless, open-ended enterprise" that works to uncover "hidden potentialities of [a] text."[20] In his letter to Schendel, though, Flusser outlines a different objective. "What I aim to do," he writes, "is to penetrate the structures of the various languages to reach a very general and depersonalized nucleus so I can, with such an impoverished nucleus, articulate my freedom." Given enough energy and time, Flusser believes that his translation exercises will provide access to a "general" core where all languages overlap, mingle, and bundle with one another, as in the Reuleaux triangle of a Venn diagram. As white light is a combination of all the colors in the color spectrum, so this nucleus, accessible only through systematic back-translation, would press together every language in the language system to transformative effect. Flusser sees creative potential in this zone of radical entanglement, which might equip him with a new way to "articulate [his] freedom." As we shall see, this freedom would be freedom not only from judgment (as in Husserl's *epoché*) but also from the structuring figure of the "I" itself.

We find Flusser already edging toward this goal in his first published book, *Language and Reality*, which uses translation to trace how different languages, and different zones of language (from small talk to concrete poetry), "permeate each other."[21] As in Bohr's quantum experiments, what Flusser records in these translation experiments is not a distant, observable thing called "Language" but his own constitutive entanglement with the observed. In a remarkable passage, he describes how the art of translation, properly practiced, overturns the ontology of the subject:

> What happens to me when I move between *vou* to *I go*? While I think *vou*, I am firmly anchored within the Portuguese reality. *Vou*, which is my thought, has definite meaning. However, during the translation, during this ontologically inconceivable moment of the suspension of thought, I hovered over the abyss of nothingness. *I am* during this transition only in the sense of becoming.[22]

To translate is to perform a quantum leap across the proximate zones that lie between languages, which Flusser here describes as an "abyss" where the "I" cannot go. Caught in the buzzing breach between Portuguese and English, Flusser is no longer a discrete subject engaging with a manipulable object. Rather, subject and object co-implicate one another to such a degree that all that is left is the event's unfolding. In this dialogical moment, Flusser "*lives* (*erlebt*) the dissolution of the Self and reality" to literally *become* the gesture of translating.[23]

Flusser's gesture of translating, then, provides a way of testifying to the dynamic processes of lived experience without framing it in terms of the subject. This is the uptake too of his intersubjective gesture of searching as he describes it in the "Crisis" essay—you'll notice, looking back at that essay, that Flusser avoids categorizing the model's moving parts as either subject or object. Instead, he draws on a wealth of descriptors that emphasize duration and convocation, from "events" and "stream of elements" to "things" and, of course, the "hollow, translucid sphere" that drifts across the screen.[24] We arrive now at the key principle of an intersubjective style, which Flusser presents to Schendel the form of a quandary. "The most terrible stylistic difficulty [of writing in the intersubjective mode]," he writes, "appears in the dialogical phase of my life, where the 'me' and the 'you' get mixed up." An intersubjective style, properly elaborated and executed, would honor the "mixed up" state of things by abandoning (the aggressive separation of) subject and object altogether; it would, as Flusser writes elsewhere, take "the interference of subject and object as its point of departure."[25]

As the passage from *Language and Reality* reproduced earlier clearly shows, the entry price to these in-between states—whether they be between languages, discourses, species, or subjects—is the "I" itself, which becomes hopelessly entangled with its object. Flusser understood this risk-factor to be the hallmark not only of the general gesture of translating but of his specific gesture of writing. In a 1967 essay titled "Essays," Flusser meditates on how his own self-proclaimed "lively style (*estilo vivo*) differs from academic convention."[26] While an academic style requires that the author "explain" their topic from a measured distance, a lively style is based in the author's radical identification with his materials. Flusser is quick to identify the ontological dangers inherent in such a procedure: "If I decide ... on my style, on implicating myself in my topic," he writes, "I run a risk. It is a dialectical risk: that of losing myself in the topic, and that of losing the topic. These are the two dangers of my identification with the theme."[27] Although Flusser labels his style "subjective"—he has yet to add Husserl's "intersubjective" to his repertoire—it is clear that he means to draw our attention away from the self-contained individual and toward the intimate zones of proximity that lie between the writer, his topic, and his "others," where "others" refers both to his interlocutors and his readers—the "before" and "after" of his own gesture of writing.

How Flusser comports himself around his others is an important aspect of his intersubjective style. His essays are mostly unencumbered by footnotes or endnotes, and he was more given to paraphrase than direct quotation. As with his translation experiments, scholars have mostly interpreted this formal quality through the lens of Flusser's own itinerant biography; as Finger, Guldin, and Bernando explain it in their coauthored book on Flusser, his "rootless biography [...] resulted in a certain synthetic rootlessness. He rarely cited his sources, and he rarely acknowledged those who influenced his thinking."[28] This is a persuasive argument, but as with his self-translation, there is also a way to read his unconventional citational apparatus (or lack thereof) as an effort to express an intersubjective, which is to say, a quantum, sensibility. In "Essays," Flusser offers this rationale for his citational minimalism:

> Let us suppose I want to write an essay on translation and translatability. It is an erudite topic, so I could choose the treatise form. In this case, I could base my argumentation on authors I have read, citing these authors in a bibliography as well as in the text in order to reduce my responsibility, although I still could add some of my own thoughts. The topic would be rendered explicit, and my readers would be informed. But I choose the essay. The problem of translation and translatability takes on the cosmic dimensions of all existential issues: it encompasses everything [...] In sum: I begin to lose my topic by having identified myself with it. And I simultaneously begin to lose myself in it, because I start to identify with its different aspects.[29]

Flusser objects to conventional academic citational practices for their adherence to Cartesian principles of separation and distance. A bibliography is a little partition machine that works to separate the writer's thoughts from the thoughts of others and in so doing models critical thinking as progressing linearly through a logic of accumulation ("I still could add some of *my own thoughts*," Flusser muses). Writing in the intersubjective style, though, Flusser cannot cite his sources or acknowledge his influences because there is no "him" left to do such work. This is not an expression of "rootlessness," quite the opposite: what radiates at the core of a Flusser essay is a fibrous topic that twists its way through and "encompasses everything." Remembering that the word "encompass" finds its root in the Old French *compas*, meaning "circle," we can add this to our growing collection of annular figures, including the "hollow, translucid sphere" and that "general and depersonalized" nucleus.

It is with the figure of the circle that this chapter curls to a close. If an academic style imagines the researcher as a straight-line drilling downward through obstacle after obstacle, then an intersubjective style imagines them to be a dense, permeable circle in a state of permanent drift through vast, open terrain. In his media theory, Flusser famously associated circles with images and prehistoric thinking, and lines with writing and historical thinking. He described the "narrow, magical circle" as a dizzying dead end that obstructed our ability to change or develop—it's all rotation, no revolution.[30] The intersubjective circle distinguishes it from the closed circuity of the "magic" world of the image by way of its radical openness. Our three examples hold up well here: the "hollow translucid sphere" is perfused with various inputs, the "general and depersonalized" nucleus is a bustling site of radical convergence, the essay's topic radiates outward until it "encompasses" the whole world. It is this emphasis on pressing, proximity, and projection that connects Flusser's intersubjective gesture of searching to a quantum sensibility, which perceives the world as a lively swirl of crossings and contaminations that cannot be properly measured or fully predicted. We do not need new media to properly enact this dynamic swirl. As we've seen, Flusser's own writing style brings into relief a mode of being-in-the-world that is neither looped, as in the circular image, nor progressive, as in linear writing, but *diffractive* in its commitment to tracing out the interference patterns that are produced when two or more "things" touch.

Notes

1 Flusser, *Gestures*, trans. Nancy Ann Roth (Minneapolis: University of Minnesota Press, 2014), 155.
2 Ibid., 147. This rotation of interest from divining reasons to imagining possibilities is one characteristic of an intersubjective style.
3 Ibid., 157.
4 Flusser, "A Utopia of Gardens: Epicurus versus Marx" (1980), unpublished manuscript, *Flusser Brasil*, December 19, 2012, 4. Accessed June 5, 2020. http://flusserbrasil.com/arte18.pdf
5 For a comprehensive overview of how Husserl and his scholars use the term, see Alessandro Duranti, "Husserl, Intersubjectivity, and Anthropology," *Anthropological Theory* 10, nos. 1–2 (2010): 16–35.
6 Flusser, *Gestures*, 156, emphases mine.
7 Ibid., 157.
8 Ibid., 25.
9 Flusser, "On the Crisis of Our Models," in *Writings*, ed. Andreas Ströhl (Minneapolis: University of Minnesota Press, 2002), 79.

10. See Haraway, *Modest_Witness@Second_Millennium.FemaleMan©Meets_OncoMouse*™ (New York: Routledge, 1997), 268.
11. In *Gestures*, Flusser riffs on the etymology of the word "stylus" to call this process simply, "style": "In the gesture of writing, the problem of style is not added on, it is the problem itself. My style is the way I write, which is to say, it is my gesture of writing. *Le style, c'est l'homme*" (24). Flusser will go on to repeat Georges Louis Leclerc Buffon's famous idiom—"the style is the man"—verbatim in the September 1974 letter to Mira Schendel that I take up shortly.
12. Flusser, "On the Crisis," 76.
13. Vilém Flusser and Louis Bec, *Vampyroteuthis Infernalis* (Minneapolis: University of Minnesota Press, 2012), 9.
14. Qtd. in Siegfried Zielinski, *[. . . After the Media]* (Minneapolis: Univocal, 2011), 112.
15. The letter from Flusser to Mira Schendel was sent to me in its original Portuguese by Rainer Guldin. The hard copy can be found in the Vilém Flusser Archive in Berlin, reference number CORRESP.79_6 [3130], 19 February 1973. This is my translation.
16. Karen Barad, *Meeting the Universe Halfway: Quantum Physics and the Entanglement of Matter and Meaning* (Durham: Duke University Press, 2002), 138.
17. Qtd. in Anke Finger, Rainer Guldin, and Gustavo Bernardo Krause, *Vilém Flusser: An Introduction* (Minneapolis: University of Minnesota Press, 2011), 67.
18. Barad, "Interview with Karen Barad," in *New Materialism: Interviews and Cartographies*, ed. Rick Dolphijn and Iris van der Tuin (Ann Arbor: Open Humanities Press, 2012), 61.
19. Flusser, "Wondering About Science," *Artforum* 27, no. 10 (Summer 1989): 4.
20. Finger, Guldin, and Krause, *Vilém Flusser*, 49–50.
21. Vilém Flusser, *Language and Reality* (1963), trans. Rodrigo Maltez Novaes (Minneapolis: University of Minnesota Press, 2018), 30.
22. Ibid., 29.
23. Ibid. This prefigures his claim from *Gestures* that "We no longer believe that we make gestures, but that we are gestures" (Flusser, *Gestures*, 155).
24. Flusser will have known that "thing" finds its etymological root in the Old English *þing*, meaning "meeting, assembly, council, discussion." It is only in its later form that the word took on the meaning of "entity" or "object."
25. Flusser, "On the Crisis," 76.
26. Flusser, "Essays," in *Writings*, ed. Ströhl, 194.
27. Ibid.
28. Finger, Guldin, and Krause, *Vilém Flusser*, 66. See also PPrexemysław Wiatr, "Between Literature and Philosophy: Vilém Flusser's Nomadic Games," *Santa Barbara Portuguese Studies*, 2nd Series, 4 (2020): 2.
29. Flusser, "Essays," 194.
30. Flusser, *Does Writing Have a Future?*, trans. Nancy Ann Roth (Minneapolis: University of Minnesota Press, 2011), 159.

"Naked Little Spasms of the Self"

In Search of an Authentic Gesture in Posthistorical Times

Dominic Pettman

The Gesture of Reading Flusser

To read Vilém Flusser is to experience an inspiring case of cognitive dissonance. So much of his writing seems bleak, belated, and sifting through broken things. And yet he never fails to provide at least a glimmer of hope or a scent of redemption. Not unlike his kindred spirit, Jean Baudrillard, Flusser's nihilism (or rather, his somewhat mimetic *diagnosis* of a nihilistic world) hides a wry smile, scanning the horizon for new insurgencies, symptoms, assignations, opportunities. Two motifs especially sustain and pulse through his work—the idea of gesture and the idea of posthistory (There are many others, of course, but these are the two we seek to put into renewed conversation here.). What indeed is the secret, or not so secret, affinity between these twinned concepts? How does one inform the other? What conditions do they embody and/or challenge?

For Flusser, *posthistory* is the general condition that follows the almost complete expropriation and programming of our gestures by functionalist logic. If *history* is the name traditionally given to the space within which our gestures unfolded, it is itself also the fruit of gestural expression. History is, so to speak, the sum total of human gestural expression and intention. And yet this "history," rather ironically, eventually led to the abdication or outsourcing of its own thrust, purpose, and momentum. So to say, Atlas shrugged many times: once, to throw off the weight of the world, and thereafter (out of resignation, more than defiance), in the mode of a world-weary and unemployed cosmopolitan. In "The Gesture of Painting," Flusser writes, "all observable gestures, in their totality constitute 'history.'"[1] Later, in the same collection, he notes that the "General Theory of Gestures" and the "Philosophy of History" are *synonymous*.[2] As it turns out then, history is not an angel, flung backwards through a chronic catastrophe, but the various traces of modest—and not so modest—gestures that sophisticated simians have made since the beginning of the very business of becoming human. In other words, the process the philosophers call "hominization", is made up of gestures which, from day one, have been made in concert and choreography with our tools. For to be human is to use prosthetics, technical objects, and techniques. The problem comes, as the familiar narrative goes, when humans begin *adapting* to their tools, rather than continually readapting technologies for new human purposes and needs. A fatal reversal thus occurs, which different thinkers date at different moments, although most agreeing of relatively recent provenance, "historically speaking." In any case, the aims and intentions of human beings are deprioritized in order to follow the logic and affordances of emerging technologies.

Of course Silicon Valley, and other technocratic centers, will still sing the song of *homo faber* and human mastery. But we "users" feel the pressures of conforming to new technical imperatives, protocols, and environments on a daily basis, even if we do not fully understand them (Marshall McLuhan's great refrain, of course). Modernity is thus presented as the prolonged primal scene for not just an epochal shift but perhaps even an evolutionary one, where so-called Man morphs into a posthuman hybrid creature: no longer the sovereign agent of its own expression—be it physical, emotional, linguistic—but one conditioned node in a socio-technical, cybernetic continuum. Communication (or the more ambiguous "interaction") now occurs in over-coded, pre-programmed ways. Our gestures are not our own (as one of Fernando Pessoa's personas puts it so passionately: "My gestures break away from me / And I see them in the air like vanes / Of a windmill, utterly not mine, and I feel / My life circulating inside them!").[3] Society mandates, through its individual constituents, algorithmic functionalized behaviors, rather than the more natural, spontaneous—perhaps even subversive—modes of action or address (that is to say, the less scripted gestures of yore). Giorgio Agamben jumps on this train with both feet, when he claims that "By the end of the nineteenth century, the Western bourgeoisie had definitely lost its gestures."[4] A state of affairs that, according to this same authority, has only intensified in the intervening 130 years or so: as if it were possible to lose something not just definitively but by almost infinite degrees. The asymptote of alienation.

Such a narrative, however, begs the question: Has modernity progressively—and now absolutely—robbed us of our gestures, leaving only limited, exquisitely sublimated profit-driven movements? Are we *really* mere marionettes, dancing for capital, or "the program industries," or "the apparatus," or "the spectacle"? Or are gestures—potentially, at least—more creative, elusive, and generative than this? Can they still represent what Flusser calls the "irresponsible enrichment of social life"?[5] Or have they been reduced to a physical tic, the somatic equivalent of what Franco Berardi calls "the crisis of social imagination"?[6]

The Gesture of Paying Attention to Gesture

But before we read Flusser's concept of the gesture through a posthistorical lens (and vice versa), we should remind ourselves what he means by that term. Etymologically speaking, a gesture entails a bearing, behavior, or mode of action. It comes from the

Latin *gerere*, meaning to *bear*, *wield*, or *perform*. Gesture is thus found within a cluster of associations connecting concepts such as *identity* (what one is), *intention* (what one will), *performance* or *expression* (how one is), and *communication* (how one signals one's selfhood to others). For a gesture to take place, one needs an agent or body, a given milieu for that body to interact with other bodies, a shared semiotic frame for the gesture to be legible, and a medium or media through which the gesture is to take place (even if that medium is the original agent or body, thereby closing the gestural loop).

We would be mistaken, however, if we simply began with an abstract agent-body, who skulks about the scene for a while, checking everything out, before deciding to experiment with this organic art of gestures. As we well know, agent-bodies (often called "subjects") are born into a world of already-existing gestures. And they learn who they are—their contours, desires, limits, and so on (or at least who they are expected to be)—through a complex network of ever-evolving gestural communication (a capacious phrase, which includes failed attempts at communication). We become who we are, in other words, by recognizing, decoding, and responding to gestures received from others (Nietzsche: "The richness of life reveals itself through a *richness of gestures*. One must *learn* to feel everything—the length and retarding of sentences, interpunctuations, the choice of words, the pausing, the sequence of arguments—like gestures").[7]

Gestures present us with a paradox, then, since they are at once personal and impersonal. Gestures are "public domain," as it were, and part of our cultural inheritance; and yet they can also be highly individual or idiosyncratic. They can be required (the soldier's salute) or unexpected (the stranger's seduction). As such, gestures inhabit the zone between agency and instinct, expression and reflex, freedom and automaticity (as Flusser notes: "a gesture is not free, but freedom is 'somehow' expressed in it").[8] The world of gesture—aka history—is a shifting grammar we inhabit and pass on to the next generation, who then further tweak the syntax as they see fit. This situation becomes properly posthistorical, however, when the motivation for a gesture comes from not only outside of ourselves, individually speaking, but external to human needs or concerns (think of the famous scene from Charlie Chaplin's *Modern Times*, when the worker's body becomes little more than a puppet of the gestures internalized from the requirements of the factory production line). For a gesture to be authentic, according to Flusser, it must move or occur in concert with a free relationship to being-in-the-world. Sticking one's tongue out—at an ogling or judging stranger, for instance—could be considered a free and real gesture, since it is a spontaneous expression of displeasure or aversion (even if this gesture was learned from others). Exchanging business cards, however, with both hands, so as not to insult the other person, is not a free or real gesture, since it is already coded into the commercial situation.

So what is Flusser's precise definition of gesture? Well, it is very difficult to say, precisely. Indeed, Flusser is quite coy about the fact that he provides such a definition only elliptically, layer-by-layer—like peeling an onion or, in fact, like trying to interpret an unknown gesture, directed at oneself. In this way, his project is performative—refusing to give us a technocratic definition: one that we can encode and apply, like some kind of fixed interpretive grid. Instead it starts to surround us, using a suggestive choreography of seduction. He promises. He teases. He reveals. Only to withdraw from the record or rephrase himself completely (gesture is, on some level, always about the power to mask or reveal the self through movement). And like a matador, he whips up the cape on which we readers tend to stampede bullishly toward a fixed figure.

On the very first page of his book dedicated to the subject, Flusser tells us that "Gestures are movements of the body that express an intention," only to immediately follow with "But this is not very serviceable."[9] He soon refines his capsule definition to "a gesture is a movement of the body or of a tool connected to the body for which there is no satisfactory causal explanation."[10] But this too is soon burdened with a series of caveats and exceptions (though this does help us distinguish a gesture from an action—the latter having its feet firmly planted in the world of rational cause and effect). Eventually Flusser tips his hand enough to provide some solid characteristics, if not a fully fledged definition. Gestures are at base symbolic, since they are representative and "concerned with a meaning."[11] And yet, this relationship with meaning is not at all straightforward, since gestures are especially open to misinterpretation ("The more information, the less communication,"[12] Flusser insists, impishly). Gestures are not at all about efficiency, then. Nor are they about clarity, since there is something inherently ambiguous about them, which—both ironically and luckily—encourages further attempts at communication. Indeed, it is the gap between the one gesturing and the one gestured to which produces the distance necessary for communication to be desirable or possible in the first place. Moreover, gestures—in overflowing rational or utilitarian activities—irrigate our affective lives ("I will proceed as if I wished to defend the thesis that 'affect' is the symbolic representation of states of mind through gestures"[13]). Gestures are thus formal, aesthetic, and "artificial" (in the sense of applying art to nature, not in the sense of simply being "fake").[14] Hence the confusion we often feel regarding a given gesture. Is it empty? Or full?

Considering our current focus, however, we might well ask: What is the purpose of all this taxonomizing by the author, when he has already effectively given a eulogy for gestures, here on the wrong side of the cusp of posthistory?

The Gesture of Endings

Put differently, what is the relationship between our sense of gesture and the sense of an ending? Flusser ascribes a negentropic power to history, in the sense that the historical drive or consciousness accumulates and transmits information, in a way contrary to "nature." History is thus exempt from the second law of thermodynamics (at least while it is in effect).[15] The crucial change happens, however, when this historical drive decides to store all this information in computational media, which—in contrast to previous storage technologies, such as books, with their analogue (i.e., analogous) relationship to their source—are simplified, transcoded, and put to work in mysterious new ways. "The mass communication apparatus," Flusser writes, "are black-boxes that transcode the messages from the trees of science, of technique, of art, of political science, into extremely simple and poor codes."[16] Moreover, "They are black-boxes that have history as *input* and post-history as *output*. They are programmed to transcode history into post-history, events into programs."[17] What we might call *an actual occurrence in reality* (history) becomes not only anticipated by computers but predetermined by them, thus changing their very essence. The new and almost numinous power of the virtual becomes harnessed, channeled, and put to the banal work of making things happen, over and over—now emptied of any "true meaning," since such occurrences are now only the industrial by-product of cybernetic feedback (a proleptic process Richard Grusin calls "pre-mediation"[18]). Things may still happen. Spectacular things that have everybody talking. But they are not, strictly speaking, historical, because they fail to carry the seal of authenticity required of a real event (according to the same logic that prompted Baudrillard to make the provocative claim that "the Gulf War did not take place"). "'Program' is 'prescription,'"[19] insists Flusser. Thus, in the posthistorical age, we may be drowning in data, but we are rapidly losing information (the kind of information that previously made up the "communicative fabric"[20] of social discourse, dialogism, and dialectics). In other words, we are losing the very texture of "the dynamic of history."[21]

One of the most corrosive elements of the new media ecology, according to this perspective, is the prevalence of image over text. "A powerful *counter-revolution of images against text* is underway,"[22] claims Flusser. And just as Catholics were never the same after Luther, these images are not the same as before Gutenberg. They are "post-alphabetic" and thus carrying a different viral strain. Where images once worked within an ontology of *scenes*, text occurs within an ontology of *process*. But the new "technical images" now threaten to appropriate process as well. In Flusserian terms, the invention of writing is the mid-wife for the birth of history, because it introduces *flow* into human thought, along with linear consciousness, and an understanding of events both before and to come. More recent images—those emerging after the invention of photography, in the nineteenth century—are technical images and thus are forged through a different mandate than paintings or sketches. They are the tempting, but ultimately rather bland and mass-produced, fruit of "the apparatus." "The apparatus has become the aim of history," writes Flusser. "It has become a dam for linearly progressive time."[23] History is dead. Long live history! Nietzsche's eternal return is thus re-presented through the anti-lens of Guy Debord, where the Spectacle absorbs everything in itself, including (and especially) our capacity to communicate in a non-spectacular way—itself a form of purgatory. "History transcoded into program becomes eternally repetitive."[24]

There is an irony, of course, in Flusser writing tens of thousands of words about the frightening new power of technical images and their immunity to the critique of textuality. Why would he bother doing this, if the situation were truly so hopeless? Is the "critical thinking" of alphabetic intelligence just an empty, reflex gesture, in the age of TV game shows and computer chess champions? We can't help but suspect Flusser harbors a clandestine hope that—through his own chronicled witnessing of the end of history—he and his fellow textual spirits can once again flip "the current inversion of the vectors of significance."[25] Flip things, that is, back to an ontology of becoming. Back to a sense of reality. And away from the "absurdity" of a situation where what is real and what is fiction is essentially a moot point (a state of affairs not only absurd but rather terrifying, in the age of Trump, Putin, and other masters of programming hyperreality—or what Adam Curtis calls "hypernormality"). "We cannot dismiss the possibility," Flusser notes, in terms that now appear touchingly quaint, "that in the future, existentially significant history will play out before an audience on walls and television screens rather than in time and space. That would be authentic posthistory."[26]

One wonders then, when Flusser writes, "Epistemological and ethical thought has been replaced once and for all by cybernetic, strategic thought and by program analysis. History is over";[27] does he *really* mean "once and for all"? As with Agamben—who likes to take away human significance, freedom, and agency with one hand, only to place it just over the horizon with the other—Flusser's apocalyptic words always seem to echo with an imminent, somewhat messianic "however . . . " And perhaps this is the spirit in which we should read his initial foray into assembling an inventory of gestures: as a record of the human being integrated into the wider *dispositif*, just before being completely absorbed into the network. In doing so, some clues might be left whereby humans, at least *potentially*, rediscover their historical relationship to prostheses. Before, that is, finding *themselves* rendered the prosthetic element.

The Gesture of New Gestations

One figure in particular is offered by Flusser as an avatar of the posthistorical condition: the filmmaker, who "due to his praxis . . . overcame the linearity of time." And how did the filmmaker achieve this feat? "The line of the filmstrip is for him a structure to be modulated. He can curve it into circles of eternal return, into ellipses, into spirals and into vectors. . . . His consciousness equally overcomes magic and history."[28] Such a power may sound like it approaches omnipotence, or a God-like agency. However, Flusser is quick to assure us that such an Archimedean vocation, or "post-historical transcendence," does not imply that the filmmaker is free from that which represents, nor how he represents it. "It is true," Flusser continues,

> that he [the filmmaker] plays with history and that he splices and glues it, but history, as raw material, offers resistance to his manipulating gesture. It imposes its own game rules. . . . As he manipulates the filmstrip, the filmmaker must take into consideration the structure of the apparatus in function of which he is operating. He must consider the technical, financial, ideological and "aesthetic" demands of the apparatus, in sum: its program. The filmmaker produces programs in function of meta-programs. In that he distinguishes himself from God. In that *he is a programmed programmer*, a played player. He transcends history, but transcends it in function of programmed events. He is a functionary, he is not emancipated.[29]

The gesture of filmmaking is therefore, according to Flusser's philosophy, an unfree gesture, one which produces a medium that itself may be considered a museum-cum-mausoleum for the gestural imperative.

In making such statements, Flusser aligns himself with other all-encompassing media philosophies, such as those of Agamben, Kittler, Baudrillard, Stiegler, and to a large degree, Heidegger and Adorno. The narrative follows the theological logic of the Fall, even if it is acknowledged that we never lived in Edenic times or places. Once we invent computational machines, however—once we outsource our thinking and doing to these machines—we produce a sinister "standing reserve" and make "unreasonable demands" of both nature and history. Our gestures become predetermined, or at least overdetermined, by the technological *gestell* (enframing). Try as we might, our palette of expression is already anticipated by the apparatus, to the extent where we are running a program through our minds and bodies, rather than creating new opportunities for new kinds of expression, communication, and action. "Beyond machines," Flusser writes, "there is nothing to do.... Where apparatuses prevail, there is nothing left to do but function."[30] In short, "We have learned that we cannot live without the apparatus or outside the apparatus."[31] A bleak diagnosis indeed. And one which leaves us little room to invent. Indeed, this scenario goes beyond theories of ideological bad faith or false consciousness, which at least allows a chance of seeing beyond the veil, to a complete erasure of the possibility of free will. Humans are now organic computers, running software programmed by the apparatus itself. Where Frances Fukuyama has admitted a *mea culpa* for his own, less sophisticated, pronouncements of the End of History, Flusser would likely see no reason to revise his thinking, due to the new political upheavals happening all around us. Indeed, these would be considered evidence of posthistorical disorientation, of unmoored pseudo-events with dire consequences, granted, but without direction, logic, or meaning. After both tragedy and farce comes blank, pointless repetition. On the macro-scale, humanity's greatest hits are replayed, all the more destructive for being advanced by a vast and ubiquitous technological infrastructure. And on the micro-scale, our own actions lack not only purpose or goals, beyond meeting the most basic of necessities, but any previous art of "savoir vivre" that we used to cultivate for our own sake.

Having thus essentially left us playing the role of neurotic marionettes ("docile and obedient," in Foucault's words), Flusser finishes his book on posthistory on a surprisingly upbeat note. After noting the cultural shift from the university to the technical school, he parrots the mandate of the technocrat: "The school of the future should be an institute of technology; creativity at the service of apparatus."[32] But just as Heidegger believed that the "saving power" grows precisely where the danger lies, Flusser too makes a cautious prophecy about "these institutes," which "are ambiguous from the point of view of the apparatus":

> They shall necessarily irradiate formal disciplines, that is: to provide a vision of the subjacent structures. And this is "theory", closer to the meaning of it according to the Ancients. The Platonic academy demanded the knowledge of mathematics and music from the students, which are formal disciplines. The technological

institutes of the future will demand the knowledge of informatics, cybernetics, set theory and game theory. This will provide the students an "ironic" withdrawal in relation to apparatus and their functionalism. And this theoretical distancing will be an invitation for a plunge toward immediate experience. An invitation to "philosophy." In other words: behind the backs of the apparatus, the students of the school of the future will transcend the apparatus.[33]

In an update of the *deus-ex-machina*, Flusser looks forward to these students of the near future learning the rules and then (through an unspecified process of reverse hypnosis) breaking the rules—creating the conditions for a dialogic relationship with our technologies, so *we* become the programmers once more. This new type of school will, as a consequence, change in the process: "it will no longer speak 'about' but 'with.'"[34] Were these massive epistemic changes to transpire, then not only would history begin to flow forward once more, but our gestures would be returned to us. And, presumably, new ones forged for the future.[35]

While Flusser concedes that the chance of living a "trans-apparatus life" is remote, he wants to keep the possibility open. In contrast to the captured gestures of the contemporary "user"—what Erving Goffman called "naked little spasms of the self"[36]—we may just reclothe our subjectivity and reclaim gesture as "an active being-in-the-world."[37] Indeed, the gestural field itself might be the incubation chamber for this decisive quantum leap, beyond the horizon of the posthistorical (as some recent critics also hope: "With enough gestures we can deafen the satellites and lift the curtains surrounding the control room").[38]

This is where Flusser leaves things at the end of his monograph on posthistory, obliging us to speculate on how gestures might evolve, in the happy event of a reboot of history. In the same sense that technical images should not be confused for those types of images which came before textual hegemony, it may well be that the reborn human gesture will not be *human* in the same way. After all, it is a supreme act of human exceptionalism, or anthropocentrism, to presume that gestures are the sole domain of our own species: especially when ethologists have been filling their notebooks with examples of creaturely gestures for many centuries (no doubt, stubborn humanists will insist any such gestures are "instinctual," and thus, not free, in the sense that we like to think of our own. Pet owners, well versed in the improvised and creative two-way communication that occurs between humans and (other) animal, would beg to differ). Of course, today our machines can appear more lively than we do—as Donna Haraway noted even before robots and artificial intelligence began to become a banal part of everyday life.[39] Any post-post-historical theory—or praxis—of gesture must thus take full account of the ways in which humans, animals, and machines mutually inform each other's gestural range and possibility. For if the human is always already a prosthetic creature—as David Wills and other persuasively maintain—then human gestures are always in concert with other objects and/as agents.[40] Perhaps a post-Flusserian thinking of gesture would not be so quick to draw a line between the person and the apparatus—or between the historical and posthistorical—but rather trace a genealogy between, say, the gestures of the contemporary actor, covered in motion capture sensors for the mapping of animated content, and the eighteenth-century coquette, using her fan as an animated weapon of seduction.

There is little question that Flusser was correct in saying our gestures have been colonized by technological imperatives. We swipe, we click, we type, or else we starve. And it's also true that if we don't invent new gestures, we will die anyway: starving from want of what Adorno called "those irreplaceable capacities which cannot bloom in the isolated cell of pure interiority, but only in contact with the warmth of things."[41] How to reprogram ourselves in ways that are "legible" to others, but that go beyond simply enabling and embodying social algorithms. How to express oneself on a different register, or in a different idiom, without swiftly being dismissed as extravagant, self-indulgent, autistic, or otherwise irrelevant, because one's mode of gestural address does not "get with the program"?[42] This is the rather urgent conceptual, somatic, and political task ahead of us.[43]

Notes

1 Flusser, *Gestures* (Minneapolis: Minnesota University Press, 2014), 66.
2 Ibid., 171.
3 Fernando Pessoa, *A Little Larger Than the Entire Universe*, trans. Richard Zenith (London: Penguin Classics, 2006), 396.
4 Giorgio Agambem, "Notes on Gesture," in *Means without End: Notes on Politics*, trans. Vincenzo Binetti and Cesare Casarino (Minneapolis: University of Minnesota Press, 2000), 49.
5 Flusser, *Post-History*, trans. Rodrigo Maltez Novaes (Minneapolis: Univocal, 2013), 154.
6 Franco Berardi, *The Uprising: On Poetry and Finance* (Los Angeles: Semiotext(e), 2012), 7.
7 Lou Salomé, *Nietzsche*, trans. Siegfried Mandel (Urbana and Chicago: University of Illinois Press, 2001), 77.
8 Flusser, *Gestures*, 175.
9 Ibid., 1.
10 Ibid., 2.
11 Ibid., 4.
12 Ibid., 8.
13 Ibid., 4.
14 See John Tresch, "Leroi-Gourhan's Hall of Gestures," in *Energies in the Arts*, ed. Douglas Kahn (Cambridge, MA: MIT Press, 2019).
15 Flusser, *Post-History*, 51. "Human communication opposes itself dialectically to the natural tendency toward entropy. History is a negatively entropic epicycle that superimposes itself over nature's tendency; its antithesis" (51–2).
16 Ibid., 56.
17 Ibid., 57.
18 Richard Grusin, *Premediation: Affect and Mediality After 9/11* (London: Palgrave MacMillan, 2010).
19 Flusser, *Post-History*, 97.

20 Ibid., 52.
21 Ibid., 96. Flusser: "Apparatus are black boxes that . . . devour history and spew out post-history" (*Post-History*, 96).
22 Ibid., 91.
23 Ibid., 97.
24 Ibid.
25 Ibid., 105.
26 Flusser, *Gestures*, 90.
27 Ibid., 18.
28 Flusser, *Post-History*, 102.
29 Ibid., 102–3, my emphasis.
30 Flusser, *Gestures*, 17.
31 Ibid., 16.
32 Flusser, *Post-History*, 148.
33 Ibid.
34 Ibid., 149.
35 See Giorgio Agamben, *The Open: Man and Animal*, trans. Kevin Attell (Palo Alto: Stanford University Press, 2004).
36 Qtd. in Natasha Dow Schüll, *Addiction by Design: Machine Gambling in Las Vegas* (Princeton: Princeton University Press, 2012), 11.
37 Flusser, *Gestures*, 171.
38 See Fenton Johnson, "The Future of Queer," *Harper's Magazine*, January 2018, https://harpers.org/archive/2018/01/the-future-of-queer/.
39 See Donna Haraway, "A Cyborg Manifesto: Science, Technology, and Socialist-Feminism in the Late Twentieth Century," in *Simians, Cyborgs and Women: The Reinvention of Nature* (New York: Routledge, 1991), 152.
40 See David Wills, *Dorsality: Thinking Back Through Technology and Politics* (Minneapolis: University of Minnesota Press, 2008).
41 Theodor Adorno, *Minima Moralia: Reflections on a Damaged Life*, trans. E. F. N. Jephcott (New York and London: Verso, 2005), 43. See Jason Read, *The Politics of Transindividuality* (Chicago: Haymarket Books, 2016).
42 For one of my own recent attempts to answer this question in practical terms, see the collaborative set of "para-academic" stories, based on Flusser's book, Carla Nappi and Dominic Pettman, *Metagestures* (Punctum, 2019).
43 On the notion of "gestural inflation," see Lauren Berlant, "Structures of Unfeeling: Mysterious Skin," *International Journal of Politics, Culture, and Society* 28, no. 3 (September 2015): 191–213.

15

The 'Pataphysical Span

Alfred Jarry and Vilém Flusser

Judith Roof

Duration is the transformation of a succession into a reversion.
I.e.:
THE BECOMING OF A MEMORY.

Alfred Jarry, "Practical Construction of the Time Machine," 218[1]

The work of media theorist Vilém Flusser often reverses, confounds, and realigns cause and effect in ways reminiscent of the tactics of 'pataphysics, the playful early twentieth-century "science of imaginary solutions" founded by Alfred Jarry and that persists to this day. As Flusser's work on media began to appear in Brazil in the 1960s, so in Paris the College de Pataphysique, established in 1948, included among its members such avant-gardists as Marcel Duchamp, Boris Vian, Eugene Ionesco, Man Ray, the Marx Brothers, and Fernando Arrabal, as well as the experimental offshoot Oulipo (the workshop of potential literature), which counts among its aficionados Georges Perec, Italo Calvino, and Raymond Queneau. The London Institute of 'Pataphysics, founded in 2000, promotes 'pataphysics in the English-speaking world.[2] Envisioning itself as an "epiphenomenon" that deploys whimsical fictions to forge "imaginary solutions," 'pataphysics offers a process through which thinkers might bring into question and imaginatively reformulate received accounts of complex phenomena. 'Pataphysics will be, as Jarry suggests in *The Exploits and Opinions of Dr. Faustroll, Pataphysician*, "above all, the science of the particular, despite the common opinion that the only science is that of the general"; and further, "Contemporary science is founded upon the principle of induction: most people have seen a certain phenomenon precede or follow some other phenomenon most often, and conclude therefrom that is will ever be thus."[3] "This is true," Jarry continues, "only in the majority of cases, depends upon the point of view, and is codified only for convenience—if that!!"[4] Introducing the example of a watch, Jarry queries, "Why should anyone claim that the shape of a watch is round—a manifestly false proposition—since it appears in profile as a narrow rectangular construction, elliptic on three sides;" and "why the devil should one only have noticed its shape at the moment of looking at the time?"[5]

Flusser's work on media, apparatus, and communication phenomena represents a reformulation of cause–effect relations and a resituation of perspective that are in many ways akin to 'pataphysics' extension of metaphysics in the ways Flusser combines phenomenology with 'pataphysical transformations. Though not an example of 'pataphysics' "imaginary solutions," Flusser's reenvisioning of the relations among apparatus, psyche, and the cultural imaginary reverberates 'pataphysics fanciful re-visioning of phenomena as well as the dynamics that operate among physics and metaphysics, succession and reversion, generation and feedback, and apparatus and psyche. Merging and reintegrating phenomenology with 'pataphysical transformations, Flusser's analyses relinquish traditional inductive assumptions and the delusion of an encompassing perspectiveless perspective to explore media phenomena from the more experiential and phenomenological aspects of its functioning, seeing media as "epiphenomena," as sets of complex interactions of apparatus, environment, and the accruing adjustments of continued operation and feedback.

Although not the "science of imaginary solutions," Flusser's presentation of media phenomena as wholistic and multifaceted challenges the typical inductive assumptions of apparatus studies, as well as offering a more wholistic exploration of the very concepts of what might constitute media in the first place. In addition to his explorations of photography, communications technologies, and other media such as writing and even gesture, Flusser's work explores the concepts and practices of design, mechanical production, the actions that contribute to the production of "technical images," and the broad complexity and feedback effects of apparatuses. These various explorations often overlap, echo, reenvision, and offer multiple perspectives on the relations among media, communication (broadly conceived), and the operations of media apparatuses and other interconnected systems. Flusser's work, like 'pataphysics, dislocates induction and an assumed detached perspective to inject issues of subjective experience, perception, and point of view resident to phenomenology as well as enlarging the field of what might constitute media phenomena themselves. In so doing, Flusser's work, like Jarry's, reenvisions the order of things in a more wholistic demonstration of the complexities, scale, and operational matrices of machines, apparatuses, and media.

One nexus where the affinities of Jarry's 'pataphysics and Flusser's analyses most obviously connect is in the realm of the "*geste*" or the "gesture," understood by both thinkers as a broad concatenation of enactment, expression, splayed motivation, contradictory impulses, and ambiguous effect. The *geste* represents the concatenation of the "pata-," "meta-," "para-," "epi-," where "pata-" refers to that which is "beyond metaphysics" and "meta-" itself is already a layer beyond physics in an environment of "epiphenomena" which occur beyond or in addition to phenomena or even paraphenomena which occur alongside, or perhaps even contrary to, a phenomenon. For Jarry, the *geste* was a 'pataphysical reconsideration of a collection of quotidian phenomena ranging from stamps to pedestrians, omnibuses, police, and the shuttlecock (among others). Flusser's collection, *Gestures*, encompasses explorations of such gestures as writing, shaving, smoking a pipe, telephoning, painting, and photographing, again among others. For Jarry, a *geste* was the act of 'pataphysically reperceiving, reorienting, reanalyzing, and writing about another gesture; for Flusser, in a similar mode of reconsideration and recontextualization, *Gestures* offers a reconsideration of mundane actions not only as media but also as complex communicative actions that often do not convey what we might assume they do.

The "Gestes" of Speculative Journalism

In 1900, 'pataphysician Alfred Jarry began publishing "speculative journalism" in magazines with substantial circulation. Speculative journalism merges fictional narrative with traditional conceptions, perceived circumstances, or even scientifically analyzed phenomena as a mode of commentary, analysis, and prediction. Such narratives often reverse cause and effect, past and future, humorously exposing the assumptions, fallacies, absurdities, and hubris of phenomena often taken for granted. In his collection of these essays, *Siloquies, Superloquies, Soliloquies and Interloquies in Pataphysics*, Jarry dubbed the first year's worth of journalistic output "*Speculations*" and those from the second year, "*Gestes*." These journalistic forays enact and exemplify Jarry's concept of 'pataphysics. In his 1911 "neo-scientific novel" *Exploits and Opinions of Doctor Faustroll, Pataphysician*, Jarry defines 'pataphysics as "the science of that which is superinduced upon metaphysics, whether within or beyond the latter's limitations, extending as far beyond metaphysics as the latter extends beyond physics."[6] He continues: "an epiphenomenon ('That which is superinduced upon a phenomenon') being often accidental, pataphysics will be, above all, the science of the particular.... Pataphysics will examine the laws governing exceptions, and will explain the universe supplementary to this one."[7] And finally: "DEFINITION. *Pataphysics is the science of imaginary solutions, which symbolically attributes the properties of objects, described by their virtuality, to their lineaments.*"[8]

Thus setting out to engage in a species of experimental thinking, Jarry's "Gestes" reconceive the gestures of common phenomena and apparatuses. For example, in "Cynegetics of the Omnibus," Jarry classes the omnibus among "the different species of wild beasts and pachyderms that are not yet extinct and which roam the districts of Paris."[9] Commencing with this reclassification, itself a gesture that deploys a different basis for classification than that used by zoologists, already incites a reconsideration of the bases for classifications themselves. The second brief paragraph enlarges the field by noting that the companies that own the omnibuses have "reserved the monopoly of the hunt for themselves," a tactic whose ostensible value the *geste* reverses by noting that such monopoly is not "logical" since "the fur of the omnibus is worthless and its flesh is inedible."[10] Thus already reperceiving and relocating the omnibus opens up a reconsideration of its municipal function, a 'pataphysical gesture focusing on both the omnibus' "virtuality" and its "lineaments." Imaginary? Reconceiving of the omnibus as a living being redefines its "properties," resituating it in another order of being and re-visioning some of its properties in ways that reveal not only the propensities of bus lines but also the behaviors of its co-inhabitants.

Because the omnibus is now an animal, Jarry introduces Darwinian reasoning to explain "the bewildering range of colours that distinguish them," explaining the colors as "accidental differences, due to habitat and the influence of their surroundings," and dismissing the white omnibuses' "mimesis" as simply akin to the denizens of polar regions. Having engaged zoological accounts of adaptation, the *geste* proposes "a more scientific division" of the omnibus into "two varieties:" "those who cover up their footprints" and "those who leave a visible track behind them."[11] Characterizing the omnibuses' modes of propulsion as the habits of beasts reenvisions transportation itself as a return to the essential capacities of all locomotion, instead of as an aspect of industrial advances. The *geste* continues with an analysis of "naturalist" interpretations of these modes, concluding that although the one with tracks is "stupider," its survival is enabled by its ferocity.

Jarry's 'pataphysical analysis continues with a description of the omnibus' "curious habit" of always taking the same "route in its periodic migrations," a potentially dangerous habit the beast instinctively mitigates by turning around just as its pursuers might attack and taking the same tracks the other direction. The omnibus, too, is threatened by "snares" consisting of "huts" of ambushing "gangs," some members of which clench the omnibus' "posterior" as it flees. And some omnibuses have been "domesticated," obeying commands to stop and go, although, as Jarry warns, "they remain wild creatures" who ingest humans. The omnibuses' digestive systems have adapted so as to excrete "their victims alive," but only after the beast has extracted "as many particles of copper as possible." The presence of these particles, then, accounts for the "joyous metallic-sounding string of loud farts which invariably precedes their meals."[12]

Jarry ends this epiphenomenal examination by noting that "nothing is known of their courtship rituals or means of reproduction," though in a "Postscript" he reveals that the omnibus' means of reproduction is the same "as certain plants" whose pollen is spread by means of "insects who penetrate their innards."[13] He only mentions this in the postscript to avoid "making what are euphemistically called the 'passengers' blush at the not very honorable role they play."[14]

Considering, thus, the omnibus from the perspective of its shared attributes with a very large animal produces a different conception of its activities. While this appears to be an effect of the operation of a simile—the omnibus is like a large beast—it is also a reconsideration of a daily phenomenon that in itself produces a set of different insights about the operation of modes of transportation and their relation to passengers. Giving the omnibus evolutionary and survival motivations offers a different perspective on the relations between humans and machines, which in turn brings into question humans' relative free will in relation to their environment. The omnibus uses its passengers just as much as the passengers use the omnibus—or maybe even more. This reciprocity ultimately recasts the relation between humans and industrial apparatuses as less a matter of human control and more a situation in which mechanical apparatuses themselves impose their own control on human users. As a species of "'pataphysical exception," the omnibus' description enacts a "universe supplementary to this one," the supplement in this case consisting of the machine's contradictory relation to its users, a relation that opens up the possibility that humans' relations to their machines are not what they seem to be.

"Beyond Machines"

In his collection of essays, *Gestures*, Vilèm Flusser lays out a history of the progressive disentanglements of states of cultural consciousness around the question of work.[15] A species of sociocultural phenomenology, Flusser's vision of the evolution from a focus on ontology to the epistemological limits of methodology performs a dissective re-vision of Western culture's conceptions of work and its relation to human beings, instating a new perspective on older concepts of historical progression. In his essay "Beyond Machines," Flusser, like Jarry but in a much broader history and more philosophical discourse, begins by adopting a different perspective on the quotidian phenomenon of "work."[16] Commencing with a scenario of prehistorical "magic," in which the three states Flusser identifies—ontology, deontology, methodology—are "not separated," he tracks the trajectory of humans' relation to work from the unquestioned values of prehistory ("magical work"), to the engaged work of classical and medieval times ("engaged work") that must decide among values, to modernity where work has become "research" and "the question of values lost its force."[17] In the present ("the time of technical work"), the issue of "values has become nonsensical."[18] But he also notes almost from the start that "most people don't work. They serve as tools in the work of others. In their alienation, they have no wish to know how the world is or how it should be. . . . They participate only passively in history; they put up with it."[19] They are, in Jarry's terms, riders on the omnibus.

Flusser locates the break from magic and ontology in fifteenth-century Italy, in a gesture "that divides practical from theoretical work by freeing epistemology from the tyranny of religion. It sets the 'good' in quotation marks and separates it from the 'true,'" suggesting that this gesture "cuts history in two." This bifurcation produces two spheres—"values" where the question is "To what purpose?" and "nature" (the "given") where the question is "Why?"[20] These two queries represent a split of culture into "the scientific" and the "humanist," separating politics from science, by the "progressive invasion of the sphere of values by the sphere of givens."[21] The transformation from questioning the value to questioning the concept of value leads, Flusser suggests, to a "methodological schizophrenia" in the nineteenth century where the conflict of "theoretical and practical work" results in the "technologizing of work."[22] Methodology triumphs, and the question shifts from issues of value and purpose—the "why" simply to "how."[23] This focus on methodology replaces questions of value with considerations of efficiency. "Value" becomes "'metaphysical' in the discrediting sense of the word" and "ethics and ontology become meaningless discourses" as they offer no insight onto questions of method.[24]

Continuing his dissection of this historical "gesture" that displaces value with method, Flusser declares finally that the concept of purposefulness and value has disappeared, and the "the gesture of work becomes absurd."[25] The worker "functions as the functionary of a function" and "this absurd gesture cannot be grasped without observing machines, for we are actually functioning as functions of a machine, which functions as the function of a functionary, who in turn functions as the function of an apparatus, which functions as a function of itself."[26] We are back to the omnibus, whose nomenclature itself points to its representative function, as the word is the Latin dative plural meaning "for all." Flusser's breakdown of epistemological stages of history ultimately outlines an epiphenomenon showing the necessary subordination of the human to the apparatus, an apparatus whose ontology the human no longer knows. Like the omnibus, the apparatus uses its unwitting users both as a means of self-reproduction and as an apparently productive mechanism that in the end sustains itself. Flusser's interpretation of the historical stages of phenomenological consciousness arrives at a similar but more philosophically reasoned conclusion as Jarry's 'pataphysical reinterpretation of the omnibus. Both reenvision and reinterpret phenomena and their interrelations by shifting perspective, restaging the phenomenon they analyze into an "epiphenomenon" and situate the foci of their analyses as "gestures," a reconceptualization of the assumptions of induction that itself participates in 'pataphysics' "science of imaginary solutions" to offer new perspectives.

"Shaving"

Flusser's essay "Beyond Machines" is one of two essays that open his collection *Gestures*, setting up the method of his epiphenomenal interpretations of the more quotidian operations that follow in the volume's essays. The other opening essay sets his method of analysis as a "Phenomenology of Gestures," in which he defines gesture as "a movement of the body or of a tool connected to the body for which there is no satisfactory causal explanation."[27] For Flusser, this lack of explanation means that a gesture's "meaning must be discovered."[28] Beginning, then, with the idea that gestures express "something," Flusser locates that meaning in "affect": "states of mind. . . . Can make themselves manifest through a plethora of bodily movements but that they express and articulate themselves through a play of gesticulations called 'affect' because it is the way they are represented."[29] Coming finally to the insight that "the absence of a theory of interpretation of gesture" means that "any judgment remains empirical and 'intuitive,'"[30] Flusser concludes by envisioning "gesture" as existing on a scale between "the 'empty' and the 'full'"[31] and that interpretations of gestures can range from "kitsch" to "those great moments in which humanity confers meaning on its actions and sufferings."[32]

Although Flusser's "rational" arguments about his method of defining and interpreting gestures seem far from Jarry's apparently random 'pataphysical interventions, they share 'pataphysics' mode of shifting perspective on phenomena, questioning presuppositions, and locating the phenomena they analyze in new and different contexts. Although Flusser is much more systematic in his accounts of method, his queries push against received knowledge by dislocating, then re-characterizing phenomena in a process similar to, but much more consciously rationalized, than 'pataphysics.

In the *Gestures*' essay "Shaving," for example, Flusser re-situates, interprets, and redefines the gesture of shaving as a gesture akin to gardening.[33] Introducing the gardening simile is itself a "gesture" similar to the tactics deployed by Jarry's 'pataphysical accounts, or "Gestes," that renders the gesture of shaving into an epiphenomenon that explores the affinities suggested by the new perspective of shaving as gardening. In seeing shaving through the 'pataphysical perspective of gardening, Flusser discerns their common element as "the questionable concept of the skin": "in light of the similarity between electric razors and lawnmowers, or between the gestures of propping up beards and bushes."[34] Focusing, then, on the common element of literal and metaphorical "skin," Flusser sees both "as *dermatological* gestures" which demonstrate "how permeable the skin is from both sides and how despite its permeability, it represents an obstacle between man and the world."[35]

Seeing skin as the "no-man's land between man and the world," Flusser's analysis of the gesture of shaving then focuses on the tools for grooming/gardening, envisioning the shaver as "an extension of the body (defining tools as artificial body organs)."[36] As in Jarry's "Gestes," Flusser envisions the line between the organic and the mechanical as traversable and reversible. Noting that the "beard hairs' ontological location has not changed in shaving but has simply transferred from one place on the body to another," Flusser concludes that the body itself may be seen "as an apparatus that is manipulated by the gesticulator."[37] The gesturer becomes the gestured, the human becomes an apparatus. As Flusser comments, "this gesture is not the biologically explicable movement but the existential ambivalence of acting and being acted on at the same time."[38]

Continuing the reversals typical of 'pataphysical reconsiderations, Flusser also sees the gesture of shaving as opposite to superficial notions of grooming. "Shaving," he says, "is exactly the opposite of self-analysis (this despite the shaving mirror into which one looks), that one does not shave to recognize oneself but to change oneself (to become other than one is)."[39] And although his analysis of the gesture of shaving commences by locating the skin as a permeable boundary, further consideration shows that "a removal of beard hair" emphasizes "the boundary between man and world. Shaving makes the skin, and not the face, visible and that means it makes the boundary between man and world visible."[40] Hence, Flusser continues, "the goal of shaving is not to make a connection with the world but to distance oneself from it and assert oneself in it."[41] Like Jarry, Flusser twists the logics of a surface to reveal the surface's functions.

Flusser, however, adds an additional epiphenomenal layer to his analysis of shaving, evoking his own methodology as a part of the gesture, a layer Jarry's "Gestes" leave aside, since their point is to incite perspective instead of analyzing its origins or philosophical effects. Where Jarry's commentaries perform colorful and local commentary, Flusser continues his analysis with an analysis of the effects of the analysis: "If I emphasize skin, that is, the difference between myself and the world, I am defining world and self, and that means I am standing above and at a distance from both."[42] In defining what he is defining, Flusser also defines the perspective which he identifies both as a part of the gesture of shaving and as a part of the gesture of reconceiving the gesture of shaving. Flusser's phenomenological commentary is ultimately a commentary on the phenomenology of phenomenology. He concludes by declaring that "the engagement with the skin is a static and, in this sense, reactionary adherence to dissociating structures. The gesture of shaving is the gesture of formalist rationalism, a classic, unromantic, and anti-revolutionary gesture"—a far cry from the opening comparison of shaving and gardening.[43]

Speculations

Flusser's *Gestures* extends the realm of interpretation from the apparently incidental to the broadly phenomenological, tracking the ways correlations produced through 'pataphysics' deployment of metaphor illuminate common assumptions. In contrast, Jarry's *Speculations* tend toward the broadly satirical, focusing on assumptions and correlations to make evident not the real "causes" of social phenomena but the striking resemblances among theoretically unrelated events.[44] In his essay "Speculations" from *Speculations*, these resemblances push toward causality via a satire on the employment of statistical data.[45] Although Jarry's tactics differ slightly from Flusser's identification of a common site—the skin—from which Flusser derives a series of epiphenomenal effects, Jarry's satire on the presumptions of statistics as a common vector for determinations of causality suggests a similar epiphenomenal joinder of inapposite processes as potentially the same.

Investigating the relation between "debt repayment by installments" and suicide, which already offers an apparently arbitrary choice in the broader realm of "commercial" phenomena, "Speculations" begins by describing how "the honest man" "following written notification three months in advance" from the "Bank" "sometimes and without apparent motive escapes the consequences of this interview by committing suicide."[46] Noting the coexistence of "debt repayment" and suicide, Jarry justifies his use of suicide as a measure since "statisticians . . . [r]ecord the fatalities every year in the same numbers."[47] But, as Jarry points out, the suicide numbers are only "*cumulatively* constant*.*"[48] Looking at graphs of incidents through time reveals that the numbers "peak" on "those days of the month fixed for the repayment of loans."[49]

Jarry's analysis, however, does not stop at merely suggesting debt repayment as a motive for suicide. The suicides become ephiphenomenal as the motive for the criminal actions on the part of bank employees. "Speculations" flips the correlation of death and loan repayment from an observation of a causal relation between the need to repay and suicide to the cause of something else. Instead of arriving at the "obvious" conclusion that loan repayments cause suicide, Jarry's essay instead divines that the bank employee who collects loan repayment actually (in a display "of bold individual initiative!")

"blows out the brains of the shopkeeper, TAKES BACK THE BILL, and having thus become the legitimate owner of the gold, returns the bill to the bank, showing it to be unpaid."[50] But the 'pataphysical consideration does not stop here. The bank, then, seeing what it believes to be a suicide (i.e., the debtor "avoided dishonour and ruin") does not worry the debtor further. What appears to be a statistically grounded cause–effect relation between debt and suicide becomes the evidence of the underhandedness of opportunistic and murderous bank employees.

Jarry's 'pataphysical satire on the effects of banking practices illustrates the same kind of re-perspectivalizing phenomena that Flusser's work develops and elaborates. Rejecting the obvious, received relationships among phenomena and adopting alternate and often unexpected perspectives enables a productive reenvisioning of phenomena, the understanding of which had typically followed the protocols of linear cause–effect relations. Both 'pataphysics and Flusser's work begin by defining and envisioning these phenomena anew and following the insights of changed perspectives.

Notes

1. Alfred Jarry, "Practical Construction of the Time Machine," in *Alfred Jarry: Adventures in 'Pataphysics*, trans. Paul Edwards and Antony Melville (London: Atlas Press, 2001), 211–18.
2. See Andrew Hugill, *'Pataphysics: A Useless Guide* (Cambridge, MA: MIT Press, 2015), 113–36.
3. Jarry, *Alfred Jarry*, 21–2.
4. Ibid., 22.
5. Ibid., 23.
6. Ibid., 21.
7. Ibid.
8. Ibid.
9. Jarry, "Cynegetics of the Omnibus," in *Siloquies, Superloquies, Soliloquies and Interloquies in Pataphysics*, in *Alfred Jarry: Adventures in 'Pataphysics*, 245–7, 245.
10. Ibid.
11. Ibid.
12. Ibid., 247.
13. Ibid.
14. Ibid.
15. Flusser, *Gestures*, trans. Nancy Ann Roth (Minneapolis: University of Minnesota Press, 2014).
16. Flusser, "Beyond Machines," in *Gestures*, 10–18.
17. Ibid., 11.
18. Ibid.
19. Ibid.
20. Ibid., 12.
21. Ibid.
22. Ibid., 13.
23. Ibid.

24 Ibid.
25 Ibid.
26 Ibid., 13–14.
27 Flusser, "Gesture and Affect: The Practice of a Phenomenology of Gestures," in *Gestures*, 1–9, 2.
28 Ibid., 3.
29 Ibid., 4–5.
30 Ibid., 8.
31 Ibid., 9.
32 Ibid.
33 Flusser, "Shaving," in *Gestures*, 105–10.
34 Ibid., 105.
35 Ibid., 106.
36 Ibid.
37 Ibid., 106–7.
38 Ibid., 107.
39 Ibid., 108.
40 Ibid.
41 Ibid., 109.
42 Ibid.
43 Ibid., 110.
44 Jarry named his second series of 'pataphysical essays, *Speculations*.
45 Jarry, "Speculations," in *Siloquies, Superloquies, Soliloquies and Interloquies in Pataphysics*, in *Alfred Jarry: Adventures in 'Pataphysics*, 244–5.
46 Ibid., 244.
47 Ibid.
48 Ibid.
49 Ibid.
50 Ibid., 244–5.

16

Flusser's New Weird

Keith Leslie Johnson

There hath he lain for ages, and will lie
Battening upon huge sea worms in his sleep,
Until the latter fire shall heat the deep;
Then once by man and angels to be seen,
In roaring he shall rise and on the surface die.

—Tennyson, "The Kraken" (1830)

The Weird, as a literary if not existential category, tends to derange and reshape intellectual histories. Ostensibly nominating fiction by H. P. Lovecraft and his "circle," its tentacles gather unto it all the morbid and supernatural obsessions of post-Gothic literature from the preceding century—from Edgar Allan Poe to Alfred Kubin. Central to these obsessions is an interrogation of the humanist subject, its pretensions to knowledge and meaning; in their place, the Weird offers "the dark frisson of the unknown and visionary."[1] Long considered subliterary, the Weird has in recent years piqued scholarly interest as an alternate, repressed, or submerged modernism, from whose pelagic depths we might dredge up all sorts of ideas and images deep-sixed by the officer class. As such, it represents "the pulpy underside of literary modernism" while at the same time "guid[ing] even the most iconic modernist thinking about time and history, from Yeats and Eliot's mythic pasts and graveyard obsessions to the archaeological mysticism haunting Willa Cather's desert plains."[2] In other words, what ultimately surfaces is the fundamental weirdness of modernism as such, "its unfamiliarity, its combination of elements previously held to be incommensurable, its compression, its challenges to standard models of legibility."[3]

Underwriting these literal/littoral reclamation efforts is, generally speaking, a renewed appreciation of speculative fiction and, more specifically, the so-called New Weird. Associated initially with writers like M. John Harrison, Thomas Ligotti, and China Miéville, it has come to signify a broad swath of post-New Wave writing that weds "low" genres (i.e., SF, fantasy, and horror) to a "high" (and often experimental) literary sensibility. Beyond that, however, the New Weird self-consciously revisits its own Lovecraftian precursors, revising their politics and rereading modernism as such.

By their lights, Lovecraft's deflationary vision is not *that far* removed from, say, Beckett's. Human meaning is either mooted or suspended, the difference being that in Beckett the obscene deity will always arrive *tomorrow*. Any number of modernist figures can be *weirded* in this way. Beckett, Borges, and above all Kafka become transitional figures for the New Weird, sluicing the currents this way or that, deforming the modernist canon. What, in short, I want to propose here is to consider Vilém Flusser's *Vampyroteuthis Infernalis* (1987) as in its own way a New Weird document, one that anticipates the New Weird's rereading or alternate version of modernism. More specifically, the rest of this chapter will consider *Vampyroteuthis Infernalis* as a framework for thinking about modernism in terms of a genealogy of rapprochement with cephalopods. For Flusser, the vampire squid has four features which are in turn epitomic of modernity: they are *infernal, disgusting, perfidious*, and *rapacious*. To understand these features of the vampire squid is to understand modernism. Put differently, modernism's anxious fascination with its own media experiments, with emergent information ecologies, and with the end of history is restaged here as a series of pulpy (*poulpe*-y?) encounters with sea monsters. To propose just one dossier: Jules Verne's *Twenty-Thousand Leagues Under the Sea* (1870), H. P. Lovecraft's Cthulhu stories of the 1920s, and John Wyndham's *The Kraken Wakes* (1953) each uncannily redact aspects of Flusser's "vampyroteuthic" modernity. In thinking about the destinies of humankind proposed by Verne, Lovecraft, and Wyndham, we can in turn imagine modernism's different survival scenarios for its infernal encounter.[4]

The Infernal

Long before the composition of *Vampyroteuthis Infernalis*, Flusser was preoccupied with the infernal. It was after all a copy of *Faust*—carried with him from Prague to London and, eventually, São Paulo—that offered something like a ready-made allegory for the unfolding enormity of the Third Reich from which he fled. His first important work, *The History of the Devil*, composed (in German) in the late 1950s and published (in Portuguese) in the mid-1960s, reads at some level like midrashic commentary on Goethe's play and perhaps also by extension something like a spiritual biography of Hitler's Germany. Indeed, Flusser seems to target the ongoing project of *Aufklarung* itself, a project that not only failed to prevent Auschwitz but passively sponsored it: "The mind that is free of all illusion, the emancipated mind, is the mind that contorts in the cauldrons of Hell ... [and its] only support ... is the Devil's trident. The paradise of disciplined enlightenment is the rotating skewer, upon which the mind spins."[5] The diabolic and infernal were not for Flusser otherworldly categories but human, all-too-human, ones. From this perspective, an apparent oddity like *Vampyroteuthis Infernalis* makes a fitting bookend to a career devoted to understanding, among other things, the infernal germ within humanity and the role of media in its fertilization.

In the titular "vampire squid from hell" (which is not actually a squid and is, in fact, like *Homo sapiens*, the only surviving member of its genus), Flusser nominates an absolute alterity but one, nonetheless, uncannily immanent to (even emerging from) human being itself, the way a photographic image emerges from its negative. Though *Vampyroteuthis Infernalis* begins as a more or less straightforward (if misinformed) ethological treatise, it soon morphs into a weird meditation on media, cybernetics, and the logic of modernity. Though Flusser frequently refers to the metaphorical, fabular nature of the argument, he insists with equal vigor upon its homological truth. In brief, Flusser contends that our new, immersive media environment—an environment essentially chromatophoric, consisting of "televisions, videos, and computer monitors . . . display[ing] synthetic images"[6]—threatens to vampyroteuthize us, if not "swallow us whole."[7] For Flusser, the "vampyroteuthic" becomes another, more totemic name for that *Universum der technischen Bilder*, that "dimensionless" world of dreamlike images, which does not "lie below waking consciousness, but above it."[8] In other words, modern humans, reduced to cephalopodic "functionaries" of systems, find themselves now floating in the depths beneath a shimmering surface of stroboscopic information. The inferno of modernity is neither Dante's icy chasm nor Milton's fiery plain, but a watery abyss in which we drift, stupefied, and bedazzled.

The Disgusting

Flusser's not entirely accurate description of the vampire squid emphasizes, with more than a little disgust, both its alienness and uncanny familiarity. Its purported scale—some 20 meters, according to Flusser—is alarming enough, but when we are informed of the creature's mouth—a horrid beak behind which writhes a tooth-encrusted tongue (or "radula"), in fact with tens of thousands of pullulating teeth extending down the esophagus into the entrails—we are confronted by nothing less than a nightmare that "surpasses in brutality all other of life's weapons."[9] Like all cephalopods, the vampire squid's head is fused to or sheathed by its foot, creating a mantle; while Flusser admires this efficient design, their spiral symmetry, with the brain at its axis, should remind us of that earlier image of a mind rotating upon a diabolic skewer. To hint at such dark forces at work, Flusser notes that cephalopods developed skulls—a "vertebrate strategy" having "no place on the evolutionary agenda of mollusks"—a fact that "warrants concern."[10] On the one hand, like all mollusks, the cephalopod is a mushy, visceral mass, literally screwy, coiled around a spiral axis; on the other hand, its nervous system, "[c]ybernetically speaking . . . represents the highest organization of life."[11] Vampire squid disgust us by virtue of this weird combination of rudimentary and complex organization.

As anyone who's ever accidentally stepped barefoot on a snail will tell you, the first stage of any phenomenology is disgust, the instinctive repulsion from the encountered world, its perception as an "irritant." At some formal level, we might say that the world doesn't really *appear* to us until it is expelled, resisted, or recoiled from; until it is othered, it is simply perceived as part of us. Disgust becomes for Flusser a category deeply bound to our *Dasein*, to such an extent that he advances the hypothesis that "[d]isgust recapitulates phylogenesis,"[12] meaning that it (i.e., disgust) is a function of perceived biological distance. Indeed, to turn one of Sianne Ngai's insights on its head (which is also, in the context of cephalopods, to set it on its feet), namely that "the ultimate index of an object's cuteness may be its edibility,"[13] what then do we make of the vampire squid, which is known to commit suicide in captivity by eating its own tentacles? Cuteness, we might say, is edged with disgust in much the same way that "the abject is edged with the sublime."[14] Far from being the hallmark of ethical or moral failure,[15] disgust for Flusser is an index of our *recognition* of otherness and the precondition for any "attempt to overcome the constraints of *Dasein*."[16]

Something like this process of overcoming seems to occur in an oft-cited passage from Jules Verne's *Twenty-Thousand Leagues Under the Sea* in which Prof. Arronax and crew conduct a symposium on the cephalopod (which happens at that moment to be gnawing through the hull of the *Nautilus*). After discussing the creatures in myth and trading several dubious anecdotes, Arronax decides at last to look out the porthole and finds, seeing the creature up close, that he cannot "repress a gesture of disgust."[17] The prodigious physical size and power of the creature, its "spindle-like body" with tentacles "twisted like the furies' hair," the horrid rows of suction cups fastening and unfastening against the windows, its "enormous staring green eyes," its chameleonic skin flashing irritably, and above all its freakish mouth—"a horned beak like a parrot's" in whose depths writhes an equally freakish tongue "furnished with several rows of pointed teeth":[18] all these features confirm to Arronax the creature's monstrosity, a monstrosity that is signaled also by a kind of crisis of nomenclature (it is referred to variously as a "squid," "cuttlefish," "devilfish," and "poulp"). At the same time, however, he cannot quite bring himself to dismiss it outright as a "failure in the purposive effort,"[19] for although it decidedly represents a confusion of the natural order—"a bird's beak on a mollusk!" he shudders—it nonetheless seems to him endowed by the Creator with extraordinary "vitality" and "vigor."[20] "I overcame the horror that inspired me," Arronax concludes, "and, taking a pencil, began to draw it."[21]

Flusser would no doubt point out the irony of a marine biologist safe in the belly of a figurative cephalopod, the *Nautilus*, fearing death in the belly of a literal one; but more intriguing still would be the way Verne strangely stages this encounter in terms of a double inscription. Before Prof. Arronax sets pencil to paper himself, he notes the chromatophoric display on the creature's skin and perceives it as a communique, "an outward expression to the inner thoughts of the organism" in Flusser's gloss.[22] The important thing for Flusser is that the cephalopod's message is intentional: it is preceded by an experience; the creature's attitude, reaction, or concept of that experience; the desire to transmit that information; and finally the information's encoding and transmission via chromatophoric inscription on the skin. This process of inscription, start to finish, is not dissimilar to photography as Flusser conceives it: "What fascinates the photographer is not the photographic paper, the object, but the information transmitted."[23] For Flusser, photography thus represents an entirely new model of inscription, an inscription not on objects—which he associates with the epoch of capital-*h* History inaugurated by linear writing—but inscription on *subjects*, an ephemeral or liquid medium. In the posthistorical epoch inaugurated by this model of inscription—which is in fact nothing less than modernity itself—"society ... shall be a society of information consumption, less and less interested in the consumption of 'goods', of objects."[24] Such a "vampyroteuthic society" uses liquid media not to concretize thought as historical record—it has less and less use for cultural memory—but rather to actualize thought "through the epistemological, aesthetic, and ethical modeling of the other":[25] the manipulation of the subject. In other words, the disgust Prof. Arronax feels when witnessing the cephalopod's chromatophoric display is hypothetically mirrored back to the cephalopod, glaring balefully at a squishy human making crude inscriptions upon a sheet of prosthetic skin. These crisscrossing signals can in turn be mapped onto Flusser's philosophical parable in which skin-writing becomes an image of photography, itself the emblematic technical practice of modernity.

The Perfidious

Skin-writing, however, is not the only kind of inscription or vampyroteuthic signaling that interests Flusser. The clouds of sepia ink that cephalopods emit to confuse predators are more than a mindless diversionary tactic, according to Flusser: "Closer observation of the vampyroteuthis's relatives has revealed that the act of sculpting the sepia cloud has nothing to do with their enemies and that, beyond self-portraits, they fabricate countless other forms that are indecipherable to us."[26] These transmissions are indecipherable for any number of reasons, their ephemerality and instability not least among them. But beyond these is the fact that "this information is exclusively intended to *mislead* its receiver."[27] Communication becomes a mendacious feedback loop. The whole of vampyroteuthic cybernetics is built around perfidy: all it can say is lies.

In the interests of science we should note that vampyroteuths do not in fact secrete sepia ink, as Flusser asserts. That is itself an untruth and a nonsensical one, obvious the moment we consider the creature's environment: the darkened abyss. Furthermore, and for similar reasons, its chromatophoric "vocabulary" or palette is limited to dark reds and browns. In both instances, however, these inaccuracies give way to uncannier truths that, if anything, bear out even more powerfully Flusser's thesis. Namely, the vampire squid compensates for chromatophoric limitations with special light-producing organs ("photophores") located at the tips of its tentacles and emits not sepia ink but a bioluminescent mucus: in other words, it is *even more* of a photographic apparatus than Flusser knew. Whatever the vampire squid's means of signaling, the point—the point of all these deceptions, their culmination—is reproduction. In fact, the only nondeceptive inscription of which the vampire squid is capable, Flusser informs us, occurs on the egg itself, "the only material for information storage that is worthy of trust."[28] Through the clouds of perfidy, it tells but one truth, but tells it slant, in the act of mating.

The terror of Lovecraft's stories is often figured in terms of a profane inscription—a "mating scene"—of this sort. Beyond the physical horror of his monstrous deities, their size and appearance, and beyond even the contemplation of human annihilation, there is often the dreadful ritual invocation of a cephalopodic creature that emerges from the depths (of either space or sea) not to rule us but simply to make an inscription—an impregnation. When, in "The Dunwich Horror," the character of Curtis Whateley attempts to describe such a monstrosity, his speech devolves into vampyroteuthic jabber about an immense, gelatinous, egg-shaped creature covered in tentacles,[29] the foul offspring, it is later revealed, of a human mother and Yog-Sothoth, a malignant cosmic entity. The semi-human twin of this creature, Wilbur, has been attempting to summon Yog-Sothoth in order to "make [his monstrous brother] multiply"[30] or, in other words, reproduce. This grim emphasis on reproduction is coupled to other scenes of uncanny inscription, from the lightning-scorched site of the altar from which Yog-Sothoth is invoked to the "tarry stickiness"[31] the creature leaves in its wake like an eldritch signature or glyph—not a cloud of sepia ink but the trail of another mollusk, the slug.

This tarry stickiness is in turn not unlike the "inky marsh" discovered by the narrator of another Lovecraft story, "Dagon." It is a stain demarking the quotidian human world from the vampyroteuthic abyss. Having escaped an Imperial German man-of-war in an unattended dinghy, the narrator finds himself marooned on a boggy island recently formed by "some unprecedented volcanic upheaval."[32] Brought up from the depths and exposed to the light of day, the island solidifies enough for the narrator to explore its infernal expanse of fetid muck, recalling to him "Satan's hideous climb through the unfashioned realms of darkness" in *Paradise Lost*.[33] At the island's center, he finds a weird obelisk covered with "inscriptions and crude sculptures": mysterious hieroglyphs; "conventionalized aquatic symbols such as fishes, eels, octopi, crustaceans, molluscs, whales, and the like"; and finally "bas-reliefs . . . whose subjects would have excited the envy of a Doré."[34]

In each type of inscription—hieroglyph, symbol, picture—it is as if we take a step away from the abstraction of linear writing that for Flusser inaugurates human history. The inscriptions become increasingly literal, from bizarre hieroglyphs (in which symbols convey conceptual and/or phonetic content) to symbols (in which pictures convey a general idea), to bas-reliefs (which attempt to mimetically represent persons and things). In the latter case, the literal nature of the images—in one instance an aquatic humanoid "killing a whale . . . but little larger than himself"[35]—beggars belief and strikes the narrator, if not exactly perfidious, then at least "badly out of proportion."[36] What seems to him a deceptive exaggeration is however soon enough revealed to be an awful truth: an enormous humanoid creature emerges from the deep and, clasping the monolith, seems, with unspeakable ululations, to worship it. From this moment the narrative shifts its interest from inscription on objects to inscription on subjects—namely, the now-unhinged narrator, whose dreams, drug- or fever-induced, seem fixed by an obscene agency on "a day when the land shall sink, and the dark ocean floor will ascend amidst universal pandemonium."[37]

If we take the inscriptions on the monolith as representative of the logic of atavism so often found in Lovecraft (devolving, ultimately, to an eldritch spoor or stain left on the mind), we approach (as it were, from the other side) Flusser's thesis about the vampyroteuthic, synthetic images that shape modernity: "The images that program us are post-alphabetic and not pre-alphabetic, as are the images of the past."[38] For Flusser, it is important that these images have "passed through" the alphabet, so to speak, so that even if they resemble "primitive" images, they nonetheless carry with them extra information, in the form of their rejection or mooting of linear writing, of history. If the images programming Lovecraft's characters are not exactly "post-alphabetic" as Flusser claims the images that program *us* are, they are at any rate post-hieroglyphic and suggest less a return to the past than the reassertion of a primordial cybernetics, overwriting the present. Inscription, in both the Lovecraftian and Flusserian sense, is in-formation, data that enters and forms us from the inside: "Whoever is programmed by technical images lives and knows reality as a programmed context."[39] The aim, in other words, of both Flusser's vampire squid and Lovecraft's Great Old Ones is simply "to inform the Other, to alter him, to impose on him particular information, knowledge, behavior and sensations."[40] And what is the nature of this knowledge? What truth conditions its perfidy? Surveying cephalopodic literature from Icelandic fables to Verne to Lovecraft and Miéville, Eugene Thacker concludes that "the cephalopod stands in as a manifestation of that indifference of the black inky abyss," an indifference that discomfits and displaces us, so that "[i]t is we who are alien."[41] The alienation, however, that for Lovecraft has its source in the unplumbed blackness of space can be found, for Flusser, in the photographer's darkroom: the skin-writing of vampire squid is an image of photography itself; photography is the art and science of technical images; technical images increasingly manipulate and program "modern" subjects; this programming dazzles and stupefies the subject and, rather than installing her in history, merely disposes her to further technical images, further perfidious derangements. It is in this sense that Rodrigo Maltez Novaes concludes that our society "is a 'Vampyroteuthian' society, a society of artifice and lies, of surfaces."[42]

The Rapacious

The alienating perfidy of cephalopods cited by Thacker is matched in its antiquity only by a corresponding reputation for morbid sexual vigor. The second-century poet Oppian observes that "[f]or the Poulpe his deadly mating goes with bitter destruction and union consummated is consummated death: for he does not abstain or cease from his desire, until he is spent and strength forsakes his limbs and himself falls exhausted on the sand and perishes."[43] When not dying outright from the act of inscription (or, if female, the travails of birth), the cephalopod is soon gobbled up by passing fish and crabs. Poets and philosophers alike have noted the double irony here, not only the coincidence of death and reproduction but the cruel reversal of predator and prey. For Flusser, however, the weirdness of squid sex lies altogether elsewhere, not in its proximity to death but rather in its proximity to *knowledge*. The male vampire squid, he notes, has not one but three penises: one for actual insemination, with a detachable "single-use" tip; a second for stimulating the female's radula and inducing ovulation; and a third, rather more mysterious member, that simply caresses the female's abdomen during copulation. When not occupied with this latter task, though, the third penis "actively feels the environment,"[44] probing, grasping, and otherwise encountering the world like any other tentacle. "All incoming bits of information have, simultaneously, a tentacular, optic, and sexual dimension,"[45] Flusser informs us: in short, the epistemology of the vampire squid is a kind of empty sexual rapacity. To grasp is to copulate is to know.

The physiological fusion of sensory and sexual organs implies a phenomenological fusion of knowledge and arousal. If the bizarre circuit forged thereby reminds us of Freud's famous image of the unconscious as it "stretches out feelers . . . towards the external world and hastily withdraws them as soon as they have sampled the excitations coming from it,"[46] this shouldn't surprise us. "As complex beings with complex brains," Flusser explains, "[squid and humans] are both partially rational and partially oneiric"; however, these two faculties are inverted relative to the other, so that "[w]hat to us is wakeful consciousness is, to it, the subconscious."[47] What our unconscious but coyly samples, the vampire squid ardently embraces; what for us is apprehension is for it orgasm.

One of the most hideous scenes in John Wyndham's alien invasion novel, *The Kraken Wakes*, seems to me to hinge precisely on this disturbing feature of cephalopodic epistemology. After a series of escalating conflicts, the deep-sea dwelling aliens (or "xenobaths," as they come to be known) eventually dispatch "sea tanks" to torment coastal populations. These biological tanks—variously described as dull, metallic eggs or "huge grey slugs"[48]—extrude bladder-like objects that "split open, as if [they] had been burst into instantaneous bloom by a vast number of white cilia which rayed out in all directions."[49] Upon contact with humans, these sticky tentacles slowly retract, dragging their human catch, "struggl[ing] like flies on a fly-paper,"[50] back toward the central body until the whole writhing mass of arms, legs, and tentacles rolls away and pitches itself into the sea, leaving behind only a "miasmic" coating of slime.[51] It is as if the xenobaths were staging a grotesque parody of the *Symposium*, in which Aristophanes claims we were once hermaphroditic, spherical beings with multiple sets of limbs and genitals, whole and complete until sundered by the gods, and ever seeking thereafter a fleeting glimpse or memory of that former wholeness in the sexual act. This coding of the assault has to be later reconciled with the realization that it wasn't exactly an assault in the ordinary sense but more of a trawling or "shrimping" expedition[52]—a foray, with no especial malice, to collect samples.

The novel's Flusser stand-in, Dr. Bocker, acknowledges that détente or mutual understanding between the two species was "very likely . . . never a possibility,"[53] not so much because they are different but because "the same urge drives them as drives us."[54] In this moment he does not concede the xenobath's humanity so much as modernity's xenobathic (or vampyroteuthic) nature. The novel's horror, ultimately, inheres less in the idea of outright human extinction than in a sense of nullity or pointlessness, one kind of inscription erasing another. But this is an erasure that humanity, enthralled by technical images, already perpetrates against itself. On the one hand, like the novel's main characters (husband and wife journalists), we lament "all the shams and the humbug, and pretending that the lies aren't lies, and the propaganda isn't propaganda,"[55] but on the other, like those same characters, we nonetheless content ourselves—perversely, bizarrely, well past the eleventh hour—with the composition of nugatory, even delusional, "scripts." But what is to be done? For Wyndham, it is as if the species were caught between a Scylla and Charybdis: the Lovecraftian thesis that "[t]here have been lords of the earth before us"[56] and the Flusserian one that "[i]t is impossible to indoctrinate the vampyroteuthis without also being indoctrinated by it."[57] This formulation expresses the stakes of Flusser's *Vampyroteuthis infernalis* and the felicity of thinking it against the backdrop of Weird fiction—precisely the sort of "apocalyptic perspective" he insists must be attained in order for "the problem of photography [to] assume the importance it deserves" as *the* crisis of modernity.[58]

As furtive as cephalopods are, their rapacity means we don't have to look hard to find evidence of their presence in literary modernism: from pre-instances in Melville, Verne, and Hugo to the nightmarish first-contact narratives of H. G. Wells, to industrial-capitalist allegories like Frank Norris's *The Octopus*, to any number of High and late Modernist specimens—in James Joyce, for example, Marianne Moore, and Evelyn Waugh[59]—the period is replete with, as Moore herself might have put it, imaginary abysses with real cephalopods in them. Even when the squid itself darts out of sight, a telltale cloud of ink marks its presence: the enervating bureaucratic gloom, say, that typifies Kafka's Poseidon, disaffected comptroller of the deeps. Much in the same way that Lyotard claims "[a] work can become modern only if it is first postmodern,"[60] we might suggest that a work becomes modern only if it is first Weird—and perhaps only properly Weird from the vantage of the New Weird.

Reading modernism with Flusser then is to discover a New Weird archive—keyed to the infernal, disgusting, perfidious, and rapacious—not only found in the generic periphery but secreted in the canonical center, obtaining not only to the regime of technical images but to the logic of modernity itself, whose one repeating message is that if and when the world ends, it will end not with a bang but a gurgle.

Notes

1 Jeff VanderMeer, "Introduction," in *The Weird: A Compendium of Strange and Dark Stories*, ed. Jeff and Ann VanderMeer (New York: Tor, 2011), xv–xx, xvi.
2 Kate Marshall, "The Old Weird," *Modernism/modernity* 23, no. 3 (September 2016): 631–49, 633.
3 Mark Fisher, *The Weird and the Eerie* (London: Repeater Books, 2016), 33.
4 For Flusser's own escape plan, such as it is, see *Does Writing Have a Future?*, trans. Nancy Ann Roth (Minneapolis: University of Minnesota Press, 2011).
5 Flusser, *The History of the Devil*, trans. Rodrigo Maltez Novaes, ed. Siegfried Zielinski (Minneapolis: Univocal, 2014), 180.
6 Vilém Flusser and Louis Bec, *Vampyroteuthis infernalis* (Minneapolis: University of Minnesota Press, 2012), 67.
7 Ibid., 73. For simplicity's sake, I will tend to cite the published German version of the text, translated by Valentine A. Pakis. However, I will occasionally draw a

felicitous passage from the (previously unpublished) Brazilian-Portuguese version, translated by Rodrigo Maltez Novaes. In these latter instances, the words "Brazilian Vampyroteuthis" will be added to the citation.

8 Flusser, *Into the Universe of Technical Images*, trans. Nancy Ann Roth (Minneapolis: University of Minnesota Press, 2011), 166.
9 Flusser and Bec, *Vampyroteuthis Infernalis*, 13.
10 Ibid., 15.
11 Ibid., 14.
12 Ibid., 11.
13 Sianne Ngai, *Our Aesthetic Categories: Zany, Cute, Interesting* (Cambridge, MA: Harvard University Press, 2015), 79.
14 Julia Kristeva, *Powers of Horror: An Essay on Abjection*, trans. Leon S. Roudiez (New York: Columbia University Press, 1982), 11.
15 As in, for example, "The Rime of the Ancient Mariner," whose sermon is to love all God's creatures, even the slimy things of the deep.
16 Flusser and Bec, *Vampyroteuthis Infernalis*, 12.
17 Jules Verne, *20,000 Leagues under the Sea* (Boston: George M. Smith, & Co., 1873), 272.
18 Ibid., 272–3.
19 Aristotle's definition of monstrosity. See Aristotle, *Physics*, trans. R. P. Hardie and R. K. Gaye, in *The Basic Works of Aristotle*, ed. Richard McKeon (New York: Random House, 1941), II.8.
20 Verne, *20,000 Leagues*, 273.
21 Ibid.
22 Flusser and Bec, *Vampyroteuthis Infernalis*, 51.
23 Flusser, *[Brazilian] Vampyroteuthis Infernalis*, trans. and ed. Rodrigo Maltez Novaes (New York: Atropos, 2011), 115.
24 Ibid., 114.
25 Ibid., 111.
26 Flusser and Bec, *Vampyroteuthis Infernalis*, 52.
27 Ibid., emphasis added.
28 Flusser, *[Brazilian] Vampytoteuthis Infernalis*, 105.
29 H. P. Lovecraft, "The Dunwich Horror," in *Tales*, ed. Peter Straub (New York: Library of America, 2005), 370–414, 409–10.
30 Ibid., 382.
31 Ibid., 396.
32 Lovecraft, "Dagon," in *The Call of Cthulhu and Other Weird Stories*, ed. S. T. Joshi (New York: Penguin, 2016), 1–6, 2.
33 Ibid., 3.
34 Ibid., 4.
35 Ibid., 5.
36 Ibid.
37 Ibid., 6.
38 Fluser, *Post-History*, trans. Rodrigo Maltez Novaes, ed. Siegfried Zielinski (Minneapolis: Univocal, 2013), 92.
39 Ibid., 97.
40 Flusser, *[Brazilian] Vampyroteuthis Infernalis*, 111.

41 Eugene Thacker, *Tentacles Longer Than Night: Horror of Philosophy*, vol. 3 (Winchester: Zero Books, 2015), 153.
42 Rodrigo Maltez Novaes, "Translator's Introduction," in Flusser, *Post-History*, xiii.
43 Oppian, *Halieutica, or Fishing*, in *Oppian, Colluthus, and Triphiodorus*, trans. A. W. Mair (Cambridge: Loeb Classical Library, 1928), 257.
44 Flusser and Bec, *Vampyroteuthis Infernalis*, 20.
45 Ibid., 40.
46 Freud, "Note on the 'Mystic Writing Pad,'" trans. James Strachey, in *Collected Papers*, vol. 5, ed. James Strachey (New York: Basic Books, 1959), 175–80, 180.
47 Flusser and Bec, *Vampyroteuthis Infernalis*, 41.
48 John Wyndham, *The Kraken Wakes* (New York: Penguin, 2008), 141.
49 Ibid., 139–40.
50 Ibid., 141.
51 Ibid., 144.
52 Ibid., 145.
53 Ibid., 180.
54 Ibid.
55 Ibid., 161.
56 Ibid., 148.
57 Flusser and Bec, *Vampyroteuthis Infernalis*, 71.
58 Flusser, *Towards a Philosophy of Photography* (London: Reaktion Books, 2000), 20.
59 See Melville's *Moby-Dick*, ch. 59; Hugo's *Toilers of the Sea*; and Wells's *War of the Worlds*, "The Sea Raiders," and "In the Abyss." See *Decline and Fall*, Part II, chapter 4. For a further roll-call of tentacular modernists, see Aaron Jaffe, "Introduction—Who's Afraid of the Inhuman Woolf?" *Modernism/modernity* 23, no. 3 (September 2016): 505–9.
60 Jean-François Lyotard, *The Postmodern Condition: A Report on Knowledge*, trans. Geoff Bennington and Brian Massumi (Minneapolis: University of Minnesota Press, 1984), 79.

17

A Philosophy of Refraction

Vilém Flusser's Speculative Biology and the Study of Paramedia

David Bering-Porter

The book *Vampyroteuthis Infernalis: A Treatise, with a Report by the Institut Scientifique de Recherche Paranaturaliste* was one of Vilém Flusser's later works, coauthored with Louis Bec, an artist and friend of the family during their time in France in 1987 where it was originally published in German. In spite of the scientific trappings of the title, the *Vampyroteuthis* text is much more of a thought experiment than it is an example of close, scientific description. *Vampyroteuthis Infernalis* translates literally as "vampire squid from hell," which is a name that is nearly as provocative as it is inaccurate. Yet, I would argue that accuracy in scientific description is not the aim of the book, nor in Flusser's argument, and to emphasize the text's deviation from reality is to miss the point altogether. This chapter is an exploration of Flusser's project of speculative biology through the conceptual lens of the *Vampyroteuthis*, functioning both as a text and as an idea that is propped up on the possibility of its own expression through living matter. Flusser's writing on the *Vampyroteuthis* may not accurately portray the living animal on which it is based, but it does plumb the depths of an ontology and a phenomenology that is both alien and remarkably compelling in its antipodean reflection of our own experience.

The *Vampyroteuthis* is, for Flusser, the way into an experiment in thought that is based in speculation, extrapolation, and design. As the subtitle of the book suggests, this is a treatise or treatment of the *Vampyroteuthis*, a term whose etymology extends backward through the French *traiter* to the Latin *tractāre*, meaning to handle, move, or manage. *Tractāre* is an embodied, manipulative verb whose recessive meanings are carried only in the more archaic English definitions of "treatment" that denotes "handling" in both a literal and figurative sense.[1] Thus, the word "treatise" is actually quite revealing as to Flusser's actual designs in treating the *Vampyroteuthis* and subjecting it to a kind of treatment that affords him the opportunity to imagine the world otherwise.

Flusser's book on the *Vampyroteuthis* is a fable of *Dasein*,[2] as he says early on: "What will be presented here is, accordingly, not a scientific treatise but a fable. The human and its vertebrate *Dasein* are to be criticized from the perspective of a mollusk. Like most fables, this one is ostensibly concerned with animals. *De te fabula narratur.*"[3] The passage in Latin translates as "the story applies to you," as all good fables should. This fable of invertebrate *Dasein* is meant to be instructive for its audience and like many fables, this one uses the figure of the animal to reveal something significant about the reader themselves. This speaks to something important about Flusser's style and method more broadly. Flusser often uses misdirection in his writing and there is a theatrical quality to the presentation of his ideas. He is an elliptical thinker and does not seem interested in bringing his arguments full circle, but rather to a new place that brings with it a new perspective on the place he started from. His is a kind of trickster theory that defamiliarizes, extrapolates, and speculates about the world we inhabit. Philosophical reflection has been replaced by theoretical refraction.

The goal of this chapter is to think about Flusser's speculative biology as a kind of phenomenological approach to media studies, an approach that draws less heavily on his writings on photography and technical images and more heavily upon his theories of design in order to open a path toward what I would like to call *paramedia*, or a speculative and embodied theory of media and mediation. This chapter will look to Flusser's *Vampyroteuthis* book as its primary example, since the text serves as the lens through which Flusser's method becomes clear—a method that Flusser uses in his own fable of the *Vampyroteuthis Infernalis* in a unique blend of phenomenology, speculation, and imagination.

The object of Flusser's analysis in the *Vampyroteuthis* book is not the squid itself, but rather the squid as an object of speculation and its imagined body as a kind of medium through which Flusser's own thinking can unfold; it is a vessel into which Flusser channels perceptions, experiences, and ideas and through which he can carry out an anamorphic analysis. It is a philosophy from a particular point of view: a perspective that necessitates a certain vantage point. It is this approach that is responsible for Flusser's mild obsession with the prefix "para-," which is borrowed from the Greek, suggesting a string of adjectives such as "to one side, amiss, aside, faulty, irregular, disordered, and improper."[4] These connotations all suggest a kind of conceptual parallelism, a set of ideas to one side of the mainstream, as well as those that fail, fall by the wayside, and seem to asymptotically follow the forms of nature that we know.

With this definition in mind, we can consider the significance of the subtitle of Flusser and Bec's book, roughly translated as "The Scientific Institute for Para-naturalist Research," a title that represents a semi-imaginary organization that would seem to be Flusser and Bec's attempt to codify their own approach and methodology. What Flusser and Bec refer to as para-naturalism might otherwise be described as speculative biology: a fictionalized field dedicated to the *Dasein* of the other. Para-naturalism might bring together into a single discipline a diverse array of works that might include the writings of Jacob Von Uëxkull, Thomas Nagle, Peter Godfrey-Smith, Gilles Deleuze, and the host of recent work carried out in the emerging area of "animal studies." Yet, while animal studies often decenters the anthropocentrism of human culture, Flusser's aim in his writings on *Vampyroteuthis* is somewhat different. It is worth repeating that Flusser's approach is one of philosophical anamorphosis and his aim, off-center as it may be, is to consider the human through its radical other. In this instance, para-naturalism bears a family resemblance to other sidelined fields, such as para-literature and para-cinema, even para-psychology, all of which embrace the heterodox over the orthogonal lines of their reflected disciplines.

Rosalind Krauss coins the term "para-literature" as a way of describing the literary criticism of Jacques Derrida and Roland Barthes. Krauss suggests the category of the paraliterary as a way of framing those texts that exist neither as literature nor as criticism but share the characteristics of both. The paraliterary is a category, then, that overlaps with established categorical boundaries but falls outside of the canon, existing instead alongside the literary. Krauss argues that "The paraliterary space is the space of debate, quotation, partisanship, betrayal, reconciliation but it is not the space of unity, coherence, or resolution that we think of as constituting a work of literature."[5] Krauss points out that this distance is necessary because of a paraliterary enmity toward more traditional accounts of literature.

The term grew to include several genres that fall outside of canonical inclusion and respectability, from science fiction, to comic books, to pulp fiction and beyond. Critics of the term, such as Ursula K. Le Guin and Samuel R. Delany, have pointed out that the term "para-literature" is arbitrary and exclusionary insofar as it perpetuates the relegation of genres like science fiction to so-called low or popular culture and puts it in a position in dialectical opposition to the "art" of literature.[6] In film theory, the category of "para-cinema" operates along similar lines, incorporating B-movies, exploitation films, sex hygiene films, and other works excluded from the realm of respectable cinema. Jeffrey Sconce points out that the category of para-cinema is elastic, able to accommodate a seemingly endless stream of cinematic production outside of the Hollywood mainstream. Sconce points out that "Para-cinema is thus less a distinct group of films than a particular reading protocol, a counter-aesthetic turned subcultural sensibility devoted to all manner of cultural detritus."[7] What Sconce and Krauss have in common in their readings of para-cinema and para-literature respectively is that they refer more to a methodology, a reading strategy, than to a genre or body of texts. As a "reading protocol," this strategy bears more than a passing resemblance to Flusser's approach to his objects of study—a way of looking at an object that steps outside of the mainstream and accepted relation and, instead, tries to posit something different and new.

Steven Shaviro also puts forward a theory of para-literature as a category that embodies some of the best characteristics of science fiction, saying that sci-fi is a type of writing that "operates through speculation and extrapolation, and that takes place (conceptually, if not grammatically) in the future tense."[8] While Flusser's speculative biology on the *Vampyroteuthis* is not cast in the future tense, it does seem to embody these values implicit in science fiction and the para-approach to an established canon or object through the spirit of speculation and extrapolation. These qualities of speculation and extrapolation seem to be at the heart of Flusser's analysis of the

Vampyroteuthis, and para-naturalism, for him, is a discipline rooted in the material conditions of sensation and experience. In other words, it is rooted in the body. I suggest that Flusser's analysis of the *Vampyroteuthis* should be understood as a theory of paramedia that emerges from Flusser's approach to philosophy as something mediated and rooted in a body. If the prefix "para-" has come to signify a parallel discourse, one that incorporates unusual and noncanonical objects, then I propose that Flusser's reading of the *Vampyroteuthis* is actually a kind of media studies, but a version of this discourse that includes the embodied experience of flesh and blood as a valid media object.

Flusser's descriptions of the *Vampyroteuthis*, provocative to the imagination as they may be, are often inaccurate. But while the text fails as a work of zoology, it succeeds in providing an account of being (or *Dasein*) that imagines a culture, aesthetic, psychology, and even an unconscious that is rooted in a body that is radically different from our own, and taken as a fable it is not clear that it matters that the *Vampyroteuthis Infernalis* is not the abyssal giant that Flusser wrote about. Rather, the project is to imagine what it is like to be a vampire squid with the associated experience that stems from that body, of existing in such an alien environment, so as to occupy the *Vampyroteuthic* world and to imagine what *Vampyroteuthic Dasein* might be like. It is through the eye of the *Vampyroteuthis*, which like all the members of its genus possesses an eye remarkably like our own, that Flusser's anamorphic philosophy can take place. Flusser's speculative project depends on the sheer otherness of the *Vampyroteuthis*: a member of the cephalopod family most distant from us, both physiologically and geographically.

Flusser is not alone in lighting upon the cephalopod as an example of alien intelligence on earth. Peter Godfrey-Smith has described cephalopods as "an island of mental complexity in the sea of invertebrate animals."[9] Both Godfrey-Smith and Flusser are quick to point out that our common ancestor with the cephalopods existed approximately 600 million years ago, meaning that we and the cephalopods have been on parallel tracks ever since, evolving independently of one another. But for all that, our encounters with cephalopods—like octopuses, squids, and cuttlefish—result in the distinct feeling that we are *meeting* someone, a subject radically different from ourselves who regards us from a place in the world that we cannot occupy. As Godfrey-Smith puts it, "this is probably the closest we will come to meeting an intelligent alien."[10]

Flusser gives a vivid description of the vampire squid's body, its perceptual apparatuses, and its imagined capacities, all of which grow together into a series of insights and speculations about the *Vampyroteuthis*' experience of its own being. This turn toward phenomenology is quite explicit in the text as Flusser argues that he must "follow a 'phenomenological' train of thought" which necessarily departs from abstract poles of organism versus environment.[11] In this section of the text, Flusser's method is strictly comparative. Before extrapolating the *Vampyroteuthic* world, he must first articulate yet again how we rely on the foundational capacities of our bodies as the primary medium through which we engage with our environment.

On the human side, Flusser is quick to point out "the case of the erection of the human body carriage [. . .] [a]s an example of an alteration of the 'ego-world' relationship."[12]

This upward growth, this verticality of the human body, is the mediator between ego and world that frees the hand to grasp what is ready and present to it and frees the eye and the gaze to orient itself upward and out, toward the horizon. For Flusser, it is this change in our bodily orientation that affects not only our epistemology but our ethics and aesthetics as well.[13] The body tempers our relationship to space and time, and its orientation and biology provide the ground from which our psychology and culture grow (even this metaphor is rooted in our terrestrial position in the world, as would be our affinity with trees). The body is the medium through which our world is apprehended and understood; perception gives shape and form to the type of world that we occupy.

In this crucial moment of comparison between human and *Vampyroteuthic Dasein*, Flusser turns to both Heidegger and Marx. The debt to Heidegger is clear in speculative biology's investment in phenomenology, and it is even more apparent in Flusser's use of the term "*Dasein*" throughout the text. Flusser argues that the heart of human *Dasein* lies in the literal and metaphorical grasping of both concepts and matter; thus, he makes the bold correlation between Heidegger's "ready-to-hand" and "present-at-hand," the past and the future, and Marx's definition of science as that which has already been grasped, versus ideology, as that which has yet to be grasped.[14]

In contrast to this, the *Vampyroteuthis* does not grasp with two hands at all but with ten tentacles, formed in a radial fashion between the mantle and the mouth. If we humans grasp the world with fingers and hands, the *Vampyroteuthis* touches the world in a more labile fashion, with its tentacles having evolved not from arms or legs but from tissues that share an evolutionary history with our own lips and tongue. Indeed, this is no exaggeration since many cephalopods can taste with their skin, blending the haptic with the gustatory. Flusser argues that both our world and the world of the *Vampyroteuthis* are fundamentally object-oriented. But whereas our objects are encountered and used, the objects of the *Vampyroteuthic* world are tasted and tested—an act that Flusser describes as one of "digestion and discrimination."[15]

Vampyroteuthic culture, as Flusser imagines it, does not hold its objects at arm's length but seeks to incorporate them; we grasp a concept through an act of unveiling, but the *Vampyroteuthis* "irradiates the world with its own point of view."[16] In a way, we might see this moment in the text as one in which Flusser lets slip the mechanics of his own speculative methodology: Flusser's attempt to imagine the *Dasein* of the *Vampyroteuthis* seems to fall somewhere between speculating about its alien point of view and imposing a sense of what it must be.

Heidegger not only provides some of the conceptual raw material for Flusser's fable, as it rests heavily on the notion of *Dasein*, but Flusser also takes up ideas from Heidegger's metaphysics that address the question of whether or not we, as humans, can transpose our being onto the place of another. Heidegger points out that this transposition "is not an actual process but rather one that *merely transpires in thought*. And this in turn is easily understood to mean not an actual transposition but an '*as if*,' one in which we *merely act as if* we were the other being."[17] Heidegger's description of the process of self-transposition seems to perfectly describe Flusser's method in the *Vampyroteuthis* text, which makes its most valuable contributions as a kind of thought experiment. Heidegger goes on to say that "[t]ransposing oneself into this being means going along with what it is and how it is."[18] Once again, this seems to speak directly to Flusser's method, but perhaps the most important contribution that Heidegger makes to Flusser's thinking on the *Vampyroteuthis* appears in the notion of "going-along-with" which is central to Heidegger's question of our relation to the other as both human and animal.

For Heidegger, this project of self-transposition is not about imposing one's own perspective onto the other but occupying the space of relation between the two. Heidegger argues:

> This moment does not consist in our simply forgetting ourselves as it were and trying our utmost to act as if we were the other being. On the contrary, it consists precisely in we ourselves being precisely ourselves, and only in this way first bringing about the possibility of ourselves being able to go along with the other being while remaining *other* with respect to it. There can be no going-along-with if the one who wishes and is meant to go along with the other relinquishes himself in advance.[19]

The notion of "going-along-with" is particularly significant in relation to Flusser's writings on the *Vampyroteuthis* since it speaks to the speculative project that he undertakes and returns us to the notion of paramedia. Recalling that, for Heidegger, *Dasein* is always *Mitsein*—in other words, that being emplaced within the world is always a matter of being-with, this "going-along-with" also gestures toward the parallel worlds of *Vampyroteuthis Infernalis* and *Homo Sapiens*, a version of embodied experience that mediates a radically different perspective, one that stands to one side of our own. In the end, Heidegger is more suspicious of this project of transposition, but Flusser takes this idea and runs with it. He uses this method of transposition in his reading of the *Vampyroteuthis* and elsewhere in his engagements with speculative biology, embodied experience, and a philosophy of design.

Paramedia follows from this line of thinking, as it embodies a more oblique relationship to more traditional media. Paramedia is also a "going-along-with" more traditional media forms, a media-in-parallel that emphasizes the material conditions of a medium, even when those are flesh and blood, alongside orientation, speculation, and even failure. The *Vampyroteuthis* is both a body and a system that mediates, in time and space, the relations between ego and environment: a form of media arrived at through phenomenology.

The project of speculative media undertaken by Flusser in this text begins with genealogy, since the evolution of the *Vampyroteuthis*' body informs the entire project. Speculative biology reminds us about the organic roots of mediation itself, and Flusser imagines that the evolutionary trajectory of the *Vampyroteuthis* as a central part of his analysis. However, the *Vampyroteuthis* of Flusser's imagination is quite different from the *Vampyroteuthis* as it actually exists, and it is worth attending to these differences.

The actual *Vampyroteuthis Infernalis* lives at a depth between 600 and 900 meters (or between 2,000 and 3,000 feet) below the surface, a literal twilight zone that is reached by less than 1 percent of sunlight. This aphotic or "shadow zone" of the ocean has some of the lowest oxygen saturation, generally too little for complex organisms supporting an aerobic metabolism.[20] The *Vampyroteuthis* occupies a dark and suffocating place, starved of light and under immense pressure, yet the *Vampyroteuthis* thrives here, albeit not in the ways that Flusser imagined. While Flusser described the *Vampyroteuthis* as the pinnacle of cephalopod evolution—claiming for it the same lofty position among invertebrates that we humans hold within the vertebrate side of the phylum—in fact, the *Vampyroteuthis* is a living fossil.[21]

Like many deep-sea animals, the *Vampyroteuthis* has become so well adapted to its harsh environment that it has remained largely unchanged for nearly 300 million years and has seen the rise and fall of the dinosaurs. Unlike its phylogenetic cousins nearer the surface, *Vampyroteuthis* is small and biologically conservative, relying on the marine snow that drifts down from the higher regions of the ocean for food. Because of the scarcity of food, light, and oxygen, the *Vampyroteuthis* is actually quite small, only reaching a size of 6–12 inches, not the 30-foot behemoth that Flusser describes.

Reading Flusser's account of the *Vampyroteuthis*, one gets the sense that he was influenced by works of Victorian science fiction, like Jules Verne's *20,000 Leagues Under the Sea* and that, perhaps, he really had in mind the *Architeuthis*, or Giant Squid, which does reach lengths of 30 feet or more and whose appetites are notoriously more voracious. *Vampyroteuthis* lacks several of the key characteristics upon which Flusser bases his argument: the *Vampyroteuthis* lacks the complex social behavior that Flusser imagines as the ground out of which *Vampyroteuthic* culture grows; it lacks the ink sacs upon which Flusser pins the embodied writing and signification of the *Vampyroteuthis*; and the *Vampyroteuthis*, living as it does in such abyssal depths, does not employ the complex signifiers that the chromatophores, located in the skin of many cephalopods, use to manipulate color and texture. These chromatophores mediate both the social relations and the environment in the lives of many squids, octopuses, and cuttlefish. Despite its actual limitations, the *Vampyroteuthis* becomes the fantasmatic nexus point of its entire phylum—an aggregate of characteristics and bodily mechanisms that are combined in the imagined *Dasein* of the *Vampyroteuthis*.

Taken more broadly, the project of speculative biology opens a way for thinking about questions of being, embodiment, and mediation. Flusser's book on the *Vampyroteuthis* is so compelling because it works as a kind of philosophical fiction, positing a project of knowledge production based precisely in the kind of theoretical refraction and anamorphosis that I mentioned earlier in this chapter. The artist Pinar Yoldas has argued that speculative biology is deeply rooted in a theory of design.[22] For Yoldas, speculative biology lies at the intersection of "speculative design, synthetic biology, and cultural criticism," continuing further to suggest that critical approaches to design that are involved in the project of speculative biology serve as a counter to the industrialized and instrumentalized nature of the field, as it so often appears in academia and the arts.[23] Yoldas's point about the significance of design within speculative biology is prefigured by Flusser who, in his writings on the philosophy of design, argues that the roots of design lay once again in the body's capacities combined with deception.

Flusser argues,

> Who and what are we deceiving when we become involved with culture (with art, with technology—in short, with Design)? To take one example, the lever is a simple machine. Its design copies the human arm; it is an artificial arm. Its technology is probably as old as the species *Homo Sapiens*, perhaps even older. And this machine, this design, this art, this technology is intended to cheat gravity, to fool the laws of nature and, by means of deception, to escape our natural circumstances through the strategic exploitation of a law of nature.[24]

This description is decidedly McLuhan-esque, casting the lever as a kind of media-machine that extends the existing capacities contained in the human arm. The weirdness of this passage is, of course, that if the lever is a form of technical trickery, a strategic exploitation of the law of nature, then so too is the human arm upon which it is based—itself a form of natural exploit. Life itself seems rooted in the design principles of exploitation and trickery in Flusser's vision.

Flusser's book on the *Vampyroteuthis* is something of a transitional object. The *Vampyroteuthis*, in all its imagined glory, becomes a medium through which Flusser begins to think through a set of ideas that are central to one of his last works, in which he imagines the transition from a kind of subjectivity toward what he describes as a *projectivity*. As Siegfried Zielinski has pointed out, "the roots of *projection* for him led back to the Latin verb *proicere*, meaning to throw out, down, or forward and denoting a constructive action. It also has the meaning of projecting in the sense of shaping and changing the form of something. A projector is not only a machine that throws images, but also a planner or designer."[25] For Flusser, *projectivity* was a space of being, a way of inhabiting the world in ways that were actively creative and not simply *subject* to the underlying principles of the environment. The sex, art, and culture of the *Vampyroteuthis* as Flusser imagined it, while not an example of *projectivity* per se, certainly incorporated elements of the next phase of his thinking with explicit reference to trickery, design, the projection of light and ink into darkness. The *Vampyroteuthis* was a mediator, for Flusser, between human subjectivity as we know it and something new. It was a sidestep or detour of his thinking but a necessary one that reveals something important about the method of speculation that he employed. Thus, the *Vampyroteuthis* text is an example of a study in paramedia that simultaneously illustrates the usefulness of paramedia: a detoured position through which one can dialectically approach a subject otherwise while stepping outside the familiar framework of subjectivity altogether.

Notes

1 "Treat, V.," *Oxford English Dictionary*, 2019, https://www-oed-com.libproxy.newschool.edu/view/Entry/205381?rskey=gQUO8Q&result=3&isAdvanced=false#eid.

2. The term "*Dasein*" (literally translated as "being-there" or "presence") is a term borrowed from Martin Heidegger and is a central idea in his philosophy referring to the experience of being that is unique to humanity. While *Dasein* is automatically human *Dasein* for Heidegger, Flusser expands on this concept to suggest that every being experiences its own particular form of *Dasein*.
3. Vilém Flusser and Louis Bec, *Vampyroteuthis Infernalis* (Minneapolis: University of Minnesota Press, 2012), 10.
4. "Para-, Prefix1," in *Oxford English Dictionary*, n.d. "Para-, Prefix1." *Oxford English Dictionary*, 2019, https://www-oed-com.libproxy.newschool.edu/view/Entry/137251?rskey=d4C0Bn&result=10#eid.
5. Rosalind Krauss, "Poststructuralism and the 'Paraliterary,'" *October* 13 (Summer 1980): 37.
6. Ursula K. Le Guin writes on this in "Conversation with Ursula K. Le Guin, Victor Reinking and David Wellingham/1994" from *Conversations with Ursula K. LeGuin*, ed. Carl Freedman (Jackson: University of Mississippi Press, 2008), 110. Samuel R. Delany discusses this idea in "The *Para*Doxa* Interview: Inside and Outside the Canon" from *Shorter Views: Queer Thoughts & the Politics of the Paraliterary* by Samuel R. Delany (Hanover and London: Wesleyan University Press, 1999), 204–5.
7. Jeffrey Sconce, "'Trashing' the Academy: Taste, Excess and an Emerging Politics of Cinematic Style," in *The Cult Film Reader*, ed. Ernest Mathijs and Xavier Mendik (Berkshire and New York: Open University Press, 2008), 101.
8. Steven Shaviro, *Discognition* (New York: Repeater Books, 2016), 8.
9. Peter Godfrey-Smith, *Other Minds: The Octopus, the Sea, and the Deep Origins of Consciousness* (New York: Farrar, Straus and Giroux, 2016), loc. 99. Kindle Book.
10. Ibid.
11. Flusser and Bec, *Vampyroteuthis Infernalis*, 32.
12. Ibid., 36.
13. Ibid., 37.
14. Ibid., 36–7.
15. Ibid., 39.
16. Ibid.
17. Heidegger, *Fundamental Concepts of Metaphysics: World, Finitude, Solitude*, trans. William McNeill and Nicholas Walker (Bloomington and Indianapolis: Indiana University Press, 1995), 202.
18. Ibid.
19. Ibid., 202–3.
20. Brad A. Seibel, Fabienne Chausson, Francois H. Lallier, Franck Zal, and James J. Childress, "Vampire Blood: Respiratory Physiology of the Vampire Squid (Cephalopoda: Vampyromorpha) in Relation to the Oxygen Minimum Layer," from *Experimental Biology Online* 4, Issue 1 (December 1999): 1–10.
21. B. H. Robison, K. R. Reisenbichler, J. C. Hunt, and S. H. Haddock, "Light Production by the Arm Tips of the Deep-Sea Cephalopod Vampyroteuthis Infernalis," from *Biological Bulletin* 205, no. 2 (2003): 102–9.
22. Pinar Yolas, "What Is Speculative Biology?" https://medium.com/@pinaryoldas/what-is-speculative-biology-c35a57de6990
23. Ibid.

24　Flusser, *The Shape of Things: A Philosophy of Design* (London: Reaktion Books, 1999), 19.
25　Zielinski, "Introduction II—Vilém Fluser: A Brief Introduction to His Media Philosophy," presented at the _Vilém_Flusser_Archive: Flusser's View on Art. Mecad Online Seminar, n.d. Accessed October 9, 2019.

18

Everything Quantizes[1]

Kate Brideau

What calculation is all about is computing cold sums into new things that have never existed before. This white heat of creativity is closed to people who do not go in for calculation as long as they see calculation merely as a question of numbers.
—Vilém Flusser[2]

Vilém Flusser once asked the question, "Why do typewriters go 'click'?" His simple answer was: because everything does. Everything stutters. "Everything quantizes."[3]

The world he describes is one that has been cobbled together through calculation. At the world's own request, we take the units of which everything is made and we gather them into heaps. This world is made up of parts and series, and in it we're reliant upon stuttering machines. The heaps are not immutable; and the machines, rather than being a hindrance, are simply the state of affairs—what we now have would be unsustainable without them (though it may also be unsustainable with them). Flusser recognizes the temptation to assume that we have a quantized world only because we, wanting to count and measure, divided it into parts. And he recognizes the temptation to characterize calculation as cold and divisive. But, he counters, calculation has always been about synthesis, and our machines reveal this fact—the sounds, colors, and shapes that numbers now create reveal "the beauty and depth of calculation."[4] The line that is writing, on the other hand, doesn't synthesize or stutter; it rolls, it leads, it demarcates. And in Flusser's view, the line won't survive into the assembled future.

The typewriter goes "click" because it is a machine, but also because it is a means for writing to survive in a world of parts and heaps. For Flusser, the handwritten word is *about* the world it describes, but the number, the unit, the characters created by the typewriter are *of* the world. Type is of the world. He identified typography as the source of Enlightenment thinking, that which taught us the world is not made up of immutable Platonic ideals, but rather of "types" that we can manipulate in order to manipulate the world in turn. Typography achieved this by treating alphanumeric characters as three-dimensional objects—not altering their nature but revealing the topology that had always been there.[5] Flusser's reading of typography illustrates the significance of how media are designed. In his work he studied the topology of media to see how they invite us to organize and communicate the world and, in doing so, invited new ways of seeing and understanding that *Lebenswelt*. Thought, for Flusser, is modeled, materially informed, spatial; its limitations and possibilities reflect its media. And so, thought in this age is also quantized; some of the thoughts below might be formed into heaps.

Perception

Consider the idea that humans have, to varying degrees, alienated ourselves from the world—that we watch our surroundings pass by through the windows of moving trains; we drink water from pumps, faucets, and processing plants; we wear clothing; we have language. Beyond being ways in which we are alienated, this is a list of ways in which we mediate our existence—ways in which we bridge the gap between us and the stuff outside of us. So, following from this is the idea that the vast majority of our experiences are mediated. Whether automobiles, representations, or eyeglasses, there is almost always something between you and that thing over there.

These kinds of ideas can easily lead us to idealist thoughts, that the world exists through these mediations—that the properties of objects exist only insofar as we observe them, or that we think or name the world into existence.

Mediations as apparently omnipotent and omnipresent as language can cause us to believe that there is nothing outside of them. Although it is only a link between our perception (nonconceptual sensory experience) and our apperception (conceptual and/or motivated understanding), language has the habit of making us believe there is no nonconceptual sensory experience available to us. Language has been viewed as that which defines us, as well as that which confines us. It has been viewed as the measure of reality—naming something makes it official, makes it real. And it has been viewed as a necessary tool for thought. In light of all this we can see how it might come to usurp the place of objective reality.

But if language sits between objects and minds, or things and thought, what reason would there be that this mediation could annihilate objects yet leave the mind untouched? We seem to allow the medium—language—to destroy the object and preserve the mind because in our mediation, our aim is not to relate to the object but to relate the object to us. We want to locate ourselves, reassure ourselves (a move that, it seems, would actually increase the alienation rather than remedy it).

Perhaps if we leaned toward perception rather than apperception we would more easily understand there to be real objects with real properties that are not reliant upon us. We could see that being unnamable or unknowable has no bearing on existence. We would perhaps even see forms of growth and change (human-made or not) that do not depend upon historical, cultural, or subjective context. Perhaps most importantly, we would see that for an object to have properties all its own does not mean that those properties must be necessary or that they have anything to do with truth—truth being one of the words we invented to help us find our place. Even contingent properties can belong to the object itself.

This should not be read as an argument against some corrupting human force in favor of an ideal, pristine nature. If we were to grant independence to things, why couldn't this be done for both "natural" things and human-made things? Why couldn't a thoroughly human invention like typography have an order and movement to it that does not reveal itself in a cultural history? Sure, humans make type, but once made, what more need does it have for us? Once made it enters into relations with other similar and dissimilar things—other type, other marks, other shapes. And it may outlast us all, not even needing us to read it in order for it to be what it is.

Just as this is not an argument against culture in favor of nature, this is also not an argument for experience at the expense of meaning. This choice between a phenomenological presence and a hermeneutic search for meaning is an unsatisfying one. Experience need not be limited to the specificity of context, and meaning need not be fixed. One can perceive the ways things are and the way things are can change. This is only an argument for the abandonment of various kinds of anthropocentrism.

But what would it mean to lean in the direction of perception? If we take visual perception as an example, what is it that we see? Perhaps we see objects; we see a skull, a quill, a stack of papers. This does seem the intuitive answer, but our perception is not so simple as that. First, as soon as we recognize that which we see as nameable objects, this is no longer just perception but apperception as well. "Skull" is a concept. But even if we did not name the things we see, we still do not see objects. This is not to say that there are no objects before our eyes, only that what we see is more complicated than objects. Imagine that you are attempting to turn your perception into a drawing rather than into a verbal description. If you approach visual perception in this way, you'll see shapes. If you were to draw "a skull," "a quill," and "a stack of papers" the result would look more like pictograms than what is actually before your eyes. If you try, then, to draw something as near to what you see as possible, you'll find you are not drawing objects, you're drawing a dark shape next to a lighter shape, and so on. (See Figure 18.1)

Figure 18.1 Drawn after still life by Pieter Claesz. Source: Kate Brideau.

Wittgenstein's House

Do not be troubled by the fact that languages (2) and (8) consist only of orders. If you want to say that this shows them to be incomplete, ask yourself whether our language is complete;—whether it was so before the symbolism of chemistry and the notation of the infinitesimal calculus were incorporated in it; for these are, so to speak, suburbs of our language. (And how many houses and streets does it take before a town begins to be a town?) Our language can be seen as an ancient city: a maze of little streets and squares, of old and new houses, and of houses with additions from various periods; and this surrounded by a multitude of new boroughs with straight regular streets and uniform houses.[6]

In his *Philosophical Investigations* Wittgenstein gives language a material form, that of a city that is built up as need be and in which people live. In this metaphor, language is presented as something that performs a function, something that is useful not just in logic but in everyday life. In this account the language of logic would likely be a suburb of the ancient city, though in Wittgenstein's earlier work logic was central. In his *Tractatus Philosophicus* it is through a proper examination of the logic of language that the limits of the expression of thought could be discovered.[7] He argues that the facts we picture to ourselves share with reality the same logical structure. And going further, he argues, that anything that contradicts logic cannot be represented in language.

In the *Tractatus*, logical thought reigns, while in *Philosophical Investigations* it is use that defines language. And between these two works, Wittgenstein designed a house for his sister. The design was influenced by Adolf Loos, who famously declared ornamentation to be criminal.[8] As such, the house is stark, geometric, disciplined, and free of ornamentation. It perhaps looks like the *Tractatus*—one carefully constructed logical proposition upon another. And yet, this house was not a logical exercise but a space in which people were to live, a space that would be used.

Writing on "Wittgenstein's Architecture," Flusser creates a metaphor that takes after Wittgenstein's own metaphor of language as a city. In this case, though, a landscape is made of philosophical and literary works. It includes the snow-covered mountains of Homer's texts and of the Bible; the calm lake of Aristotelian texts; and the housing blocks and factories of Modernist thought. Dominating Flusser's scene are two buildings: in the old city center is the Cathedral of St. Thomas Aquinas's *Summae*; and alone, off in the suburbs, Wittgenstein's *Tractatus*.[9]

The Cathedral is described from the outside as a towering structure with stained glass windows. It sits surrounded by the rooftops of Baroque thought and points our attention to heaven. It is the embodiment of Aquinas's view (after Aristotle) of God as a static mover—a mover of things that is itself not moved. The *Tractatus*, on the other hand, is a small house that looks like scaffolding. Its interior is organized by six pillars (propositions), each leading to the next, and a seventh that lifts the building off the ground. In his description, Flusser takes us inside this building, describes a person walking through it, proposition to proposition, until one step falls out from under him and he falls into an abyss.

Flusser argues that the heaven to which the *Summae* points and the abyss to which the *Tractatus* leads may be the same hole. But in their differing architecture, he portrays differing thought. The Cathedral is experienced from outside and below, the little house is experienced from within and through a passage of time. One is towering and stable; the other precarious to move through, yet also protected. In his description of the *Summae*, we can see Aquinas's certitude about God. And in the description of the *Tractatus* we can see Wittgenstein's belief that the ladder of propositions he's built has to be discarded after one has climbed it. This imagined landscape of thought supports the idea of theory one can live within or at the very least theory one can use to orient oneself.

Otl Aicher does not imagine architecture for Wittgenstein, but rather discusses the actual house the philosopher designed. His essay on "use as philosophy" doesn't present a metaphor of thought but discusses the house as thought itself. For Aicher, Wittgenstein's house is a bridge between the *Tractatus* and *Philosophical Investigations*— its form is logical, but the building of it, he argues, is what leads Wittgenstein to realize the importance of use. Aicher argues that the only architecture that exists is that which has been built, and that which architecture successfully creates.[10] Perhaps best known for designing a nonlinguistic sign system for the 1972 Olympics, Aicher views Wittgenstein's house as a testament to the value of use. Here use is not the opposite side of theory, rather "use is itself cognition."[11]

In Flusser's work the structure of a thought—the kind of model it is—matters, but he also maintains that it is the theory underlying such a model that matters most. It's the theories that form models, not the other way around.[12] For Aicher, it is the process of making, acting, or using that forms the theory. It seems there are no "paper architects" in his world. He approaches the issue of cognition from a designer's perspective, that is, from the perspective of a problem-solver or of someone who doesn't simply manifest ideas through images and shapes but who thinks through images and shapes. According to Aicher, the meeting of shape and use is what moved Wittgenstein's thought.

In Flusser the thought built the house, while in Aicher the building of the house reforms the thought. What transcends these views is the fact that thought is not monolithic and that the variety of thought one uses matters.[13] They raise questions about the means of thinking, but also about the end of thinking. Is there value in thought alone or does thought need to lead to doing? Or better yet, is there any thought outside of doing? They deal with different kinds of problems and cause us to wonder what it means to be useful, yet both thinkers seem to view use broadly as the ability to live within an idea. There are cities of language in which we can live, but there are also cities of shapes, cities of images, and cities we haven't considered yet.

On the I-It of Technology

First, consider that both Martin Buber and Martin Heidegger influenced the ideas of Vilém Flusser. Then, that Buber wrote, "What is essential is lived in the present, objects in the past."[14] Finally, that Heidegger wrote that the conception of technology that reduces it to man means we "fail to hear the claim of Being which speaks in the essence of technology."[15] That is, for Heidegger, Being and man are linked in technology; while for Buber, Being (presence) is only through You (in relation to I), and not through objects (which exist only in the past). How then does Flusser join these two philosophers in his own thought?

Certainly, there are similarities between Buber and Heidegger—both, for instance, reject isolationist views of existence. For Buber, man is always twofold. And for Heidegger, Being involves thrownness, a relation to others and to things, and is known through experience not through some sort of Cartesian contemplation. But already we begin to see differences. Buber argues that man has a twofold attitude because there are two basic (compound) words that man can speak: I-You and I-It. There is no I before I-You, nor is there any present without the presence of You. It is clear from this that Buber values the relation of I-You over the experience of I-It. In fact, the It does the unfortunate work of transforming unity (I-You) into multiplicity (I and You each with our own separate qualities). Two differences emerge here: first, unlike Heidegger, Buber views man's relation to things, that is, to It, as a negative or corrupting relation. Second, even to call this a relation, in Buber's view, is wrong. I does not have relations with It, rather I experiences It. I has a relationship only to You. So, again unlike in Heidegger's work, *experience* is not valued. Whereas experience and the questioning of experience is one of the cornerstones of phenomenology, Buber sees experience as a distancing from You, because experience is inward; it is not a relation with the world.[16] In Buber's thought there is a primal unity which is broken—he laments the fact that in our world every You unfortunately becomes an It. Our striving, then, seems to be to regain this unity; and objects and technology work against this unity. For Buber, we are misguided in making things (including the You as It) to relate to.

Heidegger might have considered this view to be one of those corrosive views that reduces technology to man. His own view of technology was more conflicted than this. On the one hand he saw technology as oppressive, as enframing. For him, technology forces man to gather resources to himself for the sake of technology. In this incarnation, a technology is damaging—it redefines the world in terms of what is useful to humanity. However, there is a more essential role that technology plays. In its role as techne, technology is a revealing of that which is the case. Our technology makes us aware.[17] Or as Bernard Stiegler's interpretation of Heidegger puts it, technology allows *Dasein* (which, for our purposes, we can simply say is Heidegger's anonymous human being) to both encounter and avoid its own mortality. *Dasein* exists toward death, and it is this fact (that I will die, and only I will experience that death) that *Dasein* knows best. According to Stiegler, technology is a means (one of many) for *Dasein* to avoid the fact of its mortality. It is a distraction, from the Being of *Dasein*, but more than this it is an attempt to preserve *Dasein* (to record, to construct, to enframe the world for humanity). Technology is identified as a means of approaching that mortality. In this view technology is a recognition that one will die and that the daily lived experiences that have been accumulated in an existence will be lost if they are not recorded. In this interpretation, we use technology not to attempt to live forever, but rather to ensure that *Dasein*'s past is always ahead.[18]

While for Buber technology is a division of the primal relation of I-You, for Heidegger technology is a central, if sometimes problematic, part of Being. So then how does Flusser manage to bring these two thinkers together in his own thought? In large part his view of technology is in line with Heidegger's. For Flusser, technology—particularly in his contemporary moment—is a substantial aid to the existence of humans. But rather than considering technology's relation to being-toward-death, Flusser takes entropy as the dominant force with which humans compete. We do not work against the impending and ultimately individualistic experience of mortality, rather we work against a larger force of nature that threatens to reduce everything to sameness or un-informativeness. Technology helps us create and preserve information in opposition to entropy, and for Flusser this process is a collective or social process. And whereas for Heidegger das Man (the "They") is a means of avoiding *Dasein*'s mortality, for Flusser dialogue with others, or our social existence, is less of an avoidance and more a perpetuation of the new. The relation of I-You—so important to Buber—in Flusser's thought.

We see, then, that much of Flusser's social philosophy comes from Buber rather than from Heidegger (we can also say that Edmund Husserl's phenomenology rather than Heidegger's influences Flusser's view of society).[19] From Buber, Flusser adopts the I-You relationship, but there are also some important differences between their philosophies. One such difference is that Flusser doesn't see the I-It relationship as corrosive. In Flusser's philosophy there is a separation that creates the divide between subject and object, and our various forms of representation are attempts to regain the human being's connection to the material world. But a dialogic, if not seamless, relationship of I-world is as important to Flusser's thinking as that of I-You.

This first difference is perhaps due to the second significant difference between Flusser and Buber, namely that Flusser does not posit a primary unity. Whereas Buber argues humans have worked to create multiplicity out of unity, Flusser views the world—humans and objects alike—as multiplicities, as fragmented, quantized collections of particles. Our goal in representation is not to regain a lost unity but to create some concreteness, temporary and malleable as it might be, to allow us to comprehend and live within the fact of our fragmentation. For Flusser, technology is what helps us to coalesce the collections of dust that we are, so that we can be in dialogue with one another and with the world.

These divergences from Buber's thought are vital, since to view technology as a hindrance to the Being of humans is to misunderstand technology. This is perhaps one of Karl Marx's greatest contributions to philosophy (rather than to economics or history)—drawing our attention to the social relations that are concealed within technology. Not only did Marx identify the development of technology (or production) as a key point in defining the human species (as Stiegler and Flusser later would), he also saw uncovering the central role technology plays in defining social relations as a necessary step in achieving a more equitable society.[20] While under the force of industrial capital, technology maintains social relations that are oppressive for the majority of people. The important idea to take away from Marx, Flusser, Stiegler, and even Heidegger is that technology is less a hindrance to Being than it is a central part of being human. Certainly for Flusser there is as much (if not more) creative possibility in technology as there is corrosive potential. Perhaps the question philosophers of technology and ontology should consider most is not whether the subject–object, human–technology, relationship is beneficial, but rather whether our relationship to all technologies is the same.

Notes

1 The following are fragments taken and revised from a self-published zine, *Everything Quantizes*, inspired by both the subjects and style of Vilém Flusser's writing. That writing has an admirable brevity and denseness, and a free and often playful borrowing from fields that might be seen as outside his own.
2 Flusser, "Why Do Typewriters Go 'Click'?" in *The Shape of Things* (London: Reaktion Books, 1999), 64.
3 Ibid., 62.
4 Ibid., 64.
5 See Flusser's unpublished essay, "On Typography;" many of the ideas in that essay also appear in "Print," in *Does Writing Have a Future?*, trans. Nancy Ann Roth (Minneapolis: University of Minnesota Press, 2011), 47–53.
6 Ludwig Wittgenstein, *Philosophical Investigations*, trans. G. E. M. Anscombe (Oxford: Blackwell, 2001), 8e.
7 Ludwig Wittgenstein, *Logico Philosophicus*, trans. D. F. Pears and B. F. McGuiness (London: Routledge & Keegan Paul, 1961).
8 Adolf Loos, "Ornament and Crime," in *Programs and Manifestoes on 20th-Century Architecture*, ed. Ulrich Comrads (Cambridge, MA: MIT Press, 1970), 19–24.
9 Flusser, "Wittgenstein's Architecture," in *The Shape of Things*, 76–7.
10 Otl Aicher, "Use as Philosophy," in *Analogous and Digital* (Berlin: Wilhelm Ernst & Sohn Verlag fur Architektur und Technische, 2015), 123.
11 Ibid., 130.
12 Flusser, "On the Crisis of Our Models," in *Writings*, trans. Erik Eisel (Minneapolis: University of Minnesota Press, 2002), 82–3.
13 See "Hannah Arendt on Hannah Arendt," in *Thinking without Banisters*, ed. Jerome Cohen (New York: Schocken Books, 2018), 472–3.
14 Martin Buber, *I and Thou*, trans. Walter Kaufmann (New York: Touchstone, 1970), 64.
15 Martin Heidegger, *Identity and Difference*, trans. Joan Sambach (New York: Harper & Row, 1969), 34.
16 Buber, *I and Thou*, 56.
17 Heidegger, "The Question Concerning Technology," in *The Question Concerning Technology and Other Essays*, trans. William Lovitt (New York: Harper & Row, 1977), on enframing, see 16–21; on techne as revealing, see 13–14.

18 See Bernard Stiegler in *The Ister*, dir. David Barison and Daniel Ross (Icarus Films, 2005); and Martin Heidegger, *Being and Time*, trans. John Macquarrie and Edward Robinson (New York: Harper Perennial, 1962).
19 In his essay "On Edmund Husserl," *Review of the Society for the History of Czechoslovak Jews* 1 (1997): 91–100, Flusser uses Husserl's philosophy to argue that the individual human is no longer a viable way of understanding politics, but rather that in politics neither the human nor society are concrete. Each is defined purely by knots of relationships (an idea he saw being fully developed in the development of telematics).
20 See Karl Marx, *Capital*, vol. 1, trans. Ben Fowkes (New York: Penguin, 1990), 492–508 and 544–53, for the social relations of the machine and the factory; and on the species being, see "Economic & Philosophical Manuscripts of 1844," in *Early Writings*, trans. Rodney Livingstone and Gregor Benton (New York: Penguin, 1992), 328–30.

19

Religious Telematics and the Archives of Memory

K. Merinda Simmons

We make culture this way, entirely in retrospect.
—Simone White, *Dear Angel of Death*

The older I get, the more Jewish I get.
—Vilém Flusser

Social-media platforms and pop culture essays are probably not the first venues that come to mind when looking to identify traces of philosopher Martin Buber's intellectual legacy. But thanks to Twitter, something like a "philosophical tradition" can find company with a teen music idol in a platform accessible across the globe. From circa 2011 to 2015, @Justin_Buber served a mash-up of pop star Justin Bieber and Martin Buber, exclaiming, "I'm just a regular teenage kid. I make good grilled cheese and I like girls. One cannot approach the divine by reaching beyond the human."[1] Joining the ranks among such luminaries as Kantye West (@Kantye_West) and Kim Kierkegaardashian (@KimKierkegaard), the young YouTube icon made possible by the digital age proves an effective, if not particularly clever, counterpoint to Buber's religious existentialism. Zadie Smith's 2018 book of essays *Feel Free* imagines the same mash-up in another form with "Meet Justin Bieber!" Smith muses about the phenomenon of *being* Justin Bieber: "What does it feel like? Does it still feel like being a person? If you met Justin Bieber, would he be able to tell you?"[2] While the connection between Bieber and Buber might seem tenuous at best outside a bit of fun at the sound of their surnames, the arbitrariness nicely demonstrates a key element of unavoidable interrelatedness in Buber's work on dialogic exchange—work that would later influence Flusser's.

My task here is to elucidate the strain of religious thought that appears in Vilém Flusser's work. Specifically, the phenomenological emphases of philosophers like Martin Buber show up in Flusser's attempts to think through the coextensive nature of users and systems, artists and apparatuses, human subjectivity and memory. Like Buber, whose famous I/Thou construction offers a theological framework for the importance of intersubjective relationships, Flusser stresses the importance of dialogical human interaction. Whereas Buber sees the dialogical communication between humans as allegorical—a stand-in for the ultimate relationship to God—however, Flusser does not rely upon a traditional understanding of divinity or relational transcendence. On the contrary, Flusser presses the implications of dialogic exchange so as to take stock of temporal dynamics and telematics. Specifically, I will discuss how Flusser's notion that "we shall survive in the memory of others"[3] suggests an interrelational archive—one whose dialogic technologies suggest productive renderings of time and subjectivity that avoid linearity and ontological stasis, instead making generative use of the inevitable interruptions and indirect translations. I will close this chapter with a consideration of critical improvisation studies as a subset of contemporary performance and media theory, whose recent turns offer analytical inroads for thinking about the archive of relationality and memory.

Martin Buber's philosophy of dialogue as outlined in his now-classic 1923 essay *I and Thou* remains a foundational example of religious existentialism and phenomenology, a quick overview of which is useful before discussing Flusser's deployments, extensions, and contraventions thereof. Steven Kepnes offers this concise description of Buber's I/Thou dynamic: "Because an individual becomes an 'I' through another, through a 'Thou,' because the self is recognized and confirmed only by and through the other, to ask the question of individual identity is to ask the question of relationship to others."[4] What for Flusser would become a discussion of "dialogical programming"[5] finds a predecessor in Martin Buber's "dialogic life," characterized by this irreducible relationality.

For Buber, the starting point and ultimate purpose of such situatedness is squarely theological. As David Forman-Barzilai notes, "[A]ccording to Buber's philosophy of dialogue, the source of humanity as well as the human dialogical partnership is God."[6] Buber states his formulation as follows: "What concerns me fundamentally is that our relation to our fellow man and our relation to God belong together, that their basic character, that of the reciprocal I-Thou relation, joins them to each other."[7] The reciprocal relation he mentions is what he saw as the one intrinsic to humans-in-contact, with recognitions of the other (the Thou of the pairing) being also necessarily invocations of the self (the I). Put simply, in *I and Thou* "Man becomes an I through a You [Thou]."[8] While this dialogical exchange is necessary for societal/civic equanimity, the most important part of the dynamic for Buber is what it reflects about a believer's relationship to God: "in each *Thou* we address the eternal *Thou*."[9]

Flusser's *The Freedom of the Migrant: Objections to Nationalism* spells out not only his adoption of a Buberian mode of relational phenomenology but also his pressing of the same into telematically infused new directions:

> In other words, when I identify myself, I do so in relation to someone else. In terms of an existential analysis, one would say that "I" is simply that of which someone else says "you." ... From the point of view of neurophysiology, what I term "I" is a computation by the central nervous system, which computes an I-consciousness out of incoming stimuli, whether these arise in the environment or from inside.

In short, a biography cannot be about some sort of "I." And it seems to me that anyone who tries to describe his own life history has never lived. Rather, I think that a biography consists of the listing of networks through which a current of experiences was run.[10]

With this emphasis on an experiential current running through a series of networks, we see one of the more interesting revisions Flusser makes to a philosophical approach influenced by Buber: namely, the addition of a vital computational element that lends concrete systems analysis to erstwhile theological strands of phenomenology. Whereas Buber located the meaning of dialogic exchanges in their divine corollary, Flusser attempted to take serious stock of their paradoxes and inconsistencies without attempting to extract or translate a teleological Grand Meaning from them. For Flusser, the answer to this dilemma is straightforward, albeit not entirely simple: theology simply is not possible, as one cannot talk about God but only to God.[11] Meanwhile, the only image one has of God comes by way of another person. Thus, synthetic computer images allow access points for people to love their neighbors.

For both Buber and Flusser, the self and the other are not distinct ontological spheres but are modalities for mutual reference/knowability. However, for Buber, the relationship is figurative, reflecting the ultimate dialogue one has with God, while Flusser does not ultimately rely upon a concept of divinity. Instead, he invokes dialogue by way of computational interface that rejects abstraction. Consequently, Flusser identifies what he calls the "religious aspect of telematics."[12] I suggest the inverse is likewise worth considering: the telematic aspect (or, more appropriately, the telematic structuring) of religion. While academic studies of religion are typically treated as studies of an inescapably human enterprise (in the name of escaping the metaphysical and confessional trappings of theology), Flusser's work brings into the mix a consideration of nonhuman exchange between humans without slipping into mysticism. His contribution to the self/other, religion/telematics Möbius strip that I want to take up here is his emphasis on temporality, not just regarding a moment of mutual recognition but more specifically in relation to the idea of surviving in the memory of others.

Buber points to the temporal conditionings of intersubjective dialogue implicitly in one of his later essays, "Distance and Relation":

For the inmost growth of the self is not accomplished . . . in man's relation to himself, but in the relation between the one and the other . . . that is, pre-eminently in the mutuality of the making present—in the making present of another self and in the knowledge that one is made present in his own self by the other—together with the mutuality of acceptance, of affirmation and confirmation.[13]

Flusser's intervention on this front challenges the presumed frameworks of mutual awareness and recognition, shifting the emphasis from subject position to subject processing. What kinds of temporalities and technologies are assumed by and implicit in ideas about presence, about the moment of recognition of and by the other? In inviting the question, Flusser offers an answer that constructively troubles the notion of a clear and present process. His *History of the Devil* (1965), for example, "playfully approached history and the creation of linear time, as the work of the devil."[14] Simone Osthoff describes his point in that book as follows: "If we abandon the idea of possessing some identifiable hard core, and if we assume we are imbedded within a relational network, then the classical distinction between 'objective knowledge' and 'subjective experience' will become meaningless."[15]

This emphasis on a relational network could easily slip into the theo-phenomenological approach Buber espoused,[16] but Flusser's contributions regarding technologies, systems, computation, and apparatus keep a useful eye on structural *forms as content*. In other words, the network and the relationality are coextensive. In a move analytically akin to Buber's claim that individual identity comes into relief only by virtue of relationships to/with others, Flusser discusses the "other program" that telematics necessitates: "telematics allows a dialogic programming of image—producing apparatuses."[17]

If we take Flusser at his word—that he became "more Jewish" as he aged—his rendering of Judaism (particularly the distinction he draws between it and Christianity regarding the concept of life after death) is worth clarifying.[18] While Christian dogma relies upon an idea of a material spirit or soul that will survive death, Jewish ideology suggests that people survive in the memory of others. The Jewish tradition of saying when someone dies, "May their memory be a blessing," reflects for Flusser the extent to which everyone plays both codependent and co-constitutive roles in relation to each other's immortality. The other is not the only possible image of God but also an archive, subject to its own system processing. In this way, Flusser's religiosity (or the metaphysical vein of this idea) is operationalized by way of an archive of intersubjective memory that productively blurs the boundary between subject and object, self and other. He grounds such a claim in an insistence on the concrete over the abstract. In his 1990 interview with Láslo Beke and Miklós Peternák, he goes as far as to describe a "Jewish utopia" in terms of information revolution, artificial memories, transference, and transmissions. As Andreas Ströhl suggests, "Flusser's utopia proves to be profane: The only chance for survival and viability lies in the collective memory of culture set up by dialogical networks."[19] "Memory" is thus not an abstract realm floating in the ethers but is rather a mode of media and computational systems. "Immortality" as such is a curated archival relationality. And the archive is more a dialogic technology and system function than it is a repository.

"Without recourse to any mystical or religious view, the intellect *lives* (*erlebt*) the dissolution of reality and of the Self," Flusser suggests in *Language and Reality*.[20] So to survive in the memory of others is to accept that the survival is always inevitably and unavoidably a process of mnemonic translation of one person's experiences into another's system processing. In this way, although "[a]ny translation is annihilation,"[21] there is in the process a certain mode of ontology made thinkable/possible:

> During this process, the intellect annihilates itself provisionally. It evaporates when leaving the territory of the original language so as to be condensed once again when it reaches the language of the translation. Each language has its own

personality, providing the intellect with a specific climate of reality. Translation is therefore, strictly speaking, impossible. Translation is approximately possible.[22]

The series of filters and translations present in memory processing are akin to how Kate Wells talks about the "cultural archive," which, "thought of as a spatial medium, orients itself towards an open future of multiple uses and multiple repetitions that do not bear allegiance to an original."[23] Thinking about memory as a media archive that annihilates an objective past by translating a subject into an open future of multiple repetitions invites us to consider such a space as a necessarily improvisational one. With what remains of this brief chapter, then, I want to connect Flusser's work with contemporary performance/media theory by way of critical improvisation studies. As an avenue of inquiry, this subfield attends to a certain mode of call and response between self and other—I and Thou—but forestalls a linear or symmetrical dispensation or exchange. Instead, the context-specific performance keeps at the fore its particular media situation.

The formal elements of improvisation are an example of Flusser's "dialogic programming": Flusser suggests what he calls the "religious attitude" as a tool for programming anew. In his calibration, and in a move similar to Buber's understanding of the individual coming into being through and by virtue of the other, telematics necessitates "the other program." "Future man won't judge according to a program," he suggests, "but will judge by programming."[24] Importantly, the emphasis here is on the action or performance—the form as constitutive of the content. Critical improvisation studies asks us to think about community and interaction, performance and reception, without appealing to a stable sense of community or collective identity. In fact, it asks us to think about performance and dialogic interaction from places of seeming foreclosure and impossibility. Ted Gioia thus discusses artistic improvisation (especially jazz) as "an 'imperfect' art, governed by an 'aesthetic of imperfection.'"[25] Flusser anticipates this methodology's emphases by way of his focus on inhuman computational apparatuses to think about interpersonal dialogue. I want to posit this approach as a way to access the archive in different theoretical terms, shifting focus from content/history to form/temporality and, in so doing, suggest a productive way to trouble the boundary between the two. For Flusser, after all, the silences and gaps within the archive of memory are productive problems if we attend to them structurally—if we see the improvisational work embedded in our dialogic projects.

Additionally, scholars working in critical improvisation studies share Flusser's focus on time—how its arrangements and interventions orchestrate the programming in a foundational way. Flusser's paradigm of intersubjective dialogue and dialogic exchange is not marked by direct or seamless linearity. Flusser's religio-philosophical leanings, despite their occasional reliance upon theological concepts, are not so much a Buberian emphasis on contact with the divine as they are an attempt at thinking about the silences and interruptions. Flusser's discussion of Sabbath is a good example of this.[26] What marks the Sabbath as sacred, in his reading, is not its inherent value but its social effects (not the program but its programming). Specifically, it is "sacred" not because of a sui generis substance making it so but because of its effectively interrupting a temporal schema. So, too, does improvisation rely upon interruptions and contraventions of a certain structural order. Put simply, the silences are as important as the sounds. As such, they are programming exercises all their own. Increased attention to how interruption and forestallment function in Flusser's corpus—especially in regard to temporality, religion, subjectivity, and programming—would be a fruitful endeavor. After all, the Sabbath's interruption of a linear temporal schema is akin to memory as a storehouse of life after death. Memory is a computational system that is at once a site of afterlife and renewal and of revision, subject always to the processing of another's mnemonic filter(s). Dialogic exchange is never a direct transference but is always an approximate translation. It is an archive and, as such, an improvisational mode of computation whereby humans engage in an endless process of narrativizing performances that memorialize and project simultaneously. Instead of thinking of selfhood as something that is ordered across a linear timescape with clear origins and manifestations, there is potential in recasting the notion of subjectivity as a series of fits and starts within a mnemonic archive that interrupts traditional orderings by way of its pauses, silences, interjections. Traditional appeals to memory and relationality, then, are also appeals to chrono-normativity. A more nuanced look at what conditions are necessary in order for something to be deemed "present"—for the language game of presence to be agreed upon intersubjectively—challenges the notion of an archive as historical repository and posits it instead as improvisational performance piece.

The connective tissue here between critical improvisation studies and analyses of memory as archive is the shared emphases on and engagements with the idea of presence. While improvisation suggests a spontaneity always sounding into the future and archives suggest a history always grounded in the past, they both present constructively thorny questions of legibility and reception in the present. Michael Gallope, in asking whether improvisation is present—and whether philosophy and improvised music are compatible in the first place—suggests that the questions wrapped up in that endeavor "allow us to see more precisely how improvised music grounds its sense of virtuosity not on the basis of a singular immediacy or self-presence, but in remaining mediated after having done away with any single proper idiom. This view allows us to affirm an unconditional absence or the lack of common ground at the heart of musical practice itself."[27] In relation to Flusser's interest in our surviving in the memories of others, the same can be said for the lack of common ground about the subject being remembered. As a corollary, we might think of Arjun Appadurai's claim that "the archive, as an institution, is surely a site of memory. But as a tool, it is an instrument for the refinement of desire."[28]

The pauses, silences, spaces, gaps in the archive interfere with the flow of dialogic access. If we leave alone the idea of direct or pure translation, what methodologies are available for this different kind of work? We should consider (and complicate) our presumptions about the objects of our interpellations. How do we imagine the relationship between the subject of memory and the computational system remembering? Fred Moten's notion of "jurisgenerative grammar" is useful here. For Moten, there is a "fugitive poetics" in Heidegger's *commercium*—"a social space marked by the propensity for song, chatter, and idle talk." It is within such mundane speech acts, broken and nonlinear, that Moten suggests "a place for thought and thoughtful creation."[29] Taking serious stock of the archive as such a place—not at all cohesive but instead characterized by rumors and fragments—allows a mode of scholarship that can more substantively name and theorize the inevitable improvisations we bring to our studies of memory and subjectivity rather than seeking to cover them over with an illusion of wholeness or recuperation. Likewise in the interstices and interruptions that characterize dialogic exchanges and translations thereof, there is performative potential that helpfully contravenes the presumed structural integrity of an idea like memory. These silences and slippages force an altered practice of listening and engaging, opening new hermeneutic avenues in the process.

Tracy McMullen's discussion of the "improvisative" as a way to emphasize the self's capacity for generosity rather than the other's ability to recognize is another example of how such questions might be addressed.[30] I find the shift in focus she proposes—from recognition of the Other to generosity of the self—misleading, but there is nonetheless something potentially constructive about the self-reflexivity and analytical mindfulness bound up in the self's attempts at giving rather than the Other's abilities to recognize. Following Stephen Best in *None Like Us: Blackness, Belonging, Aesthetic Life*, the challenge becomes "to figure out frameworks for reading that postpone interpretation, that defer saying what the bewildering acts we stumble upon in the archive mean and leave the gnawing dissatisfactions alone to see whether they might be fluid and continuous with other social experience"[31] (95).

Bringing critical improvisation studies to bear on considerations of the archive makes more apparent the ways in which ideas about subjectivity rely upon negotiations of media, technology, and futurity. In many configurations of the archival process, the techno-textual record is taken to serve as metonym for social agents whose *humanity* is the very notion ideally and presumably located and maintained. The archives of memory wherein which people continue, then, are simultaneously paleofuturistic fantasy and nostalgic projection. They are not librettos for histories and subjectivities performed. Rather, they are more productively seen as a series of curations and repetitions, inside of and between which there are spaces that render impossible easy translations and interpretations. Grappling with these spaces, with the objects that remain indiscernible and the narratives that remain incomplete, and avoiding inclinations toward filling them or covering them over are vital for theorizing forward.

In an amusing collapse of temporal and religious ontologies, Flusser tells Láslo Beke and Miklós Peternák in their interview (just a little over a year before he died), "The older I get, the more Jewish I get." In that same interview, he suggests that "The older I get, the more I think about and reflect on the information revolution, the more I remember my roots which I had forgotten." A consideration of innovation is what prompts his return to forgotten roots. The religious self-reflexivity he points to here is not adequately addressed by traditional appeals to an individualist, interior model of belief-based dogma. Instead, it points to programs that beget other programs. The media interface that projects Justin Bieber is the same that remembers Martin Buber.

Speaking the self into existence is, in the process, always a narrative about the past. Or as poet Simone White suggests in *Dear Angel of Death*, "We make culture this way, entirely in retrospect."³²

Notes

1. March 21, 2012. https://twitter.com/justin_buber?lang=en.
2. Zadie Smith, *Feel Free: Essays* (New York: Penguin Books, 2018), 381.
3. Flusser discusses this idea in a 1990 interview with Láslo Beke and Miklós Peternák, https://vimeo.com/162279023.
4. Steven Kepnes, *The Text as Thou: Martin Buber's Dialogical Hermeneutics and Narrative Theology* (Bloomington: Indiana University Press, 1992), 110.
5. In fact, "one can only speak of dialogic programming," he suggests in "Celebrating." From his collected *Writings*, ed. Andreas Ströhl, trans. Erik Eisel (Minneapolis: University of Minnesota Press, 2002), 170.
6. David Forman-Barzilai, "Agonism *in* Faith: Buber's Eternal Thou after the Holocaust," *Modern Judaism* 23, no. 2 (May 2003): 156–79, 159.
7. Sydney Rom and Beatrice Rom, "Interrogation of Martin Buber," in *Philosophical Interrogations*, conducted by Maurice Friedman (New York, 1970), 99 (qtd. in Forman-Barzilai, "Agonism *in* Faith," 160).
8. Buber qtd. in Kepnes, *The Text as Thou*, 109.
9. Martin Buber, *I and Thou*, trans. Ronald Gregor Smith (New York: Scribner, 2000), 22.
10. Flusser, *The Freedom of the Migrant: Objections to Nationalism*, ed. Anke K. Finger, trans. Kenneth Kronenberg (Champaign: University of Illinois Press, 2003), 89.
11. See the 1990 interview with Láslo Beke and Miklós Peternák mentioned earlier.
12. Flusser, *Writings*, 167.
13. Buber qtd. in Kepnes, *The Text as Thou*, 109–10.
14. Simone Osthoff, "Performing the Archive and Vilém Flusser," *Flusser Studies* 24 (December 14, 2017): n.p., para. 3.
15. Ibid., para. 4.
16. He goes as far as to identify "false media" in this regard: "Every single human is my only 'medium' to God, and I can only arrive at God if I go to him 'through' the other. All other 'media' are false media.'" Flusser, *Writings*, 171.
17. Flusser, *Writings*, 170.
18. See Beke and Peternák interview.
19. Andreas Ströhl, "Flusser und der Dialog: Negentropische Klimmzüge über der Bodenlosigkeit," *Flusser Studies* 1 (November 1, 2005): n.p. Abstract, para. 3.
20. Flusser, *Language and Reality*, trans. Rodrigo Maltez Novaes (Minneapolis: University of Minnesota Press, 2018), 29.
21. Ibid., 31.
22. Ibid., 31.
23. Kate H. Wells, "Ancestral Irrepressible: Marshall McLuhan and the Future of the Archive in Derrida's Archive Fever," *Flusser Studies* 06 (May 2008): n.p., para. 23.
24. Flusser, *Writings*, 169.

25 Gioia qtd. in the Introduction to *Critical Improvisation Studies*, ed. George E. Lewis and Benjamin Piekut (New York: Oxford University Press, 2016), 4.
26 See Flusser's essay "Celebrating," in *Writings*, ed. Ströhl, 165–71.
27 Michael Gallope, "Is Improvisation Present?" in *The Oxford Handbook of Critical Improvisation Studies*, ed. George E. Lewis and Benjamin Piekut (Oxford: Oxford University Press, 2016), 156.
28 Arjun Appadurai, "Archive and Aspiration," in *Information Is Alive: Art and Theory on Archiving and Retrieving Data*, ed. Joke Brouwer, Arjen Mulder, and Susan Charlton (Rotterdam: NAI Publishers, 2003), 24.
29 Fred Moten, "Jurisgenerative Grammar (For Alto)," in *The Oxford Handbook of Critical Improvisation Studies*, ed. Lewis and Piekut. Abstract.
30 Tracy McMullen, "The Improvisative," in *The Oxford Handbook of Critical Improvisation Studies*, ed. Lewis and Piekut, 115–27.
31 Stephen Best, *None Like Us: Blackness, Belonging, Aesthetic Life* (Durham: Duke University Press, 2018).
32 Simone White, *Dear Angel of Death* (Brooklyn: Ugly Duckling Presse, 2018), 71.

20

The Challenge of Vilém Flusser

Latinidad and Its Others

John D. Ribó

Vilém Flusser has been described as a writer, a philosopher, a media theorist. He is praised as an autodidact, a polyglot. The expansive and idiosyncratic range of Flusser's work has been linked to his nomadic life as refugee and migrant—his Jewish heritage, his Czech origins, his German education, his Brazilian citizenship, his final French residence. With the full complexity of these many aspects of Flusser in mind, this chapter contemplates his life and work through the lens of yet another label: Latinx. At first glance, Flusser and Latinx may seem an odd coupling and indeed they are. Flusser's strongest connection to Latinidad comes via Brazil, the single country in which he lived the most years of his life. Yet Brazil's relationship to Latinidad is complicated, to say the least, and Flusser, who never claimed to be Latinx, ultimately left his adopted homeland to return to Europe. Despite these facts, considering Flusser's life and work through the lens of a speculative, even counterfactual Latinidad queries the place of whiteness, Europe, and Brazil in Latinidad and highlights complexities, ambiguities, and limitations of "Latinx" as a contested category that has come under increasing critique as anti-Black and anti-Indigenous in practice if not theory.[1]

Latinidad's Whiteness

"Latinx" and "Latinidad" are capacious and contradictory terms. On the one hand, for some these words evoke collective aspirations of peoples of Latin America and of Latin American descent throughout the world. On the other, the terms are rooted in a European language of empire. Like the fasces or the motto "E pluribus unum," Latinx and Latinidad raise questions about who benefits from collectivity, to what ends are the many made one, and who ultimately gets left out of the bunch. Although in popular and critical discourses whiteness and Europe are increasingly viewed as taboo components of Latinidad that some would prefer excised altogether, the European provenance of "Latinx" lies at the root of the ethnonym itself, and as recently as 2010 the majority of US Latinxs identified as white in the US census.[2]

Latinidad's fraught relationship with whiteness and Europe was on full display in reactions to a red carpet interview at the 2020 Oscars. During a short, pre-show segment, Ryan Seacrest asked Salma Hayek what the nomination of Antonio Banderas for Best Actor for his performance in Pedro Almodóvar's *Dolor y gloria* (2019) meant to her. Hayek responded, "I started with Antonio. I think he was the first Latino that really made being Latino sexy in Hollywood, and it's amazing to survive so many years [and] still be thriving in this world where it looked impossible to us."[3] Immediate reactions to Hayek's comments among Latinx scholars and journalists were not positive. American studies scholar Arlene Dávila tweeted, "Listening to Salma Hayek say Antonio Banderas is the first 'Latino['] to make 'Latinos sexy' in [sic] the red carpet. Dios mio [sic], I don't think I can keep watching."[4] If Dávila's tweet leaves room for interpretation, the scare quotes intimate objections to the characterization of Banderas as "Latino" and to the celebration of the hyper-sexualization of Latinxs in film and other media. Journalist Yara Simón's response to Hayek is less ambiguous. In a short post on the website *Remezcla*, Simón wrote:

> I can't believe I have to do this again, but here's your pre-Oscars PSA: Spaniards ≠ Latinos. Those from Spain are considered Hispanic because they speak Spanish, but they are not Latinos. It's why Brazilians, who speak Portuguese, are not Hispanic. But they and people from Latin America are Latinos. Spain, which is in Europe, therefore does not fit the definition.[5]

Despite Simón's unambiguous geographic taxonomy excluding Spaniards from and including Brazilians in Latinidad, an extensive body of scholarship demonstrates that the history of who has been included and excluded from Latinidad is considerably more complicated.[6] Moreover, though US academic and popular discourses increasingly identify Brazilians, and particularly Brazilian Americans, as Latinxs, this is a relatively recent phenomenon, and both groups have tended historically to distinguish themselves from, rather than group themselves with, Latinxs.[7]

These reactions to Hayek nevertheless form part of a shift in academic and popular discourses toward critiques of the dominance of whiteness in media representations of Latinidad. This trend responds not only to Hayek but to Hollywood's long history of casting European actors—from the Portuguese Carmen Miranda to the Spanish Antonio Banderas—as sexy Latinxs. Such European performances of Latinidad are not restricted to film. The conversation about Banderas came in the wake of debates about Catalan Flamenco singer Rosalía's rise to prominence in Latin music after her 2019 crossover hit single "Con Altura," recorded with Colombian reggaetonero J. Balvin. Petra R. Rivera-Rideau, author of *Remixing Reggaeton: The Cultural Politics of Race in Puerto Rico* (2015), describes Rosalía's success as part of the music industry's modus operandi of promoting "artists that are white even if the musical practices that they're performing are rooted in black communities."[8] Rivera-Rideau explains that "The people who are getting promoted to be at the higher echelons of these media industries, like popular music, tend to be Latinos who embody a kind of whiteness . . . a mestizo whiteness."[9] In distinction to Anglo-American formations of whiteness, mestizo whiteness includes those who may be of mixed race but who have light complexions and European features that cannot easily be identified as "obviously black or indigenous."[10]

The dominance of mestizo whiteness in contemporary media representations of Latinidad originates in Latin America's colonial history exemplified in the *castas*—eighteenth-century pseudoscientific illustrations naming, describing, and charting hierarchies of mestizaje, or mixture of European, African, and Indigenous peoples. In these colonial schema, Spaniards and other Europeans occupied the apex of Latin America's racial hierarchies and of humanity itself. Today Banderas, Rosalía, and others embody the racial ideal of mestizo whiteness not despite but indeed *because* of their Spanishness, their Europeanness, and their whiteness. In other words, Spaniards overrepresent Latinxs in contemporary global popular media precisely because European whiteness functions, in practice, as master-signifier structuring Latinidad as a hierarchical ethno-racial category.[11]

In the North American context the whiteness of Spaniards, however, is distinct and particular. In *Spain's Long Shadow: The Black Legend, Off-Whiteness, and Anglo-American Empire*, María DeGuzmán explains the origins of what she calls Spanish 'off-whiteness' writing:

> Anglo-American imperial discourse took the Moors, Gypsies, and Jews that the Spanish Empire had endeavored to expel from the Iberian Peninsula and Native Americans and Africans whom the Spaniards in the Americas had enslaved and used as labor, including sexual, and inscribed them under the skin of or transformed them into physical marks on the imagined body of the Spaniard.[12]

Rivera-Rideau's and DeGuzmán's work underlines how Latinxs and Latinidad are ambiguously situated at the convergence of multiple, competing racial formations rooted in intra-European conflicts that played out through settler-colonial history and layered migrations of the Americas—a phenomenon Maylei Blackwell terms "hybrid hegemonies."[13] Ambiguities and slippages between these racial formations allow Spaniards and other Europeans marked as "ethnic" to perform multiple forms of whiteness simultaneously for different audiences throughout the Americas and beyond. Spaniards such as Banderas and Rosalía thus represent both Latinx and Latin American whiteness at the same time that they embody a subordinate though nevertheless privileged off-whiteness in the Anglo-American context. What better way, after all, to reinforce the supremacy of Anglo-American whiteness and maintain white supremacy in Latinx and Latin America communities than to simultaneously denote and erase the ethnic and racial diversity of Latin America through the off-whiteness of a vaguely ethnic European surrogate Other.

Flusser's Latinidad?

Flusser's biography and oeuvre cut across these multilayered, ethno-racial hierarchies in challenging and complex ways. As a Jewish refugee who fled Prague while the rest of his immediate family died in Nazi concentration camps, Flusser escaped the horrors of white supremacist genocide in Europe only to become, in the Americas, a citizen of a settler-colonial nation founded on the lands of Indigenous peoples and the labor of enslaved Indigenous and African peoples. Flusser, then, was at once refugee and settler, migrant and colonist—a predicament at the heart of contradictions that run through all of his writings, especially his essay "The Challenge of the Migrant," and particularly that essay's passages about the creation of a Brazilian heimat.[14]

Before analyzing passages from "The Challenge of the Migrant," it is worth noting that in the English reception of Flusser, his biography at times seems inescapable. Texts bringing Flusser to the Anglophone world often include a summary of the philosopher's life. To give three examples, *Vilém Flusser: An Introduction* (2011) parallels his work and life opening with an introduction-cum-annotated bibliography before recounting his biography in depth in its first chapter. The introduction to the English translation of *The Freedom of the Migrant: Objections to Nationalism* (2003) similarly begins by linking the concepts developed in the collection of essays to the events that shaped the author's life. Finally, the paratext accompanying the English translation of *The History of the Devil* (2014) also frames Flusser's philosophical allegory within the intrigue of the writer's migrations from Europe to Brazil and back again.

Death of the author aside, such biographical frameworks make sense in the case of Flusser for reasons practical and philosophical. While Flusser remains understudied in the Anglo-American context, the events of his life are remarkable and his trajectory as a thinker atypical. The impact of the Holocaust and the Second World War on Flusser's life is often presented as paradigmatic of an entire epoch; as Anke Finger puts it, "Flusser's life and work embody the turmoil of the twentieth century."[15] There is also a certain satisfying if circular logic to the idea that Flusser might not have been Flusser—a transnational, polyglot outsider theorist with a body of work that is at once sprawling and fragmented—were it not for the historic circumstances that forced him to flee Prague, forego formal education, and chart a circuitous path back to Europe through the fruit of his own often underappreciated intellectual labor. These facts form a compelling and legible narrative for newcomers to Flusser.

Flusser's body of writings, which includes *Bodenlos: Eine philosophische Autobiographie* (1992) and other provocative allusions to his biography throughout, also productively plays with tensions between philosophical objectivity and subjective experience in ways consonant with what Alex Brostoff and Lauren Fournier are calling autotheory, or work "[f]using self-representation with philosophy and critical theory ... [that] moves between the worlds of 'theory' and 'practice,' often exceeding disciplinary boundaries, genres, and forms."[16] Yet while the most famous Latinx example of autotheory that Brostoff and Fournier provide—Gloria Anzaldúa's *Borderlands/La Frontera: The New Mestiza* (1987)—writes the self from a place of authoritative authenticity where the personal is not only political but nearly undeniable, Flusser remains playful, contradictory, detached, and skeptical when theorizing his own life.

The opening sentence of "The Challenge of the Migrant" exemplifies Flusser's ludic and enigmatic engagement with theorizing the self. He writes that "Although it goes against my usual practice and steers us away from the subject of heimat and its loss, I would nonetheless like to tell the reader about my own loss of heimat."[17] In one breath Flusser disavows the imminent distraction of the autobiographical detour while in the next admitting that his life experience is entirely germane to the topic of his essay. "The Challenge of the Migrant" plays a similar contradictory sleight of hand at the collective level as well. As the original German title—"Wohnung beziehen in der Heimatlosigkeit" or "Taking Residence in Homelessness"—indicates, Flusser's essay ultimately rejects heimat as an antiquated concept. Yet Flusser's essay nevertheless rehashes a summary of Brazilian history that positions the genocide and enslavement of Indigenous and African peoples as the unfortunate but necessary preconditions for the creation of a new Brazilian heimat.

Thus, although Flusser draws upon personal experiences of loss and uprootedness to advocate for new understandings of identity and collectivity in "The Challenge of the Migrant," his reflections on Brazil as a nation of immigrants conform to settler-colonial narratives. Flusser imagines the Americas—particularly the United States and Brazil—as a "New World" upon which European and Asian immigrants must inscribe novel, transnational, hybrid identities. In "The Challenge of the Migrant" Flusser twice describes Brazil as a "no-man's land" and writes:

> [Brazil] was not like an African, Asian, or Andean colony in which colonists ruled natives; it was more like the United States, an empty land from which the natives were driven. This was why the immigrants were received not as detested foreigners but rather as comrades who shared the fate of being without heimat.[18]

While this comparison of Brazil and the United States with other colonies can be read as an implicit critique of different forms of equally unjust settler-colonial violence, the result of that violence—the supposed emptiness of the United States and Brazil—makes possible the openness to immigrants and the intermingling of cultures that Flusser's essay celebrates.

These "New World" narratives that run through Flusser's essay rely on the irrevocable rupture of transatlantic connections among people of African descent and the supposed disappearance of Indigenous peoples. Of these groups, Flusser writes:

> Africans constituted the largest portion of the population, but they had no conscious relationship with Africa. The human beings who were disgorged naked from slave ships on the Brazilian shore possessed in their inner selves, numbed by hard work, only the memory of the patterns of their lost culture. These manifested themselves in music, dance, and religious rites, forming the foundations of any future Brazilian heimat. The indigenous Indians, who were pushed ever further into the forests, were never included as genuine Brazilians: they were relegated to the background, sometimes celebrated as mythic objects, occasionally brutally raped.[19]

While Flusser's recapitulation of Brazilian history does not shy away from the violence of the transatlantic slave trade or of settler colonialism, it also deprives peoples of African and Indigenous descent agency in the intellectual life of modern Brazil.

This marginalization of Black and Indigenous peoples is a crucial if unspoken precondition to the intellectual community of global migrants Flusser once dreamed capable of articulating a new Brazilian heimat. Flusser writes that "As long as Brazilian society welcomed new waves of immigrants, this weaving of a secret code, of a future Brazilian heimat, this transformation of adventure into habit and this hallowing of habit, remained charged with excitement."[20] Describing this community Flusser lists the intellectual contributions of migrants from Europe, the Middle East, and Asia, writing,

> the philosophical institute in which Italian students of Croce, German Heidegger scholars, Portuguese followers of Ortega, Jewish positivists from Eastern Europe, Belgian Catholics, and Anglo-Saxon pragmatists took part had to open itself up to Japanese students of Zen Buddhism, a Lebanese mystic, and a Chinese literary scholar, and it had to make room for a Talmudist from Western Europe as well.[21]

If this transnational intellectual community actually had the opportunity to imagine the nation anew, that opportunity was only made possible by Brazil's settler-colonial history.

However remarkable and complex Flusser's biography and work may be, his story is not completely unique. Rather, Flusser's case can be understood as paradigmatic of the complexities and contradictions of transatlantic, transpacific, and transamerican migrations of populations fleeing persecution in their countries of origin only to arrive in host countries with structural inequalities rooted in past injustices. Moreover, rather than disqualifying Flusser from Latinidad, Flusser's European roots, and the presence of settler-colonial ideology in his work puts Flusser squarely in line with much of canonical Latin American letters from the colonial encounter to the present. More pressing is the issue of fully reckoning with how a Holocaust survivor becomes enlisted, even temporarily, in the nationalist project of articulating a modern, settler-colonial Brazilian heimat while simultaneously resisting the totalitarian military dictatorship of his newly adopted homeland. Such questions require nuanced approaches that disentangle layered histories of collective trauma and complicate facile binaries of victim and perpetrator.

Ethnic studies scholars are currently developing frameworks to address such hybrid hegemonies that arise from complex, layered histories of oppression, genocide, and migration. For example, in the introduction to their 2017 special issue of *Latino Studies* on "Critical Latinx indigeneities," Maylei Blackwell, Floridalma Boj Lopez, and Luis Urrieta Jr. advocate following "the lead of Asian settler colonial scholars in Hawai'i (Fujikane and Okamu, 2008) by recognizing that im/migrants arrive on homelands and nations of Indigenous peoples and that this awareness brings with it responsibilities and the possibility of new relationships of tension and solidarity."[22] Though Flusser ultimately abandoned Brazil, his time there transformed his life and work and offers generative points of entry for analyzing shifting formations of ethnicity and race across complex trajectories of global migrations. I would argue that ultimately the most compelling questions emerge not from adjudicating whether Flusser may be considered Latinx or not, but rather in exploring how the life and work of a thinker such as Flusser epitomizes the inherent contradictions of categories such as Latinx and Latinidad, categories that in attempting to address historic erasures, injustices, and inequalities inevitably inscribe others.

Notes

1. Latinidad, or Latinness in Spanish, describes the diverse, collective qualities of peoples of Latin America and Latin American descent regardless of nation, race, or ethnicity. Though Latinx studies scholars have engaged Latinidad critically since the term emerged in the mid-1980s and some prefer the plural Latinidades to signal the instability, multiplicity, and proliferation of ways of being Latinx, in US popular culture today there has been shift toward critiques of how Latinidad often centers white Latinxs and thus contributes to the erasure of peoples of Indigenous and African descent in the Americas. For examples of such popular critiques, see Miguel Salazar, "The Problem with Latinidad," *The Nation*, September 16, 2019, https://www.thenation.com/article/archive/hispanic-heritage-month-latinidad/.
2. Karen R. Humes, Nicholas A. Jones, and Roberto R. Ramirez, "Overview of Race and Hispanic Origin: 2010," United States Census Bureau, March 2011, 6, https://www.census.gov/prod/cen2010/briefs/c2010br-02.pdf.
3. "Salma Hayek Celebrates Antonio Banderas' Oscar Nomination For Him," E! Red Carpet & Awards Shows, February 9, 2020, video, 0:15, https://www.youtube.com/watch?v=XNDh3261Ds4.
4. On an informal, hyper-immediate social-media microblogging platform such as Twitter, typos as those found in Dávila's tweet are often the rule rather than the exception. Arlene Dávila (@arelendavila1), "Listening to Salma Hayek . . . ," Twitter, February 9, 2020, https://twitter.com/arlenedavila1/status/1226664593839263744?s=20.
5. Yara Simón, "Despite What Salma Hayek Said on Oscar Red Carpet, Antonio Banderas Isn't Latino," *Remezcla*, February 9, 2020, https://remezcla.com/film/salma-hayek-calls-antonio-banderas-latino-red-carpet/.
6. Critical analysis of the complexity of Latinidad, including its vexed but nevertheless fundamental relation to Spain and Europe, is one of the primary functions of Latinx studies as a field of scholarship. For contemporary journalism grappling with Latinidad's complexity, see Daniel Hernández, "Is Oscar Nominee Antonio Banderas a 'Person of Color'? It's Complicated," *Los Angeles Times*, February 7, 2020, https://www.latimes.com/entertainment-arts/story/2020-02-07/oscars-antonio-banderas-person-of-color-latino-hispanic.
7. For examples of scholarship on Brazilians' relationship to Latinidad, see Helen Marrow, "To Be or Not to Be (Hispanic or Latino): Brazilian Racial and Ethnic Identity in the United States," *Ethnicities* 3, no. 4 (2003): 427–64; Antonio Luciano de Andrade Costa, "The Hispanic and Luso-Brazilian World: Latino, eu? The Paradoxical Interplay of Identity in Brazuca Literature," *Hispania* 87, no. 3 (2004): 576–85; and Silvio Torres-Saillant, "The Unlikely Latina/os: Brazilians in the United States," *Latino Studies* 6 (2008): 466–77.

8   Justin Agrelo, "Rosalía and the Blurry Boundaries of What It Means to Be a Latin Artist," *Mother Jones*, October 11, 2019, https://www.motherjones.com/media/2019/10/rosalia-and-the-blurry-borders-of-what-it-means-to-be-a-latin-artist/.
9   Ibid.
10 Ibid.
11 I emphasize the white supremacist function of Latinidad "in practice" because many contemporary Latinx studies scholars argue precisely the opposite—that Latinidad represents the formation of a potentially liberatory collectivity theorized and actualized precisely to resist white supremacy.
12 María DeGuzmán, *Spain's Long Shadow: The Black Legend, Off-Whiteness, and Anglo-American Empire* (Minneapolis: Minnesota University Press, 2005), xxviii.
13 Maylei Blackwell, "Líderes Campesinas: Nepantla Strategies and Grassroots Organizing at the Intersection of Gender and Globalization," *Aztlán: A Journal of Chicano Studies* 35, no. 1 (2010): 13–48.
14 Though often translated as home or homeland, the German "heimat" is a loaded and in many ways untranslatable term in English. For this reason, Kenneth Kronenberg leaves heimat untranslated in his translation of "The Challenge of the Migrant." Vilém Flusser, "Challenge of the Migrant," in *Freedom of the Migrant: Objections to Nationalism*, ed. Anke K. Finger, trans. Kenneth Kronenberg (Urbana: University of Illinois Press, 2003).
15 Anke Finger, introduction to Vilém Flusser, *The Freedom of the Migrant: Objections to Nationalism*, ix.
16 Alex Brostoff and Lauren Fournier, Call for Papers for *ASAP/Journal* Special Issue on "Autotheory," http://asapjournal.com/call-for-papers/.
17 Flusser, "The Challenge of the Migrant," 1.
18 Ibid., 9.
19 Ibid., 8.
20 Ibid., 9.
21 Ibid.
22 Maylei Blackwell, Floridalma Boj Lopez, and Luis Urrieta Jr., "Special Issue: Critical Latinx indigeneities," *Latino Studies* 15, no. 2 (2017): 126–37.

21

On Synthesis and Synthetic Reality
Post/Modernism in Flusser's Thinking

Rainer Guldin

In his famous article "Toward a Concept of Postmodernism," Ihab Hassan introduced a table of terminological oppositions in an attempt to distinguish postmodernism from modernism.[1] Hassan concedes that the table of dichotomies remains "equivocal" and "insecure," and that possible inversions and exceptions abound, suggesting that the two positions are different but overlap in places and that the border between them is porous. The following pairs, in which the first term designates modernism and the second postmodernism, are of particular interest with regard to Flusser's philosophy: finished work versus process, totalization versus deconstruction, centering versus dispersal, and last but not least synthesis versus antithesis.

Starting out from these dichotomies and their interconnectedness, this chapter argues that Flusser's work and its unfolding over time can be described in terms of a constant unresolved conflict between modernist and postmodernist positions. A few examples shall illustrate this. Flusser's practice of multiple successive self-translations and the philosophy of translation he elaborated and refined over the years are both an attempt at a final totalizing synthesis and an open-ended process. Similarly, his early language theory describes our visions of reality in constructivist terms. Each language allows for another perspective onto the world. At the same time, each individual language possesses an irreducible kernel that ensures its uniqueness and guarantees its untranslatability. This idea resurfaces in the essay "Das Heilige im Abgrund zwischen den Wörtern" ("The Sacred in the Abyss between Words") published as late as October 1991.[2] Finally, the notion of *Pilpul*, a multilingual Jewish thinking strategy used in the Babylonian Talmud, presupposes the coexistence of a meaningful center and a swarm of opposing points of view that beleaguer and surround it.[3] The different, often-diverging, and openly conflicting centrifugal commentaries on the central core revolve around the same gravitational focal point: they are a field of circling points of view that attract and repulse each other.

These ambivalences also determine Flusser's work as a whole. The early Brazilian work of the 1950s and 1960s shows a strong modernist bias centering on synthesis and totalization, whereas the later work of the 1970s and 1980s is characterized predominantly by a postmodernist stance focusing on process and dispersal. However, in both cases the prevailing theoretical position is constantly questioned and reshaped by the other perspective. The two positions not only question and contradict each other but are generally contained within one another. In this sense, Flusser's self-contradictory style of thinking and writing is neither simply modernist nor postmodernist, but both modernist and postmodernist from the very beginning and up to his last publications and conferences. This situation also accounts for recent research highlighting Flusser's postmodernism and deconstructivism *ante litteram*.[4] Flusser's wavering between the two theoretical positions is well in tune with the overall unclassifiability of his writings situated on the border between discourses and different styles, ranging from the essayistic to the philosophical and the literary.

To illustrate this continuity in discontinuity with an eye on the evolution of Flusser's thinking, I will focus on the etymologically related terms of "synthesis" and "synthetic." "Synthesis" comes from the Greek *synthesis* (composition, putting together) and the verb *syntithenai* (to combine), from *syn-* (together) and *tithenai* (to put, to place). "Synthetic" comes from Greek *synthetikos* (skilled in putting together), from *synthetos* (constructed and compounded), past participle of *syntithenai*. In the late nineteenth century, synthetic was used in reference to substances made artificially by chemical synthesis. The notion of "synthetical material" was first used in the early 1930s for synthetic fibers like nylon. The notions of synthetic and synthesis are also used for digital and analog electronic musical instruments. Synthesizers produce a sound synthesis through an assemblage of individual tones. They can imitate traditional musical instruments, reproduce human voices and natural sounds, or generate completely novel electronic timbres. In this sense, both synthesis and synthetic refer to the compositional side of constructive and creative processes.

"Synthesis" is not only one of the central concepts of Flusser's early work, but it also plays an important role in the 1970s and 1980s. "Synthetic," on the other hand, first appears in the course of the 1980s in connection with computer-generated images—a specific variant of what Flusser called *Technobilder*, technical images.[5] Computer-generated images, similar to electronic music created by synthesizers, compute new worlds from single components. From the dot-like structure of computer screens and the swarms of notes of the synthesizer emerge new visual and acoustic realities. "Synthesis" and "synthetic," thus, articulate two complementary but distinct sides of Flusser's thinking: a modernist striving for a final unity and reconciliation and a postmodern admission of artificiality and ultimate dispersal and failure. Even if the concept of synthesis appears earlier in his work his understanding of the term has a synthetic dimension to it from the very beginning, and conversely his later notion of the synthetic still gestures toward a possible overall convergence.

The modern meaning of synthetic as artificial, opposed to natural, introduces a new essential dimension to Flusser's concept of synthesis, but in a way, only confirms a central tenet of his earlier thinking: all forms of "synthesis" are ultimately "synthetic," that is, projections of meaning, *Sinngebung*, onto the canvas of the world. The digital world reveals something that was there from the start. In this sense, Flusser defines the notion of "digital reality" as a tautology. His notion of the ultimate artificiality of the real is more akin to Slavoj Žižek's than Jean Baudrillard's philosophy.[6] In a conversation with Ulrich Gutmair and Chris Flor on October 7, 1998, Žižek points out that "What was so shocking about virtual space was not that there had been a 'real' reality before it and now only a virtual one. It was only through the experience of virtual reality that we realized, retroactively, that there had never been any 'real reality.' Reality was always virtual; we just did not notice it [translation RG]."[7]

In the 1950s, Flusser uses synthesis in connection with different projects that unite different contradictory discourses and worlds. He connects this synthesizing strategy directly with his own multilingualism and his liminal existential position between the European origin and the new Brazilian environment. A similar vision linking the individual to the collective is developed in the early 1970s in the autobiography *Bodenlos* where Prague is defined as the very origin and model of all future existential and intellectual attempts at synthesis. Prague is a city on a border, a synthesis of three different cultures: Jewish, German, and Czech. Plurality is transformed into wholeness and singularity. Flusser describes this cultural synthesis as a representation of his own identity using the Hegelian notion of *Aufhebung* that results from the interaction of thesis and antithesis. The collective cultural synthesis of Prague has been transcended, sublated, into a synthesis of one's own identity ("in ... der 'eigenen' aufgehoben").[8]

On August 27, 1951, Flusser writes in an unpublished letter to Columbia University, in which he introduces the writing project that was to occupy him for the next years:

> Having spent much time on problems of philosophy, I have been impressed, on the one hand, by the ever widening gap between Continental and Anglo-Saxon philosophy, and on the other hand, by the inability of recent philosophy, to digest the imminent, or even accomplished, downfall of European civilisation. As the establishment of links between Anglo-Saxon and Continental thought seems to me imperative, if the European heritage is not to be lost altogether, and as I have been subject to both influences during my studies in Prague and London, I might possibly be able to contribute something. The eighteenth century seems to be at the same time the climax and the beginning of the decline of European civilisation and I am therefore planning a book on 18th century thought as seen from our present position. . . . The introduction to that book is now ready. It discusses the concept of logic as developped [sic] in England and America, and the concept of history, as developped [sic] in Germany, and tries to bring both concepts into an *organic connection* (emphasis added).

This is also the case with his first full-length book finished in late 1957, which bears the notion of synthesis in the subtitle. *Das Zwanzigste Jahrhundert. Eine subjektive Synthese* (*The Twentieth Century. A Subjective Synthesis*) is among other things an attempt to bring Western and Eastern thinking together, especially modern physics and Buddhism, which share a similar vision of the world. The fusion of science, philosophy, and art also plays a central role in Flusser's vision of an overall code convergence to which I will come back at the end of this chapter. Both Buddhism and modern physics emancipate humanity from a naïve belief in objective reality by revealing the emptiness of the world and the constructedness and artificiality, that is, the synthetic nature of all our visions about it. Thanks to Buddhism, we also recognize that even the alleged innermost core of our being is nothing but a "Nullpunkt."[9] Interestingly enough, Flusser uses the related notion of zero-dimensionality as a point of departure for his later theory of media evolution. In *Vom Subjekt zum Projekt* (*From Subject to Project*), written in the late 1980s, he describes reality and identity as comparable to a swarm of particles, "Partikelschwärme," that possess the same numerical dot-like structure.[10] The anticipatory character of the deconstructive and postmodern tendencies in Flusser's early work ties in with the parallels between Eastern mysticism and modern physics that he described in *Das Zwanzigste Jahrhundert. Eine subjektive Synthese*. In a way, this book anticipates Fritjof Capra's *The Tao of Physics* published nearly twenty years later.

Flusser's attempts at cultural and linguistic synthesis from the 1960s combine the utopian vision of a new hybrid culture on Brazilian ground with the development of a theory of translation that tries to build a bridge between Continental phenomenology and Anglo-Saxon pragmatism in order to reach a new overarching philosophical and linguistic synthesis. In 1967, he reattributed this synthesizing task to the communication theory he was developing at the time. As he argues in an interview, the phenomenon of communication brings formalists and existentialists together.[11]

In *Bildnis des neuen Menschen als Säugling* (*Picture of the New Man as a Baby*) from 1974 to 1975, Flusser described a millenarian rebellion in the state of Santa Catarina that proclaimed the end of history in an apocalyptic vision of generalized brotherhood. This apparent primitivism was an attempt at synthesis, a process of crystallization "welding together completely heterogeneous elements," similar to the creation of the Christian belief in the first centuries of our era.[12] The same conception can be found in *Brasilien oder die Suche nach dem neuen Menschen* (*Brazil or the Search for the New Man*) also written in the early 1970s. In the baroque churches of Ouro Preto "Portuguese, oriental (Chinese and Indian), and Negroid elements have been generating a true synthesis of apparently contradictory elements."[13] The complex linguistic situation in Brazil, which Flusser describes as a trialectic ("Trialektik")— an interaction between three different sociolects: the language spoken in the interior of the country, the proletarian and the bourgeois language of the cities—results in a chaotic centrifugal setup.[14] At the same time, however, this opens up the possibility of a new creative synthesis that may radically transform the weaknesses of the Brazilian language and its partial archaism, thanks to its capacities for assimilation.

The passages discussed so far show that the notion of synthesis is pervasive throughout Flusser's work from the 1950s to the early 1970s. The centering totalizing modernist dimension generally prevails. Flusser speaks of an *organic* form of synthesis, of a *welding together* of disparate apparently contradictory elements, of the *forces of assimilation* that suspend centrifugal dispersive tendencies and use synthesis also in the Hegelian sense of *Aufhebung*. Despite this, even if not always explicitly, the synthetic dimension keeps reappearing between the lines. In the following, I will focus on the work of the 1980s, which is characterized by a shift toward more explicit forms of deconstruction, decentering, and dispersal. The totalizing component does not completely disappear but is redefined and recast in new postmodernist terms. Flusser's overall work, to use his own description of his multiple consecutive self-translation practice, might be described as an expanding spiral,[15] in which new elements are constantly ingested and older components redefined and repositioned. In this sense, modernist and postmodernist components, and points of view, are caught up in a continuous dialogue, inseparably enmeshed in repeated processes of reciprocal translation.

In the last part of this chapter,[16] I would like to discuss the relationship between the terms "synthesis" and "synthetic" in connection with Flusser's idea of a final code convergence. The notion of digitally calculated technical images that he developed in *Into the Universe of Technical Images* (1985) represents another combination of the two notions of synthesis and synthetic and the theoretical stances they imply. This new synthesis is conceived as a synthetic code: "synchronization." In *Towards a Philosophy of Photography* (1983), Flusser develops his first version of a history of media evolution, which is based on three interconnected codes each defining a specific universe: images, texts, and technical images. These three codes are related to each other through processes of translation and re-translation. Synthesis is conceived here as a tripartite form of nesting. The third most recent code contains the two previous ones. Technical images are based on texts and texts, in turn, on images. In *Into the Universe of Technical Images*, Flusser adds two more codes: numbers and sounds. In the chapter "Chamber Music," he uses "to compose" and "to compute" explicitly as synonyms, bringing the world of music, mathematics, and technical images together. "The world of music is a composed universe." It is "calculated and computed as that of technical images."[17] The universe of technical images is a two-dimensional universe of surfaces, but like the musical universe, and contrary to that of traditional images, "it is a pure universe, free of any semantic dimension. . . . Since the beginning of computing, technical images have *rushed spontaneously* to sound, and from sound spontaneously to images, *binding them* (emphasis added)."[18] Flusser does not explain this reciprocal spontaneous tendency of images and sounds to bond and fuse into one another, but defines this inclination as a characteristic of both pretechnical images and pretechnical music. The technical image is "the first instance of music becoming an image and an image becoming music."[19] This seemingly organic synthesizing fusion is not to be understood as a simple juxtaposition of the visual and the acoustic, or as a form of nesting, as with images, texts, and technical images. Flusser intends a complete reciprocal penetration and fusion of the two codes creating something radically new, unheard-of, and unseen so far. This synthetic synchronization is made possible by computing which breaks down sound and sight into small bits and reassembles them again into a new coherent form. As the Persian poet Omar-i-Chajjam, who Flusser quoted on different occasions, puts it: We shatter the existing world into bits to remould it nearer to our heart's desire.[20] Flusser uses the English word "bits" in a double sense: in the general sense of bits and pieces and in the more restricted sense of binary digit, the basic units of information theory. By synthesizing bits, we can recreate the world according to our own wishes and project new composite synthetic realities of a completely new kind.

An example of this new form of synthetic synthesis can be found in the work of the photographer Nancy Burson,[21] who creates photographic chimeras that are not like the traditional ones from Greek mythology. Her pictures are not assembled like a collage, through simple juxtaposition. The mythical chimera was composed of different heterogeneous elements: a lion with the head of a goat and a tail with the head of a snake. If Bellerophon had kicked its backside, the lion's head would have tumbled to the right and the snake tail to the left. This is not possible with Burson's synthetic computed chimeras. Her portraits of politicians—combining Hitler, Stalin, and Mussolini into a single face—and her ironical composite of female beauties—a cocktail mixed out of Audrey Hepburn, Bette Davis, Grace Kelly, Sophia Loren, and Marilyn Monroe—are based on computer programs that work according to a specific algorithm.

In a similar way, neither the concept of the audiovisual nor the existence of electronic intermixers that translate images into sounds or sounds into images correspond to the new level of integration that has become possible with the invention of calculated technical images.

> In a sounding image, the image does not mix with music; rather both are raised to a new level.... Contemporary approaches to making music pictorial and pictures musical have had a long preparation. They can be seen, for example, in so-called abstract painting and in the scores of newer musical compositions.... So-called computer art is moving toward sounding images and visible sound.[22]

As Flusser points out, this trend can be detected in all synthetic images "even those that present themselves as scientific or political documents rather than art."[23] Technical images manage to get rid of the earlier representative character of images and to become pure art, the same way music always was: immaterial and without an object to refer to.

> But only synthesized images are really conceived musically and made musical with visualizing power. It will be pointless to try to distinguish between music and so-called visual arts because everyone will be a composer, will make images.... Once they have both become electronic, visual and acoustic technologies *will no longer be separable* (emphasis added).[24]

In this sense, they are syntheses of a new kind operating on a completely different level.

Flusser ends his description with a reference to German Romanticism. The new code convergence is a collective projection of a world that is completely artificial, an utterly fictitious world, in which to live with complete self-consciousness:

> I think this new aspect can be grasped at its tip in the dreamlike quality of the emerging image world. It is a dream world in which the dreamers seem exceptionally alert... a dream world... that does not lie below waking consciousness but above it, conscious and consciously constructed, a hyperconscious dream world. It will therefore be pointless to try to interpret dreams: they will mean nothing beyond themselves, and they will be tangible—a world of pure art, of play for its own sake. "Ludus imagines"... as ludus tonalis... and the emerging consciousness of the power to imagine as that of homo ludens.[25]

This dreamlike vision of a final synthesis that synchronizes images, texts, technical images, numbers, and sounds is associated with a synthesis of another kind that recalls the synthesis of Buddhism and physics, and that of Continental and Anglo-Saxon philosophy from the early work. In "The Photograph as Post-Industrial Object: An Essay on the Ontological Standing of Photographs," Flusser sums up his idea of an encompassing cultural convergence stemming directly from technological evolution: the meeting and fusion of the natural sciences and the humanities, of art and science, and of imagination and precision. In the following passage, he links this evolution to the work of Leonardo da Vinci and the notion of Gesamtkunstwerk as it appears in the music of Richard Wagner:

> Ever since the fifteenth century, occidental civilization has suffered from the divorce into two cultures: science and its techniques—the "true" and the "good for something"—on the one hand; the arts—beauty—on the other. This is a pernicious distinction. Every scientific proposition and every technical gadget has an aesthetic quality, just as every work of art has an epistemological and political quality. More significantly, there is no basic distinction between scientific and artistic research: *both are fictions in the quest of truth* (scientific hypotheses being fictions). Electromagnetized images do away with this divorce because they are the result of science and are at the service of the imagination. They are what Leonardo da Vinci used to call "fantasia essata." A synthetic image of a fractal equation is both a work of art and a model for knowledge. Thus the new photo not only does away with the traditional classification of the various arts (*it is painting, music, literature, dance and theatre all rolled into one*), but it also does away with the distinction between the "two cultures" (it is *both art and science*). It renders possible a total art Wagner never dreamt of (emphasis added).[26]

Notes

1 Ihab Habib Hassan, "Toward a Concept of Postmodernism," in *The Postmodern Turn: Essays in Postmodern Theory and Culture* (Columbus: Ohio State University Press, 1987), 84–96.

2 Flusser, "Das Heilige im Abgrund zwischen den Wörtern," in *Basler Zeitung*, nr. 230, 3.10.1991, 35.

3 Flusser, Pilpul (2), in *Jude sein. Essays, Briefe, Fiktionen* (Bollman: Mannheim 1995), 143–53.

4 Especially the work of the Czech-Brazilian scholar Eva Batličková, *A época brasileira de Vilém Flusser* (São Paulo: Annablume, 2010) and *Saul de Vilém Flusser. Diálogo e subversão* (São Paulo: Annablume, 2019). See also Rainer Guldin, "Derrida and Flusser: On the Concept of Writing and the End of Linearity, Annual MLA Convention Philadelphia (USA) 27–30 December 2004" (December 27, 2004), https://www.researchgate.net/publication/291294862_Derrida_and_Flusser_On_the_Concept_of_Writing_and_the_End_of_Linearity.

5   See Guldin, "Bilder von Texten: Zur terminologischen Genealogie von Vilém Flussers Technobild," in *Technobilder und Kommunikologie. Die Medientheorie Vilém Flussers*, ed. Oliver Fahle, Michael Hanke, and Andreas Ziemann (Berlin: Parerga, 2009), 141–60.
6   See Rainer Guldin, "Simulakrum und Technobild: Modelle der Gleichzeitigkeit bei Jean Baudrillard und Vilém Flusser," in *Simultaneität. Modelle der Gleichzeitigkeit in den Wissenschaften und Künsten*, ed. Philipp Hubmann and Till Julian Huss (Bielefeld: Transcript, 2013), 335–51.
7   Ulrich Gutmair and Chris Flor, "Hysterie und Cyberspace. Im Gespräch mit Slavoj Zizek," http://www.heise.de/tp/artikel/2/2491/1.html.n.
8   Flusser, *Bodenlos. Eine philosophische Autobiographie* (Bensheim: Bollman, 1992), 77.
9   Flusser, "Das Zwanzigste Jahrhundert. Eine subjektive Synthese," *Flusser Studies* 25 (May 2018): 212, www.flusserstudies.net/sites/www.flusserstudies.net/files/media/attachments/flusser-das-20-jahrhundert.pdf.
10 Flusser, *Vom Subjekt zum Projekt. Menschwerdung* (Bensheim and Düsseldorf: Bollmann, 1994), 10.
11 Flusser, *Zwiegespräche. Interviews 1967-1991* (Göttingen: European Photography 1996), 9.
12 Flusser, "Bildnis des neuen Menschen als Säugling," in *Brasilien oder die Suche nach dem neuen Menschen. Für eine Phänomenologie der Unterdrückung* (Mannheim: Bollmann, 1994), 191.
13 Ibid., 72.
14 Ibid., 149.
15 See also Flusser, "Retradução enquanto metodo de trabalho," *Flusser Studies* 15 (May 2013), http://www.flusserstudies.net/sites/www.flusserstudies.net/files/media/attachments/flusser-retraducao.pdf.
16 This part of the chapter is based on excerpts from an earlier essay: Rainer Guldin, "On the Notion of Code Convergence in Vilém Flusser's Work," http://2013.xcoax.org/pdf/xcoax2013-guldin.pdf.
17 Flusser, *Into the Universe of Technical Images* (Minneapolis and London: University of Minnesota Press, 2011), 164.
18 Ibid., 164–5.
19 Ibid., 165.
20 See, for instance, Vilém Flusser, "Nancy Burson: Chimären," in *Standpunkte, Texte zur Fotografie* (Göttingen: European Photography, 1998), 146.
21 Ibid.
22 Flusser, *Into the Universe of Technical Images*, 165–6.
23 Ibid., 166.
24 Ibid., 165.
25 Ibid., 166.
26 Flusser, "The Photograph as Post-Industrial Object: An Essay on the Ontological Standing of Photographs," *Leonardo* 19 (1986): 331.

Fascism, Iconoclasm, and the Global Village

Guy Stevenson

Like so many post-1960s theorists of media, Vilém Flusser owed a debt to Marshall McLuhan's *The Medium Is the Massage: An Inventory of Effects*. Not long after it was published in 1966, McLuhan's book had become an enormous global sensation, and Flusser made no secret of that text's influence on his thinking. Next to Roland Barthes, he told an interviewer in 1988, McLuhan had been his "most important point of departure."[1] Methodologically, anthropologically, and in terms of style the lineage is plain to see—from their shared provocation to take the image instead of its contents as message to a long historical view of modern man as released wonderfully, precariously, from his linear, text-bound solipsism.

If Flusser's Central European and South American backstory has tended to obscure his links to the Anglo-American intellectual milieu, his similarities and debts to McLuhan have not gone unnoticed.[2] Sloukje van der Meulen, for example, considers Flusser a "European Marshall McLuhan"—someone who brought his training in continental philosophy to bear on the digital-era discoveries of that totemic figure in late twentieth-century media theory.[3] In their *Vilém Flusser: An Introduction*, Anke Finger, Rainer Guldin, and Gustavo Bernardo connect Flusser's attempt "to explain specific historical settings by the predominant way of communication" to McLuhan's before him.[4] And in her recent dissertation on Flusser, Martha Schwendener notes not only the many McLuhan-coined concepts and terms Flusser used (the "medium," "the message," "the box") but their shared cultural-theoretical "interdisciplinary" approach.[5] As such critics have also suggested, however, the two differed in important ways. Informed by post-structuralism and his own multilingualism, Flusser displayed a fluidity of thought and an engagement with "socio-political setting" that were at odds with the older theorist's older-fashioned "formalism."[6] In the pages ahead, I'll consider the implications of these differences between disciple and master, focusing particularly on that political dimension—which is touched on here and there in accounts of Flusser's work but rarely afforded explicit analysis.

My own departure point is Flusser's unlikely proposal—in the same interview in which he paid homage to McLuhan—that there was something "fascistoid" about McLuhan's exhilarating analogy between prehistorical, preliterate man and his posthistorical, postliterate late twentieth-century ancestor.[7] The claim is provocatively, typically counter-intuitive. Besides paving the way for much of Flusser's own politically progressive philosophy, McLuhan had been synonymous in the 1960s with a countercultural movement that posited the new televisual world as a system of collective mind control, in need of resistance. His irreverent, best-selling study *The Gutenberg Galaxy: The Making of the Typographic Man* (1962), which probed the impact of new media and looked ahead to a future of "retribalization," was taken up as a manual by young idealistic North Americans eager to stay hip against the system.

Flusser's improbable reading of McLuhan as fascist-like therefore stands to reveal not only important differences between thinkers often presumed to be kin but something larger about the Cold War period both were analyzing. It allows for a political reading of ambivalences in McLuhan's work that, while troubling to many in his time, have lately become less fashionable to point out, such as his unclear position between optimism and pessimism about the "global village" produced by digital technology, and his detached, often amused feint-and-dodge approach to the masses of people in shock at digital technology's new ability to reconnect the world. That McLuhan's ideas on media were shaped by elitist and in fact fascist-sympathizing high moderns like Ezra Pound and Wyndham Lewis, and Flusser's were shaped by leftist continental philosophies (but also the notoriously Nazi-sympathizing Martin Heidegger), puts the worry about "fascistoid" undertones into a longer intellectual-historical context.

Flusser's facility with German, Czech, Portuguese, French, and English led him to take great care over etymology—always grounding his analysis of media terms in their specific linguistic origins. It may be significant then that he called McLuhan fascist*oid* rather than fascistic or plain fascist. Like the android to the human, he suggests, here was a way of thinking other to fascism, but resembling it in strange, unsettling, and advanced form. Flusser shared McLuhan's mixture of excitement and trepidation at the return of the image to the center of human experience. Both believed that the invention of photography in the nineteenth century had been the first step toward a way of seeing and engaging with a world that pre-dated writing. For Flusser as for McLuhan, this ontological shift was enormously disruptive *and* liberating—it represented a painful but productive wrench out of the "visual world of lineal organization" and historical consciousness and toward a posthistorical, tribal existence of image, myth, and the aural.[8] It also represented the liberation of the image—of icons, in fact—after millennia of subservience to the written word. What Flusser intuited in McLuhan was that this celebrated celebrator of the technical image—scourge, as John Barth put it, of "print-oriented bastards" everywhere—was inveterately opposed to it.[9]

Evidence for this lies first in McLuhan's background as a scholar of modernist literature—his Ezra Pound and Wyndham Lewis-like tendency to ape simultaneity in the modern experience while disdaining its mass cultural sources and recipients. Rather than the idolater he claimed to be—a revolutionary acceptor of digital images in a world too timorous to lay down its books—he was in fact as old-fashioned in his inclinations as the mainstream he criticized and as eager by extension to re-intern those images on the margins. More evidence—and what Flusser probably means when he refers to McLuhan as a "technological determinist"—is his pronounced lack of concern at the abuse or misuse of icons in mass culture.[10] Where Flusser worried about "a return to 'cult' and 'magic' in a posthistorical guise" and the "reversal of [the] 'image-reality' relationship, which caused people to live in the function of images," McLuhan described but drew no moral conclusions about the "tribal drum" beaten by public broadcasting companies to summon people en masse to the televisual fireside.[11] Like Heidegger, whom Flusser admired despite his Nazism, McLuhan felt little ire at modern man's immersion within his technological environment—coding it simply as the latest stage in eighty thousand years' of Homo sapiens' relations with media.

Flusser's own writing is full of McLuhan-like, perhaps McLuhan-learnt paradoxes, but he interpreted this deadpan apolitical attitude as dangerous. As van der Meulen points out, in 1973 he wrote to his friend and fellow theorist René Berger to suggest a new "communication theory of media against McLuhan," from "the point of view of the (phenomenologically conscious) receiver."[12] Like McLuhan, Flusser trod a line between warning of the damage new media could cause and celebrating its humanistic potential. Unlike McLuhan, however, Flusser behaved as if humans—and theorists—had the power to make some sort of active difference. By extension, while Flusser borrowed elements of McLuhan's showmanship, his enigmatic anti-academic pizzazz, and his provocative play with words and concepts, he stopped short always of goading or poking fun at his readers.

This difference between their styles reflects a larger geographical and temporal departure. Flusser's comments on media come out of a knowing European avant-garde tradition going back to Walter Benjamin, whereas McLuhan sits somewhere between the arch skepticism of the modernists he read as a doctoral student at Cambridge and the consciously naïve, outrageous countercultural scene he entered onto in 1950s America. Where Flusser followed Benjamin and the Frankfurt School by identifying systems of control behind an increasingly technical, automated world, McLuhan echoed Wyndham Lewis's justification for indifference to questions of politics and morality: that it was absurd to pass personal judgment on anything as pervasive and inevitable as media. Flusser's response to that side of McLuhan was a more sensitive and much better-informed version of the common criticism leveled at *The Gutenberg Galaxy* when it was first published: that amoral objectivity was a disingenuous excuse for fatalism. Faced with bewildering technological change, it wasn't enough to point out how television was altering thought, perspective, and behavior; some effort needed to be put into considering—and countering—its qualitative psychological, political, and social impact.

Their different political backgrounds go some way to explaining why Flusser's work seems concerned where McLuhan's is lackadaisical about the quality of the information technical images end up transmitting. Rather than "fascistoid," we might be better off thinking about the reactionary implications of McLuhan's media theory in light of a politics about which he was clear—that of traditional, pragmatic conservatism. Responding to accusations from Norman Mailer during a televised debate, first that he took "a great, kindly pleasure in outlining the lineaments of this [appalling] electronic world" then that "in all of McLuhanland you never find the words good and bad," McLuhan calmly, and in his best schoolmaster's voice, quoted Edmund Burke back at him. Recalling Burke's response to the French Revolution, he told Mailer "I do not know how to draw up an indictment against a whole people."[13] In other words, facts—and particularly facts on the scale of the evolution of human technology—can be observed but not altered, no matter how upset the observer might be about them. Crucially, he did find hope—a glimmer of it if you go by his published writings and a great blinding shaft if you look deeper at his private correspondence—by way of yet another perverse analogy. A convert to Catholicism in his twenties, McLuhan believed quite seriously that the corporate human community television was creating would replicate Christ's vision of a brotherhood of man united through his body. As Michael Darroch and Martha Schwendener have pointed out, his faith extended to an early optimism about computer code as the universalizing answer to a linguistically, culturally divided world—the harbinger of a "Pentecostal condition of universal understanding and unity."[14]

McLuhan might have been defensive against the messaging of televisual and advertising industries, but he also trusted digital media itself as a God-given and ultimately unifying development. If he understood that the "global village" would be cruel and violent (saying often that "there is no one more cruel than the villager"), his delusion—rumbled by Flusser—lay in believing it would uphold a rough and self-regulating, pastoral civic order. Humanity's digital future, Flusser wrote in his *Kosmologi*, would indeed be marked by the proliferation of "cosmic" connections McLuhan had prophesied, but it would look more like an anarchical "circus" than a rule-observant "village."[15]

Flusser was also partial to a religious parable—in his first book, *A historia do diabo* (1965, first written in German as *Die Geschichte des Teufels* in the late 1950s), he compared humanity's fall under the spell of the written word to Adam and Eve's under the Serpent's. But his prelapsarianism left less to fate—or indeed *to God*—than McLuhan's. Like his forebear he used provocative words to encourage new ways of thinking but was tempered by both a duty of political care toward his readers and a healthy skepticism about the new configuration of order this posthistorical, post-ideological age was about to usher in. The circus Flusser envisioned was directed by genuine and sinister "ampitheatrical senders," whose manipulative messaging it was not enough to simply decode.

In Flusser's uneasiness about McLuhan—a man whose thinking and style had made his own possible—and in their very different responses to potential problems with the digital worlds they were critiquing, we get a sense of the older man's dereliction of that same political duty. Finally, tentatively, the ambivalence between amoralism and utopianism in McLuhan's approach might also provide clues as to an equivalent irresponsibility in the 1960s counterculture that took him to heart, and whose attitude toward technology and the masses he helped to mold.

Notes

1 Flusser, "1988 Interview about Technical Revolution (Intellectual Level Is Lowering)," accessed February 23, 2018, https://www.youtube.com/watch?v=lyfOcAAcoH8.

2. The collections I refer to are a special issue of the online journal flusserstudies.net (*Flusser Studies* 06 (2008), http://www.flusserstudies.net/archive/flusser-studies-06-may-2008) and *Marshall McLuhan and Vilém Flusser's Communication + Aesthetic Theories Revisited*, ed. Tom Kohut and Melentie Padilovski (Winnipeg: Video Pool Press, 2015).
3. Sloukje van der Meulen, "Between Benjamin and McLuhan: Vilém Flusser's Media Theory," *New German Critique* 110 (Summer 2010): 180–207, 197.
4. Anke Finger, Rainer Guldin, and Gustavo Bernardo, *Vilém Flusser: An Introduction*. (Minneapolis: University of Minnesota Press, 2011), 89.
5. Martha Schwendener, "The Photographic Universe: Vilém Flusser's Theories of Photography, Media, and Digital Culture" (Ph.D. thesis, City University of New York, 2016), 96.
6. Ibid., 237.
7. Flusser, "On Writing, Complexity and the Technical Revolutions: Interview in Osnabrück," September 1988. European Media Arts Festival, Osnabrück, Germany. https://www.youtube.com/watch?v=lyfOcAAcoH8.
8. Marshall McLuhan, *Understanding Media: The Extensions of Man* (Cambridge, MA: MIT Press, 1994 [1964]), 83.
9. John Barth, "The Literature of Exhaustion," in *Postmodernism and the Contemporary Novel: A Reader*, ed. Bran Nicol (Edinburgh: Edinburgh University Press, 2002 [1967]), 38–47, 144.
10. Flusser, quoted in Finger, Guldin, and Bernardo, *Vilém Flusser*, 96.
11. Flusser, quoted in van der Meulen, "Between Benjamin and McLuhan," 195.
12. Ibid., 186.
13. "Marshall McLuhan and Norman Mailer Go Head to Head," *The Summer Way* (Toronto: CBC, 1968), https://www.cbc.ca/player/play/1809372202.
14. Schwendener, "The Photographic Universe," 236–7.
15. Flusser, *Komunikologie*, quoted in Finger, Guldin, and Bernardo, *Vilém Flusser*, 100.

23

The Future of Writing

David Golumbia

Vilém Flusser belongs to a small group of thinkers whose ambition and range recall those of polymaths of earlier ages. He shares with those thinkers a sweeping historical vision that refuses to take for granted the nature of historical evidence itself, so that the means by which history is represented becomes one of Flusser's chief concerns. With the thinkers he most resembles—especially Marshall McLuhan, Harold Innis, and Walter Ong—Flusser shares a strong inclination toward epochal pronouncements, an attention to the specificities of media forms and to their centrality in determining the foundations on which all history and even chronology rests, and a profound interest in not just the past but the present and future.

Of the four, Flusser is by far the most interested in and aware of the details of the advent of digital media. Though his focus in this regard most resembles McLuhan's, Flusser offers far more detailed thoughts than does McLuhan about how the affordances of a wide range of specific digital (and other new) media affect perception and communication. *Into the Universe of Technical Images* (1985) is especially noteworthy in this regard, and in many ways the work of Flusser's that I find the most useful, because it draws attention to a whole range of phenomena that are inarguably media but have rarely ever been considered in that mode. Further, the technical images Flusser points to are not supplementary or occasional, but in many ways they are core parts of everyday contemporary perception and action, often more so than other media to which scholars pay almost undivided attention.

Flusser's writings on language too are valuable because they reflect so much on the ways in which digital technology is changing and will change linguistic practice. His reflections are all the more remarkable given how early in the digital revolution he realized what these changes might be. Flusser's argument about the relationship between writing and futurity has two primary aspects. First, he worries that written language will in some fundamental way disappear, perhaps in favor of video and audio: "the alphabet will be abandoned as an ineffective code and society will be informed (benumbed) exclusively by programmed images with sound."[1] Second, he argues that writing has a specific relationship with chronology, determining both the past and the future, and that the disappearance of writing per se, or of some relevant parts of it, means that we will lose access to history as writing gets supplanted by other forms of communication: "Writing consciousness should be referred to as *historical consciousness*."[2]

In both cases, Flusser's background assumptions make these theses a little hard to parse. By "written language" Flusser does not mean the existing and well-known range of written languages but *exclusively* languages that are expressed in alphabets. Indeed, Flusser explicitly rejects as "writing" what he calls ideographic or pictographic scripts like those in which Chinese and Japanese are written, but he rarely goes into any more detail about how these scripts work. He does not mention other categories of script, such as syllabaries, that are not typically understood as either ideographic or alphabetic.[3] Flusser's insistence that only the West has alphabetic scripts and that therefore only the West has writing ("Letters are fascinating because they are symbols for the initiation into the history of the West")[4] and consequently only the West has history is one of the more troubling features of his work: "The alphabet is a clear rejection of ideographic writing. Despite all the ideogram's advantages, writing was to be in letters."[5]

Flusser rarely attempts to specify what he means by "letter," by "ideograph," or by "alphabet." These might seem obvious matters to nonspecialists, but to linguists they are anything but. Contrary to what Flusser seems to assume, specialists have long determined that the boundaries between "alphabetic" and "ideographic" writing are far from clear, and that, speaking only of contemporary scripts, the alphabetic script in which English is written has many "ideographic" characteristics, and the scripts in which Chinese and Japanese are written have many of the characteristics associated with alphabets, especially the correspondences between symbol and sound which Flusser considers central. Indeed, one of the most famous lines of research on ideographs in contemporary scholarship comes from the Sinologist John DeFrancis, who has long argued that "Chinese characters are a phonetic, not an ideographic, system of writing," and that perhaps even more surprisingly, "there never has been, and never can be, such a thing as an ideographic system of writing."[6] DeFrancis expands on this argument in a later book, *Visible Speech* (1989). While these arguments remain controversial, most linguists accept their general outlines: thus, the most authoritative scholar on world writing systems, Florian Coulmas writes that "Chinese characters are very inadequately described as ideographs, if this notion means that the written symbol refers to an idea rather than to a linguistic unit. In modern treatments of Chinese writing the notion of ideography is therefore often avoided."[7] Further, as DeFrancis among many others has noted, Western ideas about ideograms often express cultural prejudice about China that date back at least to Leibniz: "a sort of Exotic East Syndrome characterized by the belief that in the Orient things strange and mysterious replace the mundane truths applicable to the West."[8]

Flusser's argument about the future of alphabetic writing therefore must be tempered with a more grounded and less parochial notion of what writing itself is. Even if all writing systems are not functionally equivalent, they are more alike than different. Further, if we turn to another influential theorist of writing, Jacques Derrida, we find an argument according to which "writing" itself cannot be effectively isolated from language per se. In his best-known series of works including *Of Grammatology* and *Writing and Difference*, Derrida develops the notion of *arché-writing*, according to which all language, indeed all cognition, requires an activity that resembles the physical practice we call writing, and all or most forms of physical writing in a more or less metaphorical sense embody this fundamental linguistic practice.[9] Derrida's expanded view of writing and language is arguably compatible with the radically expanded view of language developed by the philosopher Charles Taylor, who describes language itself as "making possible new purposes, new levels of behavior, new meanings, and hence as not explicable within a framework picture of human life conceived without language," functions about which Flusser has little to say.[10]

With this in mind, the second aspect of Flusser's thinking about the relationship between writing and futurity deserves careful consideration. Flusser argues that history itself is only possible in the regime of alphabetic scripts; even if we push aside some of the Eurocentrism of this thesis, it is harder to gainsay the idea that writing plays a crucial role in history and historical consciousness; indeed, the word "prehistory" is commonly used to mean something like "before history could be written down." If we follow Derrida, we are going to reject the idea of human society without writing as incoherent, attributing the idea of historical consciousness less to writing per se than to the medium in which history is written down, a factor to which Innis (1951) is also particularly attuned. While writing in many forms does not merely persist but seems to proliferate in digital technology, the media in which it is stored and accessed have changed rapidly and in multifarious ways, with consequences for both language and history.

A remarkable number of forms of writing, broadly construed, have emerged since Flusser developed his arguments. He was certainly prescient in noting the emerging pervasiveness of video and audio media; indeed, among the most suggestive parts of Flusser's work are those where he seems to have grasped what platforms like YouTube would look like, decades before any such platform existed. "The newspaper will disappear as soon as video- and audiotapes and records from electromagnetic senders flow, cheap and plentiful (perhaps free), into all homes to be stored in video and audio libraries," Flusser suggested, and while we could debate for a long time about what "newspapers" are, what Flusser meant by them, the extent to which something like newspapers persist today, and their resemblance or lack of resemblance to the newspapers of earlier times (while noting that they were also not static media forms, nor uniform across geographies), it would be impossible to argue against Flusser's comments about audiovisual media.[11] We are, in fact, flooded by audiovisual media, and there is much to be said about the relationship between YouTube videos and podcasts, to take two notable examples, and "writing" tout court. Flusser seems not to observe that many forms of audio and audiovisual media are themselves not just abstractly written in a Derridean sense but literally written, in the sense of being scripted beforehand. Many YouTube videos are unscripted, but many are scripted, and many exist in between these two poles. Further, all of these modes, if not the particular media that embody them, existed in robust form while Flusser wrote: thus in our time as well as his, the relationship between writing and audiovisual media is more complex than some of his theoretical pronouncements would suggest.

Nevertheless, some forms of what it seems fair to call "writing" have emerged since Flusser wrote that neither Flusser nor any other theorist I am familiar with predicted. Each of them combines some functions of written language with some functions of imagery; each of them raises questions about the nature of linguistic precision and the correspondences between written form and spoken language. Two in particular appear at this point to have widespread influence: *emoji* and *memes*.

Emoji seem unanticipated in Flusser's theory. Emoji are largely imagistic in nature, yet it would be inaccurate to think of them as asemic or as registering meaning identically to the way visual images that have been more fully theorized work.[12] At first, it seems plausible to claim that emoji function as something like the long-sought after "universal" language, not unlike the Orientalist way in which Leibniz famously characterized Chinese writing: each emoji corresponds to one and exactly one idea. Yet even brief reflection shows that the situation is far more complicated. The simple smiling face represented in ASCII as :) and in emoji as ☺ may well be understood as a cross-linguistic mark indicating "smile," and it is no doubt the case that most texting systems that provide the service offer to seamlessly substitute the ☺ emoji for the local equivalent of the word "smile." Yet even in this simple example, it is apparent that the ☺ emoji and the word "smile" are not at all equivalent. The ☺ emoji would seem to have a greater range of uses in practice than does the *word* "smile," and in many cases its exact meaning is neither clear nor required to be clear. The more complex the emoji, the more polyvocal its semantics appear to be—thus the same assumption made about apparently ideographic writing systems applies in a surprisingly parallel way to emoji. Writing about the "poop" emoji, Jonathan Abel notes that we are easily tempted by the idea that it too has a single meaning:

> The idea presupposes that a picture is self-evident, in a one-to-one correspondence, with what it represents. At least some degree of fidelity is hence taken as given, even as certain details are left out or local flair, color, or cuteness is added. Following this assumption, rebus-like communication could not rise to the level of complex literary forms. Emoji, one could assume, would "dumb down" language and its nuances. And yet, at the moment when a policeman is presented as equivalent to a "pile of poo," we have the most basic and necessary component of a literary language: a metaphor.[13]

However, it is also fair to say that emoji do realize one of the principles that Flusser is most concerned with: the absence of a phonetic system. Unlike the putatively ideographic system of Chinese writing, it is at this point impossible to argue that there is a linguistically salient phonetic component to emoji. Whatever 👀 might *mean*, it serves as a kind of placeholder for the English term "eyes," the French term "les yeux," the Hindi "आंखें," and the Telugu "కళ్ళు," just to pick some ready examples using Google Translate. It can fairly be suggested that few universal cross-linguistic scripts of this sort have ever before existed, let alone been put into wide use. Yet nothing in 👀 tells us anything about how to pronounce it: the fact that it points to different words in English, French, Hindi, and Telugu proves this beyond doubt.

Thus although emoji do not exist in a one-to-one correspondence with specific *ideas*, it is also clear that emoji are not an alphabetic script of the sort to which Flusser attaches the name *writing* (perhaps, as we have seen, to the detriment of his theory). Because of their loose correspondence to spoken language, they can't be used, at least not easily, to compose phrases and sentences of much complexity, at least not of the sort we experience routinely in spoken and written language. Though it is true that there are many popular practices involving the use of many emoji combined in many different ways, there does not seem so far to be evidence of the kinds of regular combinatorial syntax emerging that would in ordinary terms be referred to as a "new language," and it seems likely that detailed investigation of complex multi-emoji expressions would be unlikely to reveal regular syntactic patterns independent of the spoken and written languages used by the emoji writers.

Even if emoji are not writing per se, it is still hard to register them as entirely imagistic either.[14] After all what is usually taken as their primary usage specifically involves their function within written languages, even if those functions may be supplemental. Once computers were able to process written text (vs the mathematical and symbolic input and output modes of the earliest machines), it became possible to leave typewritten script messages for other users, but with informational content that would have typically been expressed verbally. Emoji could be used to add emotive inflection to written messages that could tell readers something about the tone in which the message was meant.[15] Written language in this sense, and perhaps unlike the affordances of longer-form written communication such as personal letters and even memos, apparently lacks features of spoken language that help us to generate charity (in the Gricean sense) and mutual understanding; the "winking face" and the "smiling face" tended to soften messages that might in the absence of context be interpreted as hostile or otherwise challenging.[16]

In this sense, whether or not it would be right to call emoji a writing system of their own, it is the case that emoji have played a critical role in not just the survival but the dissemination of writing across many different technologies and practices; it is hard to read Flusser as anticipating the remarkable proliferation of texting technologies, let alone that they would become one of the leading modes of usage for digital devices.[17] While in the abstract the meaning of emoji may be ambiguous, in situ their meanings are often far clearer, offering a variety of affective shadings to text that may otherwise lack clear emotional cues, although still remaining less exact than written language per se.[18] In this sense it would seem that even though emoji may point away from writing continuing in its alphabetic form, in other ways emoji allow alphabetic text to persist and even expand its range of uses.[19]

If their standardization by the Unicode Consortium suggests at least one way in which emoji might be viewed as a form of writing, memes display no such systematicity.[20] Memes are by definition visual; a great deal of their power stems from their visual components, and in general their visual features persist more regularly as memes spread than do their written ones, although there is more to say about this. Does the proliferation of memes provide evidence for Flusser's contention that "the alphabet will be abandoned as an ineffective code and society will be informed (benumbed) exclusively by programmed images with sound"?[21]

Like emoji, memes seem to suggest both forms of writing that Flusser did not anticipate and to offer at least gentle counterarguments to his strongest arguments. Perhaps in line with the proliferation of comments on "pure" images, moving and still, in social media, memes suggest that we are less prepared to abandon writing than Flusser thought. But Flusser's contention compels us to ask: Why is writing important to memes? Which functions of writing persist in memes, and which have been supplanted or supplemented?

Limor Shifman, in the most comprehensive work on memes to date, comments on the visual component of memes:

> digital memes are much more visual than their predecessors. This has two main implications. First, visual display allows greater integration between politics and pop culture. While it may take some ingenuity to invent a verbal joke in which Barack Obama meets Luke Skywalker, it is easy to Photoshop the president's head on a Jedi's body. A second implication of the visual nature of Internet memes relates to their polysemic potential—that is, their tendency to be open to multiple readings. Whereas in verbal jokes the target of mockery and its scorned feature are often clear, visual images' openness and lack of a clear narrative may invoke contrasting interpretations.[22]

"Polysemic" seems the wrong word to capture this aspect of the visual component of memes; indeed, the word "polysemy" is used canonically to point at the fact that language itself is already subject to such multiplicity of meaning that it threatens (or offers) to explode beyond comprehension, something Derrida frequently discusses.

Rather than polysemy, the quality Shifman points at seems to entail the simultaneous or near-simultaneous juxtaposition of multiple elements, a feature of visual culture familiar to art historians and others who study visual media. Even though the viewer cannot help but perceive the visual object in somewhat ordered fashion—moving from one part of the object to another—the viewer can also perceive aspects of the object in toto, in a way that it is difficult (but not impossible) to attribute to the visual processing of writing. It would be tempting to suggest that the chronological ordering of speech provides a sharp contrast with this kind of simultaneous processing, and this may in large part be correct, but it is one of the fascinating features of sign languages that they incorporate so-called simultaneous grammar that takes advantage of the way visual processing can take in several elements at once.[23]

This leads to one aspect of memes that seems distinct from emoji. While there is certainly not (or not yet) a clearly identifiable grammar of memes, it does seem plausible that individual memes include a series of steps or steplike elements that produce something like a grammatical construction. For example, in the famous "distracted boyfriend" meme, three major elements coexist: the woman on the right tagged with an "old" idea; her distracted boyfriend in the center, not looking at her, but instead at the woman on the viewer's left, wearing a red dress (Figure 23.1). In order to understand the meme, the viewer has to understand the sequence-like arrangement of elements; once she does, the meme forms a kind of template not unlike what scholars of

Figure 23.1 Distracted boyfriend meme example by Reddit user dankiger. Source: Hathaway 2017.

grammar call "constructions," or grammatical forms that provide additional meaning to words and phrases based on their arrangement.[24] The construction for this meme might be articulated along these lines:

[subj] ignores [old idea] because [subj] is distracted by [new idea]

This far exceeds the somewhat limited rebus-like combinatorics of emoji and suggests further ways in which writing that is fundamentally image-based can also take up features more usually associated with spoken language. Whether this kind of memetic grammar might be useful for historical knowledge seems less clear.

Given these new developments in writing, in addition to others not covered here, Flusser's basic questions remain serious ones without obvious answers. Even if we reject the idea that history can only be conveyed and preserved in phonetic writing or that phonetic writing, in so far as it is a coherent concept, is in decline thanks to digital media, it is clearly the case that writing in toto is experiencing remarkable changes thanks to digital technology, and that these changes involve movements toward phatic and image-based forms that are frequently even less exact in their implied meanings than are the vast majority of representations found in lexical writing systems. Further, it is very clear for reasons unrelated to language use in particular that historical consciousness has come under significant attack in recent years, in no small part due to at least some of the affordances of digital technology in general and specific digital platforms in particular. From Twitter to Facebook to Reddit, feeds oriented toward "most recent" and "most popular" tend to swamp attempts to comprehend the past in the more linear fashion Flusser describes; the much-touted "eternal September" of digital media is itself an artifact of the tremendous orientation toward the immediate and coordinate hostility toward the past that seem to saturate digital platforms. Despite the important ways in which digital media seem to make it impossible to forget, they seem to exert an opposing pressure to forget everything, to live in a very much front-brained, highly affective present that makes cooler reason about anything, but especially the past and future, difficult to exercise.[25] This "always on" characteristic of digital technologies seems directly correlated with the rise of fascistic and proto-fascistic politics across the world, for all such politics must exert pressure against contact with real experience, especially contact that has the ring of authority. It seems no accident at all that in the age when more "information" is available to the people of the world than ever before, by several orders of magnitude, it is also the case that the greatest crisis of our contact with reality occurs. Surely if it were true that freely available information creates a populace more responsive to material facts, we would not be watching a majority of politicians and citizens denying in various ways the implications of anthropogenic climate change.

Viewed in another way, our comprehension of anthropogenic climate change is itself partly a matter of writing and futurity. Scientists construct models that predict the future, largely in probabilistic terms, and largely with quantitative methods. For those of us trained in the sciences and the logical thinking methods that underlie them, these numerical methods of writing the future are largely convincing. To others, less versed in or less committed to the connections between such quantitative methods and the material world, these assertions may have a character of mythical thinking. They may appear as little more than assertions of authority by distant masters that include with them an inherent condescension toward those who do not consider themselves competent in such methods, and as such produce a psychological backlash in which a contrary authority is asserted, one that asserts the primacy of a qualitative, narrative form of consciousness over one determined by a commitment to number and purely logical rationality.

In this sense it is hard not to wonder whether we should also be asking Flusser's questions about writing and futurity in inverted form. Could it be the case not that writing is diminishing in the face of digital technology, but instead that its power and influence are expanding? Might it be that however we define it, "writing," and therefore "language," especially in Taylor's sense, has many different forms and functions, and that some of these are being exaggerated while others are being diminished in our media environment? Might it be the case that some of the most fundamental forms of writing—those particularly important to a thinker like Derrida, those that he argued were present in all cultures and all histories—retain their strong connections to power, and that they themselves trouble historical consciousness as much as they enable it? Might the problem be that some writing does very much have a future, but that this future mitigates against the collective future of humanity? While this despairing question, depending on the angle of view, appears to be both similar to and different from the ones Flusser asked, it does suggest a different way of addressing the worry: Might we need to work harder on discriminating among various kinds of writing, functions of writing, and to think harder about how humanness itself is predicated on some of them, and how certain forms of technological thinking, ones overly committed not to number but to the stories humans tell themselves about number, might inevitably produce other forms of writing as resistance—a resistance that politics need learn not to dismiss, but instead to recognize as an other of quantitative writing that the polis can afford neither to scapegoat nor to quarantine? If writing in this more Derridean sense is something like "the human thing," it surely is the case that the human future becomes unthinkable without coming much more fully to grips with its nature, its functions, its resistances, its historicity, and its futurity.

Notes

1 Flusser, *Does Writing Have a Future?* (Minneapolis: University of Minnesota Press, 2011), 42.
2 Ibid., 7, italics in original.
3 See Florian Coulmas, *The Blackwell Encyclopedia of Writing Systems* (Malden and Oxford: Blackwell Publishing, 1996) and *Writing Systems: An Introduction to Their Linguistic Analysis* (New York: Cambridge University Press, 2002), and Steven Roger Fischer, *A History of Writing* (London: Reaktion Books, 2001).
4 Flusser, *Into Immaterial Culture* (São Paulo: Metaflux, 2015), 16.
5 Flusser, *Does Writing Have a Future?*, 30.
6 John DeFrancis, *Visible Speech: The Diverse Oneness of Writing Systems* (Honolulu: University of Hawai'i Press, 1989), 133.
7 Ibid., 82.
8 DeFrancis, *The Chinese Language: Fact and Fantasy* (Honolulu: University of Hawai'i Press), 37.
9 Jacques Derrida, *Of Grammatology* (Baltimore and London: Johns Hopkins University Press, 1976) and *Writing and Difference* (Chicago: University of Chicago Press, 1978).
10 Charles Taylor, *The Language Animal: The Full Shape of the Human Linguistic Capacity* (Cambridge, MA: Harvard University Press, 2016), 4.
11 Flusser, *Does Writing Have a Future?*, 116.
12 Here I use "emoji" as a generic term for what are variously referred to in scholarship as emoticons, *kaomoji*, and emoji; for more on the history of these forms and the distinctions among them, see Marcel Danesi, *The Semiotics of Emoji: The Rise of Visual Language in the Age of the Internet* (London and New York: Bloomsbury, 2017), and Elena Giannoulis and Lukas R. A. Wilde, eds., *Emoticons, Kaomoji, and Emoji: The Transformation of Communication in the Digital Age* (New York: Routledge, 2020).
13 Jonathan E. Abel, "Not Everyone's: Or, the Question of Emoji as 'Universal' Expression," in *Emoticons, Kaomoji, and Emoji*, ed. Giannoulis and Wilde, 35–6.
14 See Lukas R. A. Wilde, "The Elephant in the Room of Emoji Research: Or, Pictoriality, to What Extent?" in *Emoticons, Kaomoji, and Emoji*, ed. Giannoulis and Wilde, 171–96.
15 See Luke Stark and Kate Crawford, "The Conservatism of Emoji: Work, Affect, and Communication," *Social Media + Society* 1, no. 2 (July 2015), https://journals.sagepub.com/doi/10.1177/2056305115604853.

16 In addition to Stark and Crawford, see David Crystal, *Txting: The Gr8 Db8* (New York: Oxford University Press, 2008).
17 Crystal, *Txting*.
18 See Hannah Miller et al., "'Blissfully Happy' or 'Ready to Fight': Varying Interpretations of Emoji." Association for the Advancement of Artificial Intelligence (2016), https://grouplens.org/site-content/uploads/Emoji_Interpretation_Paper.pdf.
19 See Crystal, *Txting*, and his *Language and the Internet* (New York: Cambridge University Press, 2006).
20 See Giannoulis and Wilde, *Emoticons, Kaomoji, and Emoji*.
21 Flusser, *Does Writing Have a Future?*, 42.
22 Limor Shifman, *Memes in Digital Culture* (Cambridge, MA: The MIT Press, 2014), 150.
23 Mark Aronoff, Irit Meir, and Wendy Sandler, "The Paradox of Sign Language Morphology," *Language* 81, no. 2 (2005): 301–44.
24 William Croft, *Radical Construction Grammar: Syntactic Theory in Typological Perspective* (New York: Oxford University Press, 2001).
25 See Kate Eichhorn, *The End of Forgetting: Growing Up with Social Media* (Cambridge, MA: Harvard University Press, 2019) and Viktor Mayer-Schönberger, *Delete: The Virtue of Forgetting in the Digital Age* (Princeton: Princeton University Press, 2011).

Vilém Flusser's Linguistic Briefcase

Tatjana Soldat-Jaffe

> [...] The structure of the external world is precisely the structure of our intellect, and the structure of our intellect is the structure of our languages.
> —Vilém Flusser, *Philosophy of Language*[1]

In an essay about "Essays" in 1967, Vilém Flusser ponders the difference between the nature of a treatise and an essay. He reaches the conclusion that the former are written in "an academic style," whereas the latter are written in "a subjective one":

> [in] a treatise, I will think about my subject and I will discuss it with my others. In an essay, I will live my subject and I will have a dialogue with my others. [...] In the treatise, I do not take on myself, I take on the topic for my others. In the essay, I submerge myself in the topic and in my others. [...] In the essay, I and my others are the topic within the topic. [...] It is a dialectical risk: that of losing myself in the topic, and that of losing the topic.[2]

More pointedly, Flusser narrows down these elaborated different approaches of writing as he argues that the aspect of translatability requires the essay. He expounds on the point:

> [...] I choose the essay. The problem of translation and translatability takes the cosmic dimensions of all existential issues: it encompasses everything. For example, it encompasses the problem of knowing, which is an aspect of translatability. It includes value, which can be considered an aspect of the validity of the translated sentences. It encompasses the problem of meaning and of the absurd, part of the limits of translatabiltity. In sum: I begin to lose my topic by having identified myself with it. And I simultaneously begin to lose myself in it because I start to identify with its different aspects. For example, I find that I myself am a translation problem, that is, a multiplicity of systems to be translated among themselves into a metasystem.[3]

Flusser's distinction between these two notions of compositional techniques explains his logic and reasoning; his writing and thinking are fundamentally determined by experience. The fact that Flusser prefers the essay over the treatise on translatability indicates that language is intrinsically connected to the correlation between oneself and the unfamiliar. This factor remains a recurring theme in the debate about translation and translatability as scholars question to what extent the target text can and must deviate from the source text with respect to the particular cultures in which they are respectively embedded. But the question goes deeper for Flusser: Is translation merely a transaction or a process? And a process to what end? While we are more familiar with the first question, the second question was new of a kind. Taking aside Walter Benjamin's work in "The Task of the Translator" (1921) and Roman Jakobson's in "On Translation" (1959), most scholars who have had an impact on translation studies entered this very same conversation at least twenty years later: Jacques Derrida's "Des Tours de Babel" (1985), Umberto Eco's *Experiences in Translation* (2001), along with other theorists such as Emily Apter, Sandra Berman, or Lawrence Venuti.

Reflecting on Flusser's approach to language, one would perhaps hesitate to call him a linguist because he appears to resist language as an object of scientific study: he is not interested in how language influences social life, what the relationship between language and society is, or to what extent language is a system of interconnected units; to quote him, "the narrower concepts of language are forced and artificial."[4] Instead, as a phenomenologist, Flusser investigates how language experiences the world. Rather than calling him a traditional linguist or a traditional language philosopher, he is a *philosopher of communication* with its premise that communication is its own affirmation in and through its language use to investigate and reflect raw data. Anke Finger, Rainer Guldin, and Gustavo Bernardo claim that for Flusser reality is "raw data" that materializes through the senses. This raw data only becomes real within the context of language. However, as languages are plural and differ in their structure, the realities created by them also vary.[5] Flusser narrows down his approach to raw data by the types of languages—that is, "the worlds within which the human intellect lives." The three kinds of worlds are fusional, agglutinative, and isolating languages. As the raw data needs to be cognized through language, and language is not a fixed variable but an experience, the method needs to be beyond any language-centered approaches. As such, communication takes place and does so continually; it must continue to demonstrate how to engage with the raw data. He states that we need to understand that "our view of language in all its plenitude [. . .] is to regain a naivety in the face of language, a naivety lost in the course of the history of thought."[6] Language has to be experienced as we are supposed to "approach language without such knowledge." Translation, then, for Flusser, is a theory of knowledge as it represents a means to investigate realities—translation *is* communication. As Flusser claims, "translation and polyglotism were recognized as the only intellectual methods for overcoming the limits of language."[7]

In Flusser's writing, experience, culture, and the self are in a constant, fluid dialogue with each other like a "jazz quartet" that is informing as well as engaging with other subjects. The cornerstone of his work is motivated by his philosophy that culture determines habitual ways of thinking and acting. Cultural determination becomes a modus operando. This philosophy echoes Benjamin Whorf's work on linguistic relativity, who surmises that

> in linguistic and mental phenomena, significant behavior [is] ruled by a specific system or organization, a "geometry" of form principles characteristic of each language. This organization is imposed from outside the narrow circle of the personal consciousness, making of that consciousness a mere puppet, whose linguistic maneuverings are held in unbreakable bonds of pattern.[8]

Whorf's philosophy of language connects with Flusser's idea of translation studies echoing the principle of the chronotope. Flusser postulates that identity is contingent on the multilingual and multicultural setting as he reveals above that the translation problem emerges from relations across a multiplicity of systems.[9] Resembling Mikhail Bakhtin's theory of the chronotope, Flusser's idea of translatability depicts and challenges the intricate relationship between time and space in human experience: that is, how context affects identity. More specifically, Flusser anchors time and space linguistically insofar as he concludes

> words allow for consideration both within and outside of sentences. Considered outside of sentences, these words can be inflected. I will consider two kinds of inflection: declension and conjugation. Declension is the inflection of words called nouns or other words similar to nouns, whereas conjugation is the inflection of verbs. There are inflections that transform words from one type to another. [. . .] Declension is responsible for that aspect of our outside worlds that we call "space," and conjugation for that aspect that we call "time." Languages with another structure cannot result in worlds that have aspects of time and space in our sense of these terms.[10]

Conjugation of words, namely verbs, establish reference to time as past tense, present tense, future tense, past within the past, and future within the past. The difference between the sentence "I see the child" as opposed to "I saw the child" is not a difference in semantic but in temporal meaning. Declension, on the other hand, refers to space, as grammatical information indicates number, case, and gender about nouns, pronouns, adjectives, adverbs, and articles. By changing the form of a word, it occupies different positions in the sentence, and the word gets charged with a different meaning. For example, the difference in the German pronoun in subject, indirect object, or direct object will not only reflect the change in grammatical information within the word (number, gender, case) but also the configuration of the so-called *emes* to each other within a sentence; the subject is the agent while the indirect versus the direct objects assume different agent-object dichotomies.[11] An indirect object, if present, is the recipient of the direct object. Here is an example in German using the masculine singular noun for the last point made:

Ich schenke *den Ring* [I give the ring]
Der Ring → den Ring: accusative, singular, masculine
Ich schenke *dem Mann* X [I give X to the man]
Der Mann → dem Mann: dative, singular, masculine

Putting the two sentences together using the respective pronouns shows how the declension reflects the arrangement of the emic units in their particular forms.

Ich schenke dem Mann den Ring → *Ich schenke ihn ihm.*

A German speaker knows the reference for each pronoun. The morphosyntactic change in form from noun to pronoun, as well as the positions to each other, elicits spatial information within its sentence. For Flusser, living in exile and surrounded by more than one language and culture, language is a system within the two paradigms, but he rejects the idea that the language user settles down for just one system; as a matter of fact, languages are more likely to be of different systems, and multilingualism accommodates different competing systems. Therefore, (the essential distinctive nature of) translation provides and gives transparency to a platform for an ongoing dialogical relationship between the subject, its language, and the cultural environment. Flusser's chronotopic approach to language specifically suggests that while language is informed through the spatial and temporal paradigm illustrated earlier, language refuses to be restricted ipso facto to the spatial and temporal boundaries because language is not a means to an end but a means without an end.

Flusser's linguistic credo is formed through his own personal experience. Living as a migrant most of his life, he became proficient in Portuguese, German, Czech, and English. His fluid multilingualism is essential to understanding how polyglotism informed his pragmatism as well as his perception of culture and the human. Just as his multilingual competency has been instrumental to his learning and awareness of multiculturalism, so did his writing become experiential as well as experimental; his writing is known for being open-ended and interdisciplinary, communicating phenomenologically through perceptual experience. Trying to understand what constitutes language and how language is determined according to Flusser is like going down the rabbit hole: it transports us into a wonderfully (and sometimes confusing) surreal state because his understanding of language is multifold: he explains it empirically through philosophy, belief, and different manifestations of culture. He does not use theory but creates it. And, as such, it is impossible to classify him into a particular school of thought. His early assessment of himself ("I begin to lose my topic by having identified myself with it [and] I simultaneously begin to lose myself in it") translates into a ludic abundance of writing that is informed through a concoction of poetry, anthropology, philosophy, and language studies. This recipe applies specifically to the latter: Flusser moves from language structure, to the study of semantics, to language relativism (i.e., linguistic anthropology), to language philosophy, to pragmatics. As Anke Finger, Rainer Guldin, and Gustavo Bernardo insightfully argue, "not only does Flusser's multilingual style of writing prevent such a solidification of one text in relation to others, but it also would undermine each text's potential multireferentiality and disciplinary or interdisciplinary interpretations."[12]

Flusser's fundamental understanding of language seems at first highly confusing. His approach appears uncomfortably binary. He sees the nature of language as a system: an enclosed organized interconnected order. Like a structuralist, he maintains that "[l]anguages are systems of signs, and from now on signs within languages shall be called symbols."[13] Despite his claims not to be impressed by Saussure, one cannot dismiss that both, Flusser and Saussure, seemingly shared their approach to the phenomenology of language.[14] They both believed that linguistic entities are parts of a system and are defined by their relations to one another within that system. Flusser posits that

> given the structure of this type of languages, discourse consists of phrases composed of words that obey rules. The rules have two levels: they regulate the form of the words within the phrase, and they regulate the form of the phrase within discourse.[15]

For Flusser, like Saussure, the meaningful symbols are arranged in a network that connect with one another as Flusser asserts that "[a] situation is meaningful when it contains signs, and it is an ordered situation when it has symbols contained in languages."[16] As a matter of fact, borrowing Saussure's well-known chess analogy, where the current value of any piece depends on all the others and moving one piece has an effect on all the other pieces, Flusser also argued analogously in a published piece called "*Schach*" (chess), originally in Portuguese in 1972 and translated into German by his wife, Edith Flusser. This short introspective essay illustrates the linguistic affordances for the human mind in terms of the situation of the chess player:

> *Nehmen wir den Bauern als Beispiel. Das Essentielle ist nicht, dass er aus Holz ist, weder, dass er gelb ist, noch, dass er die Form einer karikierten Pagode hat, nicht einmal, dass er mit der Absicht erzeugt wurde, Teil des Spiels zu sein. Das Essentielle an ihm ist folgendes: vertikal sich nach vorne bewegen zu können und diagonal fressen zu können. Seine Essenz ist, mächtige diagonale Paare und wichtige vertikale Paare zu bilden und sich mit einem dialektischen Sprung auf die letzte Reihe zur Dame machen zu können. Diese Essenz, dem Bauern eigen, offenbart sich beim Spiel und beim Nachdenken (wie jetzt). [. . .] Sollten wir die Essenz dieses Spiels entdecken wollen, in dem wir die Steine sind, müssen wir versuchen, seine Regeln kennenzulernen.*[17]

> [Let's take the Pawn as an example. The essential thing is not that it is made of wood, nor that it is white, nor that it has the shape of a caricatured pagoda, not even that it was created with the intention of being part of the game. The essential thing about it is the following: being able to move vertically forward and being able to eat diagonally. Its essence is to form powerful diagonal pairs and important vertical pairs and to be able to make yourself a Queen with a dialectical jump to

the last row. This essence, inherent in the pawn, is revealed in play and thought (as here). [. . .] If we want to discover the essence of this game in which we are the pieces, we have to try to learn its rules.][18]

This metaphorical narrative echoes the linguistic relationship between the emes as meaning distinguishing discrete units in its system whether it is a phoneme, morpheme, tagmeme, or sememe. For example, the phoneme /a/ in an English word is only charged with meaning in its context of a word and in its contrast to another sound such as /i/ in its own respective context. For example, the meaning of the sound /i/ in /kit/ as opposed to the sound /a/ in /kat/ [cat] is not due to its inherent phonetic features but due to its meaning distinguishing constituents. Comparably, the pawn represents a unit that comprises a function, or to use Flusser's word, a code. It is a code that is not always fully conscious of the artificial character of communication but that it perceives in the process and facilitates.

> After learning a code, we have a tendency to forget its artificiality. If one has learned the code of gesture, then one no longer recognizes that that head nodding signifies "yes" only to those who make use of this code. Codes (and the symbols that make them) become second nature, and the codified world in which we live [. . .] makes us forget the world of "first nature" (the signified world).[19]

Flusser refers to the process itself, "the tendency to forget its artificiality," and that the word consists of a sequence of sounds as "negentropic tendency of human communication."[20] It is the human intention that wants to understand the accumulation of information. The meaning of the pawn is not what it is made of but rather how it moves in the process because it experiences and evaluates as a becoming, or as Flusser articulates "it is revealed in play and thought" ("*offenbart sich beim Spiel und beim Nachdenken*").[21]

The structuralist dimension of Flusserian thought takes language as a coherent system of formal units placed in peculiar systematic arrangements. Naturally, nothing illustrates this approach better than a telling anecdote from Flusser's own experiences, which provides a conceptual key to his linguistics. Documented in a newspaper article, Flusser describes an incident in Paris in which a briefcase of his was misplaced—or more specifically pilfered from a rental car. The briefcase contained his notes and unpublished work. Ultimately, it was recovered, recovered but a few streets away. Brimming with irony, Flusser states that the briefcase was discarded with nothing removed, because the contents were judged unimportant: "The burglar decided it worthless . . . a shattering literary verdict" [*Der Einbrecher hatte sie als wertlos befunden. Ein niederschmetterndes literarisches Urteil*].[22] He connects the briefcase to a piece of his memory which resembles a miniature version of his travelling library now housed in Berlin ("*Die Tasche kann als ein Teil meines 'Gedächtnisses' angesehen werden*" [The briefcase can be understood as a part of my memory]. The lost and now found briefcase, he reports, is a "rich hunting ground for structuralist analysis," containing thirty unpublished articles along with then published articles that had been published in Portuguese, English, or German, copies of his own letters and letters by others to him, some letters that he responded to and others that had not been responded to yet, and a manuscript of a book that is due to be published in Paris the same month. What seemed to be a messy arrangement turns out to be a deeply organized, "bureau on the go." Every single document is categorized in multiple ways: letters are chronologically ordered, published articles are organized by date of publication, large manuscripts are labeled by either place or title (if there is one): "*La Force du Quotidien*," "*Ca esiste, la Nature?*," "New York," "Rio," "*Vorträge*" (lectures), "*Bodenlosigkeit*," "*Bienal Documentos*" (*general documents*). The document files in the briefcase are organized syntactically, semantically, and structurally. The only decision Flusser didn't make organizationally is an alphabetic order, which, as he points out ironically, would have led the criminal to believe that the briefcase owner had cognitive defects:

> *Allerdings fehlt in der Tasche eine 'formale Struktur vom Typ 'alphabetische Ordnung'. Aus diesem Fehlen hätte der Einbrecher auf einem Defekt meiner Denkart schließen können. [. . .] Überhaupt bietet die Tasche einen ergiebigen Jagdgrund für 'strukturalistische Analysen.*
>
> [A formal structure of the alphabetical order type is missing in the bag. The burglar could have deduced from this lack of a defect in my way of thinking. [. . .] In general, the bag offers a rich hunting ground for structuralist analysis.]

For Flusser, the meaning behind this briefcase is not ideolectical (idiotic, idiosyncratic) but follows its powers for extending concepts, thinking, and memory. "The files," he writes, "are at last organized according to their relationship to the briefcase itself and as such come in two classes: (A) the files that are stored there to stay in the memory, and (B) the files there to recall things that are not there."

> *Schließlich seien die Mappen nach ihrem Verhältnis zur Tasche selbt geordnet: Hier ergeben sich zwei Klassen. (A) Mappen, die in der Tasche sind, um im Gedächtnis zu bleiben. (B) Mappen, die dort sind, um Dinge, die nicht dort sind, ins Gedächtnis zu rufen.*
>
> [After all, the folders are sorted according to their relationship to the briefcase: There are two classifications. (A) Folders that are in your pocket to keep in mind. (B) Folders that are there to recall things that are not there.]

Flusser's emphasis on conceptual thinking explains the second part of the binary in his linguistic theory. He thinks that the meaning of language unfolds through reality as the language user comprehends language through conception: understanding language is through conceiving and interpreting it through the environment. Again, we see a link between Saussure and Flusser as they both believed that there is an alliance between language and culture. This idea of language as a social fact crystallizes itself in Saussure's two concepts of *langue* (the structure of language) and *parole* (the experienced language). Saussure maintained that "language is not complete in any speaker; it exists perfectly only within a collectivity."[23] Similarly, Flusser argued that "language is a product of a covenant: that it is conventional: that it is the product of an accord in relation to its meaning. Language [. . .] is the articulation of a covenant, due to which I find myself."[24] Saussure's demonstration of the two levels of language corresponds to Flusser's suggestion of the horizontal and vertical translation. According to Flusser, horizontal translations are mutual adequations between languages of similar structures, whereas vertical translations refer to two language systems or dissimilar structures that communicate different realities.

As discussed previously, translation is a form of communication. Accordingly, translatability cannot be understood without understanding language. Flusser, likewise, sees language into two layers: the spoken and the written language. The system of symbols that represent the sounds of spoken language (the alphabets) are the result of the effort to translate the meaning of spoken language onto the two dimensions of the plane (i.e., space and time).[25] Spoken language can be codified through symbols (alphabets) but while "[t]he alphabets translate the meaning of spoken language, it cannot translate every meaning," as "the ideograms of the written languages of the East are independent from spoken language."[26] The lack of translation between the alphabet and the spoken language is due to the disparity between language and reality: language falls short of reality—reality exceeds language.

This conclusion takes us to the conversation about the horizontal and vertical translation. According to Flusser, languages of the same kind, sharing the fundamental structural identity and the same reality, are possible for translation.[27] But, if languages are of different realities, translations will be impossible.[28] He gives the example of Semitic verbs that realize time conceptually differently ("[i]n the Semitic reality, the present is not time"):

> If I translate the Portuguese phrase "eu falo," [I speak] to the Hebrew phrase "ani omer," the situation of reality will have been entirely changed. The situation of "eu falo" is dynamic because it involves time. The situation of "ani omer."[29]

A horizontal translation between Portuguese and Hebrew would "reveal itself as a complicated case of successive vertical translations."[30] Vertical translation means to simplify by translating to the layer of symbolic logic (systems of different kinds) and retranslating to the corresponding conversational layer (reaching the systems of the same). It is a progressive exhaustion of meaning, to impoverish the language, to find an economically simpler language with less meaning and less reality.[31] Again, less reality means reality of the same kind.

The linguist J. R. Firth once stipulated that "[o]f all human studies, the study of language is probably the most heterogeneous and heteroclite."[32] This assessment that language is constitutively anomalous and different is what fuels Flusser's work. It is a conglomerate of information and knowledge. The only way to understand this enigma is through linguistic activity. He states that "language is an experience through philosophy as philosophy is a linguistic activity and philosophy is a conversation."[33]

As an element of experience, it derives from the inherent organizing function of human knowledge. Labeled as a phenomenologist, Flusser's writing was informed as a philosopher, writer, and media theorist, but language was the epicenter of his thinking. Everything that we do, the way we conceive the world, according to Flusser, is integral to the experienced language:

> We cannot do [conceive the world through other than structure of our worldview], because the structure of the external world is precisely the structure of our intellect, and the structure of our intellect is the structure of our languages. [. . .] We may oscillate between these worldviews, but we may not conceive of the world through a different structure. We cannot do it, because the structure of the external world is precisely the structure of our intellect, and the structure of our intellect is the structure of our languages.[34]

What is compelling about Flusser's theory of language is a new approach to Whorf's linguistic relativity hypothesis; it is not just that reality has an unspecified impact on language, but *how* it impacts language. Here, we watch Flusser entering the conversation with Saussure through philosophy arguing that philosophy is "a linguistic activity" as the universe, knowledge, truth, and reality are linguistic aspects. Rather than ceasing the symbol as an arbitrary sign that obtains the meaning through a sociocultural consensus, he argues that the meaning of a symbol acquires through the participation in linguistic activities (also known as progressive thought). For him, "philosophy turns toward the symbol to discover the symbol's meaning" in order to discover that it is "through linguistic activities that we understand how symbols 'seek something external' which is 'reality'": language is reality; language gives form to reality; language creates reality; language disseminates reality.[35]

Just as Flusser's approach to language exceeds Whorf's linguistic relativity hypothesis, his theory also expands Saussure's principles of language. Flusser augments Saussure's theory of the signifier and the signified by putting the external reality into the foreground. Language is not, as Saussure would have it, a mere community of distributed dictionaries—a grammatical system existing *virtuellement* in each brain, and in its tangible written form binding on all members of the community by virtue of a *contrat passe*, a system of agreed code signs. The difference between Flusser and Whorf or Saussure is the last part of his proposition: *language disseminates reality*.

Why is epistemology so influential to Flusser? Flusser's work is informed through his own experience, his work, and the epistemological positions from which he observed the phenomena he encountered: as a migrant, refugee, and, ultimately, an intellectual nomad.[36] *Bodenlos* (bottomless) is not only the title of his intellectual autobiography but also a reoccurring and repeated image in his work on language. Flusser believed that knowledge arrives through reason, the study of nature, and the limits of knowledge. He described himself as "disoriented," which was induced by vulnerability and lack of grounding. We know that the epistemologies of Kant and Russell both had a profound impact on Flusser, but it may be best to think of these epistemologies as willfully disoriented—distorted, displaced, and damaged—epistemology.[37]

From them, he absorbed that it is crucial to understand the conditions of the possibility of human understanding by appealing to sensory experience. A certain strain of distorted Heideggerian thinking is also obvious. According to Flusser, borrowing from Heidegger, culture can only exist through "*Vorhandensein*" (ready at hand) and "*Mitsein*" (existing with). Language as a tool is to experience so that culture can be perceived (*erkennen*) and experienced (*erleben*).[38] To summarize, language is experience and experience is through language. If Flusser is intellectually closest to sociolinguistics, how is experience understood sociolinguistically? His approach is closer to Karl Vossler[39] than, let's say, Leonard Bloomfield. While Bloomfield postulated that society is a group of people who interact (i.e., experience) by means of speech, Vossler maintained through his concept of the "experienced language" that we see language as a product of achievement and subjective value. Vossler, and by extension Flusser, would postulate that language represents an inner form as a community of interests and of experience. Vossler calls it a common *sentimentis*. Hence, language is not merely a mirror of culture, nor a multiplication of echoes of it because language is not merely coexisting with culture but a process.

So, how is meaning ultimately created through experience? Language as a process is through indexicality. Let's take this to the discussion of translatability: what Flusser refers to as the poorer in meaning of the word and closer to the layer of form, the easier translatable, he means that the indexicality of languages belonging to the respective external worlds is similar or analogous.[40] "Poor" means "the same" as the indexicality of the respective words is enough of a simple denotation to share the same meaning. If reality impacts the language system (different realities—different systems as described in the comparative example between Portuguese and Hebrew), and if language systems share the same reality or similar realities, then the meaning of a word means that the word carries the same indexicality to the external world. Words have meanings because they index meanings. The meaning of the word, the experience, can then be either alike or different. Flusser's briefcase manifests this point: his meticulous labeling of his work by type, by date, by name in one bag builds the reference to the respective work worth eighteen months. It is his order of system, his labeling, that reflects his intellectual world. Flusser has been a linguistic pioneer of his own kind. It all starts with the postulation of the bottomless (*bodenlos*) that seems to be simultaneously impotent and creative. To him, the external world is a preexisting grid that comes as raw data through time and space in which language as experience is the intermediary between reality and human. Language is experience so that culture can be perceived (*erkennen*) and experienced (*erleben*).

Notes

1 Flusser, *Philosophy of Language*, trans. Rodrigo Maltez Novaes (Minneapolis: Univocal, 2016), 40.
2 Flusser, "Essays," in *Writings*, ed. Andreas Ströhl, trans. Erik Eisel (Minneapolis: University of Minnesota Press, 2002), 193.

3 Ibid., 194.
4 Flusser, *Language and Reality*, trans. Rodrigo Maltez Novaes (Minneapolis: Univocal, 2018), 6.
5 Anke Finger, Rainer Guldin, and Gustavo Bernardo, *Vilém Flusser: An Introduction* (Minneapolis: University of Minnesota Press, 2011), 21.
6 Flusser, *Language and Reality*, 6.
7 Ibid., 53.
8 Benjamin Lee Whorf, "Language, Thought, and Reality," in *Selected Writings of Benjamin Lee Whorf*, ed. John B. Carroll (New York and London: John Wiley and Sons, 1959), 257.
9 Flusser, *Language and Reality*, 26.
10 Flusser, *Philosophy of Language*, 89.
11 An emic unit, also referred to as '-emes' is an abstract unit in linguistics that represents the meaning distinguishing nature of language. This means that a given emic unit is considered to be a single underlying object that may have a number of different observable "surface" representations. Examples are phoneme, morpheme, or lexeme.
12 Finger, Guldin, and Bernardo, *Vilém Flusser*, 221.
13 Flusser, *Philosophy of Language*, 8.
14 Flusser, *Writings*, 201.
15 Ibid., 23.
16 Ibid., 8-9.
17 Flusser, "Schach," in *Dinge und Undinge: Phänomenologische Skizzen* (München: Hanser, 1993 [1972]), 53–62.
18 All translations are mine unless otherwise noted.
19 Flusser, *Writings*, 2–3.
20 Ibid., 6.
21 Flusser, "Schach," 53.
22 Flusser, "Die Tasche/strukturelle Analyse," *Dolomiten* 283, nos. 15–17 (Samstag/Sonntag, Dezember 1973): 15.
23 Ferdinand de Saussure, *Course in General Linguistics*, trans. Reuben A. Bower (New York: Columbia University Press, 2011), 14.
24 Flusser, *Philosophy of Language*, 74.
25 Ibid., 47.
26 Ibid., 48.
27 Ibid., 48–9.
28 Ibid., 49.
29 Ibid.
30 Ibid., 53.
31 Ibid., 55.
32 J. R. Firth, "The Spirit of Language in Civilization," *Philosophy* 8, no. 30 (1933): 234–6, 235.
33 Flusser, *Philosophy of Language*, 26–7.
34 Ibid., 40.
35 Ibid., 7–10.
36 Ibid., 23.
37 Flusser, *Writings*, 201.

38 Flusser, *Philosophy of Language*, 26–7.
39 Karl Vossler, *Positivismus und Idealismus in der Sprachwissenschaft. Eine sprachphilosophische Untersuchung* (Heidelberg: C. Winter, 1904), 63.
40 Flusser, *Philosophy of Language*, 51.

The Depressed Person and the Vampire Squid
Sonic Gestures in the Work of Vilém Flusser and David Foster Wallace

Edward P. Comentale

Ring, ring!

I should probably let you know upfront that this chapter emerged out of a deep aversion to telephones, an irrational fear—a telephonophobia—that I have convinced myself has many rational sources. In fact, if you're still waiting for a call from me (and I know it's been awhile), please note here in my defense: (1) the immediate panic I feel in response to the making and receiving of unexpected phone calls; (2) my queasy uncertainty about the interest and responsiveness of the invisible other on the line; (3) all of the anxiety regarding my personal performance in relation to the device's unique social performance protocols, whether vocal, visual, or textual; (4) my complete failure to resist the phone's aggressive infiltration of my most personal spaces and the ceaseless battles waged with loved ones about its presence in the home; (5) my revulsion to the microscopic filth and germs that apparently collect on cell phones and make each a feared vector for contamination; and (6) the anger and guilt I feel in response to the shamelessly programmed obsolescence and overwhelming environmental problems caused by an irresponsible telephone industry.

Yes, it's true, I turned my ringer off long ago,[1] and, just so we're all clear, I remain completely flummoxed by the device. As this chapter suggests, I can only seem to respond to the questioning ring of the phone with more questions. In what perhaps neurotically follows, I pursue a media archaeology of sorts, one that traces the vexed existential climate of the phone call by focusing on the phenomenological foundations of human communication. Lurking behind my approach is a set of rather cranky questions about the ideology of connectivity: *Is genuine and sincere face-to-face conversation possible or really desired by anyone? What role does the telephone play in not just facilitating face-to-face conversation but fabricating the very idea of it? What does a media archeology of communication technology look like when it refuses to start from the ideal of greater connectivity?* I want to know what the phone is doing if it's not connecting us, what do we hear from it if we're not using it to speak and listen to each other, and for this, I have to connect the phone to other forms of communication—the novel and philosophical writing specifically—in which issues of sincerity, fidelity, connection, and mimesis do not hold such powerful sway.

Dialing into these other media allows me to define the nature of the "sonic gesture" at the heart of all communication—telephonic or otherwise—and determine whether my pessimism exists in response to the communication industry, communication devices, or simply communication as such. Also, in distinguishing between different media technology—with the recent evolution of the telephone and the smartphone as this chapter's limit case—I can begin to track and weigh transformations in the human willingness and capacity to communicate. Ultimately, connecting the fiction of David Foster Wallace with the media theories of Vilém Flusser provides a glimpse of contemporary telephonic subject positions—the diametrically opposed depressed person and vampire squid—by which a call might be more or less productively received. My hunch is that the telephone is permanently vexed by decisively human desires and anxieties, rather than the reverse, but moreover, as a mode of telematic connection, it exposes these desires and anxieties as the basis of a more creative form of communication. Perhaps the smartphone, at least through a Flusserian lens, provides a way of hearing something new in the good old-fashioned telephone call.

In *Gestures*, his most well-known phenomenology of communication, Flusser describes a range of physical practices by which the body engages in communication and inscribes cultural meanings.[2] Whether typing out an essay, smoking a pipe, or listening to music, the human body partakes in a range of semiotic practices, each lending an intention and meaning to the world that exceeds mere nature, the brute cause and effect of physiology, biology, desire, and so on. While such gestures might directly involve certain forms of communication—whether speech or writing—they each rely on a different kind of code, a certain performance of meaning or "symbolic movement" that raises the significance of the body itself and implies an investment or value apart from any explicit "expression."[3] Flusser, in fact, saves his most ecstatic language for the gesture of speaking, but he privileges the sonic gesture apart from anything actually said. Here, value resides in what speech accomplishes in its material sounding. The speaker is never simply connecting words to objects; he or she always speaks to another and does so in a decisively physical space of people, objects, and obstacles. As Flusser claims,

> Speaking is an attempt to bypass the world to reach others but in such a way that the world is absorbed, "spoken" in the move. . . . The speaker grasps the world in words he directs toward others . . . chooses his words as a function of this particular space, the space of graspable problems and reachable others, in short, the political space.[4]

The telephone holds a special place in theories of communication, specifically for what it allows or disallows in terms of connectivity, and Flusser's work, with its emphasis on "grasping," is no exception in this regard. In *Gestures*, he distinguishes the embodied and rapturous "gesture of speaking" from the horrifically insufficient "gesture of telephoning." He bemoans the telephone's "archaic, paleotechnical character," arguing that the device's utopian promise of free, multidirectional dialogue has been constrained by technological underdevelopment and corporate manipulation of the telematic network.[5] Every medium separates that which it connects, he notes, but the phone seems particularly dangerous in this regard, both delimiting and restructuring any social relations within its reach. He bemoans the mechanization of speaking as a loss of physical presence and then lists all the technical problems of the developing medium—the impoverished telephone code, the acoustic limitation of the transmission, and even the bulky, unnerving presence of the device itself.[6] But, as in many such accounts, Flusser never questions the original ideal of human connectivity, and his account seems to suggest that the gesture of telephoning only exacerbates the intersubjective problems inherent to any communicative gesture. He begins with the asymmetrical positions of the caller and the called, lamenting the nervy aggression of the former and the hapless victimization of the latter. He then lists all of the unsettling feelings attendant to the ring—impatience, fear, hope, nausea, grace—which grant the call a near "theological" status in its effect. He is mostly concerned, however, about the uncertain demand that the call places on its connected parties and how the ensuing burden of responsibility for successful dialogue generates an overwhelmingly "existential climate." Ultimately, a massive frustration vexes the call in ways that ultimately exceed its technology. The intrusion of the phone attenuates anxieties pertaining to "mutual recognition" that precede any "actual dialogue" and existed *long before* the telephone and the larger telephonic network entered the picture.[7] In this revelation, perhaps, in the failure of connection, we can begin to pinpoint the more productive aspects of the sonic gesture.

In other words, no greater amount of technological mediation or mimesis would alleviate such problems. No bigger data plan or finer pixilation grid could secure the directness and immediacy of the sonic gesture, or any other kind of gesture, if they can be grasped at all. Here, our media archeology makes its first leap, for this impossibility and its creative potential is perhaps best addressed in a short story titled "The Depressed Person" by David Foster Wallace, a writer of the telephonic era who, driven by his own frustrated experiences with the device, explored the ability of his own medium to generate a more direct human response.[8] Wallace's story focuses on a chronically depressed young woman and her tortured efforts to communicate her pain to a support group of friends over the telephone. A marvel of free indirect speech, the story takes the form of an extended and tediously recursive first-person monologue that mimics the self-absorption of its subject. The reader is placed in the position of one of the captive members of the depressed person's telephonic support group, forced to listen to her nonstop chatter of childhood slights, adolescent embarrassments, adult humiliations, self-abuse, passive-aggressive apologies, and long-winded justifications. Throughout, what the depressed person thinks is her great inability to communicate her pain becomes an extension of pain for herself and her listeners. She communicates plenty, often about this very inability, but her chatter ultimately serves a vehicle for augmenting her loneliness and dispersing it throughout her circle. The first joke of

Wallace's story is that while the depressed person is relating her pain to her friends at her therapist's advice, her so-called sharing leads only to more difficult exchanges that then become, recursively, material she brings back to therapy. The second joke is that the depressed person, in her solipsistic "omnineediness," clearly has no regard for the pain and suffering of her support group, a slowly dwindling number of friends and confidantes from college; eventually, all of her listeners abandon her, including her therapist, who commits suicide, until only one is left, a divorced mother of two suffering from terminal cancer who, given her state, has a ton of free time for phone calls. Clearly, for Wallace, no amount of connectivity leads to genuine revelation and release; in fact, all communication proves narcissistic and entropic, with the call merely serving to repeat the caller's own traumas.

A certain depressive solipsism marks all of Wallace's writings, and these problems of intimacy and communication always exceed the technology that conveys them. The phone, though, plays an important role in his story's recursive loops, and in many ways the depressed person's symptomology would not be possible without its technological mediation. Wallace, a child of the pre-internet age, writes frequently about the fantasy-sustaining power of the traditional phone. In *Infinite Jest*, his narrator explains that

> Good old traditional audio-only phone conversations allowed you to presume that the person on the other end was paying complete attention to you while also permitting you not to have to pay anything even close to complete attention to her. . . . This bilateral illusion of unilateral attention was almost infantilely gratifying from an emotional standpoint: you got to believe you were receiving somebody's complete attention without having to return it.[9]

Similarly, in "The Depressed Person," the members of the support group remain unheard and unseen, and, eventually, the physical presence of the phone itself seems to disappear, with the protagonist—a Lacanian chatterbox, for sure—spending most of her phone time using a hands-free headset at work.[10] For Wallace, though, if the telephone represents the wireless solipsism that marks all human exchange, that doesn't make it redundant or merely reflective. Rather, in black boxing the other, it exacerbates issues of sincerity and motive and thereby generates its own second-order realism. In one key scene, the protagonist recalls a college memory in which she observed her roommate speaking on the phone. While seeming to encourage the boy on the other end of the line with her attention, the roommate silently gestured to the depressed person for help getting off the phone. This traumatic experience, in which the depressed person was able to witness the call from the perspective of the person called, generates awareness of her own solipsism as well as empathy for the other caller, the unseen and unheard boy on the other end of the line. Paradoxically, the unknown-ness of the other occasioned by the phone call generates a more radical, if uncomfortable, form of knowing and responsibility. To explain this fraught demand, we might adopt Avital Ronell's account of the call, derived from Derrida, as a debt, a duty or tax that undermines the metaphysical certainties of the self and redefines "being" as a tortured state of "being-called" to and by the other. In this line of thinking, perhaps the heart of deconstructive thinking as occasioned by media technology, the phone always entails another of itself, and thus dislocates its user in space and time, raising a certain alarm about his or her own self-presence as well as its shaky dependence on another.[11] Thus, despite her solipsism, the depressed person is awakened to her situation and surmises the attitudes of her listeners. She feels great shame about her behavior—"horror and empathic despair"—but this awareness only seems to fuel her manic condition, leading her right back to the phone and extending her time on the line.

This is an odd circuit of desire and gesturalism. The anxiety that defines the call—at once existential and communicative—seems generative, perhaps even creative, and thus, oddly, contradicts or counteracts its own tendency toward entropy and death.

Wallace's text, which figures as a series of telephonic demands that extend to the reader as well, recalls us to Flusser's theory of gesture as an expressive movement of the body that demands attention and interpretation—both response and responsibility. The telephone call raises complicated demands and requires of the receiver something more than a functional approach to communication as exchange, an interpretive shift to meanings, investments, and productions that reside in the very act of calling itself. I would not try to map Wallace's analysis of the call onto a strict material history of the telephone, but it certainly recalls the early commercial development of telephony and industry efforts to manage these vexed feelings. Here, I have in mind Jonathan Stern's *The Audible Past* as it tracks how the open possibilities of early sound reproduction technology developed into the recognizable media systems that confront us today as self-determining and natural.[12] Early investors, Sterne reminds us, originally promoted the telephone as a business aid and entertainment device, and only after confronting its technical limits began pushing for its use in personal communications. Early listeners, however, feared the intrusion of the phone as a potential loss of privacy and thus needed to be taught new ways of understanding and using it. As Sterne explains, the industry responded to their anxieties by developing and promoting what he calls "audile techniques." Through ads, demonstrations, and other forms of industry PR, early telephone users were trained to value and listen for an authenticity that they never associated with the phone in the first place. As Sterne explains, a medium does not neutrally mediate relations between preexisting things but constructs those things in its own terms. The phone network determined caller and called as well as any talk between them, while the industry constructed new notions of "fidelity" and "authenticity," and thereby presented the device as a "supplement" for deficiencies of hearing and being, a certain auditory quantum through which listeners could shape, direct, and orient a sense of self.[13] In this, authenticity proved highly creative. Sounds were made for and through the machine; callers performed versions of identity according to the restrictions of the network. Thus, today, we are all experts in "auditory realism," trained to produce certain kinds of listening experiences that guarantee presence where there is none.[14] In other words, connectivity via the phone has always been an aesthetic project. Our use of the device entails a whole set of manufactured expectations and commitments. The personal responsibility that is radically raised and troubled by the call gets redesigned as a sort of second-level faith in authenticity along with a related series of more or less inhuman poses and postures.

Wallace's *Infinite Jest* animates something of this lost history as well as those aspects of the call that potentially disrupt it. Written in 1996, the novel is set in a near future which is actually, now, our own recent past. It includes a faux report on the rise and fall of networked videophony that has in some ways actually come true. As a form of media archeology written for a high school media studies class, the report comically traces the public's initial excitement for videophony and their immediate panic as the new visual phones burst the narcissistic fantasy of good old aural-only telephony. The new technology leads many users to experience what Wallace calls Video-Physiognomic Dysphoria (VPD), the horror of seeing one's own face as it truly appears to another person's face, which in turn leads to a series of compensatory technologies and increasingly bizarre masking products. Confronted with the responsibilities of face-to-face communication, users initially resort to acting and make-up in order to present their best selves to each other, artfully producing authenticity according to current social tastes. Then, however, the market kicks in, tapping into this anxious production by providing first high-definition digital masks, then form-fitting polybutylene-resin masks and stylized tableaux of various exotic locales, and eventually footage of filmed b-list celebrities who serve as videophone avatars, all of which serve to restore users' narcissistic fantasies of complete attention without having to return it. Thus, under the guise of greater intimacy and sociability, which its users all secretly dread, communication via the videophone proves highly artificial and even whimsically creative and ultimately turns into what investors' originally sought for the telephone, a business/entertainment device not unlike the internet itself. Here, again, realism proves to be something that is not only impossible but deeply frightening. Like the call itself, the network functions in a viciously recursive way, heightening user self-consciousness and asociability, leading, after a brief period of manic inventiveness, to its eventual collapse, and, most importantly, a return to traditional telephone and perhaps its narcissistic fantasy-making as a source of more immediate comfort and pleasure.

It's easy to read this as a jaded parable; in the end, commercial greed conspires with consumer vanity and insecurity. However, Wallace's novel elsewhere affirms the state of being "invisible" as not only a profound material realization of human solipsism but also a freedom from the manic performative demands of postmodern culture and its tyranny of the image. The users who reject videophony return not to any more immediately present or intimate relation but to the telephone, a form of interaction without vision, which, in Wallace's account, entails, if only dimly, the deeper kind of awareness and responsibility described previously. In other words, the opposite of artifice in this case is not realism but a more conscious attention to the ways in which human exchange is mediated and the possibilities and demands it raises for each participant, even if such remain only as postulations. As I'd like to show, Flusser comes to a similar, if more optimistic, position through a more precise phenomenology of communication. By insisting on the role of the body and specifically the ear at the center of perception and thought, he proposes a model of communication that first raises the mutual responsibility of speaker and listener and then affirms the creative potential of their exchange. I return to his work in order to locate the fragility of the "sonic gesture" within a larger theory of human exchange and an overwhelming ecology of communication devices, one in which the "depressed person," the traditional communicative subject of the Western philosophical tradition, appears transformed as the radiant media-bearing "vampire squid" of the current communications revolution.

In *The Surprising Phenomenon of Human Communication*, Flusser defines the "irrepressible" urge to communicate as both distinctly human and, insofar as it cuts against humanity's innate alienation, profoundly antihuman.[15] As we saw in his study of gestures, communication endows form and meaning to existence where it does not naturally exist; it tends toward a progressive increase in information and thus fights against nature—specifically *human* nature—as it tends toward entropy.[16] The human body enters this formulation as a site of information storage and a node of transmission in a process that blurs the boundary between not just sender and receiver but public and private. Communication, Flusser explains, is the method by which information is shared between bodies as memory storage devices, and its structure determines the relative health and creativity of a community. Here, the theorist distinguishes the one-way transmission of communication as *discourse* from the game-like exchange of *dialogue*. He argues that most modern technology—television, radio, and so on—aids a totalitarian spread of *discourse*, by invading the home, cracking open the body of the receiver, and forcing the public into the private. In bypassing traditional forums of public exchange, in obliterating mutual or face-to-face exchange, such technology moves society toward a radical depoliticization and entropic sameness.[17] Conversely, Flusser advances a model of *dialogue* based on the Greek agora in which the body actively enters the public sphere. Describing the agora as a site where both goods and ideas were exchanged, he sees it as a productive space for sharing information, establishing norms, and setting governing principles, a place of mutually constructed reason—"ratio" or measure—across a wide range of practices (83–4). For the Greeks, Flusser argues, dialogue was always essentially political; it brought private information into the public as the foundation of political life as well as, in its productive capacity, of creative life, of *poiesis* (84). Consequently, the theorist demands responsiveness as well as responsibility in and through contemporary media technology. "Dialogue," he writes, "is not only to get a message and to reply to it; dialogue is also to recognize oneself in the other . . . dialogue is also the admittance of the other, 'Eros.'"[18] We get plenty of messages today, Flusser argues, but not the other person, and so, in the catastrophic depoliticization of modern communication, in the diminishing exchange between actual bodies, we have grown "irresponsible."[19]

But what does it mean to recognize oneself in the other, to communicate through "Eros"? What role does the body and its specific appendages and organs play in this process? And, finally, what kind of gestures might give access to that body and its role? Here we return to *Gestures*. The body's participation in the semiotics of gesture guarantees human recognition in dialogue, Flusser argues. The body's gestures give expression to interior states of mind, to more or less inexpressible or unknown affects, and thereby provide an anchor for mutual recognition. One's difficulties knowing and understanding the "state of mind" of another are not so great, Flusser admits, because we each have a criterion for such knowledge and understanding rooted in our own physical experience.[20] Thus, Flusser's text argues for a better dialogue of gestures, a more passionate and even inflamed system of physical gesture as the latter seems to be disappearing from the human world. In this regard, Flusser is positively *epiphanic* about the spoken word. It is at once an embodied and spiritual manifestation of inner being, radiant and exultant amid the silence that both surrounds it and gives it value.[21] It locates the speaker's body in an exchange of information and, in forging a connection between sender and receiver that is both physical and semiotic, it ensures the kind of "responsiveness" and "responsibility" that defines effective dialogue.[22]

Interestingly, Flusser scholars have debated what seems to be a lack of interest or failure to consider issues of sounds and listening in his work, characterizing this apparent lapse as characteristic of the ocularcentric nature of most Western philosophy.[23] However, as Annie Goh suggests, the theories outlined earlier suggest that a strong case can be made that listening serves as the phenomenal basis of his general theory of communications and that the ear itself figures in his work as the key human organ for navigating what he famously theorized as the "universe of technical images."[24] In *Gestures*, listening implies a primal connection and openness to the world, one in which the human body adapts to the message and in turn becomes a point of transmission. Similarly, in *Into the Universe of Technical Images*, sonic exchange—musical or otherwise—becomes the basis of any progressive/critical existence within a world saturated by digital media.[25] Here, Flusser notes that "Musical information does not depend on the receiver's ability to decode it (such as an ear linked to a brain); rather it permeates the receiver's body with vibrations, which bring this body into resonance (sympathy)."[26] He then turns to chamber music as "pure play," a creative dialogue between musicians who are "improvising with continually reprogrammed methods." This specifically sonic dialogue—at once physical and semiotic, rule-based yet fluid—serves as a model for open and creative existence within the ever-expanding, self-renewing telematic "super-brain" of contemporary society.[27] Listening and the ear figure centrally in this fantasia of cybernetic dialogue. By emphasizing the materiality of sound and its phenomenological effects, Flusser elevates sonic experience to the center of human communication in its political dimension and as the basis of any potential freedom within it.

Thus, we come to the vampire squid, Flusser's fabulistic avatar for life within our contemporary mediascape, a hypersensitized information processor whose impassioned engagement with the world could not be farther from the posture of Wallace's depressed person and the subjective traumas of empathy and authenticity.[28] Flusser compares the squid's existence in the deep oceanic abyss to our life amid the densely packed technosphere, as a model for our own existence in a dematerialized world of wireless media technology. To survive amid the crushing pressure of his environment, the squid has developed a body and strategies for managing the information and impressions that would otherwise destroy it. It moves about its world as a hollow sac, passively receiving massive amounts of data, carefully selecting and discarding bits as they alternately aid or hinder its aims. Open and receptive to the currents that surround it, it ceaselessly ingests and expels information in a process that is at once physical, mental, and ultimately creative and social. The squid contains one of the world's most complex and responsive nervous systems. It has developed a wide range of receptors and emitters along its surfaces for help mediating the obstacles in its environment. Its sense organs extend both inward and outward, lining all of its basic bodily functions—eating, reproduction, and so on—so that each one contributes to its vast processing of information. And, perhaps most amazingly, the squid—as gestural monster—uses these same organs to communicate with others. The chromataphores that line its surface light up the environment in response to stimuli, while its glands produce a deadly ink that it can shape into beguiling, if ephemeral, sculptures. In all this, the squid exists as a highly coordinated media vessel,[29] sending and receiving messages at an extraordinary rate, in constant dialogue with its environment and ceaselessly producing new information. In this, its experience is "passive and impassioned"; its relationship to the world is "impressionistic" and thus artistic.[30]

The squid fleshes out my understanding of the role of sound and listening in Flusser's utopian vision. It provides a way of understanding how the ear, as a "passive and impassioned" receiver of sensory stimulations, connected to a physical body in space, might awaken a more responsible and creative relationship to the messages we receive. But Flusser has other devices in mind. As he states in his study of the squid, we too are about "to overcome our dependence on material objects, to renounce artifacts for an immaterial and intersubjective art form . . . we have begun to fashion new types of artificial memory, that enable intersubjective and immaterial communication. These new communication media may not be bioluminescent organs, but they are similarly electromagnetic."[31] Our digital communications devices have grown bioluminescent in precisely this way. Unlike the clunky, poorly developed telephone of Flusser's moment, or the hyper-mimetic device that Wallace used, the phones of today reveal their inherent character as dynamic media devices. Hardly anyone uses them for phone calls anymore, but they are lit up with colors, texts, sounds, and images that users can form and reform in a sort of creative dialogue with each other. Is it possible to see the smartphone as the leading edge of a ceaselessly animated self, a complex software that allows endless recreation of our place in the world? These devices might have turned us all into mollusks, but they also provide the means of navigating—often literally, as GPS systems—that existence in an active and creative way. Drawing upon recent work in sound studies and sound art, Jan Thorben and Shintaro Miyazaki write, "With the dawn of telematic technology, we have begun to 'vampyroteuthize' our society. The technosphere is changing towards more ephemeral, time-based and wireless modes of communication. Having 'lost faith' in material media, humans in their utopian projections progressively introduce new ways of inter-subjective and immaterial communication, such as wireless technologies or brain-machine interfaces." With such devices in hand, "The gesture of listening to pure music or chamber music in the Flusserian sense might be directed towards basically all measurable energy flows, rhythms, fluctuations in all sorts of systems and entities."[32]

And yet it remains clear that human being—physically as well as psychologically— has been resistant to such changes and perhaps exists, technology-wise, at an evolutionary dead end. Current science suggests that our smartphones are quickly reshaping our bodies and physical habits, creating dangerous shifts in posture and perception, limiting cognitive capacity and disrupting established sleep patterns.[33]

More to the point, the runaway communicative possibilities of the smartphone have clearly exacerbated the negative states and feelings exposed by "good old traditional audio-only phone conversations." Researchers have traced prolonged cell phone use to increases in depression, anxiety, and stress,[34] and they have started to document a whole new series of phone-related mental health disorders such as FOMO, nomophobia, phubbing, ringxiety, and phantom ringing.[35] Most interestingly, while causality has not been sufficiently explained, they have been able to track and distinguish the excessive loneliness of people who use their smartphones to make telephone calls and the excessive anxiety of those who use them primarily to text.[36] Perhaps, given our increased addiction and dependence on the smartphone as a prosthetic device, this is precisely what it means to be a squid in the modern technoscape, but I'm not so sure that these skittish affects signal evolution, regression, or some symptomatic form of protest. Either way, given the current state of the corporately owned technoscape as well as the depressed persons with whom we are forced to communicate, it seems unlikely that we can extend the gesture of listening into other contexts, let alone make it a model for revolution. Flusser, at his most ironic, writes, "We have built chromatophores of our own—televisions, videos, and computer monitors that display synthetic images—with whose help broadcasters of information can mendaciously seduce their audiences."[37] Still, we are obliged to try, to be responsible in our listening and creative in our output, and the moment provides, just like any other, enough material to make such gestures possible. More to the point, art, literature, and philosophy, like any other form of discourse, continue to invite dialogue and new ways of grasping the world in all its stubborn resistance.

Ring, ring!

Notes

1. And I'm definitely not alone in this. See Alexis C. Madrigal, "Why No One Answers Their Phone Anymore," *The Atlantic*, May 31, 2018, accessed August 28, 2018, https://www.theatlantic.com/technology/archive/2018/05/ring-ring-ring-ring/561545/.
2. Vilém Flusser, *Gestures*, trans. Nancy Ann Roth (Minneapolis, University of Minnesota Press, 2014).
3. Ibid., 5.
4. Ibid., 30.
5. Ibid., 135–6.
6. Ibid., 140.
7. Ibid., 139.
8. David Foster Wallace, "The Depressed Person," in *Brief Interviews with Hideous Men* (Boston: Back Bay Books, 2000), 37–69.
9. Wallace, *Infinite Jest* (Boston: Back Bay Books, 1996) and Teju Cole, *Open City* (New York: Random House, 2012).
10. Jacques Lacan, *Formations of the Unconscious: The Seminar of Jacques Lacan, Book 5*, trans. Russell Grigg (Cambridge: Polity Press, 2017).

11 Avital Ronell, *The Telephone Book: Technology, Schizophrenia, Electric Speech* (Lincoln: University of Nebraska Press, 1989).
12 Jonathan Sterne, *The Audible Past: Cultural Origins of Sound Reproduction* (Durham: Duke University Press, 2003).
13 Ibid., 168–71.
14 Ibid., 234–5.
15 Flusser, *The Surprising Phenomenon of Human Communication* (Metaflux Publishing, 2016).
16 Ibid., 26–31.
17 Ibid., 78–9.
18 Ibid., 89.
19 Ibid., 87.
20 Flusser, *Gestures*, 5.
21 Ibid., 28.
22 Ibid., 29.
23 See essays collected in *Flusser Studies* 17, accessed August 28, 2018, http://www.flusserstudies.net/archive/flusser-studies-17-double-issue, especially Marta Castello Branco, Annie Goh, and Rodrigo Maltez Novaes, "Introduction: Music and Sound in Vilém Flusser's Work," and Wolfgang Ernst, "Discovering the Ears on Flusser's Face. A Respectful Revision."
24 Annie Goh, "The Dimension of Sound in Flusser," in *Flusser Studies* 17.
25 Flusser, *Into the Universe of Technical Images*, trans. Nancy Ann Roth (Minneapolis: University of Minnesota Press, 2011).
26 Ibid., 164.
27 Ibid., 161–2.
28 Vilém Flusser and Louis Bec, *Vampyroteuthis Infernalis: A Treatise* (Minneapolis: University of Minnesota Press, 2012).
29 Ibid., 21.
30 Ibid., 39.
31 Ibid., 65.
32 Jan Thoben and Shintaro Miyazaki, "Hearing Aids: Flusser's Gesture of Listening Reconsidered," *media archive performance* #5, 8, accessed August 28, 2018, http://www.perfomap.de/map7/media-performance-on-gestures/hearing-aids-flusser2019s-gesture-of-listening-reconsidered.
33 See S. I. Jung, N. K. Lee, K. W. Kang, K. Kim, and D. Y. Lee, "The Effect of Smartphone Usage Time on Posture and Respiratory Function," *The Journal of Physical Therapy Science* 28 (2016): 186–9; Adrian F. Ward, Kristen Duke, Ayelet Gneezy, and Maarten W. Bos, "Brain Drain: The Mere Presence of One's Own Smartphone Reduces Available Cognitive Capacity," *Journal of the Association for Consumer Research* 2, no. 2 (April 2017): 140–54; Sara Thomée, "Mobile Phone Use and Mental Health: A Review of the Research That Takes a Psychological Perspective on Exposure," *International Journal of Environmental Research and Public Health* 15 (2018): 1–25.
34 See, for instance, A. Višnjić et al., "Relationship between the Manner of Mobile Phone Use and Depression, Anxiety, and Stress in University Students," *International Journal of Environmental Research and Public Health* 15 (2018): 697; D. S. Bickham et al., "Media Use and Depression: Exposure, Household Rules, and Symptoms

among Young Adolescents in the USA," *International Journal of Public Health* 60 (2015): 147–55; S. Saeb et al., "Mobile Phone Sensor Correlates of Depressive Symptom Severity in Daily-Life Behavior: An Exploratory Study," *Journal of Medical Internet Research* 17 (2015): 1–11.

35 C. Yildirim and A. P. Correia, "Exploring the Dimensions of Nomophobia: Development and Validation of a Self-reported Questionnaire," *Computers in Human Behavior* 49 (2015): 130–7; E. Karadağ et al., "Determinants of Phubbing, Which Is the Sum of Many Virtual Addictions: A Structural Equation Model," *Journal of Behavioral Addiction* 4 (2015): 60–74; S. H. Subba et al., "Ringxiety and the Mobile Phone Usage Pattern among the Students of a Medical College in South India," *Journal of Clinical and Diagnostic Research* 7 (2013): 205–9.

36 D. J. Reid and F. J. Reid, "Text or Talk? Social Anxiety, Loneliness, and Divergent Preferences for Cell Phone Use," *CyberPsychology & Behavior* 10 (2007): 424–35.

37 Flusser and Bec, *Vampyroteuthis Infernalis*, 67.

Cannibalistic Animals

Posthuman Natures in Flusser and Benjamin

Erick Felinto

> *Principle of Toussenel's zoology: "The rank of the species is in direct proportion to its resemblance to the human being." A. Toussenel, L'Esprit des bêtes (Paris, 1884), p. i. Compare the epigraph to the work: "The best thing about man is his dog"— Charlet.*[1]
> [G12a, 1]
> —Walter Benjamin

History was built on a foundation of radical cleavage between nature and culture. Its main topics are the adventures and misadventures of humankind as an agent of transformation in a mostly silent and passive world. Nature and the other beings that populate the planet have usually played the role of mere supporting actors. In fact, nature offers nothing more than a pleasant background onto which the deeds of humans and their cultural achievements are projected. Yet, the exclusion of this vast domain of existence from historical narrative offers us a rather partial and incomplete picture. Only very sporadically have geography, geology, or the weather emerged as protagonists in the romance of history. It took a long time for "mountains, animals and plants" to appear as true agents and "products of specific historical processes," as Manuel De Landa writes.[2] Nevertheless, our ingrained anthropocentrism may still have a difficult time with the proposition that animals and plants are not embodiments of "eternal essences" but rather "historical constructions."[3] History is something that we, humans, used to do in order to make sense of our place in this planet. However, its epistemological borders are now being widened to include a host of nonhuman accounts, and, perhaps, it is even time to "allow physics to infiltrate human history."[4]

De Landa's *A Thousand Years of Nonlinear History* (1997) is an attempt at writing such an inclusive historical account. Matter and energy are featured in the book alongside humans as forces of transformation. Nature becomes a real character, actively determining patterns of migration, forms of life, and cultural realities. Given our difficulty dealing with narratives that empower entities other than human, reading De Landa's work turns out to be an exciting and at times even disturbing experience.

Nevertheless, it would be unfair to claim absolute originality for such an enterprise. Dorothee Kimmich demonstrates how modern artists and thinkers had to deal with the disturbing interval between the living and the nonliving. Natural and artificial beings constantly crossed their borders and seemed to problematize the very notion of life. Modern authors like Kafka, Rilke, Musil, and others faced this feeling of unease with the strange life of objects. In fact, Kimmich suggests, what is really new about the moderns is the paradoxical combination of border marking (*Grenzziehung*) between the animate and the inanimate and its repeated violation.[5]

In the specific field of the philosophy of history, Walter Benjamin can be seen as a precursor and pioneer, who confronted the issue with depth and originality. In her study on Benjamin's *Arcades Project*, Susan Buck-Morss identifies a curious process of crossing the switches between the categories of history and nature in the philosopher's thought.[6] Through a procedure by means of which the aforementioned cleavage seems to falter, signs and ideas that were customarily referred to the first domain are applied to the second and vice versa—so much so, in fact, that notions such as progress or even the production of the "new" are called into question:

> Just as there are places in the stones of the Miocene or Eocene Age that bear the impression of huge monsters out of these geological epochs, so today the Passages lie in the great cities like caves containing fossils of an ur-animal[7] presumed extinct: The consumers from the preimperial epoch of capitalism, the last dinosaurs of Europe.[8]

The short circuit between these categories engendered new, unsuspected perspectives on cultural phenomena while also revealing aspects of modern reality (its transitory, primitive state) that are difficult to perceive. By using words and ideas from the natural realm to refer to the technological world of modernity, Benjamin not only gave new meanings to the notion of technology as *second nature* but was also able to lay bare the contradictions and dilemmas of modern experience. He goes on with this series of natural images in the following pages of the *Arcades Project*: for example, when he compares the merchandise sold in the arcades to "immemorial flora" and "cancerous tissue."[9] The power of such images resides in highlighting the archaic character of the consumption forms expressed by the arcades, which were already at that time being replaced by big department stores. With this peculiar critical strategy, Benjamin also seems to anticipate certain theoretical formulations of much a later date foregrounding the aesthetics of posthumanist representation, the insights of material ecocriticism, and the Latourian transfers happening between networks of things and humans.

My goal here is sketching a few converging lines between Benjamin and Vilém Flusser, another thinker who has been garnering increasing critical attention precisely in domains connected to posthumanism and postnaturalism. After several years of relative and unjust obscurity, Flusser is now being referenced with startling frequency by scholars from diverse fields, from philosophy to anthropology and cultural studies.[10] This renewed interest in Flusser is due, at least in part, to the expressive number of translations of his works that came out recently in English (at least ten books since

2012); however, one should not overlook the fact that Flusser dealt extensively, already several years ago, with the relevance of problems and questions which became completely evident only in the context of the 2000s. Some of these questions pop up even in relatively early instantiations of his thinking. The recurrent fascination with topics of a posthumanistic tenor can be found, for instance, in a series of articles entitled "Bichos" ("Beasts"), published in the 1970s in the Brazilian newspaper *Folha de São Paulo*. There, Flusser already attempts to deconstruct certain ontological hierarchies by stating that the evolutionary scale changes according to each particular being's point of view.[11] From the beginning, Flusser's texts are thus dotted with plants, animals, and nonhuman entities of the most different kinds, often playing the role of destabilizing traditional points of view and questioning the borders between nature and culture.

This world of strange beings, angels, plants, and animals was explored by Flusser as well as by Benjamin in provocative and innovative ways. Both authors provide conceptual tools for rethinking our notions of identity and otherness while also offering interesting paths for the deconstruction of anthropocentrism. If in Benjamin, for example, the obsession with angelic beings expresses a very heterodox image—that of a cannibalistic angel (*menschenfresserischer Engel*), who would liberate men by taking them rather than making them happy by granting them some gift—in Flusser the angel symbolizes the freedom that manifests itself in the flight of birds: "For our ancestors, the bird was the link between animal and angel."[12] From the Flusserian perspective, the angel is an *extraterrestrial being*, given that its interest is focused much more on space than on land. Moreover, the angel is "a being that apprehends, comprehends, conceives, and modifies 'freely.'"[13] Flusser's angel seems to be much more domesticated and harmless than Benjamin's Rilkean angel.[14] The latter, as an incarnation of the *Unmensch* (inhuman), is distinguished by its cannibalistic drive, which announces "a new type of experience (*Erfahrung*), that of incorporation."[15] A term that was polemically appropriated from the Nazi vocabulary, Benjamin's *Unmensch* becomes the sign of an entity that "empathized with the destructive side of nature."[16] The singular power of this new creature, unlike the previous ones that rely on love, is voracity, barbarism. Destruction appears here, therefore, as a necessary moment of recreation for the overcoming of the humanistic model of man.

In Flusser's works one also finds some strange beings for which cannibalism conveys a special kind of freedom. In his philosophical fable about the *Vampyroteuthis infernalis*, the "vampire squid from hell," Flusser claims that for this peculiar creature, freedom *is* cannibalism: "the right to devour its kin."[17] Whereas we, humans, overcome our animality (our natural state) by showing love to our neighbors, *Vampyroteuthis* overcomes his when he learns to hate. Like with Benjamin, cannibalism here has a political significance. However, for Flusser, Vampyroteuthic cannibalism is like "the other side" of our own spirit. A *Vampyroteuthis* hides in each one of us, like a human spirit disguised in each vampire squid. This is the reason why, when facing the *Vampyroteuthis*, we see our own "grotesque political folly."[18] If for Benjamin the devouring angel brings a new revolutionary barbarism, for Flusser the cannibalistic aspect of *Vampyroteuthis* is perceived at once with allure and mistrust. The vampire squid from hell, with his polymorphic traits, can drag us into the most unexpected abysses: "in the exploits of Nazism, in cybernetic thinking, in works of logical analysis, and in certain theological texts."[19]

Benjamin claims that the inhuman is the correlate of a notion of history "no longer purely anthropocentric in nature or anchored solely in the concerns of a human subject."[20] In other words, a history in which animals, things, and other nonhuman beings have a decisive protagonism. Benjamin uncovers this notion in the ancient idea of natural history (*Naturgeschichte*), whose roots are to be found already in the *Naturphilosophie* of the eighteenth century. The philosophy of nature was founded on the premise that "nature has a history and this history is of mythical character."[21] If history were a uniquely human enterprise (and consequently different from nature's cyclical temporality) it wouldn't be possible to speak of a natural history. There is a mystical identity between nature and spirit, which demands knowledge of the laws of analogy in order to effect the decipherment of God's intricate scripture. Like many other of his conceptual constructs, Benjamin's proposition of a natural history was inspired by the German theosophists, mystics, and romantics. Winfried Menninghaus demonstrates thoroughly the importance of Cabalistic mysticism and theosophists, such as Jacob Boehme and Franz von Baader, for the development of Benjamin's philosophy of language.[22] The book on the German baroque drama (*Trauerspiel*), in which most of Benjamin's philosophemes on natural history were elaborated, represents a key moment of the thinker's reasoning about the so-called magic of language (*Sprachmagie*). Language is "magic" in its capacity to *immediately* express itself, or, rather, its *spiritual essence*—which can be understood as its mediality and infiniteness.[23]

This interest in mysticism as a domain for processes of conceptual appropriation, even if aestheticized—a "secularized appropriation" (*säkularisierende Aneignung*), in Menninghaus's words—has often baffled his interpreters. It is worthwhile to notice that the same strategy was extensively employed by Flusser, whose reflections on the theme of freedom and its relations to otherness are often interwoven with theological motifs. This is evident, for instance, in this stunning passage from *Kommunikologie weiter denken*:

> [God created the world with the intention of placing it at man's disposal. Man reigns over it as God's image and semblance. In order for man to reign, God was compelled to give him freedom. Freedom means the liberty to sin. Man brings into the world the possibility of sin. Maybe this is not a very orthodox interpretation. *Adama* means earth, *Adam* means man. After having modelled the earth on His image, God instilled in it the spirit, *ruach*. This is the origin of writing. Clay, Mesopotamic clay, was somehow modelled into a brick. And man inscribed into it the spirit in the shape of cuneiform writing. Adam is a slab of cuneiform writing. Therein lies, therefore, this image and semblance of God, which contains the breath, *ruach, pneuma, spiritus*, and is free to sin or not to sin. To everyone's astonishment, he sins when he differentiates. So, he must sin. He cannot but sin, after having decided. To differentiate (*unterscheiden*) contains

to decide (*entscheiden*). Adam and Eve ponder and then enter into the state of *having-to-sin*. Thereby, the whole of creation is called into question. For to what end has God created the world? Only to inscribe there His image and leave it in a state of "not-being-able-not-to-sin" (*Nichts-als-Sündigen-Könnens*)? Hence, God must unfortunately (*leider Gottes*) turn himself into man. By becoming man, God releases humankind from sin, but he also deprives it from freedom. Freedom appears, then, as a threatening danger. The believer who believes in Christ is freed from deciding, from differentiating, from sin. He is absolutely conditioned (*unfrei*: "not-free"). He can no longer sin, *pecare non posset*. This is a strange, and not always present, way of experiencing freedom, but we carry it inside of us. We still have the feeling that freedom has a bitter flavor.][24]

As a matter of fact, this notion of the ability to differentiate as sin is intriguingly close to Benjamin's idea of the original sin as a fall into the "magic of judgement" (*Magie des Urteils*), developed in the essay "On Language as Such and on the Language of Man" (1916). If before the Fall man spoke the pure language of names, in which language and knowledge were the same, after this tragic event we enter into the realm of human language, wherein we find plurality and the *differentiation* between languages. It is inside this "magic of judgement" that the *abstract* elements of language find their roots. One abandons the "immediacy in the communication of the concrete, i.e., the name" and falls into the mediated abyss of "all communication, of the word as medium."[25] In judgment we find the "original separation" (*Ur-teil*), grounded on the differentiation between good and evil. Isn't judging essentially *to differentiate*? However, if judgment appears to be a lesser form of magic for Benjamin in comparison to the pure magic of names, of immediate knowledge, in Flusser sin (which indirectly means the capacity to judge and differentiate) symbolizes the only freedom available to man—and, of course, this is not a "very orthodox interpretation" of the biblical text (neither is Benjamin's). The symbolic event of the Fall affects not only language but also nature, which then becomes sad and mute. The great sorrow of nature is speechlessness, and the task of art and philosophy is "to restore what has been altered in the Fall: the language of names."[26] For Flusser, on the other hand, nature still talks, so he extends linguistic attributes to the elements of nature. Birds, for instance, speak "in a language too imperative" for him to attribute their expression to a projection of his gaze, the buds in his orchard articulate "their own unsophisticated language," the displaced cedar "presents itself" to him if he allows it to speak, and so on.[27]

To be sure: in the project of differentiation also lurks the danger of an excessive clarity, of a desire for purification that belies the world's complex and hybrid nature. With regard to the complexity of the relationship between nature and culture, Flusser identifies two possible attitudes: the first is meant to make nature's essence more resplendent; the second seeks to highlight the idea of nature as modified by human spirit. Each one would have its particular "art." But the fact remains that "the two types of art and culture do not exist, and have never existed in a pure state [. . .] This makes it extremely problematic, not only to want to distinguish, ontologically, between several cultures, but also to want to establish a rigorous dialectic between culture and nature."²⁸ Most of the times, human spirit doesn't manage to completely impose itself over nature. We interpret, we sketch projects, we attempt to differentiate. However, it's always in a complex relationship with the natural determinations that we condition our existence. In that sense, Flusser claims that the valleys, as sites for the passage of waters, are domains of perspectivism and limit. It's not possible to "inhabit" them, only "to go through" them. For Flusser, they are "almost supernatural, almost theoretical, almost perspectival."²⁹

Possibly, valleys are places akin to those that appear in Benjamin's "science of thresholds" (*Schwellenkunde*). In his reading of Goethe's *Elective Affinities*, Benjamin uses this science to evaluate the mythical powers of spatial (like the ocean's surface or the graveyard) as well as temporal (like the rites of passage) thresholds. The threshold is a *locus* of ambiguity (*Zweideutigkeit*), an in-between (*Zwieschenbereich*). The arcades are the quintessential domains of liminality, marking the complex limits between the streets and the individual stores. Here we find an interesting paradox: "the mythical spatial form of the liminal also features as an element of Benjamin's anti-mythical utopia."³⁰ It is a question not simply of destroying the myth but rather of redeeming it—in other words, "a salvation of mythical forms" (*Rettung mytischen Formen*), writes Menninghaus. This is a consequence of the fact that the old still harbors revolutionary forces waiting for their awakening.

Myth is marked by ambiguity, it is a territory of passage, in which, along with the dream images, one must seek the physiognomy of an epoch. It is not by chance that Flusser evokes the idea according to which myths are *triggers for history*. Therefore, "if one of the basic theses of Marxism is that dreams are killed once they are realized, then the dialectic side of such a thesis is forgotten: dead dreams persist."³¹ For Benjamin, on the other hand, materialist mythology illuminates the dream world in order to lead them to the threshold of awakening. The science of thresholds is the science of myths and dreams. As Buck-Morss puts it, "Paradoxically, collective imagination mobilizes its powers for a revolutionary break from the recent past by evoking a cultural memory reservoir of myths and utopian symbols from a more distant ur-past."³²

Here we face the danger of fetishism, when the technologies into which we deposit the past's utopic dreams are taken as its realizations instead of possible means to achieve it. What we are called for is an awakening capable of redeeming the dreams. In Flusser, myths and dreams display a constitutive function. They can be a way to materialize utopias (which he classifies as positive or negative). They exist to enable the construction of alternate worlds. Within the universe of digital technologies, more than ever, we enter into a domain of projection, fictionalization. The projects for possible futures are "dreams that claim for other dreamers, so that they may be able to aggregate and become more possible."³³ With his strategy of using dreams, fictions, and myths to multiply points of view (*Standpunkten*), Flusser frequently sets side by side signs of nature and signs of culture. That's what he does, for instance, when he uses *Vampyroteuthis'* bioluminescence or his metamorphic skin in order to reflect upon our contemporary electronic media. By means of this move, the thresholds between nature and culture are called into question. *Vampyroteuthis*, like the human being, possesses "art" and "culture," with the only caveat that he materializes them in a different manner.

Flusser resorts to a very Benjaminian term—"spiritual essence" (*geistiges Wesen*)—when he brings together man and *Vampyroteuthis*.[34] More than that, *Vampyroteuthis* possesses history, he is a "historisches Wesen."[35] But while human history is basically a process of storage of acquired information onto objects, "vampyroteuthic" history unfolds in a truly intersubjective way, by means of his secreting glands.

Like in John Heartfield's photomontages, which Benjamin treasured, the narrative of *Vampyroteuthis Infernalis* is a way of short-circuiting signs of nature and culture.[36] Benjamin operated in a similar manner, but through a montage of verbal images instead of photographic ones—as is the case with *One Way Street*. In some measure Flusser combines both techniques in *Vampyroteuthis Infernalis*, by joining his philosophical fable's text with Louis Bec's intriguing images for the book. Bec states each of the drawings captures attitudes or traces of Flusser's "vampiromorphic" character; however, they could very well be read with many other different meanings, be they philosophical, political, or social. It is tempting to associate the plate describing the subspecies "Lumanter Phusagrion"—characterized by his "systematic activity of destruction of all living forms that cross his bio-ideological space"—to extractivist capitalism in its thirst for appropriation and consumption of whole ecosystems.[37] After all, Stacy Alaimo suggests that Flusser's Vampyroteuthis is like an ecological treatise that veers "away from standard modes of scientific objectivity" toward an "intimate science and impassioned politics."[38] Hence, why not read it as a philosophical fable that deals not only with man's technological dilemmas but also our relationship to the environment and nonhuman beings? Even more, why not read it as a reflection on the life of objects, those things that, with their cunning (*Tücke*), resist our attempts at informing and controlling them?

Perhaps this is the most instigating perspective of the encounter between Flusser's and Benjamin's projects. Both work with concepts of life and history that extend to things.[39] Flusser explicitly affirms that "mountains are things that have a history, or, more precisely, a biography."[40] In the same vein, Benjamin claims: "the concept of life is given its due only if everything that has a history of its own, and is not merely the setting for history, is credited with life."[41] This is the reason why one should not understand the words "survival" (*Überleben*) and "continued life" (*Fortleben*), used in *The Task of the Translator*, in a metaphorical sense, but rather in objective terms. Through this perspective we find a world immensely richer than the one we traditionally inhabit. There resides a multiplicity of gazes and networks within which the human being appears as just one more component. In fact, one could say there is not only *one* world but rather several; not *one* nature but many.

> We do not live, therefore, in *one*, but in many natures: in a nature that is graspable by the categories of our natural sciences, in an Aristotelian "*physis*," in a nature that is full of Gods, in a nature created by God. All of these natures are there, outside the window, but also in here. They "really" interfere with one another.[42]

This multiplicity of natural worlds becomes clear after what Flusser calls "post-history," when it is no longer possible to perceive reality from a single point of view.

The posthistorical moment implies a multiplication of perspectives (*Standpunkte*). Technical images helped create a new, posthistorical type of consciousness. With this consciousness, we experience a partial return of the "magic" that was present in the prehistoric era. However, it is a different kind of magic, because it is no longer founded on faith (the belief that time is structured in reversible relations and everything participates in a significant context), but rather on the programs by means of which apparatuses work.[43] If Flusser is able to repeatedly "speak" from the perspective of a mollusk in *Vampyroteuthis Infernalis*, it is because we are now, more than ever, open to a multiplicity of gazes in our dealings with the world. In this world of strange beings, hybridity supersedes our desire for purity. This includes the conflation between the animal (nature) and our supposedly post-natural technologies (culture), as well as an increased capacity to perceive the dimensions of otherness that surround us even in the most ordinary situations of our lives.[44] In fact, Flusser believes that, instead of looking for alien life in other planets, we should engage in conversation with the weird and alien creatures that populate our own planet.[45] *Vampyroteuthis* is one such alien being that is simultaneously close to and extremely distant from us.

Van den Eijnden coins the expression "*alien* natures" to refer to Flusser and his fable about the *Vampyroteuthis infernalis*. Not only Flusser's octopodal beings but also Benjamin's angels and stones may fit into this "nature that is unknown and yet imaginable, a nature that is an *elsewhere* and yet somehow present in a here."[46] These alien spaces are sites for the encounter with the *other* in all its radicalness, for an interspecies dialogue by means of which man can learn about himself and the world that surrounds him in innovative ways. Therein we no longer find the dichotomy nature/culture, so that all beings present themselves as an agglomerate of multidimensional realities. It is for that reason that Flusser manages to see Oedipus in his orchard.[47] It is also the same reason why Benjamin manages to see a biological theory of fashion in zebras and horses.[48] In times of deep ecological crisis, this other history and this other way of thinking may offer us valuable tools to imagine different futures: less dark, deserted, and lonely ones, possibilities nourished by the hope for a new humankind.

Notes

1. Benjamin, *The Arcades Project* (Cambridge, MA: Belknap Press, 1999), 195.
2. Manuel De Landa, *A Thousand Years of Nonlinear History* (New York: Zone Books, 1997), 11.
3. Ibid., 13.
4. Ibid., 15.
5. Dorothee Kimmich, *Lebendige Dinge in der Moderne* (Paderborn: Konstanz University Press, 2011), 13.
6. Susan Buck-Morss, *The Dialectics of Seeing: Walter Benjamin and the Arcades Project* (Cambridge, MA: The MIT Press, 1991), 59.
7. Buck-Morss reads the word "Untier" (monster, beast) as "Urtier" (i.e., "ur-animal"; "primordial animal").

8   Benjamin, cited in Buck-Morss, *The Dialectics of Seeing*, 65.
9   Benjamin, *Gesammelte Werke*, II (Frankfurt am Main: Suhrkamp, 1991), 670.
10 See, for instance, John Ó. Maoilearca, *All Thoughts Are Equal: Laruelle and Nonhuman Philosophy* (Minneapolis: University of Minnesota Press, 2015); John Durham Peters, *The Marvelous Clouds: Toward a Philosophy of Elemental Media* (Chicago: University of Chicago Press, 2015); and, Katherine Hayles, "Speculative Aesthetics and Object-Oriented Inquiry (OOI)," *Speculations: A Journal of Speculative Realism* V (2014), http://speculations-journal.org.
11 See Felinto and Lucia Santaella, *O Explorador de Abismos: Vilém Flusser e o Pós-Humanismo* (São Paulo: Paulus, 2012), 118.
12 Benjamin, *Gesammelte Werke*, II, 1106; Flusser, *Natural:Mind* (Minneapolis: Univocal, 2013), 27.
13 Flusser, *Natural:Mind*, 27.
14 One is reminded of Rilke's famous verse in the *Duino Elegies*: "Ein jeder Engel ist schrecklich" ("every angel is terrifying"). Rainer Maria Rilke, *Duineser Elegien* in *Rilke Werke, II* (Frankfurt am Main: Insel, 1982), 441.
15 Beatrice Hanssen, *Walter Benjamin's Other History: Of Stones, Animals, Human Beings, and Angels* (Berkeley: University of California Press, 1998), 119.
16 Benjamin, *Gesammelte Werke*, II, 1106.
17 Flusser, *Vampyroteuthis Infernalis* (Minneapolis: University of Minnesota Press, 2012), 59.
18 Ibid., 60. The German original uses the phrase "political grimace" (*politische Fratze*).
19 Ibid., 70.
20 Hanssen, *Walter Benjamin's Other History*, 48.
21 Antoine Faivre, *Philosophie de la nature: physique sacrée et théosophie XVIII-XIX siècle* (Paris: Albin Michel, 1996), 16.
22 Winfried Menninghaus, *Walter Benjamins Theorie der Sprachmagie* (Frankfurt am Main: Suhrkamp, 1995), 191. Further, Baader was only one of several theosophists studied by Benjamin. On Baader's importance for *Naturphilosophie*, see the various chapters devoted to him in Faivre, *Philosophie de la nature*.
23 Walter Benjamin, "On Language as Such and On the Language of Man," *Selected Writings, 1 (1913-1926)* (Cambridge, MA: Harvard University Press, 2004), 64.
24 Author's translation, Flusser, *Kommunikologie weiter denken: Die Bochumer Vorlesungen* (Frankfurt am Main: Suhrkamp, 2009), 228.
25 Benjamin, "On Language as Such and On the Language of Man," 68–9.
26 Rainer Rochlitz, *The Disenchantment of Art: The Philosophy of Walter Benjamin* (New York: Guilford, 1996), 19.
27 Flusser, *Post-History* (Minneapolis: Univocal, 2013), 86, 119, 40.
28 Flusser, *Natural:Mind*, 10.
29 Ibid., 20.
30 Menninghaus, *Science of Thresholds: Walter Benjamin's Mythical Passages* (Suhrkamp: Frankfurt am Main, 1986), 52.
31 Flusser, *Natural:Mind*, 24.
32 Buck-Morss, *The Dialectics of Seeing: Walter Benjamin and the Arcades Project* (Cambridge, MA: The MIT Press, 1989), 116.
33 Vilém Flusser, *Vom Subjekt zum Projekt. Menschwerdung* (Frankfurt am Main: Fischer, 1998), 42.

34 The mysterious expression appears in the essay "On Language as Such and On the Language of Man." By naming things, man communicates his spiritual essence (*geistiges Wesen*) to God, he is a name-giving being. Flusser, *Vampyroteuthis Infernalis: Eine Abhandlung samt Befund des Institut Scientifique de Recherche Paranaturaliste* (Göttingen: European Photography, 2002), 27.
35 Ibid., 47.
36 According to Buck-Morss, "the ideological fusion of nature and history when reproduced by Heartfield through an allegorical use of photomontage allows the gap between sign and referent to remain visible, thus enabling him to represent their identity in the form of a critique" (62).
37 Flusser, Brazilian *Vampyroteuthis Infernalis*, s/p.
38 Stacy Alaimo, "Unmoor," in *Veer Ecology: A Companion for Environmental Thinking*, ed. Jeffrey Jerome Cohen and Lowell Duckert (Minneapolis: University of Minnesota Press, 2017), 413–14.
39 Hanssen, *Walter Benjamin's Other History*, 33.
40 Flusser, *Natural:Mind*, 77.
41 Benjamin, "On Language as Such and On the Language of Man," 255.
42 Flusser, *Natural:Mind*, 88.
43 Flusser, *Post-History* (Minneapolis: Univocal, 2013), 97.
44 In Flusser's fable, the Vampyroteuthis not only has "art" and "technologies"; it is itself, at times, a technological apparatus.
45 In the unpublished essay "Wesen aus einer anderen Welt" ("Beings from another world," n.d., typescript). For a more detailed development of Flusser's alien argument, see Erick Felinto, "Oceanic Medium: Technology, Identity and Maritime Imagination in Vilém Flusser," *Azimuth* VII, no. 13: 37–50.
46 Ibid., 45.
47 Flusser *Natural:Mind* (Minneapolis: Univocal, 2013), 115.
48 Benjamin, *Gesammelte Werke*, II, 123.

27

Flusser's New World

Aaron Jaffe

Globalization takes place only in capital and data. All the rest is damage control.
—Gayatri Spivak[1]

As Karl Rossmann, a poor boy of sixteen who had been packed off to America by his parents because a servant girl had seduced him and got herself a child by him, stood on the liner slowly entering the harbor of New York, a sudden burst of sunshine seemed to illumine the Statue of Liberty, so that he saw it in a new light, although he had sighted it long before. The arm with the sword rose up as if newly stretched aloft, and round the figure blew the free winds of heaven. "So high," he said to himself, forgetting to disembark and was gradually edged to the very rail by the swelling throng of porters.
—Franz Kafka[2]

This was the first Presidential Inauguration that the country saw on high-definition TV. I don't care if Trump is a reality TV star who isn't politically correct. The Inauguration was great television, beautifully photographed and edited, and Washington DC looked magnificent. Melania was gorgeous and Jackie Evancho sang beautifully. Trump's speech sounds like it could have been delivered by Jeff Daniels in "Independence Day." The purpose of the Inaugural speech is to make people feel great about America, and it worked for me. I know he can't accomplish half of what he said he would do. But if he doesn't deserve respect then neither does a union boss who advocates for school funding when all of the money will go to teacher pensions.
—Matthew from Pasadena in the comments section of *The New York Times*

I.

Kafka's *Amerika* begins aboard a transatlantic ocean liner entering New York harbor, as the protagonist Karl Roßmann experiences a puzzling view of the Statue of Liberty. For some reason, the de facto symbol of America is different. Her raised arm juts a sword into the sky. Looming over an anxious arrival, the symbolic beacon styled originally as the Modern Colossus seems in Kafka's version, burnished sword at the ready, to transmit a signal about a new monstrosity of administrative authority. Under this Variant Colossus, then, at the verges of American terra firma, all of yesterday's knowledge becomes hearsay, and counted among this hearsay is the American sign par excellence of Liberty Illuminating the World itself. Instead of her famous torch—tablets of law, broken chains, scales of justice, a satchel of nuclear launch codes, or any equipment, for that matter—the arm heaves a flaming sword upwards (like the one from Supreme Headquarters Allied Expeditionary Force in *Gravity's Rainbow*).

A screaming comes across the sky... An inevitable sign, as Roland Barthes might say, the sword cuts parabolically into the stratosphere prefiguring the gigantic scissors Claes Oldenburg will later envision for the Washington Mall between the Lincoln memorial and the Capitol building.[3] Pharos becoming paper shredder, sharp edges underscoring not just that there are many versions of America—diverse opinions about the meaning of a particular symbol—but also that what is apprehended from afar is a wide-reaching circumference of America's biopolitical omnia potenta. Whether pointing inward toward the American hinterland or outward back out to sea, this much is clear about the sword. Red tape will be cut. Heads will roll. Indeed, Oldenburg's take on the Variant Colossus for Liberty Island, as an enormous desk fan, fan blades constantly churning, pushes the ships back out to sea, and wrecking them in an enormous pile near Ellis Island.[4] Instead of a beacon, this Colossus sends out warnings to newcomers: they will face hardships.[5] Similarly, Kafka's Liberty, imagined as gigantic border guard, functions also as monstrous valve for extreme vetting into America, the proper noun, the monstrous signifier of precarious exceptionalism in which people will have old national attachments cut and then at last disappear.

The most obvious meaning for a national monument is to promote exceptional feelings about a nation. All nations are unexceptional in this way. Matthew from Pasadena correctly intuits an appeal to authority in a generic sense. True for the Commander in Chief and for the Union Boss, it has less to do with honoring everything America than being insulated inside retropresentist obedience amid an explosion of national signs. How did it get so high? For an Oldenburg monument, picture a super-sized aerosol can pushing out plasticized panegyric like silly string, the kinds of "high sounding exclamations" familiar from political pep rallies in disaster movies. A former model stands by mutely on the plinth, gorgeously clothed; a recent winner of a televised singing contest awaits a cue to perform the patriotic hymn; air force jets streak far overhead.[6] For Vilém Flusser—and, for Kafka as well, perhaps—this kind of scene executes an all-too-familiar program of nationalism qua kitsch—"lust elevated to the level of social reality."[7] Ungrounded in any one nation, the migrant has a different relation to all the surface signs. The fictional event—the sudden shaft of light, the phenomenal cut—transmits a signal, a surprise disclosure at the very moment of an initial glance, orientation mediated by a landmark, an ominous message about an all-too-possible reality, gauged from afar.

At a distance, Kafka, who never visited America himself, gets the communiqué only from hearsay, from postcards, perhaps, from pictures on stamps on letters from friends or from family members who emigrated. Still, there can be no doubt that Liberty Illuminating the World broadcasts a certain telematic signal to him carrying particular super-sized bromides. Thinking with Kafka, Maryam Monalisa Gharavi imagines Karl R. as an alternate version of Kafka himself—a younger brother, perhaps, receptive to the signals from America.[8] The variant K., who never was, is more adaptable and eager to please, a better escape-artist, with a heartier stomach, more robust lungs, and a better singing voice. Unlike the actual Kafka, this one finds the escape hatch out of Central Europe into a "land of open pathways and immensely charted skies that the seduction of being what one was not in the beginning holds the most power."[9] For those who arrive, the bottom falls out. The Colossus above, following Vilém Flusser, resembles Kafka's Administrative God. The Higher-up, "[a]pathetic and disinterested in our fate," "pedantic, over-organized, ridiculously incompetent, sick and tired of himself is nothing other than the increasing accumulation of man's reflection on nothingness," the administrative Colossus raises the generalized anxiety about nothingness to "gigantic proportions," like the giant adenoid in *Gravity's Rainbow*.[10] The Administrative God is a God of platforms—format, bureaucratic technicity, dimensionality: "the apathetic higher powers show their indifference towards us when they play with our lives absurdly and regardless of rules—or, we might say, idiotically."[11] If nothing else, Karl R., the would-be migrant, is an avant-garde receiver for indifferent, absurd, and idiotic information—noise, feedback, signals—which are, in Flusser's word, always "premature," "distorted and unconvincing."[12] (This is why, Flusser writes, the rest of us are in a new world and "waiting for Kafka.")

Indeed, Karl R. closely resembles the actual, real-life Vilém F., the same peripatetic Jewish, Czech-born Brazilian media theorist who fled the Nazis in the late 1930s and spent at least some of his time in Brazil thinking about "waiting for Kafka" and these very themes, writing in English as well as German, Portuguese, and French, and trying to crack open the door—cut through the skies—into the North American academic world. Significantly, his writing of the mid-1960s is preoccupied with the precarious exceptionalism of nationality, the hazardous existence of the migrant, the mutating effects of conflicting signals, media, and telematics. For Flusser, the disorienting experiences of the migrant—the receiver of premature, distorted, and unconvincing information—register feedback about national signification from loss of grounding, different signal to noise ratios, and conflicting frequencies that yield potential for critical experimentalism. The troubles with the term *America* for criticism are familiar. Not just a sobriquet for one country—it also designates various pluralities, two contiguous continents, and proximate lands. With particular reference to its tendentious place in Flusser's career, my chapter explores the role of America in the genesis of his ideas of experience and migrancy. The very status of nationality—American or otherwise—is a reified aesthetic frame rebuked by the instable experiences of the migrant who shows the notion that the signifiers of national values are plastic, subject to disorienting re-signification, available for possible variation as well as pre-programmed for data-throughput and colossal, monstrous projections.

Somewhere beneath the skin of Liberty—inside the folds of the drape—is the Eiffel Tower, or Roland Barthes's interpretation of it. Gustave Eiffel himself did in fact also design the real Statue of Liberty's support structure. For Barthes, the Eiffel Tower is a Semiotic Colossus that surpasses any attempt to restrict its meaning—including any conventional national meaning. It functions as the ultimate sign. Touching every upward glance, its form becomes the supreme specimen, recognizable everywhere—Paris, France, the World—abundant with associations and with potential meanings. A gigantic monument to signification as such, the Tower taps into the "general human image-repertoire," Barthes writes:

> its simple, primary shape confers upon it the vocation of *an infinite cipher*: In turn and according to the appeals of our imagination, the symbol of Paris, of modernity, of communication, of science or of the nineteenth century, rocket, stem, derrick, phallus, lightning rod or insect, confronting the great itineraries of our dreams, it is *the inevitable sign*; just as there is no Parisian glance which is not compelled to encounter it, there is no fantasy which fails, sooner or later, to acknowledge its form and to be nourished by it; pick up a pencil and let your hand, in other words your thoughts, wander, and it is often the Tower which will appear, reduced to that simple line whose sole mythic function is to join, as the poet says, *base and summit*, or again, *earth and heaven*.[13]

For Barthes, in a sense, semiotic universalism comes with a particular French twist, tinged with the emancipatory language of its Enlightenment discourse and its revolutionary glancing blow for universal emancipation. A lightning bolt that comes to the ground, infinite and inevitable, the Eiffel Tower is the sign that is also a signal. It stands for an amiable semiotic voyage out, the liberating powers radiating modernity's benefits outward in the form of pluripotent signification. Even as the insectile exoskeleton—the last, weirdest, most inhuman association Barthes suggests—the Eiffel Tower signals a power station for a new telematics, condensing and transmitting biomechanical life-force, as if the very engineered character of the wrought iron truss-work seethes raw, swarming biopower.

"The Tower," he writes, "ultimately reunites with the essential function of all major human sites: autarchy; the Tower can live on itself: one can dream there, eat there, observe there, understand there, marvel there, shop there; as on an ocean liner (another mythic object that sets children dreaming), one can feel oneself cut off from the world and yet the owner of a world."[14] In terms of its association with any one nation-state (i.e., France), the Eiffel Tower's infinitude calls forth both a way in and a way out. It is both the ladder and the fire escape. Insofar as the scaffolding collapses *being looked upon* and *being on the lookout*, the Eiffel Tower inevitably evokes Tatlin's Monument to the Third International, the famously unbuilt tribunal to internationalism, manned by Lenin, fashioned to look out for an alternative beyond nationalisms into the universe of alternative affective platforms. Yet, even if its appeals are autarchic not autocratic, there is something imperious in such messages, too.

Look upon an image of the infrastructure of the Statue of Liberty—diagrams of its inner skeletal structure, photographs of its girders and undercarriage—the Eiffel Tower exists inevitably and infinitely there, too. Invisible, inside the stretched copper skin of the inevitably and infinitely American symbol, one detects a specific semiotic provenance from elsewhere, the gift from French friends, commemorative emancipatory associations and expectations, and so on. The infrastructure recalls Barthes's point about the inevitability of more signification. Liberty means more than the meanings most obviously attached to it; more than its association with American-style liberty, for one, the self-applied exceptionalism of a national case, the beacon-lure for tourist-migrants; more than economic opportunity or political sanctuary for desperate multitudes; more than a hidden antenna for transmitting and receiving potential messages. The data invites doubt not dogma. More than this, too. Exhibited, the hidden infrastructure points to modernity as an unfinished disorientation platform. Doubt on a pedestal. Turning the Statue back into the Tower, one might revise Barthes further: under the folds of the signifier—in its hidden infrastructure—exist uncertainties, variants, possibilities, other signals. The Variant Colossus is at once Modern, Semiotic, and Variable.

Flusser himself mentions the Eiffel Tower in his essay on Landmarks, discussing the Landmark not as a sign ready-made for discourse but as a potential signal for orientation in the context of the way travel guides rate sights.[15] Travel guides, he notes, promote a binary form of accounting in which most things about a given place do not rate as sightworthy and thus do not get mentioned. What is the real place except the invisible ubiquity of everything omitted by a travel guide? What *is* worth seeing, Flusser notes—the Eiffel Tower in France, Cristo Redentor in Brazil, the Statue of Liberty in the United States, and so on—is coded in terms of its worthiness to be looked upon and ranked accordingly with stars. Finding one's way into this world gives a somewhat banal approximation of what Flusser means elsewhere when he describes the universe of technical images as pathways of disorientation:

> The disappointment we currently experience in every explanation, interpretation, and reading of the world (the discovery that there is nothing behind the world to be discovered) leads to a revolutionary new attitude toward the world. Disappointed, we stop bending, straighten ourselves up, and stretch out our arms against the world to point an index finger at it. From now on, all pointers, signs, traffic signals, and indicators point eccentrically away from us, and nothing more points toward us. From now on, we are the ones who project meaning on the world. And technical images are such projections.[16]

The passage among starred sights has no relation to actual finding aids but instead produces and is produced by a diagrammatic constellation of other starry sights. Karl R.'s disappearance in America anticipates precisely this kind of passage, a journey that deposits him, in effect, at the end of the line into an advertising poster for the Nature Theatre of Oklahoma. The first stop in an unfamiliar country begins and ends at the postcard rack from which one intuits what not to see—what sights are not worthy of experience and consequently are forever invisible. Flusser calls this practice the Guillotine method, because it cuts the head off everything *not* worth seeing. Through it, one capitulates to the supreme capability of the technical image.[17]

The value of *being looked at*, exemplified in the guide-book model, executes—in the sense of the guillotine level or the command line of a computer program. It decapitates the intellectual-experiential dimension of orientation (orientation through first-order, discovery-grade mapping) and communicates by means of rankings or ratings to receivers that mislead them into a pseudo-evaluative trance state. Tellingly, his reference is another Modern Colossus closely associated with the trance state of nationality (built in collaboration with another French engineer), namely, Christ the Redeemer on Mount Corcovado overlooking Rio, Brazil, South America, where Flusser landed in 1940:

> It is impossible to be too radical where [the image of the landmark] is concerned. Heads roll. First, it becomes necessary to review one's view of picture post cards. And then one's view of Rio. And so on: one must review one's view of the statue on Corcovado, and of the motive which has led to the construction of the statue. In another direction one must review one's views on photographing. In yet another direction one's views on the origins of views (on "opinion formation"). And possibly even must one review one's view on Salvation which the Savior means which the statue means which the picture postcard means which [the travel guide/the tourism leader] photo means.... In sum: if looked at carefully, that photo undermines all our views based on any authority of any kind, and nobody can know where this might lead to. It may even lead one to the extraordinary painful situation, in which one is forced to form one's views without any leader. Which of course one may then fix of picture post cards of one's own making.[18]

Flusser writes against the travel guide principle, against the authority ascribed to landmarks by a *Reiseführer*, for example—the German word for travel guide is translated more concretely as travel leader. Approaching a Semiotic Colossus, in Flusser's account, as anything besides a Landmark is disorientating. The approach presents a kind of asymptotic, infinite regression into *mise en abîme*, tantamount to losing one's way in a labyrinth of signs and associations. The supposed inherent meaning that the Landmark stands for—in the case of Brazil and Cristo Redentor that his outstretched arms promise to "lift the teeming millions who live there towards Salvation"—is not readily accessible at first but comes last, if at all. Indeed, if looked at critically enough, Flusser suggests, even these ends are dubious, the certitude of all viewpoints start to sound suspicious.[19]

One travels to the Landmark not to look at it—not to be touched by the sign that touches all—but to confirm the redundancy of the dataset: the view from above, the view from history, the patriotic view, the religious view, and so on. Turning from Flusser's Brazil to Kafka's America, the migrant confronts the sudden visibility of a nation-state through its ultimate Landmark as an extraordinarily painful situation. The upward glance upon a Variant Liberty with her counterfactual sword gives an alternative picture of a particular nation and the fact of variability discloses the nation-state as a container of themes. Each contingent meaning—though potent in particular ways—carries varying degrees of efficacy and value when viewed at a distance. Each nation-state comes with a different colossus of evitable and finite signals, and only the migrant punctuates the ubiquitous invisibility with questions. And, in this sense, the question mark remains paradigmatically "the mark of our times," and, to borrow from Marshall McLuhan, it stands for a generalized "revulsion against imposed patterns."[20] Finger, Guldin, and Bernardo write of the key role the question mark plays in Flusser's thought.[21] Flusser even devotes a short essay to the mark as a turn signal of sorts at the level of sentence punctuation. Connected, perhaps, to his ideas about landmarks, too, the question mark supplies a monumental form for casting doubt for Flusser. Recalling Karl R.'s apprehension of a Variant Liberty, they extrapolate that "[t]he question mark has perhaps taken on greater significance than the cross, than the hammer and sickle, than the torch of the Statue of Liberty, because it points to the atmosphere that encloses us. It is an atmosphere of suspicion, of exploration, and of doubt."[22]

II.

Three key words—American World Literature—do not appear frequently in the Flusser lexicon, yet Flusser, the perpetually unsettled, philosophically oriented writer, who lived from 1920 till 1991, might be an ideal exemplar for a particular form of American World Literature understood as the nexus of three distinct conceptual problems. What I have in mind for American World Literature is less a special patriotic container—and even less a market for some worthy literary objects in an age of US-American hegemony—and more three monumental question marks, a belated sense of need for methodological orientations for a kind of mobile "theory auteur," or wayward literatus, "in a plastic and assimilable age," to borrow Flusserian language.[23] Vilém Flusser is not very well known in the Anglophone world outside some quarters of Art and Media Studies. Yet, he belongs to a famous generation of literary drift— from the old world to the new, into the speculative space of Theory. Theory might be thought of as a name for the fitful, wayward, belated transmission of media thinking across national frontiers in second modernity. But, I will get to the comparison and this point a bit later.

American World Literature—following the Flusserian variant—is a sort of constellation of the long now as if thrown onto a hemispheric ceiling by a planetarium projector. So moving from the inside out: first, World is foremost a matter of telematics and geophysical dis/orientation, not geopolitical accident. Second, perhaps the most difficult issue for a collection like this and for Flusser as well: literature naming a critical problem of value around the necessity of reading and writing in posthistory, which is to say the future. Third, America is a kind of vexing conceptual landmark for Flusser, which he connects gesturally to the gluttonous contiguity of life support on an endless information feed, conceiving of life, as de

Man puts it, "not just in biological but [also] in temporal terms as the [special] ability to forget whatever precedes a present situation."[24] As de Man wrote of literature and modernity and history, it is not at all clear that literature and American world are in any way compatible concepts.[25]

The troubles with the term "American" are familiar. To make a somewhat stale point, it is not a sobriquet for just one political entity, the United States, but also designates various pluralities on two contiguous continents and various proximate lands. A hemisphere, half a world brain, the word designates a force field of reception—a form of quasi-nationalism attached to semi-formed, even inchoate feelings. Flusser, who spent much of his three decades in Brazil writing in English and trying to crack open the door of the North American academic world, was suspicious of nationalist hypostasis in all forms—and was particularly wary of the idea of nationalism in the United States. Despite its "many fluttering flags" and often "virulent" strains of patriotism, "the North American continent," he writes in *The History of the Devil*, "is the only place on Earth which has been spared nationalism strictu senso."[26] This book—his Portuguese opus—is at once a philosophical fable and a kind of theoretical novel about the principle of history, told via the seven deadly sins, and the injunction to move beyond the impasses of ontology into methodological layers of a multiply-stratified present. Nationalism, for Flusser, is little more than displaced lust: "lust elevated to the level of social reality," he calls it; a sublimated romantic discourse for organizing collectivity through an unthinking relation to the sham, well-worn fixities of blood and soil.[27] Schools serve as incubators for softening humans into habitual stupidities in literature and all other things, as if insulating them in warm blankets: "the history of humanity is . . . reduced to a monotonous series of fights between peoples, intercalated by brief proofs of superiority of our own people, or by events that prove how our people, in their innocence have been exploited."[28] By midcentury, writes Flusser, the explosion is past, but "the flakes of nationalism fall like radioactive ashes of the burning Earth."[29]

Flusser likens what he sees across the Americas to gluttony or its negative image, hunger—the "Americanization of the world" provides a format that overwhelms access by swallowing everything and spewing technê everywhere: "inhabitants . . . so preoccupied devouring their products that their machines spill out [and they] don't have the opportunity to open their mouths to sing [proper] patriotic hymns in the praise of the people."[30] The lust for nationalisms belongs to a decaying past—prettified kitsch, lackluster hymns and parades, the gluttony of new continents spanning things belonging to the future: "the furious advance of technology will soon catch up with the population's growth curve, and transform material misery into a mental misery of boredom and nausea," he writes.[31] Before the authoritarian turn of the late sixties, Brazil seemed to Flusser like a place full of potentialities, ready for new non-Eurocentric codes and primed for a search for new forms of "communications theory," the literary-theoretical aspect of which he explicitly opposes to natural sciences. It is, instead, "concerned with the human being's unnatural aspects." Making a prescient connection, developed elsewhere by Lyotard and more recently by Reza Negarestani, Flusser notes that "the American term humanities [best] underscores that the human being is an unnatural animal."³² Only a nonnative ear like Flusser's, perhaps, catches the weird pluralities that the suffix *-ities* calls forth from human/humanity/humanism in this peculiar Americanism (as idiosyncratic as *Theory*, in its own way).

In his intellectual biography, written in German as Flusser left Brazil in 1972 for France, Flusser remembers fleeing the gas chambers thirty years before and throwing himself into a dialogical project greedy for "new, humane and unprejudiced" orientations to the inhuman: searching for "a secret code [for] a future Brazilian *heimat* [that transforms] adventure into habit [and after the] hallowings of habit [into a residue that] remain[s] charged with excitement."³³ The network, once woven, he hoped, would remain open: "For example, [a] philosophical institute in which Italian students of Croce, German Heidegger scholars, Portuguese followers of Ortega, Jewish positivists from Eastern Europe, Belgian Catholics, and Anglo-Saxon pragmatists took part had to open itself up to Japanese students of Zen Buddhism, a Lebanese mystic, and a Chinese literary scholar, and it had to make room for a Talmudist from Western Europe as well."³⁴ He imagined taking part in a decades-long project, a second modernism, that would "attempt to synthesize a Brazilian culture out of a mixture of Western and Eastern European, African, East Asian, and Indian cultural elements."³⁵

According to Flusser's Atlas, the world—understood as the earth's flattened surface—has become increasingly uncanny. You cannot "not feel at home in any of [its] projections," he writes. In effect, actual maps work like Google Earth long before that was a technical possibility.³⁶ What you see, he writes, is "not history [marked as lines] but history hacked into chunks. Rather than showing a film, a sequence of photographs was presented. It offered not a procedural but a quantified view. The flow of history became a mass of grains of sand."³⁷ It was already "impossible to capture the connections between geographically separate regions."³⁸ Flusser's history of the devil contrasts this weak, almost skin-like atlas—and any affirmative commandment to describe superficial matter upon it (!)—with more deeply situated layers for methodological speculation. At once artificial construct and natural feature, Flusserian multidimensional space is material media topology, a strong mediator extending far away in space and way back in time. Characteristically, Flusser pushes to the bottom rather than the top: the subterranean cave, for example, functions as a paleo-dwelling place and ground zero for the art world; the arena works as a site for the staging of personae before audiences seated on steps that resemble strata cut into the earth; the table, outside the theatre, is not only the place where assorted business gets brokered but also alludes to another interface of geophysical mediation, the subterranean water table and hidden conduits for sedimented drift. These stratigraphic tropes, in effect, serve as fossilized technical images that give objective, inhuman character to aesthetic agencies over epochal timespans. Technical images, he writes, "liberate their receivers by magic from the necessity of thinking conceptually, at the same time replacing historical consciousness [and] the ability to think conceptually" with programs.³⁹

III.

Writing about Flusser's claims on American World Literature is very much an exercise in thinking about enormous subjects. Gigantomachy—a struggle for conceptual profundity between concepts in an age in which such projects are no longer legitimate. I wish to pull another conversation into this gravitational vortex, namely the current discourse about the so-called Ontological turn that often comes bundled with the conclusion that criticism has run out of steam—to borrow Bruno Latour's title.[40] Oddly, this move frequently gets further coupled with calls for a new critical humility and special antipathy to the literary-critical work associated with the lessons of post-structuralism. For instance, Rita Felski's *The Limits of Critique* argues for the necessity of a "postcritical" approach that adapts Latour's "actor network theory," a format that somehow shows how "*everything is connected*" without epistemology and in Felski's variant provides a strong positive value emphasis for the Humanities in an age of austerity.[41] That the very popular figure of the *network* has anything to do with the associated logic of capital and data must pass unnoticed. The "postcritical" may seem new (descriptive), but in its very gesture to novelty, the mask slips. As Boris Groys says, "to ask about the new"—whether this be new American studies, new materialism, new media, new humility, new realism—"is tantamount to asking about value."[42] In this light, postcritical means value—hunger that ontologizes privations of knowledge and simultaneously depends on a fantasy of authentic access to a continuous transcript of uninterrupted experience (devoid of theoretical experiment).

American World Literature functions as a *matrix* for something like database biography whereas the Flusserian method works like a *projector* of experience and experiment. Just as for de Man, the capacity for *unsettling concepts is critical*. Against the premature settlement of antagonisms, Flusser underscores the gesture of expulsion. He does so, he writes, "to stress the extent of the problem [is] not just about [a new world] of boat people, or Palestinians, or the Jewish emigrants from Hitler's Europe but also about the [relentless] expulsion of the older generations from the world of their children and grandchildren and *the expulsion of humanists from the world of apparatuses*."[43] The expulsion of humanists from apparatus follows from arrival of expulsion as a condition of being in a world "primarily organized by the exchange of and interaction with information" in which humans and things (i.e., technology) cannot be easily disaggregated. As Chadwick Smith notes: "Flusser is not [celebrating] exile [here], promoting it as a voluntary path to [so called] truth [because] those persons expelled from their homes [. . .] are likely not greeted as critical observers of the culture of their new homes and are often rather abused, hated, and detained in murderous prisons that are themselves apparatuses."[44] Every shift of dimensionality involves expulsion from habit, risks exposure to invisible agencies and hidden mechanisms of value—downshifts and upshifts in dimensionality—+1 and −1—exposures to risk and entropy at the limit of the interface. Following a Flusserian definition of American World Literature, then, is an act of expanded hermeneutics into something no less elemental than finding the future of the future in the production of new meaning.

Notes

1. Gayatri Chakravorty Spivak, *An Aesthetic Education in the Era of Globalization* (Cambridge, MA: Harvard University Press, 2013), 1.
2. Franz Kafka, *Amerika* (New York: Penguin, 1967), 13.
3. Claes Oldenburg and Germano Celant, *Claes Oldenburg: An Anthology* (National Gallery of Art and Solomon R. Guggenheim Museum, 1995), 275.
4. Ibid., 273.
5. Oldenburg's remarks quoted in Mark Rosenthal, "'Unbridled' Monuments; or, How Claes Oldenburg Set Out to Change the World," in Oldenburg and Celant, *Claes Oldenburg*, 254–5. See also Geoffrey H. Hartman's discussion of the deconstruction of monumentalism in *Saving the Text: Literature/Derrida/Philosophy* (Baltimore: Johns Hopkins University Press, 1981).
6. Flusser, *The History of the Devil* (Minneapolis: Univocal, 2014).
7. Ibid., 72.
8. The idea is presented in the context of an imaginary letter from Kafka to his Czech translator and amanuensis Milena Jesenska. Maryam Monalisa Gharavi, "A Sword in the Arm of the Statue of Liberty *As If Nearly Stretched Aloft*," *The New Inquiry* (September 18, 2012), accessed February 1, 2017, https://thenewinquiry.com/blogs/southsouth/a-sword-in-the-arm-of-the-statue-of-liberty-as-if-nearly-stretched-aloft.
9. Ibid.
10. Flusser, *Writings* (Minnesota: University of Minnesota Press, 2002), 155–6.
11. Ibid., 156.
12. Ibid.
13. Roland Barthes, *The Eiffel Tower and Other Mythologies* (New York: Hill and Wang, 1979), 4.
14. Ibid., 17.
15. Flusser, "Land Marks," unpublished manuscript.
16. Flusser, *Into the Universe of Technical Images* (Minneapolis, University of Minnesota Press, 2011), 47.
17. Flusser, "Land Marks."
18. Ibid.
19. Ibid.
20. Marshall McLuhan, *Understanding Media: The Extensions of Man* (Cambridge, MA: MIT Press, 1994), 5.
21. Anke K. Finger, Rainer Guldin, and Gustavo Bernardo, *Vilém Flusser: An Introduction* (Minneapolis: University of Minnesota Press, 2011), 27.
22. Ibid.
23. Flusser, *Writings*, 198.
24. Paul de Man, "Literary History and Literary Modernity," *Daedalus* 99, no. 2 (Spring 1970): 384–404, 387.
25. Ibid.
26. Flusser, *The History of the Devil*.
27. Ibid, 72.
28. Ibid., 74.
29. Ibid., 77.
30. Ibid.

31 Ibid.
32 Flusser, *Writings*, 3.
33 Ibid., 98.
34 Ibid.
35 Ibid.
36 Flusser, "My Atlas," *Flusser Studies* 14 (November 1, 2012), accessed February 1, 2017, http://www.flusserstudies.net/sites/www.flusserstudies.net/files/media/attachments/flusser-my-atlas.pdf.
37 Ibid., 3.
38 Ibid.
39 Flusser, *Towards a Philosophy of Photography* (London: Reaktion, 2000), 17.
40 Bruno Latour, "Why Has Critique Run out of Steam? From Matters of Fact to Matters of Concern," *Critical Inquiry* 30 (2004): 225–48.
41 Rita Felski, *The Limits of Critique* (Chicago: University of Chicago Press, 2015).
42 Boris Groys, *On the New* (Verso: New York, 2014), 8.
43 Flusser, *The Freedom of the Migrant* (Champaign-Urbana: University of Illinois Press, 2013)., 82.
44 Chadwick Smith, "'Inter, But Not National': Vilém Flusser and the Technologies of Exile," in *Escape to Life: German Intellectuals in New York*, ed. Eckart Goebel and Sigrid Weigel (Berlin: de Gruyter, 2011), 507.

Part III

Flusser's Toolkit

28

Anti-Apparatus

Melody Jue

Flusser's concept of "anti-apparatus" is a narrative mode of estrangement through the adoption of another's point of view. It first makes an appearance in a lesser-known essay entitled "Criteria-Crisis-Criticism" (1984), where he outlines the difficulty of criticizing technical images, such as photographs used in advertising. Like Roland Barthes, Flusser finds the advertising image suspicious because it encourages us to desire something, complicit with a kind of profitable cultural programming. Thus if a critic calls a photograph "beautiful," then he has not actually critiqued the sign but accepted its criteria that have already been "foisted onto" the photograph at the level of its production. In order to make visible the criteria by which criteria themselves come to be, Flusser writes that it is necessary to "invent an anti-apparatus" that will "uncover the apparatuses behind the apparatuses that program apparatuses," specifically, "the entire apparatus culture and all its totalitarian tendencies, including the apparatuses that program us."[1] Although Flusser ends the brief essay by celebrating a new photo criticism that will "emancipate the photographer" from criteria to fight against cultural programming, the essay cryptically leaves us wondering: What is an anti-apparatus within Flusserian thought?

The answer has to do with Flusser's obsession with the habitual, which he explored in *Freedom of the Migrant* and other short essays. Reflecting on the condition of fleeing the Holocaust and resettling in Brazil, Flusser found himself adrift in a sea of cultural estrangement that, to survive, he had to navigate. In an essay entitled, "Exile and Creativity," Flusser describes habit as a cotton blanket that "covers up all the sharp edges, and it dampens the noise," a comfortable home that "anaesthetizes" and "screens perceptions."[2] It is within the estranged and alienated point of view of the migrant—other, unsettled, and unhabituated to cultural norms—that "one discovers things. Everything becomes unusual, monstrous, in the true sense of the word un-settling. To understand this, it is quite enough to look at one's right hand with all its finger movements from the perspective of a Martian: an octopus-like monstrosity."[3] Through imagining a Martian point of view, even one's own hand—a defining human feature—might appear uncanny and monstrous.

However, it is the "octopus-like monstrosity" of the vampire squid in Flusser's unusual text *Vampyroteuthis Infernalis* (1987) that best exemplifies an "anti-apparatus"—*a speculative strategy for revealing the logic of apparatuses by adopting the point of view or environment that is radically other*. Related to the genres of the fable, the "it-narrative" (told from the point of view of an object) and science fiction (through the production of "cognitive estrangement"), *Vampyroteuthis Infernalis* imagines the development of human thought, culture, and society with vampyroteuthic thought, culture, and society, through differences in both physiology and environment.[4] Whereas we vertebrates experience posture like a "coat-hanger," the vampire squid evolved with an eight-armed body, with head fused to foot (hence, *cephalo-pod*). Where "our dialectic is linear," the vampire squid's "is coiled. We think 'straight', and he thinks 'in a circle' [. . .] That is because our world is a plane and his is a volume."[5] Further differences in embodiment and environment reveal different orientation to media: whereas terrestrial humans write by inscribing on objects, vampire squid could only produce ink clouds and skin paintings—ephemeral media that aim to influence subjects directly.

On this subject of media and inscription Flusser uses the vampire squid to de-ideologize the practice of photography. Rather than producing beautiful photographs as an end goal, photography turns out to be about impressing images upon viewers. Just as photographers "encode their concepts of the world into images" and seek to transmit these in order to "immortalize themselves in the memory of others"[6]—a point Flusser makes in *Towards a Philosophy of Photography*—vampire squid also model experiences as images transmitted to their chromatophores, meant to provoke the curiosity of another and "seduce the receiver."[7] Here, the information matters more than the object: "What fascinates the photographer is not the photographic paper, the object, but the information transmitted. The photographic paper is for the photographer what the skin is for Vampyroteuthis: a medium for colorful messages."[8] By dramatizing the deep ocean abyss as a kind of dark room for the development of his fable, Flusser uses the vampire squid as an anti-apparatus to reveal truths about the practice of photography—a practice concerned with the inscription of information directly on subjects (viewers), rather than the ephemerality of objects (photographs).

Although *Vampyroteuthis Infernalis* is Flusser's longest sustained anti-apparatus—an experiment that uses point of view to denaturalize a given apparatus—shorter examples occur in other writings. In an essay on "Humanization," Flusser discusses the trend in evolutionary thought whereby humans see all animal life relative to themselves. In life's tree, animals are either precursors to man, or cul-de-sacs that lead nowhere. However from another point of view, the story changes: "From the worm's perspective, the human is a degenerate worm. From the insect's perspective, the human would be recognized as a monstrous deviation from insect development. And, perhaps, from the chimpanzee's perspective, the human would be considered to be a chimpanzee embryo, an underdeveloped chimpanzee who still lacks certain specializations."[9]

If totalitarianism embodies the danger of living with one story only, one grand narrative that seeks to extinguish other competing views, then Flusser's encouragement to experiment with other perspectives—migrant or animal—constitutes an active form of dissent and, indeed, a certain epistemic humility. The anti-apparatus is not a reified object but a literary mode that considers the importance of subject ("for whom") and environment in its exploration of alternatives. In this way, the anti-apparatus shares kinship with science fiction and fable, genres that celebrate estrangement and alternate points of view as critical strategies.[10] Yet one might still have fun with this serious project—after all, "One can do gymnastic exercises with perspective."[11]

Notes

1. Flusser, *Writings*, ed. Andreas Ströhl, trans. Erik Eisel (Minneapolis: University of Minnesota Press, 2002), 49. In a glossary at the end of *Towards a Philosophy of Photography*, trans. Antony Mathews (London: Reaktion, 2000), Flusser defines "Apparatus" as "a plaything or game that simulates thought [trans. An overarching term for a non-human agency, e.g., the camera, the computer and the 'apparatus' of the State or of the market]; organization or system that enables something to function" (83). Thus, apparatuses that "program us" include a mixture of literal technologies and ideological apparatuses in a Marxist/Althusserian tradition.
2. Flusser, *Writings*, 105.
3. Ibid.
4. For a more extended analysis of *Vampyroteuthis Infernalis* in relation to metaphor, biology, and theories of mediation, see Melody Jue, "Vampire Squid Media," *Grey Room* 57 (Fall 2014): 82–105.
5. Flusser, *Vampyroteuthis Infernalis* (1987), trans. Rodrigo Maltez Novaes (New York: Atropos Press, 2011), 78.
6. Flusser, *Towards a Philosophy of Photography*, 46.
7. Flusser, *Vampyroteuthis Inferalis*, 109.
8. Ibid., 115.
9. Flusser, *Writings*, 180.
10. Darko Suvin famously defined science fiction as the genre of "cognitive estrangement" in *Metamorphoses of Science Fiction* (New Haven: Yale University Press, 1979).
11. Flusser, *Writings*, 184.

Apparatus

Blake Stricklin

What is an apparatus? What is a dispositif? These questions serve as the titles for both Giorgio Agamben's and Gilles Deleuze's essays on Michel Foucault. Agamben begins his inquiry on the apparatus with Foucault's own definition of the term, which appeared in a 1977 interview. Apparatus, for Foucault, first consists of "a thoroughly heterogeneous ensemble consisting of discourses, institutions, architectural forms, regulatory decisions, laws, administrative measures," and covers as much of "the said as the unsaid."[1] While Foucault offers a general (and generative) explanation of apparatus, media theorist Vilém Flusser searches for a more exact definition. Similar to Agamben, Flusser begins his study on apparatus with its etymology: the Latin verb *apparare*, which he translates to "pro-pare." Apparatus in this sense concerns "a thing that lies in wait or in readiness for something."[2] Yet, for Flusser, an etymological definition does not go far enough, as it fails to address "the ontological status of apparatuses" and "their level of existence."[3]

In *Post-History* (1983), Flusser sees Auschwitz as the beginning of a total apparatus takeover. While each situation appears different, all postwar apparatuses—from the scientific to the administrative—are "just like Auschwitz," as they are "black boxes that function with complex inner-workings in order to realize a program."[4] The dark interior of an apparatus remains obscure from its operators. The easier it becomes to take a picture, the more impenetrable and complex a camera's software. Even the programmers of an apparatus, Flusser writes, will eventually find themselves controlled by it. All apparatuses, then, work "toward the annihilation of all their functionaries [. . .] exactly because they objectify and dehumanize" the human subject.[5] Adorno asks whether one can go on living after Auschwitz, but Flusser speculates on life under a future apparatus. While it might appear more progressive and less horrific, all apparatuses seek total objectification and control of the subject.

The question of freedom from the postindustrial apparatus remains crucial for Flusser. Yet the path to escape requires different critical questions. Critics of industrial capitalism might reveal "secret, superhuman powers at work" behind an apparatus, but Flusser finds that such criticism takes "for granted that programming proceeds in a mindless and automatic fashion."[6] Apparatuses increasingly automate the choices and decisions of the postindustrial subject to a point where no one seems to be in control.

Foucault states in an interview that "power is no longer substantially identified with an individual who possesses or exercises it by right of birth: it becomes a machinery that no one owns."[7] Or as Flusser finds, "it is not those who own the hard object who have something of value [. . .] but those who control its soft program."[8] When software takes command, the program is in control and not its user or even its programmer. For Flusser, escape from this cybernetic totalitarianism proves impossible. This is the absurd situation we find ourselves in when confronted with a society fully determined/automated by apparatuses.

If the revolution is programmed then there can be no more revolutionaries. As Deleuze tells Antonio Negri, control societies require "new weapons" in order to sabotage an apparatus.[9] Throwing your body into a machine will temporarily clog the gears, but it will not stop the program. Now there "can only be saboteurs" who "throw sand on the apparatus' wheels."[10] A philosophy toward the apparatus, then, uncovers a place for human freedom by showing that freedom "is conceivable only after we accept politics and human existence in general to be an absurd game."[11] Game theory assumes that humans no longer make (*Homo faber*) culture but play (*Homo ludens*) within its program. Or as Deleuze finds, capitalism is "no longer directed toward production but toward products, that is, toward sales or markets."[12] Apparatuses feed on data and command subjects to speak in a universal or standard language. Yet for Flusser (and Deleuze), "the inebriated artist" does not speak in a programmed manner. Their art "turns utterable the ineffable and audible the inaudible."[13] The "inebriated artist," then, shows a "competence" for knowing the "difference between that which is redundant and that which is actually information."[14] They make poor players in a game that virtually pre/determines our every move, but artists are not interested in winning. Artists make something new when they exploit glitches in the program. Freedom in this context demands playing against the absurd apparatus. To make the apparatus ridiculous remains the only free and political act.

Notes

1 Michel Foucault, *Power/Knowledge: Selected Interviews & Other Writings*, ed. Colin Gordon, trans. Colin Gordon, Leo Marshall, John Mepham, and Kate Soper (New York: Vintage, 1980), 194.
2 Flusser, *Towards a Philosophy of Photography*, trans. Humbertus von Amelunxen (London: Reaktion Books, 2000 [1983]), 21.
3 Ibid., 22.
4 Flusser, *Post-History*, ed. Siegfried Zielinski, trans. Rodrigo Maltez Novaes (Minneapolis: Univocal, 2013 [1983]), 9.
5 Ibid.
6 Flusser, *Philosophy of Photography*, 64.
7 Foucault, *Power/Knowledge*, 156.
8 Flusser, *Philosophy of Photography*, 30.
9 Gilles Deleuze, *Negotiations*, trans. Martin Joughin (New York: Columbia University Press, 1995 [1990]), 178.

10 Flusser, *Post-History*, 127.
11 Ibid., 26.
12 Deleuze, *Negotiations*, 181.
13 Flusser, *Post-History*, 136.
14 Flusser, *Into the Universe of Technical Images*, trans. Nancy Ann Roth (Minneapolis: Minnesota University Press, 2011 [1985]), 111.

Automation

Seb Franklin

In *Towards a Philosophy of Photography* (1983), his first sustained attempt at to posit technical images as the second of two "fundamental turning points" within "human culture," Flusser identifies the camera as the pivotal technology in the emergence of so-called post-industrial society.[1] The camera, he insists, is "a prototype of the apparatuses that have become so decisive for the present and the immediate future." It

> provides an appropriate starting point for a general analysis of apparatus—those apparatuses that, on the one hand, assume gigantic size, threatening to disappear from our field of vision (like the apparatus of management) and, on the other, shrivel up, becoming microscopic in size so as to totally escape our grasp (like the chips in electronic apparatuses).[2]

How can the camera be the prototype of management and microprocessors? Since those apparatuses do not primarily function to produce an image, the basis for such a genealogy cannot be located in the phenomenon of indexicality so elegantly captured in Andre Bazin's observation that the photographic image is produced "automatically, without the creative intervention of man" and Roland Barthes's evocation of the photograph as that which "mechanically repeats what could never be repeated existentially."[3] The line between camera, management, and microprocessor, Flusser argues, extends not from the former's representational or even its optical function, but rather from its status as a black box that "encodes the concepts programmed into it as images in order to program society to act as a feedback mechanism in the interest of progressive camera improvement."[4]

This transmission of a program from technical object to "society" reveals something significant about automation, even though the automation of representation is not at the heart of that revelation. Let us parse the logic of Flusser's claim. The camera contains "concepts"; one might call these its algorithm, the technically-instituted possibilities and constraints through which it facilitates and imposes limits on image production. These concepts are encoded in the images a camera produces. And through the mediating effects of machine and image, photography programs "society" to function in service of the machine, as an interface between the programmed and the encoded concepts.

In advancing this argument, Flusser writes nothing of the technical or social histories that inform photography: the circumstances in which particular devices were devised, manufactured, and improved; the materials and the processes of extraction, circulation, and production that furnish their existence the uses to which they were put; and so on. Instead, he mentions in passing "the photographic industry that programmed the camera," "the industrial complex that programmed the photographic industry," "the socio-economic system that programmed the industrial complex; and so on."[5] The omission of material history, its substitution with a narrative of economic determination as a sequence of nested programming processes, and the larger argument about the camera as a technology for prototyping the process of programming users in advance of the larger and smaller apparatuses of so-called post-industrial society all make it clear that when Flusser writes "photography," he means a specific relationship between the abstract form of appearance of a specific technical object and the modes of seeing, feeling, and knowing with which that object is entangled.

In this respect, Flusser's philosophy of photography aligns with Jonathan Crary's theorization of the role of nineteenth-century optical technologies in the "historical construction of vision."[6] Where Crary focuses on the prioritization of subjectivity and the production of a "new kind of observer" characterized by the abstraction and reconstruction of a putatively mechanical "optical experience," though, Flusser suggests that photography programs its users for and thus automates the production of a set of expectations about automation itself.[7] This programming process allows Flusser to locate photography in a direct lineage with management and microprocessors: in each, a technical system entails not only the automation of the task it is programmed to perform, but also the automation of its user through the program that system imposes and invisibilizes (or black-boxes).[8] Photography is the prototype of those other apparatuses because it *programs its users* through *the imposition of constraints that cannot be directly observed or manipulated.*

Flusser's philosophy of photography positions the latter as an abstract-concrete thing that disseminates and dissimulates—automates—the operations celebrated by Charles Babbage when he wrote in 1832 of machinery's capacity to mitigate "the inattention, the idleness, or the knavery of human agents."[9] More significantly, Flusser's philosophy makes visible (by reproducing) *the process through which the constraints imposed through automation become intelligible as freedom.* In Flusser's history, the "smart tools" that photography foreshadows "replace human work and liberate human beings from the obligation to work." The camera thus "illustrates" the "robotization of work and the liberation of human beings for play."[10] But there is a sleight of hand here: freedom from some practical element of work does not mean freedom from the obligation to perform waged work in order to meet basic needs. Indeed, market dependency might be understood as the mode of automation specific to capitalism's market apparatus, in that it makes participation in the sale and purchase of commodities virtually inescapable. This principle remains unaffected by Flusser's insistence that apparatuses arise in the course of a shift from industrial to postindustrial society and thus render any analysis premised on proletarianization incapable of grasping their "basic function."[11] Perhaps the conceptual proximity between the two dynamics—the automation of some practical task, by machinery, and the practical automation effected by market dependency—explains Flusser's (and so many others') lamination of redundancy caused by mechanization and liberation from the obligation to work. Flusser's intervention might thus be understood not to narrate but rather to model, through its omissions as well as its inclusions, the production of the subjects around whom the most visible fantasies and anxieties of automation are articulated. It models the production of subjects who have been trained in a set of expectations related to automation—expectations organized around feelings of liberation, so that unmodifiable, programmed affordances appear to free the user to play. And, beyond the processes that Flusser makes legible, it is necessary to add that *Towards a Philosophy of Photography* models the necessary relationship between this automated training (or programming) and the prior existence of a subject whose principal association with the end of work is freedom rather than the possibility of premature death.

Jacqueline Goldsby has shown through a series of close readings of lynching photographs and their modes of circulation how the cultivation of the "experience and meaning of sight itself" rests on histories of racialized violence.[12] Working through Crary's account of the emergence of spectatorship while demonstrating the elisions that ground it, Goldsby argues that the seeing subject of technical-image modernity is premised on a certain proximity to dangers it can observe without direct exposure. The "modes of sight" forged through this relation in turn-of-the-century US "helped make lynching the distinctly visual phenomenon it was."[13] Flusser's theorization of photography mirrors Crary's while focusing on the production of perceptions and expectations centered on automation (rather than visuality). What would be the implications of mapping Goldsby's necessary extension of Crary onto this theorization? Attending to this question properly requires a much longer essay. But for now, in conclusion, I would like to suggest that the apparatuses that impose, maintain, and modulate the distinction between persons who can expect automation to mean an escape to the realm of play and those for whom this "freeing" means the threat of premature death will be central to any such inquiry.

Notes

1. Flusser, *Towards a Philosophy of Photography*, trans. Anthony Mathews (1983; London: Reaktion, 2005), 7.
2. Ibid., 21.
3. Andre Bazin, "The Ontology of the Photographic Image," *Film Quarterly* 13, no. 4 (1960); Roland Barthes, *Camera Lucida: Reflections on Photography*, trans. Richard Howard (1980; London: Vintage, 1993), 4.
4. Flusser, *Towards a Philosophy of Photography*, 48.
5. Ibid., 29.

6 Jonathan Crary, *Techniques of the Observer: On Vision and Modernity in the Nineteenth Century* (Cambridge, MA: MIT Press, 1992), 1.
7 Ibid., 9.
8 See Flusser's definition of automation: "a self-governing computation of accidental events, excluding human intervention and stopping at a situation that human beings have determined to be informative." Vilém Flusser, *Into the Universe of Technical Images*, trans. Nancy Ann Roth (1985; Minneapolis: University of Minnesota Press, 2011), 19.
9 Charles Babbage, *On the Economy of Machinery and Manufactures* (London: Charles Knight, 1832), 39.
10 Flusser, *Towards a Philosophy of Photography*, 29. This argument is a familiar one, as it has been rehearsed across periodic waves of automation fantasies and automation anxieties since the 1830s at least. For a useful overview of these fantasies and anxieties and the ways that many of the most recent instances (1) rely on a misplaced belief in the capacities of automation and (2) obfuscate fundamental structural causes of low demand for labor, namely, worsening economic stagnation, see Aaron Benanav, "Automation and the Future of Work I," *New Left Review* 119 (2019).
11 Flusser, *Into the Universe of Technical Images*, 25. For one of the most succinct formulations of this basic tenet, see "Wageless Life," *New Left Review* 66: "capitalism begins not with the offer of work, but with the imperative to earn a living. Dispossession and expropriation, followed by the enforcement of money taxes and rent: such is the idyll of 'free labour'" (80).
12 Jacqueline Goldsby, *A Spectacular Secret: Lynching in American Life and Literature* (Chicago: University of Chicago Press, 2006), 238.
13 Ibid., 224.

Cybernetics

Heather A. Love

As it is most commonly understood today, cybernetics was the brainchild of mathematician Norbert Wiener,[1] who coined the term in 1947 as part of his work with the Macy conferences.[2] Adapted from the Greek *kubernētēs*—meaning "steersman" or "governor"—cybernetics is a statistics-based and technology-driven discipline that Wiener initially described as the science of "control and communication in the animal and the machine" (1948).[3] He went on to author numerous cybernetics-related publications—some extremely controversial—that target audiences interested in everything from mathematics and technology to social systems and culture, and from warfare and commercial industry to philosophy and ethics.[4] A comparative study of Wiener and Flusser—as eclectic, paradoxical thinkers who pay little heed to traditional disciplinary boundaries as they stitch together ideas and develop counterintuitive theories of communication; and as provocateurs who prompt readers to grapple with both the technical and the ethical challenges, possibilities, and dilemmas of an increasingly networked society—certainly opens up new and productive ways of understanding their intellectual legacies.

The far-reaching field of study that eventually became known as cybernetics is notoriously difficult to define. The American Society for Cybernetics offers some helpful baseline statements: cybernetics "refer[s] to a way of thinking about how complex systems coordinate themselves in action"; it "was originally formulated as a way of producing mathematical descriptions of systems and machines"; and, it comprises "the study of systems which can be mapped using loops (or more complicated looping structures) in the network defining the flow of information."[5] Historians' more extended attempts to pin down the scope and significance of cybernetics as a discipline tend to emphasize a complex interplay of factors. In doing so, they prime us for recognizing cybernetics' influence on Flusser's theories of media and society. As Andrew Pickering explains, cybernetics' definitional challenge is a product of its attempt "to tie together all sorts of more or less independent lines of scientific development: digital electronic computing (then still novel), information theory, early work on neural networks, the theory of servomechanisms and feedback systems, and work in psychology, psychiatry, decision theory, and the social sciences."[6] Consequently, "one can almost say that everyone can have their own history of cybernetics"—Pickering's version is the tale of "a postwar science of the adaptive brain."⁷ With a similar emphasis on adaptability (though articulated as "purpose"), and a telescoping from "brains" outwards to "systems" more generally, Ron Kline reminds us that "the allure of cybernetics rested on its promise to model mathematically the purposeful behavior of all organisms, as well as inanimate systems."⁸ He argues that widespread "enthusiasm" about the potential relevance of cybernetic "concepts and metaphors" sparked conversation and innovation across fields as diverse as cognitive psychology, molecular biology, economics, and quantum physics.⁹ Cybernetics as the science of the adaptive brain, we could say, opened space for Flusser's theory of society as a global brain; and a cybernetic attempt to model the purposeful behavior of a multipart system paves the way for a Flusserian theory of telematics.

When cyberneticists cultivated their equations, theories, and technologies for large-scale, "ultra-rapid" data processing and feedback response mechanisms, they fundamentally blurred the boundaries between human and machine.¹⁰ N. Katherine Hayles targets this aspect of cybernetic thinking when she argues that one of its most "disturbing and potentially revolutionary" implications was "the idea that the boundaries of the human subject are constructed rather than given"—and more specifically, that because "cybernetic systems are constituted by flows of information," they also recast "body boundaries [as] up for grabs."¹¹ This critical angle builds from cyberneticians' claims that machines can be programmed to learn from the past, that human brains can be understood as complex computers, and that information can circulate freely along conscious and mechanical channels. For Wiener in particular, attending to the human-machine interface is paramount: he believes that "messages between man and machines, between machines and man, and between machine and machine, are destined to play an ever-increasing part" in our society's communication practices.¹² Flusser's theories build fairly explicitly from these ideas about the ways in which humans and machines increasingly interface with one another in the twentieth century. *Into the Universe of Technical Images*, for instance, imagines the utopian possibility of a world that will mobilize these ever-more-entwined relationships to create a vast field of information exchange and production.¹³ And as he puts it in the essay "Exp-perience," our future world of technical images, telematic systems, and global connectivity will be able to "compute into experience all stimuli incessantly streaming from all directions."¹⁴ As such, Wiener imagined harnessing for predictive adaptation and effective action the type of large-scale, rapid-fire computational power that sits at the intersection of human cognition and machine-based information-processing power.

Beyond these obvious connections, the lexicon of cybernetics also permeates Flusser's writing in more subtle ways. The first essay in *Natural:Mind* (1979),¹⁵ for example, presents the human subject as *Homo viator*, a "being who walks sometimes on deliberate paths, sometimes on mysterious paths, and [who . . .] does it sometimes deliberately, sometimes spontaneously."¹⁶ Although it doesn't shout at us in the same way that a phrase like "telematic society" does, *Homo viator* also represents a convergence of several cybernetic principles. In its orientation to the as-yet-unknown future, the *Homo viator*—a person on a path or a journey—is a type of "cybernetic being," responding to and adapting its course in light of the feedback it receives along the way. And in its position relative to "deliberate" choice and "spontaneous" action, *Homo viator* is caught up in the same dialectic between pattern and randomness, information and entropy, organization and chaos, that exists at the core of cybernetics' attempts to "control" communication. As *Natural:Mind* unfolds, the cybernetic echoes aren't always this subtle. Flusser regularly draws on the language of technological cybernetics: a valley "is a channel between redundancy and noise"; a cow represents "a clear, structural, cybernetic vision, informed by game theory"; and the sound of the wind is bound up with issues of "information" and "interfere[nce]."[17] Throughout the book, as in his broader oeuvre, cybernetics serves Flusser as a lexical tool for defamiliarizing and reorienting readers' perceptions of culture, technology, media, and environment. An awareness of the cybernetics framework is essential for understanding his vision of a data-rich society where humans and machines, bodies, brains and computers, environments and technologies communicate and coexist.

Notes

1. For more on Wiener's contributions to, and fraught relationship with the broader discipline of cybernetics, see Flo Conway and Jim Seigelman, *Dark Hero of the Information Age: In Search of Norbert Wiener, the Father of Cybernetics* (New York: Basic Books, 2006), and Thomas Rid, *Rise of the Machines: The Lost History of Cybernetics* (London: Scribe UK, 2017).
2. See Claus Pias, ed., *Cybernetics: The Macy Conferences 1946-1953. The Complete Transactions*, revised ed. (Berline: Diaphanes, 2016).
3. Wiener explicitly discusses his choice of the term "cybernetics" in *The Human Use of Human Beings: Cybernetics and Society* (Boston: Da Capo, 1954), 15. The full title of his 1948 mathematical treatise is *Cybernetics: Or Control and Communication in the Animal and the Machine*.
4. In addition to the two texts cited earlier, see also Wiener's 1949 letter to Walter Reuther, president of the American auto workers union, which warned of automation's potentially disastrous effects on employment rates (full text available on libcom.org), as well as *God and Golem, Inc.: A Comment on Certain Points where Cybernetics Impinges on Religion* (Cambridge, MA: MIT Press, 1966).
5. These excerpts come from a lengthy "Definitions of Cybernetics" entry where Stuart Umpleby collates selections from fifty different authors' descriptions of cybernetics (http://asc-cybernetics.org/definitions/).
6. Andrew Pickering, *The Cybernetic Brain: Sketches of Another Future* (Chicago: University of Chicago Press, 2006), 3.
7. Ibid., 3/6.
8. Ronald R. Kline, *The Cybernetics Moment: Or Why We Call Our Age the Information Age* (Baltimore: Johns Hopkins University Press, 2015), 4.
9. Ibid.
10. Wiener, *The Human Uses of Human Beings: Cybernetics and Society* (Boston: Da Capo, 1954), 157.

11 N. Katherine Hayles, *How We Became Posthuman: Virtual Bodies in Cybernetics, Literature, and Informatics* (Chicago: University of Chicago Press, 1999), 84–5.
12 Wiener, *The Human Uses of Human Beings*, 16.
13 See Flusser's *Into the Universe of Technical Images*, 1985, trans. Nancy Ann Roth (Minneapolis: University of Minnesota Press, 2011).
14 Flusser, *The Freedom of the Migrant* (Champaign: University of Illinois Press, 2003), 67.
15 This collection of short essays on natural phenomena—"Paths," "Valleys," "Birds," "Rain," and so on—sets out to unhinge the nature–culture binary. As Flusser explains, his "initial motivation was the suspicion that the existential impact of natural experiences are indistinguishable from cultural ones, and that, therefore, the ontological distinction between nature and culture is not existentially sustainable within the current context" (132). From this perspective, the Fuorn Pass (a paved mountain pathway through terrain that borders Italy, Austria, and Switzerland) may *seem* to be a distinctly "cultural," or human-made phenomenon, paved in asphalt and designed for car travel, but it is *in fact* much more "natural" than it appears: it began as a cow, horse, and reindeer path, and humans are simply following in these creatures' footsteps. *Natural:Mind* (Minneapolis: University of Minnesota Press, 2013).
16 Ibid., 10.
17 Ibid., 15, 45, 101.

32

Dasein's Design

Chris Michaels

As in so many of his writings, Flusser begins *The Shape of Things: A Philosophy of Design* with a discussion around the etymology and semantic relationships of the word "design." Design concerns itself with deception and cheating. Flusser gives the example of a lever, which is designed to cheat gravity, and extrapolates that "this is the design that is the basis of all culture: to deceive nature by means of technology, to replace what is natural with what is artificial and build a machine out of which there comes a god who is ourselves."[1] This deception extends to language, too—"design" deriving from the Latin *signum*, as Flusser notes in his etymological analysis[2]—and implicates signification and mimesis in culture's duplicities against nature. *Design* and *Dasein* thus go together, human beings inextricably tied to the artifice that surrounds and constitutes them. Yet, this statement of humanity's power is only half of Flusser's account, as he proceeds to say that culture does not just trick nature, it also tricks the trickster: "any involvement with culture is the same thing as self-deception."[3] Design is always bidirectional, a feature of reflexive modernity. When designers inform matter with a purpose, it is not simply the imposition of will outward onto an object toward which we always remain sovereign masters. Rather, as Flusser writes in his essay "The Lever Strikes Back," the tools strike back at us, informing us just as we inform them; as Flusser puts it, "we simulate that which we have simulated."[4]

As design and the philosophy around it changes, so does the human being-in-the-world. If in ancient Greek thought, humans *discover* eternal, Platonic forms that provide containers (*morphe*) for the amorphous matter of the material world (*hyle*), in modern thought humans *invent* these forms.[5] In the former, the designer is a god who has created nature to follow certain laws, whereas with the latter, humans are left to try out different designs (equations, algorithms, etc.) that correspond to nature. Modern humans, Flusser avers, have replaced God, becoming themselves the true designers of reality. But he follows these claims with some key caveats. First, he asks that if, rather than a celestial being, we "believe instead that we ourselves design phenomena, why then do they seem to be as they are instead of looking the way we wish them to be?"[6] Second, he undermines some of the hubris one might find in the ostensibly "modern" approach to design: "Is this really such a new story? What about Prometheus and the fire he stole? Perhaps we think we are just sitting at computers, while in fact we are chained to Mt Caucasus? And perhaps there are eagles already sharpening their beaks so as to peck out our livers."[7] As powerful and world-shaping as our designs may be, we are still subject to a world outside us that does not readily obey our designs and, in fact, may be quite hostile to our efforts.

Although Flusser thinks about the design of normal material forms like the ballpoint pen, the typewriter, and the factory machine, he returns frequently to the trend toward immaterial information. The nascent information economy of the late twentieth century indicates an "environment that is becoming ever softer, more nebulous, more ghostly,"[8] rendering the world of things (hardware) into mere junk and the world of symbols and codes (software) increasingly valuable. While these non-things, as Flusser calls them, are immaterial, part of what makes them so powerful is their role in creating our material world; rather than an "'immaterial culture,' . . . it should actually be called a 'materializing culture.'"[9] Yet, in consequence, all the world's material objects begin to take on the spectral quality of the progenitor non-thing. In addition to "lighters, razors, pens, plastic bottles," which "one cannot hold on to," eventually "all things will be transformed into the same kind of junk, even houses and pictures."[10] This transformation of the world into junk and the ascendance of information ultimately indicates a larger "revaluation of all values," Flusser writes, invoking Nietzsche: "All things will lose their value, and all values will be transformed into information."[11]

Naturally, this transformation of the world to non-things does not stop at the object but, in turn, produces a new human subject. *Homo faber*, the manufacturer who grasps and transforms the world with the hand, is replaced by *Homo ludens*, the player whose fingertips "become the most important organs of the body," the "organs of choice, of decision."[12] Whether with a typewriter or a smartphone, *Homo ludens* has the world at their fingertips, "emancipated from work in order to be able to choose and decide."[13] But this freedom turns out to be a false one, since the only choices available are those pre-programmed. In that case, one might conclude that the programmers are the only ones with true freedom, capable of inventing the choices themselves; however, this too is a false freedom, for the programmers too are constrained by the programs, symbols, and keys that allow them to create their content. Flusser calls this the "metaprogram," a concept that extends ad infinitum: there is always a programmer of the programmer, so that the "society of the future without things will be classless, a society of programmers who are programmed. . . . Programmed totalitarianism."[14]

Always reflexive, these essays on design frequently oscillate between grandiose projections and bleak outcomes of the present and future. The choice to design always carries potential (perhaps even inevitable) hazards with it, and thus, "everything which is good in the case of applied good is bad in the case of moral good. Whoever decides to become a designer has decided against pure good."[15] While always acknowledging the risks, Flusser does not suffer from the moralist's zeal, instead imagining and commenting upon the good, the bad, and the ugly revaluations and reinventions of the modern world.

Notes

1. Flusser, *The Shape of Things: A Philosophy of Design* (London: Reaktion Books, 1999), 19.
2. Flusser, "On the Word *Design*: An Etymological Essay," *Design Issues* 11, no. 3 (Autumn 1995): 50.
3. Flusser, *Shape of Things*, 20.
4. Ibid., 53.
5. For more on this distinction between discovery and invention, see "The Designer's Glance," *Design Issues* 11, no. 3 (Autumn 1995): 53–5.
6. Flusser, *Shape of Things*, 41.
7. Ibid., 38.
8. Ibid., 87.
9. Ibid., 28.
10. Ibid., 87–8.
11. Ibid., 88.
12. Ibid., 92.
13. Ibid.
14. Ibid., 93.
15. Ibid., 33.

Ecology

Derek Woods

"Nature writing" is usually a term for topics that are "natural in the traditional meaning of the term," like birds and bird-watching.[1] For example, Flusser's books *Natural:Mind* (1979) and *Vampyroteuthis Infernalis: A Treatise, with a Report by the Institut Scientifique de Recherche Paranaturalist* (1987) are about things like the moon, meadows, mountains, and an intelligent squid. But Flusser's nature writing is also ironic, "paranaturalist": he employs double meaning in texts framed as fictional science, as with the vampire squid; or he subjects "natural" things to a playful dialectic that questions the distinction between nature and culture.

So it would be possible to end my reading here: when Flusser's mix of nature writing, autobiography, phenomenology, close reading, media theory, dialectics, and ideology critique turns its seven heads to topics ecological, it reveals a hybrid "ecology without nature" similar to that described Bruno Latour and other critics of modernity.[2] Such an anticipatory conclusion should not be too surprising given the influence of Marshall McLuhan on Flusser. About the launch of Sputnik, the first orbiting satellite, hyperbolic McLuhan wrote that "Nature" is "contained in a man-made environment of satellites and information." From the moment "Earth went inside this new artefact, Nature ended and ecology was born."[3]

As a diagnosis of Flusser's ecology, this conclusion comes too late given a growing backlash against Latour's approach. In this intellectual climate, readers can see how Flusser returns to the concept of nature as distinct from society. He argues for a "future science" and a new taxonomy of things—not a return to Enlightenment natural history but what Erich Hörl calls "ecological encylopaedism."[4]

a) But first, two currents in Flusser's work do fit the broad meaning of ecology as nature–culture hybrids. For example, his account of photography refers to how microphysical principles and operations condition technical images. In *Towards a Philosophy of Photography* (1983), he writes that the "apparatus" of photography becomes "microscopic in size so as to totally escape our grasp," like a computer chip inscribed with thirty billion transistors.[5] Elaborating in *Into the Universe of Technical Images* (1985), Flusser argues that "technical images arise in an attempt to . . . make elements such as photons or electrons, on one hand, and bits of information, on the other hand, into images." Apparatuses "visualize the invisible, and conceptualize the inconceivable."[6] Through this analysis of scale, he claims that technical objects have a kind of agency, so that cameras program photographers. In this sense, we can see his affinity with recent materialists and ecological thinkers who argue for "thing power" or "environmental agency" because of matter's ability to exceed instrumental control.[7]

b) Some threads of Flusser's work correspond to the definition of media ecology whereby natural objects and flows carry messages: the atmosphere as a medium for radio or seawater for whalesong. Such is the chiasmic transition from McLuhan's understanding of media as environments to "environments [as] media."[8] For example, Flusser approaches natural entities as media as though unearthing the "stratified memory" of geological formations.[9] The paths and highways in "Paths" "serve as symbols" and "transport messages." "Valleys," "Rain," and "Fog" are *media* also in the sense of material bearers of messages, and Flusser interprets such messages to reveal multiple contradictory meanings. Meanwhile, in the squid's "conception of history," "media are glands" that produce a chromatic language in the ecological medium of seawater.[10]

c) Given recent skepticism toward the post-natural, however, the most relevant aspect of Flusser's ecology involves *renaturalization*. Before defining renaturalization, we need to reference his philosophy of science. Flusser's afterword to *Natural:Mind* approaches a "future science" through a narrative that begins with Galileo, Copernicus, and Newton. Science began by addressing things like the movement of planets. Over time sciences such as biology, psychology, and sociology emerged and became more rigorous. Science advanced "from the horizon toward the center" as the newer sciences gazed inward to ourselves, our consciousness, memory, and embodiment.[11] Thus science encounters barriers of self-reference: not only are subjects trying to understand increasingly complex systems, they are trying to understand themselves.

The new science should "relinquish scientific objectivity" and seek alternative epistemologies. But this post-positivist situation does not mean that science adds no truth to modern worldviews. One of Flusser's alternative methods is "fable," which is how he and Louis Bec describe *Vampyroteuthis Infernalis*. Such fables still "have little choice but to rely on the contents of scientific literature," in this case the literature of biology.[12] In *Natural:Mind*, the examples are different, but the principle is similar. Physics and astronomy were models for modern scientific objectivity. Like complexity theorist Stuart Kauffman, Flusser argues that "physics is no longer the model for all the sciences." Instead, fields like "communications theory" guide Flusserian scientists who are "as ignorant and naïve as were the first pioneers of modern science." But modernity is not erased by conditions of self-reference and hypercomplexity. This future science puts the "objective knowledge" accrued by modern sciences "under inverted commas for future use."[13]

Flusser's reading of this quote from Edmund Husserl emerges from his ironic naturalism. The "endeavor to catalog the things that surround us" is different from past taxonomies. "The things that are interesting to us must be inventoried," but "we must admit that our interest for things, although imposed on us by them, turns them into things." This double movement of imposition and transformation shows one sense in which modern sciences are bracketed for future use. The things are already there, attracting us through material presence. But our interest and attention turn them into things, carving them out from flows of matter and energy. In the language of the philosophy of science, Flusser thus refuses to choose a side in debates between constructivism and realism. "We are obliged to carry" "the weight" of scientific modernity, he notes.[14] But the paradoxical loop is unavoidable: our attention creates things that preexist us.

Thus the nature of natural things "in the traditional meaning" is neither pure scientific object nor strict opposition to culture. Flusser is both intriguing and inconclusive about the role nature continues to play in his future science. One good illustration of renaturalization is his essay "Moon." Since we opened with McLuhan's aphorisms about Sputnik rendering the Earth artificial, Flusser on the moon can provide an inversely orbital final example. His essay begins with the "pre-NASA" moon, describes the moon understood within the apparatus of NASA, then speculates about a "post-NASA moon" to come.[15] The pre-NASA moon is a mythic being and an inaccessible natural object. Similar to McLuhan's Earth encircled by satellites, the NASA moon is then a technology, "property of NASA," a tool, "a platform for trips to Venus."[16] But the post-NASA moon "would be a 'natural object' in an existentially bearable sense." Not restricted to the moon, "this transformation of culture into nature happens everywhere," and one of its methods is "applied ecology." Applied to the moon, "it would become nature"—not the moon's pre-NASA past but its post-NASA state.[17]

So renaturalization is a process that takes the denaturalizing forces of modern technological enframing into account as conditions of possibility, not something to nostalgically lament. Flusser's renaturalization rests on the keyword ecology, even as ample reason exists to see him as an early thinker of nature–culture hybridity and Anthropocene environmental media. Perhaps the alternative derived from his theory of science and his catalog of things like the moon, grass, and rain is more important now that too many are certain of pan-artificiality—that what had been autonomous natures have become the product of human agency. Flusser never writes as an environmentalist, whether of the romantic or "ecomodernist," pro-technology variety. Still, his ironic nature writing is an example for fellow travelers who no longer accept that natural things have inherent value by virtue of their autonomy from culture, but see the need for new cultures of nature that focus on the varied existential meanings of things that preexist us.

Notes

1. Flusser, *Natural:Mind* (Minneapolis: Univocal, 2013), 132.
2. Bruno Latour, *The Politics of Nature: How to Bring the Sciences into Democracy* (Cambridge, MA: Harvard University Press, 2004), 5.
3. Marshall McLuhan, "At the Moment of Sputnik the Planet Became a Global Theatre in Which There Are No Spectators But Only Actors," *Journal of Communication* 24, no. 1 (1974): 49.

4 Erich Hörl, "A Thousand Ecologies: The Process of Cyberneticization and General Ecology," in *The Whole Earth: California and the Disappearance of the Outside*, ed. by Diedrich Diederichsen and Anselm Franke (Berlin: Sternberg, 2013), 123.
5 Flusser, *Towards a Philosophy of Photography* (London: Reaktion, 2018), 21.
6 Flusser, *Into the Universe of Technical Images* (Minneapolis: University of Minnesota Press, 2011), 16.
7 See, for example, Jane Bennett, *Vibrant Matter: A Political Ecology of Things* (Durham: Duke University Press, 2010), xvi. Mark Hansen, *Feed-Forward* (Chicago: University of Chicago Press, 2015), 246–7.
8 John Durham Peters, *The Marvelous Clouds: Toward a Philosophy of Elemental Media* (Chicago: The University of Chicago Press, 2015), 3; See also Melody Jue, "Vampire Squid Media," *Grey Room* 57 (2014): 82–105.
9 Flusser, *Vampyroteuthis Infernalis: A Treatise, with a Report by the Institut Scientifique de Recerhe Paranaturalist* (Minneapolis: University of Minnesota Press, 2012), 27.
10 Ibid., 50–1.
11 Flusser, *Natural:Mind*, 136.
12 Flusser, *Vampyroteuthis Infernalis*, 73.
13 Flusser, *Natural:Mind*, 138.
14 Ibid., 138–9.
15 Ibid., 72.
16 Ibid., 66, 69.
17 Ibid., 71–2.

34

Ethics

Annie Lowe

Flusser begins his adventure *Into the Universe of Technical Images* (1985) with a warning about the uncertain terrain traversed therein: "*Utopia* means groundlessness, the absence of a point of reference. We face the immediate future [and the essay that follows] directly, unequivocally, except inasmuch as we cling to those structures generated by utopia itself."[1] A "precaution" in the Heideggerian senses of prediction and preparation, the essay that follows homomorphically clings to and criticizes the structure of technical images, transduced into a series of infinitives. Flusser is a thinker familiar with groundlessness, in exile. In 1939, the Czech-born child of Jewish intellectuals left a Prague descending into anti-Semitism, where Nazis would murder his family and raze their homes to cultivate their totalitarian state. Influenced by Husserlian phenomenology and Buberian social ontology, Flusser, like his contemporary, Emmanuel Levinas, renounced any *ethos* rooted in the ground, where the seeds of Empire and authoritarian social structures were sown across Western history, whither the philosophical ground of ontology, mingling blood and soil, bore its poisoned fruit. In this reordering of values, the private tends toward privation; the public toward plenitude. Both Flusser and Levinas pursue alternative existential revaluations of human being by prioritizing creative and intimate forms of relation over the identity of essence, but while Levinas privileges the experience of ethical immediacy in face-to-face dialogue,[2] Flusser's orgiastic scene of telematic dialogue further departs from both Judaic and Hellenic traditions' common hostility for the image whose reproducible artifice does not channel the authority of either word (*Logos*) or world but merely imitates it. Rather, for Flusser, the reproducibility of the image as copy provides a functional model for generation and fecundity that does not issue from the virile machinations of a phallic I—is not (dis)semination and gestation but communication. By *altering* telematic images, the Other dialogically *informs* the common universe of possible worlds.

Despite the obvious difference between Levinas's ethical immediacy and Flusser's telematic aesthetics, we come upon a virtual interval when the posthistory of Flusser's visionary utopia moves toward Levinas's eschatological (and Benjamin's messianic) time and the one glimpses the Face (*Visage*) of the Other, signifying some new surplus, a new form of relation and "a completely unorthodox religiosity."[3] Ratcheting up the prophetic register with the final two infinitives of his journey *Into the Universe of Technical Images*—"To Suffer" and "To Celebrate"[4]—Flusser moves to reconcile his theory of technical images to the suppression and denigration of the image in the Jewish prophetic tradition (which Levinas inherits as a Talmudic scholar), while likewise correcting those assumptions of classical Greek philosophy. In "To Suffer," the telematic society replaces the Platonic model of utopia in the *Republic* (c. 325 BCE), in which economy, politics, and philosophy are the three ascending forms of life toward the heavenly ideal of the good life. Gazing upward in heavenly contemplation, with "back turned to phenomena," Plato calls this highest form of life "*bios philosophikos*: life in the love of wisdom."[5] But Flusser points out that if the key word in this social model is leisure (Greek: *schole*; Latin: *otium*), the opposition of contemplative leisure to vulgar business and economic activity boils down to an ideal of feudalism.

He asks, if a telematic society were to automate economy and politics, freeing all people to contemplate images in leisurely philosophical repose, then would this be a realization of Platonic utopia, of life in the love of wisdom, the absolute good life? "Basically, is a situation in which everyone contemplates images (whether it be to receive, to change, or to forward them on), and in which the cycle of the economy and the process of production takes place behind people's backs, the very situation that Plato called life in the love of wisdom?"[6] He replies that even if the economy could be computationally automated, so that the once economically and politically requisite slave and market-classes now comprised only robots and artificial intelligences—elevating all people to *bios philosophikos*—the Platonic utopia remains *impossible* because this absolute human freedom is checked by suffering, by the body. It is the same argument that compels Levinas's detestation of the image, as a shadow,[7] which Flusser here redirects to the social systems that feign to represent freedom, that feign freedom as representation, while bodies suffer. So long as suffering is and will be an existential condition of human beings, the irremissible reality of bodily suffering puts a limit on absolute freedom, in which death, as Hegel described it, has "no more significance than cleaving a head of cabbage or swallowing a gulp of water."[8] This freedom to philosophize at leisure is called into question when faced with the suffering of others, when bodily suffering can throttle anyone's free play in dialogue. Just as Levinas says of the face of the Other whose suffering is impossible to ignore and to which one must respond (even turning away is a response), Flusser writes that so long as there is suffering, "it will remain impossible to ignore the economy, to philosophize, to have leisure, to live in school."[9]

Moving from "To Suffer" to "To Celebrate," Flusser tempers the classical definition of philosophy as the love of wisdom with a Levinasian movement toward philosophy as the wisdom of love. He dismisses the disinterested, scholastic atmosphere of Greek contemplation and Heidegger's self-possessed *Gelassenheit* (letting-be) to ask afresh the central question of a telematic society—the question of programming—prophesying a holiness he says Plato, in his leisure, would not have understood.[10]

Flusser envisions future "alternative programming" as a new, telematic form of Martin Buber's "dialogic life" in a Levinasian future time-of-and-for-the-Other, a new consciousness and a new temporality of the Other in active celebration.[11] With telematic society's realization of dialogic programming, "the point will be to have other programs (programs of others) to be able to change them (to suggest them to others). [. . . R]ather than our own programs, we will be discussing *alter*native programs, a neologism that strikes me as characteristic of telematic society."[12] If this society is to break out of self-involvement and into dialogue between everyone and every other, then the technical images by which they communicate must respect what Flusser, nearing Levinas, calls the "true image"—any human face. Technical images are made-up—they are true because they are not to be believed, even if we can believe in them. As improbable illusions, like stories, these images ask only to be entertained, and telematic utopia accrues not in accurate images of others but in the festive celebration of others' imagined illusions.

For Flusser, in the dialogically informed telematic society, technical images take up the excluded middle, in the absolute exteriority of I and Other. They form the medium of a common milieu, materializing meaning without fixing it, whereby the desire for the Other's desire produces a universe of possibilities, which is, in the last analysis as in the first principle, true (indicative), good (imperative), and beautiful (optative) because we collectively inform it. The final infinitive of Flusser's adventure *Into Universe of Technical Images* brings us to the opening quest of *Totality and Infinity*, where Levinas, channeling Flusser, proposes: "Concretely, our effort consists in maintaining, within anonymous community, the society of the I with the Other."[13] Taking this stand, Levinas and Flusser stand toward each other, for each other. Across the yawning nothingness of the abstract particulate universe and the nocturnal future of the *il y a*,[14] they are drawn out of abstraction by this desire, both bringing what can only come from the other. Levinas's ethics starts with the face of the Other, the revelation of existential alterity as foundational to first philosophy; in Flusser's prophetic vision of the utopian telematic society, the whole informatic endeavor of technical images turns out, to have been for the Other, in the end. *De te fabula narrator; fabulam pro vobis est* (the story is about you; the story is for you).[15]

Notes

1 Flusser, *Into the Universe of Technical Images*, trans. Nancy Ann Roth (Minneapolis: University of Minnesota Press, 2011), 3.
2 Emmanuel Lévinas, *Totality and Infinity: An Essay on Exteriority*, trans. Alphonso Lingis (Pittsburg: Duquesne University Press, 1969), 52.
3 Flusser, *Into the Universe of Technical Images*, 157.
4 The chapters or sections of Flusser's *Into the Universe of Technical Images* are organized into a series of eighteen infinitives, the last two being "To Suffer" and "To Celebrate," bookended by a "Warning" at the beginning and "Chamber Music" and a "Summary" at the end.
5 Flusser, *Into the Universe of Technical Images*, 142.
6 Ibid., 143.
7 See Lévinas, "Reality and Its Shadow," in *Collected Philosophical Papers of Emmanuel Levinas*, trans. Alphonso Lingis (Dordrecht: Martinus Nijhoff Publishers, 1987), 1–13.

8   G. W. F. Hegel, *Phenomenology of Spirit*, trans. A. V. Miller (Oxford: Clarendon Press, 1977), 360 (translation modified: Miller's original reads, "with no more significance than cutting off a head of cabbage or swallowing a mouthful of water." Hegel's German reads, "*ohne mehr Bedeutung als das Durchhauen eines Kohlhaupts oder ein Schluck Wassers.*" [G. W. F. Hegel, *Werke in zwanzig Bänden*, ed. E. Moldenhauer and K. M. Michel (Frankfurt: Suhrkamp, 1970), 111:436]).
9   Flusser, *Into the Universe of Technical Images*, 143. See also Barthes on Blanchot and the right to weariness and to silence, in Roland Barthes, *The Neutral: Lecture Course at the Collège de France (1977-1978)*, trans. Rosalind E. Krauss and Denis Hollier (New York: Columbia University Press, 2005), esp. 12–29.
10 See, Flusser, *Into the Universe of Technical Images*, 150ff.
11 Flusser, *Into the Universe of Technical Images*, 154.
12 Ibid., 155. Emphasis mine.
13 Lévinas, *Totality and Infinity*, 47.
14 See Lévinas, "There Is: Existence without Existents," trans. Alphonso Lingis, in *The Levinas Reader*, ed. Seán Hand (Oxford: Blackwell, 1989), 29–36.
15 See Flusser, *Into the Universe of Technical Images*, 167: "For this fable is a catastrophe about to break out of its shell. And we are that shell. *De te fabula narrator* (the story is about you)."

Etymology

Methodology as Adventure in the *Bochum Lectures*

Andrew Battaglia

Opening *Dinge und Undinge,* Vilém Flusser puns *Muße* (leisure) on *muß* (must), writing that the book at hand is both leisurely and necessary. He must inquire into the phenomenology of these things and non-things even as he does so at leisure. Of course, Flusser knows these words are semantically unrelated, yet their phonetic collision presents a wonderful opportunity to "make a virtue of spurious etymology."[1] In spite of his confession of playful rhetorical legerdemain, etymology preoccupied Flusser. In one of his last lectures, he defends etymology as a mode of inquiry even as he offers a legitimate history of *Muße*:

> First, the etymology, a method that is not particularly reliable but still a good way to go after a word: school means leisure, *scholae*. In antiquity, leisure was extraordinarily positive. The absence of leisure was contemptible, *ascholia*. German lacks a word for this. In English, it is called *business*.[2]

Delivering these lines for the students of the Ruhr-Universität Bochum during his residency as a visiting professor in 1991 at the age of seventy-one, at the invitation of Friedrich Kittler, Flusser understood the particular relationship between leisure time and linguistic research. Fleeing the National Socialist occupation of Czechoslovakia five decades earlier, he worked days at his father-in-law's Brazilian import-export business while reading and writing philosophy during his leisure time at night. Even though he was denied a stable academic position in Europe and the Americas, the twentieth century delivered Flusser into a polyglot linguistic playground, and the constellation of ideas that stem from his sustained etymological play suggests the vulnerability and brilliance of an intellectual life lived under the sign of *Bodenlosigkeit*.[3]

Adventures of etymology—both spurious and legitimate—serve as an apt emblem for Flusserian thinking, especially exemplified in the Bochum lectures. At one point, he explains to students that the lifeworld "is made up of nothing but futures . . . , an *aventure*, an *adventure*."[4] What he terms adventure is adventurous, because it is adventitious; it surprises, overwhelms, and irrupts, precluding anticipation or amelioration. The probability calculus determines the likelihood of any given future, but according to information theory, the more unlikely a future is, the more interesting it becomes.[5] Adventure is that future which is interesting precisely because it is unlikely. In *Dinge und Undinge*, he draws from this idea the conclusion that inasmuch as science arrogates knowledge of the world to itself, human life becomes less adventurous.[6] The unadventurous lifeworld echoes Max Weber's melancholic pronouncement on the disenchantment of modern life, but Flusser's project neither participates in the total clarification of all mysteries or the re-enchantment of quotidian modernity.

In the inaugural Bochum lecture, he tells students that he aims to overcome the distinction between exact and human sciences. Relying on C. P. Snow's notorious two cultures distinction, Flusser believes the difference between science and the humanities resolves to the form of the questions and answers unique to each. A scientist asks "why does it rain," but a humanist handles "to what end does it rain?"[7] For Flusser, this distinction "puts into a question the problem of anthropology. Where does the human being belong as an object of research?"[8] The problem is not the assignment of the human to one field or the other but rather the image of human we try to decipher: "I have come to think like so many others that the form of the question is wrong.... Perhaps in the field of research of human communication we can arrive at a new picture of the human."[9] The search for new methods for humanism—a communicology jointly derived from phenomenological and mathematical thinking, as it were—motivates and organizes the particular strands of ideas and provocations that run throughout the Bochum lectures.[10]

Fulfilling the terms of his Bochum guest professorship with three seminars, each met for three sessions.[11] The seminar Communicology as Culture Critique occupies the bulk of the original text, with five of the seven chapters devoted to its content. The aim in general is to "geometrize the circuits of communicative channels."[12] By this Flusser means an analysis of the geometric structure of communication networks from the circle—the "original form of discourse"—to the Attic amphitheater, from the pyramidal structure of the Roman Empire to the one-way bundling of television programs. Drawing on the legitimate etymology of *Kritik* (Latin *criticus* and Greek *kritikós*), Flusser defines it as "that act thanks to which a phenomenon is broken up in order to see what lies behind it."[13] Thus the titular critique derives from the assumption that the structure of a communicative system informs without fully determining the types of subjects it produces. In a particularly salient example, Flusser offers his students the provocative observation that "*Fasces* means of course bundle," with the implication being that any bundled system will have the "tendency to bundle the entire culture and lead us into a synchronized, fascistic totalitarianism without parallel."[14] Flusser's notion of critique does not, however, lead inexorably to liberation; networked communication erodes the "ideological concept of an 'I' as kernel" so there is no ordinary self to liberate.[15] Critique exposes what is hidden, but Flusser harbors no utopian dream that political and epistemological problems will dissolve simply because we catch sight of them. As he concludes his discussion of responsibility, critique leads to "a climate of disillusion in the true sense of that word, dis-illusion."[16]

The second seminar Communication Structures occupies two chapters in the German edition, and in the original seminar he "analyze[s] the saving and memory supports [*Speicher und Gedächtnisstützen*] according to their structure."[17] Like his early monographs, he begins at material culture, or "everything that the human hand has arranged in the course of the last two million years," but he tells the long story of the rise and fall of historical, linear thinking that the technical image supersedes.[18] Included in this story is everything from the first rock that *homo erectus robustus* stopped to consider as a problematic object to the modern digital pixel. The first stone began the problematic interplay of objectivity and subjectivity that culminates in the technical image via Mesopotamian jars for counting livestock with pebbles, the linear alphabet, and the photograph, to name just a few material instruments Flusser addresses. It is always and ever a question of information as in-formation which culminates in the zero-dimension of the technical image and the technologies that produce them.[19]

In the final seminar, Phenomenon of Human Communication, which occupies only a half a chapter in the German original, Flusser declares he will treat "culture—with my apologies—as an apparatus, the purpose of which is to save and process acquired information in the form of cities, countries, buildings, libraries, etc." (28). In the sections included in *Kommunikologie weiter denken*, Flusser attends less to cities and countries and more to the features of media technology like the photograph and especially television and video. Covering the prehistoric, antihistoric, and posthistoric image, Flusser tracks the affordances of latter-day apparatuses of the technical image, television and video. Video both instantiates the ancient philosophy of reflection and surpasses it in that the technology permits almost instantaneous mediation through manipulation. As he says, "Video is an invention that was made in order to make a scene immediately visible so that it can be controlled on television. . . . If everything [in a scene] is in order then it is played later; if not, then one changes something about it."[20] In short, video philosophizes on the fly.

Flusser characterizes the Bochum lectures as revisions to a philosophy as yet still in development, and he speaks from the *longue durée* that imbricates the not-yet over the no-longer. It is doubtful that we can map fully the contours of Flusser's technological eschatology—that posthistorical space at once a projection from the zero-dimension and the world in which we live. Trained in linear writing yet immersed in the universe of technical images, our position dictates—excluding provocative sloganeering—a judgement of *non liquet* because, quite simply, the effects of the digital can still surprise us.

Notes

1. *Dinge und Undinge: Phänomenlogische Skizzen* [*Things and Non-Things: Phenomenological Sketches*] (München: Carl Hanser Verlag, 1993), 7. Published posthumously; translation mine.
2. Vilém Flusser, *Kommunikologie weiter denken*, ed. Silvia Wagnermaier and Siegfried Zielinski (Frankfurt am Main: Fischer Taschenbuch Verlag, 2008), 236.

3   See Rainer Guldin and Gustavo Bernardo, *Vilem Flusser (1920-1991): Ein Leben in der Bodenlosigkeit: Biografie* (Bielefeld: transkript Verlag, 2017), 89.
4   Flusser, *Kommunikologie weiter denken*, 90.
5   Regarding information theory, Flusser says "Informatics is an exact discipline, or it wants to be. Its μάθησις (*mathesis*) is the probability calculus ... The more informative—the more interesting a piece of information is—the less likely it is to be" ibid., 49. For Flusser's treatment of the future, see "Chamber Music" in *Into the Universe of Technical Images* translated by Nancy Ann Roth (Minneapolis: University of Minnesota Press, 2011).
6   Flusser, *Dinge und Undinge*, 20.
7   Flusser, *Kommunikologie weiter denken*, 25.
8   Ibid.
9   Ibid., 26.
10 In the third session of Culture Critique, Flusser says, "I will try to gather the different strands here under the sign of anthropology in order to sketch at least fuzzy outlines of a picture of man," ibid., 213.
11 Guldin and Bernardo note the dates of each session (30 May–3 June, 21–24 June, and 27 June–1 July), but they do not mention which seminar corresponds to which dates. See *Vilém Flusser*, 336-338.
12 Flusser, *Kommunikologie weiter denken*, 32.
13 Ibid., 35.
14 Ibid., 33.
15 Ibid., 34.
16 Ibid., 87.
17 Ibid., 29.
18 Ibid., 90.
19 Ibid., 31.
20 Ibid., 187.

Surface and Simulation

Vilém Flusser and Jean Baudrillard

Thomas Tooley

In the 1980s, Flusser wrote his media trilogy: *Towards a Philosophy of Photography* (1983), *Into the Universe of Technical Images* (1985), and *Does Writing Have a Future?* (1987).[1] Across the books, he lays out his theory of the "photographic universe" and offers a history of the evolution of media and human communication. These works went largely unnoticed in the English-speaking world until relatively recently when they began to draw attention for the prescient ways they describe the contemporary, global mediascape. For Flusser, recent advancements in media and technology brought forth the era of the "technical image," a new dialogical form of communication which necessitates not only new ways of reading images but marks an entirely new way of being in the world. In their efforts to revisit and contextualize these ideas, scholars often draw comparisons between Flusser's theories and those offered by his French contemporary, Jean Baudrillard, who had more exposure, especially in the Anglophone world.

Certainly, both Flusser and Baudrillard take media seriously in philosophical terms—something Mark Poster notes was rare among theorists of the late twentieth century.[2] They even crossed paths several times in their careers—perhaps most notably in 1988 at the Ars Electronica symposium in Linz, Austria, where they sat on a panel together about "New Technologies."[3] This was an auspicious moment for Baudrillard, who was about to become "something of an academic celebrity,"[4] while in North America at least Flusser remained relatively obscure. He had just released the German version of *Does Writing Have a Future?*, but it would take another twenty-four years before it would be translated into English. Nevertheless, the two philosophers do share some ideas in common.[5] Key terms often associated with Baudrillard—such as "simulation," "simulacra," "code," "surface," "screens"—also appear as central elements in Flusser's media theory. Whereas Flusser approached these phenomena from a phenomenological and existential position, Baudrillard examined them from the vantage of post-structuralism. As a result, both thinkers viewed these terms, and their historical moment, in radically different ways. Baudrillard's early writings retain something of a neo-Marxism, where, among other issues, he argues that commodities now possess "sign-value," an effect of the consumption process that has led objects to "take on meaning according to their place in a differential system of prestige and status."[6] He would build upon this idea over the course of his career, eventually breaking entirely from Marxism in favor of the brand of postmodernism and post-structuralism associated with his idea of radical simulation. Notably, Baudrillard argues that mass media, especially television, have accelerated this differential system of sign-value, expanding it to such a degree that we have lost connection to any original referent whatsoever, now effectively "substituting the signs of the real for the real."[7] All that remains are empty, hollow simulacra, copies without originals. In terms of politics, this means that every subversive act or position has been reduced to just another differential point, the corollary of its opposite. For Baudrillard, then, the dynamic process of history, as one of struggle, has come to a halt, with any and all forms of resistance effectively neutralized by their position within a totalizing process of simulation.

Andreas Ströhl argues that "choosing the expression 'end of history' was perhaps a misleading provocation on Flusser's part. It unintentionally brought him closer to postmodern thinkers such as Jean Baudrillard and Paul Virilio."[8] Instead, Flusser's version of the "end of history" registers how modern "technical-images" disrupt the historical consciousness that emerges from the invention of linear writing. He argues in "Line and Surface" that the process of transcoding reality into text and then reading that code in a linear fashion has programmed us to think historically, as "the lines represent the world by projecting it as a series of successions, in the form of a process."[9] According to Flusser, that mode of being has now ended. "Civilization" has shifted from being text-based to our current image-based society, resulting in the formation of "surface-thought."[10] Furthermore, this era's new "technical images" differ from traditional images in that traditional images functioned mimetically, representing the world, whereas technical images come from apparatuses, such as cameras and computers, and are thereby programming.[11]

For all their superficial similarities, Baudrillard and Flusser have divergent assumptions and agendas. Baudrillard often approaches the fate of writing with a provocative fatalism that resembles "the cynical, resigned, nihilistic Man of Philosophy at world's end," as Adrian Martin puts it.[12] Flusser for all his irony is deliberately forward-looking, optimistically embracing the advent of new media and digitalization for dialogue. Whereas Flusser sees possibilities for computers and participatory media, Baudrillard seems less certain that what he calls "the third order of simulacra ... bears witness to the reflexes of a finalized universe."[13] Flusser holds out hope for agency in the activity of media makers, users, players, and transmitters, even though the deleterious effects of programs and the apparatus on human beings are undeniable and unavoidable, a position a Baudrillardian might consider naïve. At the same time, as Ströhl points out, Flusser "dismissed Baudrillard's notion of 'simulation,' [because he thought it] implied a naïve, positivistic notion of reality that was theoretically untenable."[14] This impasse may depend on a series of misapprehensions but it speaks to the conclusion that Flusser and Baudrillard have very different conceptions of reality. As Steven Shaviro nicely summarizes on his blog *Pinocchio Theory*:

Unlike other critics of the rule of simulacra, Flusser evidences no nostalgia. He has no Baudrillardian yearning for a "real" that would have supposedly existed prior to photographic reproduction. And he explicitly criticizes the Frankfurt School, for the humanist nostalgia behind its attempts "to unmask the [class] interests behind the apparatuses." Such approaches merely seek to reinstate the humanistic subject that photography and other post-industrial technical apparatuses have destroyed once and for all.[15]

In effect, informed by cybernetics, Flusser held a position likely inconceivable to Baudrillard: "There is no border line. . . . Every systematic thinking is wrong, every system is a violation. Reality is tangled and therefore interesting."[16] Baudrillard's commitments lead him to define the screen, for example, as a "nonreflective surface."[17] "Cold and obscene," it is nothing more than "a switching center for all the networks of influence."[18] Conversely, Flusser can view the screen as a real object, a concrete, meaningful surface. It offers him a new mode of communication that brings with it an entirely new mode of thought. Ultimately, the technical image, for Flusser, is both real and usable as a critical tool. Or, as he put it in a late interview:

> Baudrillard believes that we are living in a world where the simulations hide reality. I think this is a nonsensical proposition. . . . Images are just as concrete as is the table on which your machine is standing now. We do not have any ontological tool any longer to distinguish between a simulation and a non-simulation. The critical tool which we have to use is concreticity as opposed to abstractness.[19]

Notes

1. *Towards a Philosophy of Photography*, trans. Anthony Mathews (London: Reaktion, 2000), originally published as *Für eine Philosophie der Fotografie* (Göttingen: European Photography, 1983); *Into the Universe of Technical Images*, trans. Nancy Ann Roth (Minneapolis: University of Minnesota Press, 2011) originally published as *Ins Universum der technischen Bilder* (Göttingen: European Photography, 1985); *Does Writing Have a Future?*, trans. Nancy Ann Roth (Minneapolis: University of Minnesota Press, 2011), originally published as *Die Schrift* (Göttingen: Immatrix Publications, 1987).
2. Poster, Introduction to *Does Writing Have a Future?*, xi.
3. In fact, this symposium resulted in a publication, Ars Electronica, ed., *Philosophien der neuen Technologie* (Berlin: Merve Verlag, 1989). While there is still no English translation of this book, Ars Electronica's online archive houses other valuable resources regarding the Linz symposium, see "Ars Electronica Archive," *Ars Electronica*, accessed by request July 23, 2020, https://ars.electronica.art/about/en/archiv/.
4. Douglas Kellner, "Jean Baudrillard," Stanford Encyclopedia of Philosophy, The Metaphysics Research Lab in the Center for the Study of Language and Information, Stanford University, Winter 2019 edition, https://plato.stanford.edu/entries/baud

rillard. For a more thorough overview of Baudrillard's work, see Douglas Kellner, *Jean Baudrillard: From Marxism to Postmodernism and Beyond* (Stanford: Stanford University Press, 1989).
5 Martha Schwendener, "The Photographic Universe: Vilém Flusser's Theories of Photography, Media, and Digital Culture" (dissertation, City University of New York, 2016). Schwendener provides a fabulous comparison between Flusser and Baudrillard across her dissertation. But for a particularly extensive comparison, see pp. 238–51.
6 Kellner, *From Marxism*, 21.
7 Baudrillard, *Simulacra and Simulation*, trans. Sheila Faria Glaser (Ann Arbor: University of Michigan Press, 1994), 2.
8 Andreas Ströhl, "Introduction" to *Writings*, ed. Andreas Ströhl, trans. Erik Eisel (Minneapolis: University of Minnesota Press, 2002), xxx.
9 Flusser, "Line and Surface," *Writings*, ed. Ströhl, 21.
10 Ibid., 22. Rather than "follow the text of a line from left to right," as we would in a linear engagement, "in pictures we may get the message first, and then try to decompose it" (22–3).
11 For more on apparatuses, see Flusser, *Towards a Philosophy of Photography*, 21–32. Additionally, see Siegfried Zielinksi, Peter Weibel, and Daniel Irrgang, eds., *Flusseriana: An Intellectual Toolbox* (Minneapolis: Univocal Publishing, 2015), for a thorough look at Flusser's terminology.
12 Adrian Martin, "Revolution of the Head: Vilém Flusser," http://www.lolajournal.com/2/flusser.html.
13 Baudrillard, *Simulacra and Simulation*, 127. Also see Kellner, "Jean Baudrillard," Kellner, *From Marxism*, and Christopher Norris, *Uncritical Theory: Postmodernism, Intellectuals, and the Gulf War* (Amherst: University of Massachusetts Press, 1992).
14 Ströhl, "Introduction," xxx.
15 Steven Shaviro, "Vilém Flusser," *Pinocchio Theory*, http://www.shaviro.com/Blog/?p=266.
16 Flusser, quoted in Anke Finger, Rainer Guldin, and Gustavo Bernardo, *Vilém Flusser: An Introduction* (Minneapolis: University of Minnesota Press 2011), 67.
17 Baudrillard, "The Ecstasy of Communication," in *The Anti-Aesthetic: Essays on Postmodern Culture*, ed. Hal Foster (Port Townsend: Bay Press, 1983).
18 Ibid., 131, 133.
19 See "Vilém Flusser interviewed by Miklós Peternák - I (1988, unpublished)," http://www.c3.hu/events/97/flusser/participantstext/miklos-interview.html.

Technical Image

Opaque Apparatus of Programmed Significance

Anaïs Nony

> *For this is about opaque apparatuses, not transparent machines.*
>
> —Vilém Flusser

With the concept of the technical image, Flusser indicates a historical shift in the structure of Western society.[1] Technical images, as found in photographs, films, videos, computer terminals, and television screens, designate images produced by an apparatus designed to create programmed information. Contrary to traditional images which carry significance through representation as seen in paintings, technical images are surfaces that operate according to "inverted vectors of meaning."[2] The meaning of a technical image is not found in what the image signifies but in what it projects. In other words, technical images are less about the representation of the world and more about modeling the subject's relation to and vision of reality. As such, technical images are "instructional programs" designed to inculcate significance, shape behavior, and direct subjects on how to make sense of the world.[3] The surfaces of technical images move away from a mimetic representation of the real to inscribe concepts as connotative, as opposed to denotative, forms of signification. However, traditional images and technical images are not entirely disconnected from one another. Together they shape the posthistorical phase of humanity, a phase in which humans' relationship to reality is increasingly conditioned and modulated by embedded codification. This codification is produced by apparatuses that calculate probability. These apparatuses are opaque because they no longer require the knowledge of their operation by the subject that handles them. In other words: traditional images are "observations of objects," while technical images are "computation of concepts."[4]

Into the Universe of Technical Images, first published in 1985, opens a path toward critically understanding the meaning and impact of technical images in shaping the production and distribution of signification on a large scale. For Flusser, technical images carry their information on a surface that is easily replicable because it is first and foremost produced by an automated apparatus.[5] Understood as "a machine that elaborated information,"[6] an apparatus is conceived as the core element constitutive of both technical and cultural revolution. Flusser offers two paradigms from which to investigate the impact of technical images on signification: the first questions value and information together; the second addresses the relationship between intention and programmation.[7] For Flusser, technical images can only be criticized on the basis of their program.[8] The cultural critique of technical images requires the development of new criteria to unpack the programming significance of their production. These new criteria must respond to an imperative in which technical images are understood as projections that are programmed to appear as objective depiction of the real.[9] In other words, the cultural critique of the technical image is anchored in "defiance of common sense," which tends to read technical images as mirrors of reality.[10] Witnessing a cultural revolution in the dynamic encounter between subject and object,[11] Flusser aims to address the postindustrial society of immaterial information by moving away from the body or content of distributed images, to focus on the technical apparatus as producing programmable surfacelike images.[12] Flusser focuses on the photograph as a post-industrial object designed by technicians who "apply scientific statement to the environment."[13] For him, the technicians of opaque apparatuses as seen in the photographic apparatus influence the meaning of life by the proliferation of programmed vision. For Flusser, the twentieth century is marked by the advent of a posthistorical phase where technical images perform an analogic power that is slowly overcoming the rational dimension of writing that pretends to translate reality in a causal fashion.[14] The posthistorical designates the emergence of a new form of imagination that is no longer anchored in representation but in projection sustained by the proliferation of computational and automated apparatuses. Technical images are therefore the instruments for a new consciousness detached from the historical grounding of society. They break away from the theology of writing central to Western cultures because they function as "metacode of text."[15] As a dominant form of relating to reality, technical images are now moving away from an historical understanding of the real anchored in writing to a posthistorical relation to events. In this new epoch of societal consciousness, technical images "translate historical events into repeatable projections."[16]

The emerging culture of immaterial information designates a drastic shift in the formation of subjectivity. In the society of pure information, the subject is conditioned to absorb and consume technical images without paying attention. Flusser's understanding of apparatus is fundamental to building a praxis of media theory grounded on the effects and impact of posthistorical objects on both the psychic and collective functions. For Flusser, not only do objects "tend to become worthless supports of information,"[17] but apparatuses themselves tend to shift away from human intention. In this statement we sense the political commitment of Flusser's philosophy: human agency is no longer about creating and elaborating representation but deviating and emancipating humans from the projections produced by opaque apparatuses of vision. Agency is finding a margin of action left in the face of the imposition of information by apparatuses of programmed significance.[18] Technical images don't signify meaning but are instructional programs that operate on "an entirely different level of consciousness."[19] Thus, there is an urgent necessity to cultivate an active reception of technical images, one that re-invents the programmed images that are directing consciousness in postindustrial society. In other words, to defy "the mutation of our experiences, perceptions, values, and modes of behavior"[20] that are imposed by instructional programs, the subject needs to invent new fields of possibilities, from which a more collective and less programmable image of history can emerge.

Notes

1. The author wishes to thank the Govan Mbeki Research and Development Centre of the University of Fort Hare for the SARChI Chair postdoctoral research fellowship award that facilitated the writing of the present chapter. All credit for DHET purposes for this keyword entry article is attributed to the SARChI Chair in Social Change at the University of Fort Hare.
2. Flusser, *Into the Universe of Technical Images*, trans. Nancy Ann Roth (Minneapolis: University of Minnesota Press, 2011), 50.
3. Ibid.
4. Ibid., 10.
5. Flusser, "The Photograph as a Post-Industrial Object: An Essay on the Ontological Standing of Photographs," *Leonardo* 19, no. 4 (1986): 329–32, 330.
6. Ibid.
7. Ibid.
8. Flusser, *Technical Images*, 49.
9. Ibid.
10. Ibid.
11. Flusser, "Post-Industrial Object," 329.
12. Ibid., 330.
13. Flusser, *Writings*, ed. Andreas Ströhl, trans. Erik Eisel (Minneapolis: University of Minnesota Press, 2002), 128.
14. Yves Citton, *Médiarchie* (Paris: Seuil, 2017), 224.
15. Flusser, *Towards a Philosophy of Photography*, trans. A. Mathews (London: Reaktion Books), 15.
16. Flusser, *Technical Images*, 58.
17. Flusser, "Post-Industrial Object," 330.
18. Ibid.
19. Flusser, *Technical Images*, 13.
20. Ibid., 5.

Writing

Andrew Pilsch

Discussing the future of writing in a series of important mid-1980s essays, Flusser describes "a future society" that no longer writes "linear texts" because it "synthesizes electronic images."[1] For him, "this is not a future floating in the far distance" but one that has already arrived.[2] He suggests that this emergence is not due solely to digital technologies. Instead, this post-literary society comes about when the linearity of thought supported by writing (literally, underwritten) spontaneously decays as humans find that "at the core of the universe, particles no longer follow the rules . . . and begin to buzz."[3] As an example of this phenomenon, Flusser invokes a version of the infinite monkeys theorem: given enough time, a roomful of chimps randomly pecking at a roomful of typewriters would eventually write all the works of Shakespeare—or, in Flusser's case, the exact words of his essay. Extrapolating from this idea, he suggests that to touch a keyboard, at least at first, is the process of "finding something by chance" and that "this is the method chimpanzees use to write on the typewriter, the way they will eventually produce, by chance, a text identical to this one," even if it might require "a term projected into the future, potentially encompassing a few million years."[4] Flusser concludes this line of thought with a characteristic self-contradictory flourish, asserting that his typing is in fact *not* "the result of an accident that has become unavoidable"; rather he asserts, "I intentionally select my keys."[5] Clarifying Flusser's example, monkeys mashing keyboards will, in a *very* inefficient manner, eventually combine all the Latin alphabet characters, all punctuation and spacing, and all numbers into all possible combinations.

For Flusser, typing monkeys reveal that any output is merely the instance of an inevitable, random process of making information, and that language is merely a series of choices between predetermined quanta rather than a tool for unique expression. Authors' choices are never fully separate from random chance, as humans themselves are merely the product of "the aleatory play with genetic information," another randomized, mechanistic process.[6] This process of quantization means that as words—letters, characters—become individual tokens in an aleatory game, a new approach to meaning that abandons linearity becomes necessary: "apparatuses must be developed that grasp the ungraspable, visualize the invisible, and conceptualize the inconceivable."[7] These apparatuses, like the typewriter, the camera, or the digital computer, are at home among the "particles [that] are no more than a field of possible ways in which to function," like the quantified alphabet described previously. They blindly distill these quanta for us, and "that is what a technical image is: a blindly realized possibility, something invisible that has blindly become visible."[8] The blind revelations of mechanistic text precipitate a "contemporary crisis in writing": writing is the process of ordering thoughts into neat rows and straight lines, "and machines," he writes, "do this better than people do. One can leave writing, this ordering of signs, to machines."[9]

In an age of technical images, Flusser suggests that writing is no longer properly thought of as writing. Today, meaning is made by those who "write with and for apparatuses . . . the essence of writing has changed for these people; it is another writing, in need of another name: programming."[10] If writing is ordering thought into lines, the work of thought does not occur in tapping away at keys but in devising new apparatuses by which our thoughts are ordered and transmitted. Writing is replaced by programming, as we have machines for the mundane work of words. But it is worse than even that now, "the new computer codes have made us all illiterate again."[11] Yet, for Flusser, this is not a call to despair. While technical images resist traditional criticism because "digital codes synthesize things that have already been fully criticized," a process of recoding, "one that is only approximately named by the concept of 'system analysis,'" can perform the work of critique.[12] Writing becomes programming and critique becomes systems analysis, but adapting to this new world is possible: "we have to try to use a typographic way of thinking to get to grips with post-typographic 'writing.'"[13] Flusser's account of writing challenges us not to elaborate further the end of writing but instead to imagine and shape the textual cultures that come afterward.

Flusser's concept of writing mirrors certain aspects of writing studies that developed in the late twentieth century, as the field was registering the impact of new media. In 1972, Donald M. Murray diagnosed the state of writing instruction in the American university thus: writing teachers approach student work "as a product [. . .] as if they had passed literature in to us."[14] Murray's essay helped usher in "process theory," an approach to writing instruction focused not on what but *how* writers write. Murray articulates writing as "the process of discovery through language," and he identifies three key steps: prewriting, writing, and rewriting, with the pronouncement that prewriting, figuring out what to write, "takes about 85% of the writer's time."[15] This model structured several decades of research in writing instruction, creating increasingly nuanced ways of facilitating the process. In "The Gesture of Writing," Flusser considers writing a process too. However, the implications are substantially different from Murray's. After listing elements of writing—from paper and pen to grammar, semantics, and thought itself— Flusser concludes that "complexity results not so much from the number of essential factors as from their heterogeneity."[16] Writing is a process of negotiating between objects both concrete (pencil, letters) and abstract (linguistic convention, grammar, ideas). In contrast, Murray argues that writing "is the fastest part" and "may take as little as one percent of the writer's time."[17] It is "scary," though, because "you know how much, and how little, you know."[18]

Hence process theory's emphasis on prewriting and rewriting as activities that help ideas emerge by incorporating thinking into the writing process. Flusser inverts these assumptions. Contra process theory, Flusser views writing and thought as mutually determinate, claiming "writing fixes thinking. Writing is a way of thinking": "each language possesses its own atmosphere and is, as a result, a universe in itself."[19]

Flusser's ideas about writing, then, align him with post-process theory. Post-process, as discussed by Lee-Ann M. Kastman Breuch, for example, returns writing studies to flexibility and spontaneity, insisting that writing is "indeterminate, public, interpretive, and situated," all of which imply two further "principles": "the rejection of mastery and the engagement in dialogue [. . .] with students."[20] Dialogic and interpretive, post-process theory seemingly correspond with Flusser. Yet, Flusser's account of writing in the digital age is more radical and less sanguine about the future of writing, troubling any simple alignment between his ideas and the field of writing studies. The automatic flows of digital systems create a world "programmed with the codes of technical images" which "do not require reading."[21] Extrapolating from word processing, Flusser envisions future "grammar machines, artificial intelligences that take care of this order [of words] on their own."[22] In this future, writing, ordering ideas into lines, becomes obsolete, more efficiently done by machines after which "the speed and variability of writing" will increase and these grammar machines "will make better, faster, and more varied histories than we ever did."[23] In a sense, for Flusser, post-process is always posthistorical. "History," he writes, "is a function of writing and the consciousness that expresses itself in writing."[24]

"The Gesture of Writing" concludes with a warning: "the problems lying before us demand that we think in codes and gestures far more refined, exact, and fertile than those of the alphabet. We need to think in video, in analog and digital models and programs, in multidimensional codes."[25] "Multidimensional codes" also pose an ongoing problem in writing studies, where multimodal composition spreads within conversations about writing instruction.[26] What happens when writing and literacy itself are no longer seen as the bedrocks of education? One model for thinking about this issue, and for connecting Flusser to the future of composition instruction, is Gregory L. Ulmer's body of work, which develops an educational theory of "electracy," the contemporary analogue of "literacy."[27] Electrate education seeks what literacy sought in the alphabet: orienting the individual within a system of potentialities. In *Konsult* (2019), Ulmer argues that the humanities can engage students in "the invention of electracy online" rather than finding a niche for writing in the electrate world. *Konsult* documents new instructional models, analogous to practices like dialogue in literate society, that led students and teachers grapple with new communicative norms. Flusser's posthistorical account of writing highlights Ulmer's exigence. For Flusser, linearity has been "the 'official thinking' of the West," but it is being replaced by "the programming of cybernetic data banks and computational facilities."[28] The institution of the university, as Ulmer highlights, is a historical product of writing, and yet it must survive amid posthistorical cybernetic codes. Flusser provides writing studies a clear, if somewhat melancholic, account of the deep intertwining of writing (or, the attendant possibilities associated with writing's "linear alignment of signs" to "think logically, calculate, criticize, pursue knowledge, philosophize") and how writing may no longer be essential to what humans do within institutions—or, as he puts it, the form of human being.[29]

Notes

1. Flusser, *Into the Universe of Technical Images*, trans. Nancy Ann Roth (Minneapolis: University of Minnesota Press, 2011), 3.
2. Ibid.
3. Ibid., 15.
4. Ibid., 25.
5. Ibid.
6. Ibid., 27.
7. Ibid., 16.
8. Ibid.
9. Flusser, *Does Writing Have a Future?*, trans. Nancy Ann Roth (Minneapolis: University of Minnesota Press, 2011), 6.
10. Ibid.
11. Ibid., 55.
12. Ibid., 152.
13. Ibid., 56.
14. Donald M. Murray, "Teaching Writing as a Process Not a Product," in *Cross-Talk In Comp Theory* (Urbana, IL: National Council of Teachers of English, 2003), 3.
15. Ibid., 4.
16. Flusser, *Gestures*, trans. Nancy Ann Roth (Minneapolis: University of Minnesota Press, 2014), 20.
17. Ibid., 22.
18. Lee-Ann M. Kastman Breuch, "Post-Process 'Pedagogy': A Philosophical Exercise," *Cross-Talk In Comp Theory* (Urbana, IL: National Council of Teachers of English, 2003): 117–18.
19. Flusser, *Gestures*, 13–14.
20. Ibid., 24.
21. Ibid.
22. Flusser, *Does Writing Have a Future?*, 6.
23. Ibid., 8.
24. Ibid.
25. Flusser, *Gestures*, 25.
26. Gregory L. Ulmer, *Konsult* (Anderson, SC: Parlor, 2019): ix.
27. Flusser, *Gestures*, 24.
28. Ibid.
29. Flusser, *Does Writing Have a Future?*, 7, 4.

Zetetic Maneuvers: Stalking the Continuum

Adelheid Mers

Finding Flusser

Gerlinde gave me the small pamphlet, the Benteli edition of "Krise der Linearität"; she had received it from Ursula, who had met Flusser in Marseille, but was now over him, at least in terms of her thinking about New Media.[1] On the last train home across Cologne, the number one, I was able to read the entire thing. The next day I raided both the König and Müller bookstores, filled my big-wheeled suitcase, and took it all back to Chicago. He had been dead for years. Some of the German titles are *Kommunikologie, Medienkultur, Nachgeschichte, Bodenlos, Ins Universum der technischen Bilder, Die Geschichte des Teufels, Die Schrift,* and *Vampyroteuthis Infernalis*. (Silvia lent me a copy of the out-of-print *Gesten* when I returned the following year and visited the archive). Many texts are also in Portuguese and some in French. The Flusser Archive's office was a small room on the first floor of the Academy of Media Arts in Cologne (the archive has since moved to the Academy of Arts in Berlin). The setting feels medieval, windows open both onto the street and into the driveway that cuts through the front building and connects to the courtyard; this would be a fine spot for the castle's guardian. With my digital camera I shoot typewritten pages (no line breaks) from the original manuscripts, which are lined up in shelved binders. I find the word "textolatry," as I thought I might. Flusser's own library is housed upstairs. There's a copy of a book dear to me since the seventies, Benjamin Lee Whorf's *Language, Thought, Reality*. Like Mary Poppins, Silvia climbs onto a desk with an umbrella, reaching to close a transom. On a TV set on a rolling cart, DVD and VHS below, I watch a video, Flusser talks. Comfortably seated across from me, he is a cyborg now.

Reading Flusser

Towards a Philosophy of Photography, The Shape of Things, Writings, The Freedom of the Migrant are editions that are available in English. In Europe, Flusser became well known with *Towards a Philosophy of Photography*. I gather that his work is still mostly discussed in the context of media studies. Three of my favorite essays are "Celebrating," "Exile

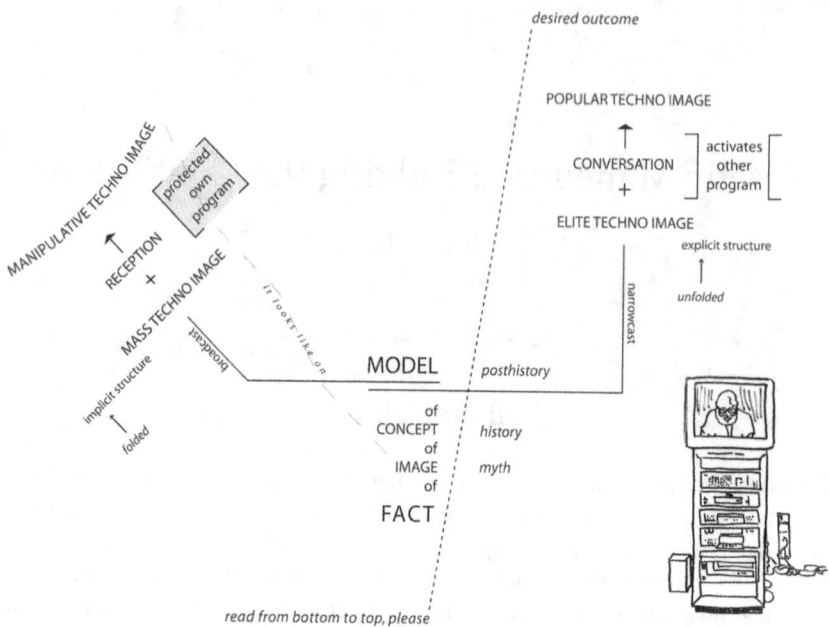

Figure 39.1 Flusserian diagrammatics. Source and permissions: Adelheid Mers.

and Creativity," and "Line and Surface" (all can be found in *Writings*). In "Celebrating," he develops the idea of an "other program" (as opposed to an "own program") that can be read as a plea for open-source software. That's a nice, frothy peak the essay whips up, but I prefer to read it through a different lens. What if the notion of the "other program" leads to a critical survey of the reader's very own premises, in preparation for a mutual exploration of contingencies that have programmed not software but individuals? How do I make sense, and what prompts me to do it just so? Celebration comes into play when ossified (implicit) structure is discerned and brought back to life (made explicit and thus again pliable), when a new capacity for absurdity supersedes habits and truths. "Exile and Creativity" describes how to be uprooted forces one to approach the above and how an embrace of permanent migranthood (the witnessing of structure) promotes conditions of creativity (the teasing of structure). What are the means available to perform and to express these operations? They are image and text. In "Line and Surface," Flusser assesses how they are intertwined. At all times, humans attend to facts. Initially, images mediate. As the notion rises that images are man-made, linear texts are invented to explain the images (iconoclasm). As the notion rises that texts are man-made, techno-images are summoned to model the texts (textoclasm) that have earlier served to explain the images and still contain their traces.

In *Kommunikologie* (not available in English), Flusser offers something that I take to bolster my art practice: diagramming, or "conducting surveys of premises." Again, an important distinction between implicit and explicit structure is performed: Flusser expands the term "technical image"—an image that models a text—into "mass-techno image" (implicit structure) and "elite techno-image" (explicit structure). The elite techno-image is what I wish to claim, but first I'd like to set up the more complicated mass techno-image. Mass techno-images are created when an operator uses a code or an apparatus to produce images. (For example, a photographer uses a camera, or the Hubble Space Telescope is programmed to record images of space.) An apparatus is not only a conduit for image-making, it is also a particular conduit. But, unless one is educated about the history that shaped the apparatus and about the limits the apparatus promotes, an image created with it does not reveal its mode of production. It just appears to show an instance of truth. A picture of a pretty girl, a cute puppy, a colorized galaxy, a compassionate conservative. Mass-techno images are not only rooted in the texts of science, but in addition they lend themselves to the ends of manipulators, and Flusser strongly advises education about their inherent framing, about their capacity to be Trojan horses for ideologies, in short, about the entirety of their implicit, man-made texts.

> "But this is not the entire truth. There also are techno-images that are not part of the apparatus-operator complex that is grinding everything into stereotypes. These elite techno-images can be seen everywhere: in science and technology, in politics and in art, and they are distinguished from mass techno-images by the fact that only specialists are able to read them. They are conscious efforts to make terminology imaginable [...]. Thus, our predicament permits two prognoses: (1) Either the apparatus-operator-complexes will imbibe all texts to recode them into techno-images and then to broadcast them around while also grinding the elite techno images into mush, (2) or the elite techno-images will lead to a new level of consciousness, from the vantage point of which it will be possible to liberate the world that is encoded in techno-images from the grip of the apparatus-operator-complex, to serve true human communication."[2]

An "elite techno-image" is a means of communication that has as its purpose to construe an existing text or even to propose new construction. A text is engaged by the person who creates the elite techno-image, who educates herself about the text's history, is aware of its artifice, of its life, and who wishes to share what she found. The elite-techno image is honest about its own premises and limitations, does not hide its own inherent ideologies, but exposes them as far as possible. Examples Flusser gives of elite techno-images are blueprints, charts, designs, or diagrams. Here is much-appreciated support of my long-standing urge (initially an artist's whim) to diagram texts. As I read it, Flusser allows that the practice of diagramming can be part of a strategy to better the world because it is well suited to point to the fact that structures are always present, hidden in plain view, waiting to be modeled. The question Flusser does not address is how best to transform an elite techno-image into a popular techno-image, but the emphasis he places on dialog throughout his entire body of writing offers guidance. One way an elite-techno-image can become a popular techno-image is if the structure it models is animated in conversation.

Diagrams

Georgia[3] had asked me to write about my research process, the work that leads up to and includes diagramming. Finding Flusser was a pivotal point in my thinking about how I work. AF (ante Flusser) and PF (post Flusser). AF consisted of recurring diagramming incidents that very, very slowly thickened into a conscious practice. I remember all of those incidents. (1) I diagrammed a bacteriophage after my biology teacher's description. None of the other kids in the class seemed to want to do it, and I was immensely proud that I was able to pull it off. (2) Wittgenstein's *Tractatus*, two pages of being lost at sea among arrows. (3) In my first year of art school, a sculpture after Benjamin Lee Whorf. A cross, knife blades protruding from each arm, a person in the center—as we order the world, it appears to show itself to us. (4) Next, I attacked not figurative language, but a painting: the angels from Altdorfer's "Birth of Mary" escaped their circle and found themselves in new arrangements with frogs, plants, and dotted lines. (5) Next, Gabo's circle sculptures were points of departure, flattened paper copies leading to hinged plywood objects whose blades could be rearranged around their empty centers. I thought at the time that the most engaging humans had empty centers, like the eye of a powerful storm, and that accidental folds provided structure. There are no backgrounds, no foundations, only configurations. (6) After moving to Chicago, the art object began to retreat forcefully, and I gave chase: not sculptures, but floor sculptures; not floor sculptures, but puddles of light; not light installations, but audiences; not audiences, but conventions; not conventions, but what seemed to be largely unexamined, underlying assumptions about art, life, politics; the retreat was halted when I ran into a wall of books. Texts were places where thoughts were temporarily arrested, so they could be examined and redeployed, records to be played and sampled. (7) Diagrams became documents of my readings. From the perspective of PF, everything that happened AF is now reframed and retold as having headed toward a diagramming practice. Pesky historical habits die slowly.

Practicing

At times I envy my colleagues, the quick-witted historians and philosophers who can swiftly build, discern, hold in mind, and traverse entire architectures of thought. In comparison, I am slow and clumsy. I stalk a prey without knowing what it is—a particular crease or fold in the continuum—following hunches along disparate lines of inquiry, picking and choosing based on criteria that seem to be physically embedded in my experience but aren't apparent unless thought matter sticks to them in a particular, site-specific way. Then I get very, very excited. There is a sense of discovery, of high drama. I want to show you, and then I want to tell you about what I'm showing you. There is no methodology, just an idiosyncratic method. That, by the way, is how I have come to define art. Given art's methodology as attention to nonliterate thought, its methods are as many as there are artists. My nonliterate thought just happened to direct me toward words, as the sources of the images seen and made and talked about today.

Notes

1 This chapter, accompanied by the author's translation of "Crisis of Linearity," appeared in somewhat different form in *Bootprint* 1, no. 1 (March 2007): 18–22.
2 Flusser, *Kommunikologie* (Fischer: Frankfurt am Main, 1998).
3 Georgia Kotretsos, founding editor of the journal *Bootprint* (2006–10).

Epilogue

Between Languages and Without Discipline: A Twentieth-Century Intellect Drafted for the Twenty-First Century

Siegfried Zielinski

Translated by Daniel Raschke

> —I am my world. (The microcosm.)
>
> Ludwig Wittgenstein[1]

"I'm not certain..." This phrase begins Roger Caillois's discussion of "Frost and Heat" in his foray on the conditions of the surface of the Earth from thirty-five years ago: "I'm not certain that the Earth easily adapts itself to the human presence. Yet, it will not be obliged to endure it forever. Only recently arrived on the planet, man acts as wild usurper unable to respect the general equilibrium. With a rapidity bordering on miraculous, he has almost completely subdued a Nature in which he was still absent yesterday."[2]

The challenges currently facing Earthlings are enormous. No wonder, for they have essentially caused the crises themselves, the consequences of which they now have to combat—from the brutal exploitation of terrestrial and maritime resources and the delusional manias of productivity and accumulation, evidently unstoppable on a global scale, to the worldwide ideological deliriums of dull nationalists, fanatical war machines, and theocratic fantasists up to the redistribution of the economic, political, and cultural balance of power in favor of the Orient and to the disadvantage of the Occident. The world is re*orient*ing itself back to that planetary region where the sun rises, from whence Hegel included China in his philosophy of world history. In this orientation is there a new chance for a planet glowing from the relentless consequences of European modernity?

The challenges are both systemic and interdiscursive in nature. They have been created by the human inhabitants of our planet and their tremendous urge to subdue everything that is not identical with their very limited ideas of Life. From this perspective, the Earthling has also created the subjects of his own species that were needed for the respective hegemonic conditions. Undoubtedly, the challenges are closely related and form an interdependent network of fundamental problems for which solutions are long overdue. The network of relationships is thwarted by a central desideratum: that is, as it were, the philosophical and ethical adhesive for the network of economy and ecology, culture and politics—namely the urgent need to work out new concepts of subjectivity.

How will the individual move in the future on the whole that we call our world? How does the One and the Other adapt to nature and technology, which has become part of our existence? What is the future communality that neither oppresses us nor tears us apart as individuals, nor simply welds us together under the sign of some bogus universalism (be this the market, religion, or ideology)? What kind of concept of freedom can be projected into the future that does not stray in the ethical emptiness of Heidegger's fundamental ontology (as Flusser himself was captivated by his early preoccupations with Heidegger), but which can be linked to responsibilities we must face? What does it mean in concrete terms to think freedom not as freedom *from* but as freedom *for*, as Flusser later demanded in his existential-philosophical considerations? Karl Löwith, nearly a contemporary with Flusser, who studied with Heidegger in Freiburg and habilitated with him in Marburg, has excellently formulated the strange emptiness of an absolute thinking of freedom in his autobiographical account. Heidegger was highly attractive to students in the 1920s precisely because of his

> indeterminate content and the mere appellative nature of his philosophical will: his intellectual intensity and concentration was on "the one thing that is necessary." Only later did we realize that this one thing was actually nothing, a pure determination for an uncertain purpose. *I'm determined but I don't know for what!* as one of the excellent student jokes put it. Yet, Heidegger's tireless and at the same time pathetic demand of his students was that "the mental work must be as *hard* and *jagged* as this dangerous Bergwelt" in which he loved to live.[3]

The unconditional *Ego*, the ostensibly sovereign ego of European modernity, has passed expiration by the end of the twentieth century, when Europe, shamelessly, still strives to export it as the highest ethical good, even though its historical half-life has long since passed and the intellectual commodity loses its exchange value daily on the theory market. The proletarian equation of Man & Machine, which the Russian Revolution proclaimed as a modernist bargain a good hundred years ago, did not work out as a calculation and check. Likewise, the unconditional *We*, as practiced and developed in contemporary China as an uncompromising identity formation, seems to be an unappealing alternative for all circumstances.

That unconditioned *We*, synthesized from didactic Confucianism and Maoist Marxism, frightens us. Not least because it emerged from the rigid subject machinery that Mao Zedong and his brutal gang of four installed with the Cultural Revolution. It is not only a stark contrast to the unconditional Ego of the West and its grandiose promises of freedom, but it has a completely different face than that which we are familiar with when we look in the mirror. We don't understand it. And there are only a few Western intellectuals, like François Jullien, who have serious access to it. It is inconceivable to the satiated portion of humanity that tens of millions had to starve miserably only sixty years ago in what is one of the richest and most powerful countries on Earth now. When Alberto Moravia published his 1967 report on the Cultural Revolution (*La rivoluzione culturale in Cina*) he began his haunting account with a fictional interview; when asked about the thing that had impressed him most in China, he replied: "Poverty."[4]

I interpret Mao's Cultural Revolution as a strong synthesis of Marxism and Confucianism. The kind of subjectivity, which was at stake to be generated anew, was *not the proletarian human machine*. Instead—and in opposition to Stalin and his Soviet Union—the Cultural Revolution celebrated the concept of a technological sociality based on *equality*. Possibility of social ascent (*Aufstieg*) was given neither through consumption as the primary source for capitalist profit (like in the United States) nor through prosperity as gratification for power, but through the quality, variety, and distribution of talent and capabilities, especially technological capabilities.

The Little Red Book with important phrases formulated by Mao did not have the status of a pure object of learning and knowledge, which one is storing in his or her shelf at home and occasionally takes out for reading. Much more it functioned as a "handbook" in the true sense of the term—it was a *manual*, which you always have in your pocket to see how the machine is running, how you can synchronize with it, how to correct or how to repair it (or yourself). This very special handbook for correct behavior and acting is highly comparable with the instructions of the Confucian rites, which easily can be read as a program. In fact, Mao's *Red Book* and the instructions for practicing and celebrating Confucian rites work supplementarily as advanced subject generators, as manuals for the new subject-identity of the unconditioned *We*.

In the Chinese form of sociality (*Gesellschaftlichkeit*), existences are poised situationally from emergency to emergency in tumultuous permanent revolution and are subjected without compromise to the regime of voluntary governmentality. Instead of *The Little Red Book*, everyone now has an Eyephone in their hands, demonstratively held for public attention as a sign of belonging and controlled in all its functions by the techno-avant-garde institutionalized by the central committee. (This is a very good example of the aberration that a technical *a priori* implies in media criticism. Internet technology is not organized per se and not necessarily in a decentralized way, as Flusser also propagated. Centralization and networking are not antagonisms, but rather constitute a tensional relationship.) And, at the same time, we are also rehearsed in the so-called Western world in a planetary, digital consumer communism that is characterized by extensive control and observation of our behavior, transparency of our technical existence, accelerated isolation, and equally voluntary submission to power. The pandemic to be endured in 2020, which dominates all discourses, not only causes a huge surge in virtualization but also promotes the tendency toward the complete dissolution of the boundaries between the private and the public, which Flusser spoke of under other auspices and which his contemporary, the British cofounder of Cultural Studies, Raymond Williams, so aptly demonstrated in the early 1980s with the term "mobile privatization."

What could be an alternative to that unconditional Ego that has so lastingly ruined planet Earth that the rich and powerful are already thinking of second and third realms outside the atmosphere that the Earthlings have poisoned?

From the rich cabinet of curiosities of Flusserian epistemes, I aver the risky concept of an identity of the Individual, the singular, in unconditional dialogue with the Other, as can be derived in different variants from the dialogical philosophies of Martin Buber, Emanuel Lévinas, Gianni Vattimo, or Edmond Jabès and inserted into the existing civilization of technically based existences and communication relations—at least as a working hypothesis. Individuals communicate like crazy, like in a constant race against each other: who can do it more, faster, more beautifully through even more intensive and noiseless connection? But, as Guy Debord already noted in his *Society of the Spectacle* in the early 1970s: telecommunication connects, but it can only connect what is already separated. The "unconditional dialogue" of which we are talking here explicitly includes the intensive exchange with other subject identities, but also with nature and technology.

The Situationist gesture, the deep inner dialectic of separation in the real and connectivity in the imaginary and symbolic inscribed in the advanced system of telematics, shaped Vilém Flusser's thinking as it moved through the technically based communication relations of Western civilization. (And it was only about this that Flusser spoke and wrote intensively. Although he lived in Brazil for thirty years, the southern hemisphere and the Orient did not really interest him very much.) The undecided in-between is characteristic of an intellectual existence that is almost magically interwoven with the phenomena of the medial itself and the way we try to think about them.

This also applies to a second paradigm that many historians even consider to be the decisive one of modernity—*movement*. The modern fairs of the nineteenth century were primarily created as gigantic kinetic machines. Acceleration and the intoxication of speed, rotation, and circling delirium—metaphors also for the entire industrial-capitalist system—occupied the public places of entertainment and found expression in a multitude of artifacts and more complex technical arrangements in which the bodies and the imagination were sent on voyages to distant countries, on excursions to hell and heaven. Machines moving themselves and others, natural and technical bodies in motion, moving images, rhythmic texts. Cinematography, for example, established itself as part of this complex apparatus, at a time when the space-time continuum and the n-dimensional were already being brought into play in advanced thinking, before and with Einstein, above all by Russian artists and thinkers such as Vasiliev, Khlebnikov, Uspensky—that n-dimensional which, in everyday simplification, now constitutes our networked communicative existences.

In five aspects, I would like to sketch in the following, in a fragmentary way, how Vilém Flusser's intellectual existence has designed a subject identity that could become characteristic, and in some aspects perhaps even valuable, for the further course of the twenty-first century. In this brief reflection, my Flusser becomes a model that goes beyond the person for whom the model stands and points to a time to come. This going-beyond-oneself is an essential dimension for understanding the mystery of why some intellectuals can be effective beyond their death and others not. "We shall survive in the memory of others," as Flusser modestly noted during his lifetime.[5]

No Fatherland: No Own Territory—Permanent Change of Place of Living—Synthetic Identity

Everything that has become dear to those who were essentially socialized by the advent of committed critical theory in the media theories of the twentieth century was not (or at least not primarily) developed in classical academic contexts and certainly not while employed on permanent university chairs: Hugo Münsterberg, Dziga Vertov, Lev Kuleshov, Bela Balazs, Walter Benjamin, Bertolt Brecht, Siegfried Kracauer, Rudolf Arnheim, René Fülöp-Miller, Herbert Marcuse, Adorno, and Horkheimer were—forced by the historical violence of the conjuncture—passers-by, exiles, fugitives, travelers.

"Bodenlos"—the titular maxim in Flusser's intellectual autobiography plays above all with the metaphorical power of this word to describe a floating existence, spiritually uprooted in the loss of God and humanism. But, it is also to be understood quite literally, namely as a rejection of a *dispositif* that at the beginning of the twenty-first century is again increasingly invoked and propagated as fatherland. The land of the fathers became a chimera, a phantasm, a projection screen of ideologies that alone turned backwards, due to the violence of context that unfolded mercilessly in the twentieth century. Flusser left his father's city and country, and none of the countries where he later lived took its place.

There is a direct interaction here: the compulsion and inclination to flee in a hurry, to constantly cross borders, to overcome walls, barbed wires, identity and customs checkpoints is symbiotically linked to the lack of discipline in thinking. The most thought-provoking critics and theorists of the twentieth century have always understood media discourses as intermedial discourses, shifting between classical forms of artistic expression and the means of technical reproduction, between painting and photography, theater and cinema, music and performance, written and networked image-writing media—just as much as between philosophy and the history of technology, sociology and aesthetic critique, informatics and semiology, psychoanalysis and critique of ideology. The internet, for example, as a *dispositif* in a comprehensive sense, is at the intersection of all these forms of expression and thought activities, in terms of both its material foundations and its aesthetic and ethical implications. Any media are to be thought of from only one of these analytical perspectives merely administratively, but not vividly. In order for something to change, it is always necessary to take a layman's or rather an amateurish view of what is stuck in disciplines, says the endo-physicist and theoretical chemist Otto E. Rössler, who, among other things, has calculated one of the complex motion attractors in chaos theory. The cofounder of apparatus hermeneutics in French cinema theory, for example, Jean-Louis Baudry, was a dentist and novelist in his bread and butter profession.

Neither productive creative work with the fluctuating media nor their intensive and constantly vigilant reflection are compatible with local or regional or intellectual ties. When they were still allowed to travel at will and in fast planes and trains, the nomads of the scene, of which Flusser was also a member, were severely scolded for bouncing back and forth between symposiums and congresses, exhibition openings and seminars, and in these movements, which were both energetic and power-sapping, they had hardly any time to (re)formulate their respective lectures stringently. Vilém Flusser, Florian Rötzer (one of his great patrons in the 1980s and early 1990s), Peter Weibel, Norbert Boltz, Gerburg Treusch-Dieter, Dietmar Kamper, Friedrich Kittler, Slavoj Žižek—at the end of the twentieth century they were among those who seemed to be constantly on tour. Their concert halls were the academies, museums, and university auditoriums; their more intimate clubs, the seminar rooms and galleries, hosted debates on criticism and the shaping of communicative conditions and their possible perspectives. The printing presses of the small publishing houses, which fought over their texts, rotated faster than thoughts could be written down. "On the Road Again" (Canned Heat, 1968)—not least of all, the early media-critical gang (I refer here to the Deleuzian term) was a generation of intellectuals that had been socialized to a large extent by rock music and the culture of the street. Many of them founded bands in the 1960s, singing as front men or women, playing drums, bass, or guitar, tinkering with electro-acoustics or synthesizers.

The fatherland has no future. As a concept it belongs to the past and thus becomes more and more unreal. We live—often only temporarily—in regions that are thwarted by different cultures of knowledge, religion, and politics. With regard to the essence of philosophical activity—thinking—in this context Hannah Arendt does not speak of everywhere but of nowhere: "Essences cannot be localized . . . the 'essential' is what is applicable everywhere, and this 'everywhere' that bestows on thought its specific weight is spatially speaking a 'nowhere.' The thinking ego, moving among universals, among invisible essences, is, strictly speaking, nowhere."[6] The thinking self, which moves among universals, among invisible essences, is, strictly speaking, "nowhere." A seductive form of Heideggerian thought that Flusser would certainly have liked: we are where we think.

Vilém Flusser lived the identity of the migrant suffering, but also with conviction. And he was equally resolute in his role as an ambassador between different disciplines. In academic or even scientific matters, he was an amateur in each of the fields in which he was active. In other words, he had an affection for fields of knowledge and activity such as philosophy, linguistics, anthropology, theology, or the history of science, without deepening them or even contributing to their administration in academic institutions. His strength lay in liaisons and in creating surprises through collisions of heterogeneous fragments of knowledge. Flusser was thus the ideal media thinker, but he did not like to be called one.

A film produced by Caecilia Tripp and Karen McKimmon for B3 Media in London's Brixton in 2008 could help us with the subject design of the stateless journeyman. The short but powerful video is called *Making History*. In it, Linton Kwesi Johnson, inventor of Dub Poetry, and the poet-philosopher Édouard Glissant develop a dialogue on the meaning of "roots" within a possible politics of identity of Black people. Both sitting relaxed on the backseat of a taxi gliding through Manhattan in New York, Johnson says: "This sense of rootlessness [. . .] is the post-modern experience, for everybody," and referring to a famous poem by Michael Smith with the title "Roots" he continues that "everybody is looking for roots. It is part of the dialectics of globalization." Rejecting this term as hostile to the poetics of relations, Glissant suddenly interrupts: "That is what I call the unity-diversity of the world. Unity is bad, when it is only unity. Diversity is bad when it is only diversity." Johnson responds: "My understanding of diversity is that we respect each other's culture [. . .]." After a while Glissant says: "The question remains, what is it what they call identity?" Johnson responds: "We have different identities, we are British, we are African, we are Afro-Caribbean, we are Asian, we are Chinese—we are all these things," and Glissant falls into his words again: "You think it is possible that we are having a kind of synthetic identity?" Johnson: "Well, it is becoming increasingly so, and I think America is a good example of a synthetic identity."

The extreme balance between the individual and the world as a whole and synthetic identities, which also means that they are generated by culture and technology—it makes at least some sense to think the actual concept of Cosmopolitanism as an adequate expression for the technologically advanced mondial community. The new socialities cogenerated by telematic connectivity, which are so difficult to grasp, can be characterized by a similar permanent act of balance. The non-place of the internet offers and generates permanently superfluous identities beyond classes, races, political parties, beyond binding/compulsory social, cultural, political movements. With a specific arbitrariness vibrating inside, that Giorgio Agamben tries to define with the Shakespearean phrase "quodlibet" (*As You Like It*, 1600). It is essentially imagined, gliding along the borderline to the imaginary and the symbolic.

No Mother Tongue: Thinking in Permanent Translation—Language as Code

In 1985, Vilém Flusser was invited to a conference in Weiler in the deep provincial Bavarian Allgäu to speak about "homeland and homelessness" (*Heimat und Heimatlosigkeit*). He must have felt the bizarre paradox of this situation and made no secret of how uncomfortable he was about being there and the cultural context of his speech. Flusser spoke in an unusually sharp, yes, cold voice that seemed literally to cut through the atmosphere in the room:

> My wife and I were born in Prague. And my ancestors seem to have lived there for over a thousand years. I am a Jew and the phrase "next year in Jerusalem" has been with me since childhood. I was brought up in German culture and have been actively involved in it for a few years. I spent over a year in London trying to flee to Brazil, and then have been to England and the United States repeatedly for long periods of time, and Anglo-Saxon culture has become part of my way of thinking. I lived in Sao Paulo for well over 30 years, I currently live in a Provencal village

and have been incorporated into the fabric of this timeless settlement. I am native to at least four languages and see myself challenged and forced to translate and re-translate all of my writings over and over again. Every language is wonderful in its own way. And this glory is particularly evident when I translate a text from one language into another. The mother, father, or what-I know uncle language is therefore every language. Anyone who loves a language loves all of them. But that doesn't mean anything. Because it is not enough to love a language if you want to write it. You have to master them too. And that means forcing them to do something that they don't want to do on their own. This love-hate relationship, this *odi et amor*, characterizes everyone who has something to do with language and writing. In short—I have become acquainted with homes and lost homes. This is my experience and the daily practice based on it may be one of the motives that led me to study communication problems. I saw and see in human communication the ever failing attempt to bridge the abyss between people and human groups.[7]

I deliberately had this quote translated by machine, the free version of DeepL, and made no change to the translation from German. With the English words and the English syntax, the machine excels, presenting the semantics and language style of the writer Flusser quite accurately. I would like to demonstrate a special aspect of his language that follows from what he did in the deep southwest Bavarian province of the Allgäu.

The migrant from Prague had no mother tongue and he did not want to acquire or learn such a mother tongue. In this respect, too, he differed from Hannah Arendt, who, as a philosophical writer who grew up in Germany, initially suffered greatly from being cut off from her mother tongue in exile. For Flusser, language was above all a code for mediatizing his thoughts for others, more precisely: for an audience. His activity as a speaker and as a writer followed the idea of a permanent connection between what was and is separate. Glissant used the phrase "poetics of relations" for this purpose, which can certainly also be assumed by Flusser as a relevant intellectual paradigm between poetry and theory. For his particular way of connecting was on the one hand pragmatically determined. Depending on where he was—in Brazil, in Germany, in France—his writing and speaking were primarily intended to move people to act and not primarily to think. That is why his texts were so much appreciated by the makers, the artists and designers. They are *anti-philosophy* in the sense of Boris Groys—that is, primarily oriented toward action (*Handlung*) and not primarily toward thinking. Moreover, his spoken and written works always had the character of something artificially produced, of something specially created, in keeping with the character of the poetic. "Languages are fields of Kosmoi's poetic work," he wrote in the Spritz essay of 1967, thus creating his specific world, his cosmos, which ran, so to speak, transversely to the individual languages as event fields.[8] *Always the same, but never myself*—the Prague Jew with the cosmopolitan and cosmo-cultural context was recognizable in every language, regardless of whether he was in German, French, English, or Portuguese; he did not write Czech, but he dreamed in the language of the country, where he was born, as Harun Farocki wrote in a review of Flusser's book *Das Universum der Technischen Bilder*.[9] Through the divisions he was always recognizable in his real presence. Person is derived from the Latin verb *personare*. It means that someone penetrates through the mask of imposed culture, of which language is an essential part, and becomes recognizable. Flusser was a charismatic personality and cultivated this identity with the utmost care.

Flusser follows a subject blueprint as we have come to know it from the time of the first avant-garde of the twentieth century in the form of outstanding thinkers, artists, and poets and as it is reactivated in a modified form at the beginning of the twenty-first century. "I contain multitudes": in 2020 Bob Dylan quotes the crucial line from the 51st sequence of the poem in parentheses in Walt Whitman's "Song of Myself." (Dylan has deliberately omitted the preceding "I am large.") "I am the many" was the title of Elisabeth von Samsonow's first book about Egon Schiele, and in doing so she interpreted, among other things, his shifting between the sexes. Franz Kafka, whom Flusser adored above all else, was as unifying and homogenizing a writer as Igor Stravinsky or Arnold Schoenberg was in music. "Das Subjekt gehört nicht zur Welt, sondern es ist eine Grenze der Welt" ["The subject does not belong to the world: rather, it is a limit of the world"]—wrote the young Wittgenstein in his legendary *Tractatus Logico-Philosophicus* toward the end of the First World War.[10] In consequence, subjectivity is an activity at the limit. This has not changed. On the contrary: only the boundaries have shifted. The fact that such limits exist has not been eliminated. The small book of the *Tractatus* had been a divine text for Flusser.

Language as code, used in mastery as poetic code, can be defined as the mode in which synthetic identities are expressed that have consciously passed through different cultural *dispositifs*: "the sources of his thought arise from foreign languages, especially French, English and German, and he has to direct these sources into Portuguese channels," Flusser writes about the task of the intellectual at the beginning of his proposal "For a field theory of translation."[11]

Even at the beginning of the structuralist movement, however, Claude Lévi-Strauss already expressed the other side, which I indicated earlier with the instructions for action and which had nothing to do with the love of language that Flusser liked to invoke. In *Tristes Tropiques*, Lévi-Strauss linked this legal and economic function of language to the written word: "Writing is a strange thing . . . it seems to favour rather the exploitation than the enlightenment of mankind. . . . If my hypothesis is correct, the primary function of writing, as a means of communication, is to facilitate the enslavement of other human beings."[12]

Dialogical Existence: Dialogue as Life Saving—As a Principle That Cannot Be Achieved

> When I find myself, and whenever I find myself, I find myself in dialogue. The dialogue is the situation I find myself in and I find me as I find myself in dialogue. The dialogue is actually the first thing I find when I am trying to find myself. So I have to start from the dialogue to find everything else.[13]

What Flusser formulates here in the early stages of his intellectual career gives expression to everyday life practice on the one hand. He regularly held his private academy on the terrace of his family's house in São Paulo. He invited thinkers from science, philosophy, and the arts and from very different provenance to discuss with him—not the other way round: he with them; such conversations were gladly dominated by the philosophical writer Flusser, who was in love with his own thoughts and his way of speaking, certainly also in reference to the great idols of the history of philosophy Socrates and Plato and their preference for dialogue as a form of conveying complex philosophical thoughts.

On the other hand, Flusser's remarks about the conversation expressed a deep longing that can be hermeneutically connected with the Habermasian utopia of a community that is constantly being reestablished through tireless and unconditional communication, and which was—in a different way—also shared by the eccentric of dialogue philosophers, Lévinas: philosophy is an activity that can only develop its meaning in practice. Philosophy has to be done. And this fulfilment is the dialogue with others and the Other.

Flusser's life plan of an intellectual existence after the failure of classical modernity and its concept of humanism expresses a necessity in an exemplary way: to be constantly on the move between different countries, languages, everyday cultures, academic worlds requires the benevolent active affection of many—a kind of unfolding economy of friendship and hospitality, even if the latter should only last until the next invitation to lecture, the next seminar or the next publication opportunity. For the exhibition "Without Firm Ground—Flusser and the Arts" (2015–17), we have tried to present such a way of life diagrammatically in a topo-chronographic access. In Flusser's working biography there was a heterogeneous diversity of people at different times and places, which enabled him to develop and publish his many different ideas. Flusser thought of the network not only as a communicative *dispositif*. He *existed* in a network, was integrated into a dense wickerwork of artists, intellectuals, and academics as well as representatives of new emerging institutions accepting the challenge of actively shaping future presences. His extensive and intensive correspondence documents excellently how hard he constantly tried to maintain and expand this network.

Thinking in Freestyle/Without a Banister: Moving into the Open

Elsewhere, I have already described Flusser's thinking as an activity that one could call "thinking without a banister" in the sense of Hannah Arendt, but which I would like to summarize more precisely for myself as thinking in freestyle. In swimming, freestyle refers to the antipode to the modes, which are defined by strict rules, in which the athletes are allowed to move through the water. Freestyle offers the possibility to unfold the creativity of the swimming body beyond disciplinary determination. Freestyle is an absence of discipline condensed into virtue, that is, discipline.[14]

This seems to me to be the decisive factor in Flusser's spiritual activity. It is neither interdisciplinary nor transdisciplinary thinking that he cultivates, for it has never moved vertically through one or even several disciplines, as is the intensive gesture of professionally oriented research. Flusser, a passionate text writer and orator, has never gone to the bottom of a discipline in order to master it—neither in the natural sciences or mathematics nor in the humanities or philosophy. Flusser was not an expert in the literal sense of the word and did not want to be one. His library was manageable. His favorite literature—as his wife Edith Flusser assured me several times—were the impressive volumes of the Encyclopaedia Britannica and other encyclopedic works of European intellectual history. He possessed a broadly diversified knowledge full of epistemic clichés arranged horizontally.

Flusser was working within liaisons and thus a typical thinker on those plateaus that Gilles Deleuze and Félix Guattari interpreted in their intellectual cosmos. In the form of surprising associations and connections, collisions and living contradictions, he was always able to recall this knowledge in his mind and adapt it to the respective situation of his intervening actions.[15] This also had—I assume—an external existential dimension. After his return to Europe in 1972 Flusser lived essentially from the lectures he gave. He was forced to constantly adapt them to the situation—from the association for the production of instruments for the hearing impaired to mass lectures at popular universities and colloquiums in elite intellectual circles of philosophy, the arts, and the media. The same applies to publications. He could not live on the books of the publishing houses that were founded in Germany specifically for publishing his works. Money was more likely to come from the countless articles he wrote for daily and weekly newspapers and a plethora of different magazines as applied philosophical thinking.

There has not yet been any systematic research into this, which is why I am speculating here. But I venture the hypothesis that, on the one hand, current academic texts are characterized by the fact that they have passed intensively through the knots, the interdiscursive intersections of networked knowledge and through an infinite number of publications, usually accessible on the internet, and contain in themselves strongly correlated, networked knowledge. On the other hand, they often lack a strong, recognizable authorial position of their own, a particular perspective of (re)presentation, a decisive argumentation for an originally elaborated context or set of facts. This is not a culturally pessimistic assessment but an observation that has to do with specific effects of the digital and networking as a general cultural technique. We often forget that individual media or media facts do not last forever in history. Technical media are interludes in history. This necessarily means that the digital is also only a passage. So we would do well not to endow the cultural technology of the digital with eternal values. The digital revolution already came to an end in the twentieth century.

The desideratum to be stated is above all an autonomous and generous horizon thinking, as, for example, a contemporary of Flusser, Hans Heinz Holz, formulated it for German postwar philosophy.[16] This attitude of mind is closely linked to what Ernst Bloch, who lived in Flusser's Prague while fleeing the Nazis from 1936 to 1938, called "dreaming ahead" (*vorwärts träumen*). For the political philosopher Bloch, "thinking ahead," as he tried to formulate it in his main work *The Principle of Hope*, and dreaming ahead were closely connected.[17] In his special construct of the history of philosophy, he furnished the dream with a luxurious open space with many windows. "The dream forward" is the movement that is privileged to belong to the youth and is closely connected with *becoming*. Particularly in "Zeitwenden" ("turning times"), favorable opportunities to create something new open up the possibility of giving priority to the sense of possibility over the sense of reality, as Robert Musil described almost in parallel in *Man without Qualities* (1930-43). The Jewish philosopher Bloch's idea of the transgressive character of thinking corresponds to Flusser's idea of transgression from subject to project, but the media anthropologist renounced any political dimensioning. In the 1980s and early 1990s, politics was frowned upon in the intellectual scene of the Federal Republic of Germany. Possible horizons in the existence of the Earthlings will only become a pressing issue again in the new twenties of the twenty-first century.

Philosophy in Motion—Transferring the Most Important Motif of Modernity into Thinking: Movement. No Sitting Out, but Dancing

What Dietmar Kamper—one of the few philosophers who wrote a decisive critique of Flusser's operative anthropology during his lifetime—noted in his *Geschichte der Einbildungskraft* (*History of the Imagination*) in 1989 in a rather anticipatory manner began to assert itself more and more in the twenty-first century: "New forms of contemporaneity will establish themselves across the disciplines that participate as subjects in the delusion of domination of space."[18] The true place of reflection is no longer the desk and no longer the professorial chair but rather a journey through time. Those who set themselves in motion in this way can contribute little to the "state of research" and must develop a precarious relationship to knowledge as "possession." The specific sedentariness as a dominating figure of research and teaching has discredited itself. It is not even up to the consequences it has caused itself. The demand that arises from the current degree of complexity of social development, namely that every sociological theory must apply the rule it establishes to itself, cannot be met with the mobility that sitting allows.[19]

Vilém Flusser developed his ideas without a stable university position. In Brazil he taught as a flexible and interdisciplinary lecturer between the humanities and engineering sciences; in the United States and Europe he gave lectures in many places and was invited to lead individual seminars. The only guest professorship he filled was received shortly before his death in 1991 at the invitation of Friedrich Kittler at University of Bochum.[20] Flusser was extremely restless. Even during colloquiums and congresses he seldom sat firmly on a chair. During his lectures he repeatedly measured the space that was given to him as a stage. He seemed to take literally the mode of dancing that Friedrich Nietzsche had wished for the new philosophical activity of the new man. Flusser wanted to be as close as possible to the audience. On the public stage there was a gifted philosopher-actor who seemed to handle Greek and Latin phrases with sovereignty, who swayed his head back and forth while speaking, nodded his head violently in agreement with a thought (preferably his own), and nestled his chin in the right hand in the thinking pose even when standing. Theoretically and media anthropologically he had a disturbed relationship to the body. To think the physical or even the corporeal of the human being radically was not compatible with an eschatology in which the material definitely dissolved into pixels and abstraction. What the new concretization that was to follow could look like, he owed us no description. But each of his thoughts seemed to express itself through his own body in motion.

Education and university studies have been highly mobilized for the twenty-first century at various levels. Biographies in which school or vocational training, university studies, and first professional practice are spread over different countries and regions of the world are by no means privileged experiences of children and young people who are descended from the wealthy or diplomats. Uprooting is becoming increasingly systemic—for political, economic, religious, individual-biographical reasons. The departure or expulsion from the land of the fathers and the weaning from a mother tongue to the Esperanto of the present, a mundanely functional American English, characterizes biographies that develop their mobile identities between different knowledge cultures. The cosmopolitan remains less the notion of longing of a few extremely sedentary philosophers like Immanuel Kant, but the lived practice of many between Hong Kong and Shanghai or Shenzhen, New Delhi, Abu Dhabi, Copenhagen, Oslo, Barcelona, St. Petersburg, Amsterdam, Paris, London, Beirut, or New York. The populist nationalists in Eastern Europe, Brazil, or the United States are already reacting to such a development. They are more likely to push this process forward internationally. For the future present is shaped by those whose lives are not essentially determined by the memory of the past. Dreaming ahead is in principle the privilege of the younger generations.

From this perspective we can sum up: Vilém Flusser helps us to sketch a subject identity that is possibly able to mediate between the unconditional ego and the unconditional we. Freed from the heavy inheritances of the motherlands and mother tongues, the project for the twenty-first century, which is just beginning, is in constant and intensive dialogue with the other, not identical to us—the other of nature, gender, cultures, religions, knowledge, and technology.[21] The modes in which this dialogue may unfold are potentially infinitely diverse. Two paradigms can help give orientation and confidence to the provisional: freedom of movement and the courageous development of fields of knowledge, of faculties in the direct sense of the word, beyond the established disciplines.

And, yes—this should not be underestimated in such a departure: "The wanderer must not have 'property'; he who possesses is not free to wander."[22] The Italian philosopher Massimo Cacciari, who also became involved as a politician by ruling the city of Venice for many years, noted this in his study of the poet-philosopher Edmond Jabès. Jabès not only wrote the most beautiful book on the poetics of subversion, which he described as "the movement of writing," as an exposure to an unknown face; he is also one of the most outstanding thinkers of unconditional dialogue.[23]

Notes

1. Ludwig Wittgenstein, *Tractatus Logico-Philosophicus* (Berlin: Suhrkamp-Ausgabe, 1921), 90 (trans. D. F. Pears and B. F. McGuinness [New York: Routledge, 2001], 68).
2. Roger Caillois, Streifzüge, in Caillois, *Patagonien und weitere Streifzüge* (Graz: Droschl 2016), chapter "Frost und Hitze," zit. 68 (French Original: Montpellier 1986). Approximately ten years before Flusser's *Vampyrotheutis Infernalis*, Caillois published *Le Pieuvre* (*Avatars of the Octopus*) with the suggestive subtitle *Essai Sur La Logique De L'imaginaire (Essay on the Logic of the Imaginary)* (1974).
3. Karl Löwith, *Mein Leben in Deutschland vor und nach 1933. Ein Bericht* (Stuttgart: Metzler, 1986), Zit. 29–31.
4. Alberto Moravia, *Die Kulturrevolution in China* (Reinbek: Rowohlt, 1971), 5.
5. Miklòs Péternak and I used this phrase as the title for the DVD of interviews that Flusser had given shortly before he died. It was produced by the Vilém Flusser Archive together with the Center of Culture and Communication (C^3) in Budapest and distributed by the Walther König publishing house in Cologne.
6. Hannah Arendt, "Wo sind wir, wenn wir denken?," in Arendt, *Denken ohne Geländer. Texte und Briefe* (Munich: Piper, 2014), 16. *The Life of the Mind*. One-Volume ed., Harcourt, Inc (1981), 199.
7. The lecture was later released on CD by Klaus Sander: Vilém Flusser, *Heimat und Heimatlosigkeit* (Köln: supposé, 1999).
8. Flusser " Für eine Feldtheorie der Übersetzung," *Spritz* (Sprache im Technischen Zeitalter), journal edited at the Berlin Technical University by Walter Höllerer, No. 24 (Stuttgart, 1967), 347.
9. Harun Farocki, "Vilém Flusser: Das Universum der technischen Bilder," *Zelluloid*, no. 25 (Summer 1987): 77–80.
10. Wittgenstein, *Tractatus logico-philosophicus*, paragraph 5.632, 90 (Routledge, 69).
11. Lévi-Strauss, *Tristes Tropiques* (1955). Quote here after the German version, *Traurige Tropen*, übers. v. Eva Moldenhauer (Frankfurt: Suhrkamp, 1978), 293–4.
12. Lévi-Strauss, *Tristes Tropiques*, trans. John Russell (New York: Criterion Books, 1961), 292.
13. Flusser, *Spritz* (1967), 350 (see footnote 8)
14. See Zielinski's and Peter Weibel's "Introduction" to the volume *FLUSSERIANA—An Intellectual Toolbox*, ed. Siegfried Zielinski, Peter Weibel, and Daniel Irrgang in three languages—English, German, Portuguese (Minneapolis: Univocal, University of Minnesota Press and Karlsruhe: ZKM, 2015), esp. 17–18. Of course, *freestyle* is used today in different contexts like Jazz or Rap music, dance, or wrestling.
15. Katrin Weiden wrote an excellent dissertation dedicated to this topic: *Ökologik des Und. Kreative Verbindungen in der Maschinen- und Apparatetheorie bei Deleuze, Guattari und Flusser* (Paderborn: Fink, 2017).
16. The DVD *Hans-Heinz Holz: Spekulatives Denken. Vorlesungen zur Geschichte der Philosophie von Parmenides bis Marx* offers a good introduction to the work of the philosophical lateral thinker, who is quite unknown outside of Germany. Lectures

on the history of philosophy from Parmenides to Marx, initiated by the Friedrich Nietzsche College with the ZKM Karlsruhe (Fridolfing: absolut Medien, 2019). It is worth reading again in this thematic context *Widerspruch in China: Politisch-philosophische Erläuterungen zu Mao Tse-Tung* (München: Hanser, 1970).

17 Ernst Bloch, *Das Prinzip Hoffnung*, vol. 1, esp. chs. 13–15, quotations pp. 84–5. Bloch wrote the three volumes mainly in a library at Harvard University in the 1930s. English translation *The Principle of Hope* (Boston, MA: MIT Press, 1986).
18 Dietmar Kamper, *Körper-Abstraktionen. Das anthropologische Viereck von Raum, Fläche, Linie und Punkt. 1st International Flusser Lecture* (Cologne: Walther König, 1999), reprinted in *Erkundungen im anthropologischen Viereck*, ed. Daniel Irrgang and S. Zielinski (Munich: Wilhelm Fink, 2018).
19 Ibid., 276.
20 See the extensive biography in *FLUSSERIANA—An Intellectual Toolbox*, 452–519.
21 See Michel Serres's great texts on the philosophy of communication (Hermes I-V, 1968-1980), especially his book *Le contrat naturel* (Paris: Bourin), which significantly influenced Bruno Latour in his intellectual movement toward the terrestrial. This orientation led to the exhibition *Critical Zones* at the ZKM Karlsruhe in 2020.
22 M. Cacciari, "Die Weiße und die Schwärze," in *Migranten*, ed. Nils Röller (Berlin: Merve, 1995), 46.
23 E. Jabès, *Le petit livre da la subversion hors de soupçon* (Paris: Gallimard, 1982), Zit. o.P. The German translation of this wonderful text, *Das kleine unverdächtige Buch der Subversion*, was provided by the Swiss writer Felix Philipp Ingold, with whom Vilém Flusser maintained a lively correspondence.

Contributors

Alexander B. Adkins is currently Professor of English at San Jacinto College in Houston, Texas, USA. He has published articles on Chinua Achebe, Salman Rushdie, and Aravind Adiga. His current book project examines the cynicism of the postcolonial world following failed revolutions.

Andrew Battaglia is a PhD candidate at Rice University. He received his B.A. in English and philosophy from Seattle University and his M.A. in English from Rice University. He has studied at the Freie Universität in Berlin and the Karl-Franzens-Universität in Graz, Austria, and he has served as a Fulbright Scholar in Germany. He is currently working on a translation of the Bochum lectures.

David Bering-Porter is Assistant Professor of Culture and Media at the Eugene Lang College of Liberal Arts at the New School, USA. His work at the intersections of race, technology, and media has been presented internationally and has appeared in *Flow*, *MIRAJ*, *Culture Machine*, and the *Los Angeles Review of Books*. His current book project is on "undead labor" and the ways that race, labor, and value come together in the mediated body of the zombie.

Kate Brideau is an instructor of Media, Culture, and Communication in the Stern School of Business at New York University, USA.

Edward P. Comentale is Professor of English and Associate Vice Provost for Arts and Humanities at Indiana University, USA. His research focuses on modern art and literature, popular music and culture, and media studies. He is the author of *Modernism, Cultural Production, and the British Avant-Garde* and *Sweet Air: Modernism, Regionalism, and American Popular Song*, as well as the coeditor of *The Year's Work in Lebowski Studies* and *The Year's Work at the Zombie Research Center*.

Erick Felinto is Professor for Media Theories at the State University of Rio de Janeiro (UERJ), Brazil. He was a visiting scholar at Universität der Künste Berlin, Germany, and New York University, USA. His current research interests cover Vilém Flusser's theories of media and identity, political imagination, and media aesthetics. He has authored several books and articles on media theory and film studies in Portuguese, German, English, and French.

Anke Finger is Professor of German Studies, Media Studies and Comparative Literary and Cultural Studies at the University of Connecticut, USA. She has published books on the total artwork, digital scholarship, and intercultural literature. A cofounder of the open access journal *Flusser Studies*, she coauthored the 2011 *Introduction to Vilém*

Flusser, and she is a member of the Flusser project team at Greenhouse Studios at the University of Connecticut. The University of Minnesota Press will publish her translation of Vilém Flusser's twenty-two futurist scenarios *Angenommen/Supposed*.

Seb Franklin is Senior Lecturer in Contemporary Literature at King's College London, UK. He is the author of *Control: Digitality as Cultural Logic* (2015) and *The Digitally Disposed: Racial Capitalism and the Informatics of Value* (2021).

David Golumbia is Associate Professor of English department at Virginia Commonwealth University, USA. He is the author of *The Cultural Logic of Computation* (2009), *The Politics of Bitcoin: Software as Right-Wing Extremism* (2016), and many articles on digital culture, language, and literary studies.

Rainer Guldin is Lecturer for German Culture and Language at the Faculties of Communication Sciences and Economics of the Università della Svizzera Italiana in Lugano, Switzerland. He is Editor-in-Chief of the peer-reviewed, open access e-journal *Flusser Studies*. Recent publications include *Vilém Flusser: Einhundert Zitate* (together with Andreas Müller-Pohle) (2020); *Metaphors of Multilingualism. Changing Attitudes towards Language Diversity in Literature, Linguistics and Philosophy* (2020); *Translation as Metaphor* (2016).

Daniel Irrgang is a research associate at Weizenbaum-Institute, Berlin, Germany, where he is part of the research group "Inequality and Digital Sovereignty," coordinated by Berlin University of the Arts (UdK Berlin), Germany. From 2013 until 2016 he has been research supervisor of the Vilém Flusser Archive at UdK Berlin. He has published extensively on Vilém Flusser and holds a PhD in media studies with a thesis on diagrammatics in relation to Flusser's concept of technical image.

Aaron Jaffe is Frances Cushing Ervin Professor at Florida State University, USA. He researches modern and contemporary literature, culture and media theory, and his publications include *Modernism and the Culture of Celebrity* (2005), *The Way Things Go: An Essay on the Matter of Second Modernism* (2014), and *Spoiler Alert: A Critical Guide* (2019). He co-edits a book series on cultural theory with Indiana UP called the Year's Work.

Melody Jue is Associate Professor of English at UC Santa Barbara, USA. Drawing on the experience of becoming a scuba diver, her book *Wild Blue Media: Thinking Through Seawater* (2020) develops a theory of mediation specific to the ocean. She coedited (with Rafico Ruiz) *Saturation: An Elemental Politics* (2021) and *Informatics of Domination* (under contract) with Zach Blas and Jennifer Rhee. Her articles appear in *Grey Room*, *Configurations*, *Women's Studies Quarterly*, and *Resilience*.

Keith Leslie Johnson is Senior Lecturer of English and Film & Media Studies at William & Mary, USA. He is the author of *Jan Svankmajer: Animist Cinema* as well as essays on Beckett, Kafka, Huxley, and other modernist figures. Apart from works of criticism, he is also a translator of Japanese, having published short fiction by Haruki Murakami and Akira Yoshimura.

Heather A. Love is Assistant Professor of English at the University of Waterloo (Ontario, Canada), and her research draws on the interdisciplinary field of cybernetics to explore connections between early twentieth-century literary and technological discourses. Her work has appeared in *Modernism/modernity*, the *Journal of Modern Literature*, and the *IEEE Technology and Society Magazine*.

Annie Lowe is a PhD candidate at Rice University, USA, where she researches and writes about the cultural history and literary tradition of hoaxing. Her work reconsiders critical developments in the history of logico-mathematics, philosophy of language, and literary theory, understood as a narrative playfully doubled in hoaxic literature from the early avant-garde to our contemporary period.

Rodrigo Martini is Lecturer in English at the University of Georgia, USA. He works in the intersections of animal studies, media theory, and modernism. His work on Vilém Flusser is forthcoming in *Comparative Literature Studies*.

Frances McDonald is Assistant Professor of English at the University of Louisville, USA. Her research and teaching focus on twentieth-century American literature and film, critical theory, and affect studies. Her work has appeared in *American Literature*, *LARB*, *Post45*, and *The Atlantic*. She is also the coeditor of *thresholds*, a digital journal for creative/critical scholarship.

Adelheid Mers is a visual artist who works through Performative Diagrammatics, a practice that includes elements of installation, facilitation with publics, and video. Her research draws on close work with others, exploring arts ecologies, and knowing differently, or epistemic diversity. Educated at the Kunstakademie Düsseldorf, Germany, and the University of Chicago, USA, she is Associate Professor and Chair of the Department of Arts Administration and Policy at the School of the Art Institute of Chicago, USA.

Chris Michaels is a teaching fellow at Florida State University, USA, whose research focuses on modernism, critical theory, and environmental studies. He is currently at work on a monograph called *Terraforming Modernism* that seeks to develop a distinctly modernist ecocriticism.

Michael F. Miller is Visiting Lecturer in the Department of English Language and Culture at the University of Amsterdam, USA. His work has appeared in *Contemporary Literature*, *Arizona Quarterly*, *symplokē*, *boundary 2 online*, *Modernism/modernity print+*, and *The Journal of Film and Video*, among others. He is currently completing a book, titled *Proximity by Proxy: Contemporary Literature in the Age of Social Media.*

Anaïs Nony is Lecturer in Media Arts and Politics at University College Cork, Ireland, and Research Associate of the H.A.R. Lab (Histoire des Arts et des Représentations) at the Université Paris Nanterre, France. She specializes in aesthetics and politics and researches the function of media technologies in shaping transcultural exchanges in and outside of the West. Since 2014, she is an editorial board member of *La Deleuziana*, a multilingual online journal of contemporary philosophy.

Dominic Pettman is University Professor of Media and New Humanities at the New School, New York City, USA. He is the author of numerous books on technology, humans, and other animals, including *Creaturely Love*, *Sonic Intimacy*, *Metagestures* (with Carla Nappi), and *Peak Libido*.

Andrew Pilsch is Associate Professor of English at Texas A&M University, USA, where he teaches and researches rhetoric and the digital humanities. Pilsch's first book, *Transhumanism: Evolutionary Futurism and the Human Technologies of Utopia*, was released in 2017, when it won the Science Fiction and Technoculture Studies Book Prize for that year. His research has been published in *Amodern*, *Philosophy & Rhetoric*, and *Science Fiction Studies*.

Rita Raley researches and teaches in the domains of new media studies, language technologies, electronic literature, the digital humanities, and cultural theory in the Department of English at the University of California, Santa Barbara, USA. Her most recent work appears in *symplokē*, *Amodern*, *ASAP/Journal*, *PUBLIC*, and *The Routledge Companion to Media and Risk*.

Daniel Raschke is a PhD student in English literature, media, and culture at Florida State University, USA. His current research focuses on modernisms, cybernetics, and speculative realism. He holds an MA in American Studies from Johannes Gutenberg University Mainz, Germany.

John D. Ribó is Assistant Professor of English at Florida State University, USA. His work has appeared in *Chiricú*, *The Journal of Haitian Studies*, *Cuban Studies*, and *ASAP/J* and is forthcoming in *Teaching Haiti beyond Literature: Intersectionalities of History, Literature and Culture* and *The Bloomsbury Companion to Edwidge Danticat*. He is currently completing his first manuscript *Haitian Hauntings*, which traces the genealogy of Haiti's spectral presence in contemporary US Latinx literature, music, and popular culture.

Laurence A. Rickels currently divides his time between Berlin and Palm Springs. His psychoanalytic and philosophical reflections on what he coined in earshot of the uncanny "unmourning" can be followed in many books, from *Aberrations of Mourning*

(1988) to *Critique of Fantasy* (2020). Rickels was Professor of German and Comparative Literature at the University of California, Santa Barbara, USA, for thirty years. *The Vampire Lectures* (1999) is the document of his most famous course of instruction.

Judith Roof is the author of eight monographs, including most recently, *The Comic Event* and *Tone: Writing and the Sound of Feeling*. She has published essays on a range of topics in film studies, modern drama, narrative theory, sexuality studies, and on the work of such authors as Samuel Beckett, Harold Pinter, Marguerite Duras, Virginia Woolf, Percival Everett, Richard Powers, Nicole Brossard, Tom Stoppard, and, well, Rabelais. She is Professor and William Shakespeare Chair in English at Rice University, USA.

Nancy Roth studied art, history, and German language at the University of Minnesota, USA. She earned a doctoral degree in art history at the Graduate Center of CUNY, USA. Around 2002, she became a committed student of Flusser's writing. She works as a critic, columnist, editor, and lecturer, and maintains a website at www.nancyannroth.com.

Russell Samolsky is Associate Professor of English at the University of California, Santa Barbara, USA. He is the author of *Apocalyptic Futures: Marked Bodies and the Violence of the Text in Kafka, Conrad, and Coetzee* as well as a number of articles and book chapters. His current research focuses on animality and ecology, J. M. Coetzee, the graphic novel, reception studies, and the way in which the Anthropocene now conditions literary analysis.

Martha Schwendener is Visiting Professor at New York University/Steinhardt School of Art, USA, and an art critic for *The New York Times*.

K. Merinda Simmons is Professor of Religious Studies at the University of Alabama, USA. Her books include *Race and New Modernisms* (coauthored with James A. Crank, 2019), *The Trouble with Post-Blackness* (coedited with Houston A. Baker, Jr., 2015), *Changing the Subject: Writing Women across the African Diaspora* (2014), and *Race and Displacement* (coedited with Maha Marouan, 2013). She is working on a monograph tentatively titled *Sourcing Slave Religion: Theorizing Experience in the Archive*.

Tatjana Soldat-Jaffe is Associate Professor at Florida State University, USA, Department of Modern Languages and Linguistics. Her research focuses on language and identity, migration literature, and translation studies. She is the author of *Twenty-First Century Yiddishism: Language, Identity, and the New Jewish Studies* and the coeditor of the special issue of *Centennial Review* "Translation and the Global Humanities." She is currently working on the study of translations in migration literature in Germany.

Guy Stevenson is Lecturer in Literature at Goldsmiths and Queen Mary Colleges, University of London, UK, and a recent postdoctoral fellow at the Institute of

Advanced Studies in the Humanities, the University of Edinburgh, UK. He specializes in modernism and the 1960s American counterculture and has published widely on both--including pieces in the journals *Textual Practice* (in a special issue he guest edited) and *The European Journal of English Studies*, the cultural magazine *The Los Angeles Review of Books*, and a monograph, *Anti-Humanism in the Counterculture* (2020).

Blake Stricklin is Lecturer at the University of Houston-Victoria, USA. He has work published in the *Journal of Modern Literature*, *American Book Review*, and *symplokē*. He is the author of *American Paraliterature and Other Theories to Hijack Communication* from Anthem Press (2021) in its Anthem *symplokē* Studies in Theory series.

Andreas Max Ströhl was born in Munich, West Germany, in 1962. He earned an MA in German Literature, Theater and American Studies from the University of Munich in 1987. Since 1988 he has worked for the Goethe-Institut. He met Vilém Flusser in Prague in 1991, and has published (about) Flusser and taught media theory ever since. From 2003 to 2011 he was director of the Munich Filmfest. In 2009 he completed a PhD on Flusser and European Ethnology at the University of Marburg, Germany. Since 2016, he has been Director of the Washington-based Goethe-Institutes in North America.

Thomas Tooley recently received his doctorate from Florida State University, USA, and now teaches in the English department at Valencia College, USA. His research focuses on non-realist forms of narrative in twentieth- and twenty-first-century literature and cinema. Currently, he is completing a manuscript that reexamines the simulacra in novels and films since the 1960s.

Charles M. Tung is Professor and Chair of English at Seattle University, USA, where he teaches courses on twentieth- and twenty-first-century literature, temporal scale, and representations of racial anachronism. He is the author of *Modernism and Time Machines* (2019). His recent work on time and modernity has appeared or will soon appear in *Timescales: Ecological Temporalities across Disciplines*, *Modernism and the Anthropocene*, *Time and Literature*, *ASAP/Journal*, and *Modernism/Modernity*.

Geoffrey Winthrop-Young teaches in the German and Scandinavian Programs in the Department of Central, Eastern and Northern Studies at the University of British Columbia (Vancouver), Canada. His major research and publication areas include media studies with a special emphasis on German Media Theories, the relationship between war and media, studies in cultural evolution, modern German literature, chronopolitics, and the Third Reich.

Clint Wilson III received his PhD in English from Rice University, where he was a fellow with the Center for Environmental Studies and currently serves as an instructor with Rice's Program in Writing and Communication. His work has appeared or is forthcoming in *Twentieth-Century Literature*, *ASAP/J*, *Modern Language Quarterly*, *Resilience*, *Environmental Philosophy,* and *The Eighteenth Century*, among others.

Derek Woods is Assistant Professor of English at the University of British Columbia, Canada. He writes about ecology, technology, and modern narrative in relation to the history of science. With Karen Pinkus, he recently edited an issue of *diacritics* on the topic of terraforming.

Siegfried Zielinski is Michel Foucault Professor of Media Archaeology at the European Graduate School, Saas-Fee, Switzerland; Professor Emeritus for Media Theory/Archaeology and Variantology of the Media at Berlin University of the Arts, Germany; honorary doctor and professor, University of Arts, Budapest, Hungary; rector of the Karlsruhe University of Arts & Design, Germany (2016–18); founding rector (1994–2000) of the Academy of Media Arts Cologne, Germany; director of the Vilém Flusser Archive (1998–2016). His latest monograph in English is *Variations on Media Thinking* (2019).

Index

Note: *Italic* page number refer to figures.

Abel, Jonathan 214
abstraction 4, 64, 276, 292, 326
  aesthetic 85
  complexity and 27
  irony and cynicism and 84, 86, 88
  phenomenology of 85
  rejection of 183
  of thought 6
actor network theory 264
Adorno, Theodor 52, 137, 272, 318
aesthetics 3–6, 10, 40, 107, 155, 166, 204, 237, 257, 318
  apparatus and 136
  gameplay and 64
  games and 59–61
  gestures and 134
  of imperfection 185
  irony and cynicism and 85–7, 89, 90
  modernism and 26
  posthumanism and 246
  simulations and 45
Agamben, Giorgio 132, 136, 137, 272, 320
"Age of the World Picture, The" (Heidegger) 69
A historia do diabo (Flusser) 209
Aicher, Otl 176
Alaimo, Stacy 251
algorithm 3–6, 54, 106, 132, 139, 203, 275
alien 20, 63, 76, 157, 252, 254 n.45
  narration 107, 109 n.29
  refraction and 162, 165, 166
Alien (Scott) 76, 121 n.13
alienation 132, 145
  artificial intelligence and 18–20
  -as-freedom 85
  irony and 87
  posthistory and 85
  religious 86
  robots and 19–20
  of unhappy consciousness 89
  vampire squid and 153, 157
Almodóvar, Pedro 191
alphabetic and ideographic writing, comparison of 212
alphabetic code 16
  technical image and 16–17
Altdorfer 312
alternative worlds 62, 63
American Society for Cybernetics 279
American World Literature 261–4
Amerika (Kafka) 255–6
Anderson, Benedict 105
Andrade Costa, Antonio Luciano de 196 n.7
angel, metaphor of 247
Ant Farm 31, 32
anthropology 3, 44, 206, 246, 295, 297 n.10
  design/shape and 24, 25, 28
  language and 325, 326
  video image and 31, 33
anti-apparatus 269–71
anti-philosophy 321
Anzaldúa, Gloria 193
Appadurai, Arjun 186
apparatus 2, 69–71, 98, 252, 277, 301 n.11, 311
  alphabetic 18
  anti-apparatus and 269–70
  artificial intelligence and 15–21
  Auschwitz 272
  camera as 78, 275–6
  categorical 78
  computational 185

culture and   296
definition of   271 n.1
ecology and   286-7
expulsion of humanists from   264
Foucault on   272
freedom and   272, 273
gesture and   134-8, 140 n.21, 147
human beings and   59, 61, 63
information   4, 5
intersubjectivity and   126, 128
irony and cynicism and   91-2
mass communication   134-5
media   5-6, 9, 83, 142
omnibus and   146
opaque   302-4
pataphysics and   142, 144
perceptual   165
photography and   78, 89, 155, 286-7
quantization and   305-6
technical image and   21, 299-300, 302-4
technology and   30, 137-8, 254 n.44
telematics and   184
Apter, Emily   222
Aquinas, Thomas   175, 176
Arcades Project (Buck-Morss)   246
arché-writing   213
architecture   57, 176
archive and improvisation   186, 187
Arendt, Hannah   73 n.22, 319, 321, 323
Aristotle   160 n.19
Arnheim, Rudolf   318
Arrabal, Fernando   141
Ars Electronica Festival (Linz, Austria)   39, 298, 300 n.3
  cybernetics and   41-6
  importance of   40, 41
Artforum (journal)   3, 126
Artforum Essays   3, 49, 50, 52-4
artificial intelligence (AI)   15
  alienation and   18-20
  in Flusser's corpus   16-18
  future reader and   20-1
artificial memory   119-20, 241
"Art Sociologique"   31
attention   54, 62, 105, 178, 211, 288, 312
  to gesture   132-3
  sonic gestures and   236-8

Auden, W. H.   113
Audible Past, The (Stern)   237
audiovisual media and writing   213
"Auf der Suche nach Bedeutung" (Flusser)   25
Auschwitz   76, 272
automata. *See* automation; technical image
automation   275-7, 281 n.4. *See also* technical image
  definition of   278 n.8
  fantasies and anxieties of   278 n.10
  Platonic utopia and   291
autotheory   193

Baader, Franz von   248, 253 n.22
Babbage, Charles   276
Badiou, Alain   6
Bakhtin, Mikhail   223
Balazs, Bela   318
Balvin, J.   191
Banderas, Antonio   191
Barad, Karen   125
Barbrook, Richard   34
Barth, John   207
Barthes, Roland   164, 206, 256, 258-9, 269, 275, 293 n.9
Barzyk, Fred   32
Bateson, Gregory   58, 65 n.1
Batličková, Eva   204 n.4
Baudrillard, Jean   2, 39, 42, 44-5, 72, 131, 135, 137, 200, 298-9
Baudry, Jean-Louis   318
"Baukasten zu einer Theorie der Medien" (Toolkit for a Theory of the Media) (Enzensberger)   33
Bazin, Andre   275
"Beasts" (Bichos) (Flusser)   247
beautiful soul syndrome   87
Bec, Louis   5, 162, 251, 287
Beck, Ulrich   51
Beckett, Samuel   152
Being and Time (Heidegger)   68
Beke, Láslo   184, 187
Benanav, Aaron   278 n.10
Benjamin, Walter   89, 92, 117, 208, 222, 245-52, 318
Berardi, Franco   132

Berger, René 33, 208
Berlant, Laura 140 n.43
Berman, Sandra 222
Bernardo, Gustavo 8, 128, 206, 222, 224, 261, 297 n.11
Best, Stephen 187
Beuys, Joseph 31
"Beyond Machines" (Flusser) 145–6
Beyond the Pleasure Principle (Freud) 113, 116
Bieber, Justin 181
Bildung 87
biography, notion of 5
biopolitical junkyards 51
bios philosophikos 291
"Birth of Mary" (painting) (Altdorfer) 312
Birtwhistell, Ray 58
Black, Max 68
Black and indigenous peoples, marginalization of 194–5
black box 77, 140 n.21, 236, 272, 275, 276
Blackburn, Jeremy 106
Black Lives Matter movement 106
Blackwell, Maylei 192, 195
Blanchot 293 n.9
Bloch, Ernst 324–5, 328 n.17
Bodenlos (Flusser) 7, 193, 200, 318
bodenlos, concept of 86, 96
body
    ego-world relationship and 165–6
    gestures and 239
Boehme, Jacob 248
Bohr, Niels 125–6
Böhringer, Hannes 39, 42, 43
Boj Lopez, Floridalma 195
Bolz, Norbert 3, 319
boogaloo bois group 106
Borderlands (La Frontera) (Anzaldúa) 193
Borges 152
Bradlyn, Barry 106
Branco, Marta Castello 243 n.23
Bratton, Benjamin 104
Brazil 2, 4, 5, 9, 24–5, 34, 54, 58, 117, 141, 190–1, 193–5, 196 n.7, 198, 200–1, 257, 262, 263, 325

Brazil or the Search for the New Man (Brasilien oder die Suche nach dem neuen Menschen) (Flusser) 201
Brecht, Bertolt 6, 33, 318
Breuch, Lee-Ann M. Kastman 307
Brod, Max 71
Brostoff, Alex 193
Brown, Wendy 92
Bruner, Jerome S. 33
Buber, Martin 31, 68, 70, 181, 291, 317
    and Flusser compared 181–4
    and Heidegger compared 176–8
Buck-Morss, Susan 246, 250, 254 n.36
Buddhism 200–1
Buell, Lawrence 49
Buffon, Georges Louis Leclerc 130 n.11
Burke, Edmund 208
Burson, Nancy 202

Cacciari, Massimo 326
Caillois, Roger 97, 314
Calvino, Italo 141
camera, as apparatus 78, 275–6
Camus Albert 71
cannibalistic animals 245–52
    angel metaphor and 247
    natural history and 248
    nature and culture and 249–51
Capra, Fritjof 201
Carnap, Rudolf 68
Cartesian worldview and quantum physics 125–6
Cassirer, Ernst 68
Cather, Willa 151
Cavalo Azul (journal) 68
"Celebrating" (Flusser) 309, 310
Center for Media Study (SUNY Buffalo) 32, 33
cephalopods 153–5, 157, 159, 165
    epistemology and 158
Challenge of the Migrant, The (Flusser) 193–4
Chernobyl disaster 51, 53, 55
Christ the Redeemer (Mount Corcovado, Brazil) 260
chronotype 223
Chun, Carl 96
citational minimalism 128–9

Index

closed games 60
code 226, 299
  alphabetic 16–17, 20, 103
  convergence of 200, 202, 203
  language as 320–2
  multidimensional 307
codification 45, 91, 98, 141, 163, 226, 228, 302
cognition 44, 98, 176, 213
  human 21, 42, 58, 280
College de Pataphysique (Paris) 141
commercium 186–7
commodities and sign-value 298–9
communication 52–3, 201, 226
  gesture and 132–4
  networks, geometric structure of 295
  phenomenology of 81, 234, 238
  technologies of 107
  translation as 222, 228
  vampyroteuthic 99
  "wiring of channels" of 80, 81
Communication Structures (seminar) (Flusser) 8, 296
communicology (*Kommunikologie*) 80–1
"Communicology as Culture Critique" (seminar) (Flusser) 8, 295, 297 n.10
composition 23, 199, 222, 307
computation 17, 20, 75, 106, 278 n.8, 280, 291, 307
  gesture and 134, 137
  religious telematics and 182–6
  technical image and 302, 303
conjugation 223
constructions 217
Conway, Flo 281 n.1
Coulmas, Florian 212
cows, metaphor of 95–6
Crary, Jonathan 276, 277
"Criteria-Crisis-Criticism" (Flusser) 269
critical improvisation 182, 185–6
  archive and 186, 187
critical theory 8, 89, 193, 318
critique
  cynicism and 89–92
  notion of 295
cultural archive 185
cultural criticism 52
cultural determination 223

cultural memory 44, 155, 250
culture
  anti-apparatus and 269
  Ars Electronica festival and 40, 45
  of art 118
  cybernetics and 283, 284
  design/shape and 23, 26, 28
  etymology and 295, 296
  games and play and 58, 63
  language and 319, 320
  linguistic features and 222–4, 230
  nature and 245, 247, 249–52, 282 n.15, 286, 288
  posthistorical 106
  posthistory and 104–6
  refraction and 164–6
  religious telematics and 184, 188
  significance of 2, 4, 5, 8, 9, 20, 34, 52, 71, 76, 85, 99, 145, 207, 238, 263, 264, 275, 279, 303, 306
  synthesis and synthetic reality and 201, 204
  of vampire squid 118–19, 166, 169
Cultures, Carriers, and the Outbreak Narrative (Wald) 105
"Curie's Children" series 49, 51, 54
Curtis, Adam 136
cyberculture 40
cybernetics 41–6, 279–81
  dialogue and 240
  fractals 44–5
  perceptions and 43
Cybernetics; or, Control and Communication in the Animal and the Machine (Wiener) 42
"Cynegetics of the Omnibus" (Jarry) 143
cynicism 83–4, 87, 89–90. *See also* irony
  postcritique and saboteur and 89–92

Danesi, Marcel 219 n.12
Darroch, Michael 209
Dasein (being-in-the-world) 27, 68–9, 163, 165, 166
  design of 283–4
  disgust and 153–4
  importance of 170 n.2
  technology and 177–8

da Silva, Dora Ferreira 68
da Silva, Vincente Ferreira 58, 68
Das Universum der Technischen Bilder (Flusser) 321
date-mark 115
Dávila, Arlene 191, 196 n.4
da Vinci, Leonardo 204
Davis, Douglas 32
Dawkins, Richard 105
daydreaming 115
Dear Angel of Death (White) 188
death drive 113, 116
death wish 113, 116
Debord, Guy 317
declension 223, 224
DeFrancis, John 212
DeGuzmán, María 192
De Landa, Manuel 245
Delany, Samuel R. 164, 170 n.6
Deleuze, Gilles 4, 72, 163, 272, 273, 324
de Man, Paul 261-2, 264
demonologies 113-20
 transference and 114, 116
 vampire squid and human interactions in 117-20
denaturalization 87, 270, 288
"Depressed Person, The" (Wallace) 235
Derrida, Jacques 69, 164, 212, 222, 236
Descartes 69, 123
description free of theory principle 79
design/shape 23, 26
 advantages of 27
 of Dasein 283-4
 language and 24-5
 Latour on 27-8
"Des Tours de Babel" (Derrida) 222
Devil Notebooks, The (Rickels) 113
diagrams 312
dialectics 52, 117, 128, 139 n.15, 270, 281, 286
 irony and cynicism and 85, 89
 language and 221, 225, 317, 320
 posthuman natures and 249, 250
 quasi-phenomenology and 75, 76, 81-2
 refraction and 164, 169
 video image and 31, 33
dialogical communication 182

dialogical life 70
dialogical model, of agora 239
dialogical moment 127
dialogical programming 70, 182, 184, 185, 188 n.5
dialogic life 182
dialogue
 discourse and 80, 81
 Greeks on 239
 as life saving 322-3
 net 75
 perceptions and 43
 sonic 240
 translation and 186
 unconditional 317
 video images and 30-1
"Digitaler Schein" (Flusser) 62, 63
digital media 16-17, 99, 209, 211, 217-18, 240
digital reality 199-200
digital revolution 211, 324
digital technology 99-100, 207, 213, 217-19, 250, 305
 language and 211
Dilthey, Wilhelm 68, 103
Dinge und Undinge (Flusser) 294, 295
discourse 6, 31, 88, 225, 239, 295
 Ars Electronica festival and 40-2, 46
 critical 41, 190
 as cultural requirement 76
 design/shape and 23, 24
 dialogue and 80, 81
 homogenization of 52
 Latinidad and 191, 192
 media 34, 40, 42, 84, 318
 as necessity 76
 philosophical 42, 145
 phrase and 225
 synthesis and 199, 200
 toxic 49
Discourse Networks 1800/1900 (Aufschreibesysteme) (Kittler) 42
dispositif 318, 323
"Distance and Relation" (Buber) 183
Does Writing Have a Future? (Flusser) 5, 7, 15, 20-1, 22 n.8, 38 n.33, 62, 298
Dolor y Gloria (film) 191
doubt 99, 259, 261

Index

Duchamps, Marcel 141
Duranti, Alessandro 129 n.5
Dylan, Bob 322

Eco, Umberto 222
ecology 286–8
   renaturalization and 287, 288
eidetic variation (*Wesensschau*) 79–81
Eiffel, Gustave 257
Eiffel Tower 257–8
Eijnden, Van den 252
Elective Affinities (Goethe) 250
electracy 307
Electronic Arts Intermix, Inc. 32
electronic memory 44
elite techno-image 311
"Emerging Viruses" (conference) 105
emic unit/emes 223, 226, 231 n.11
Emmott, Stephen 109 n.29
emoji 214, 219 n.12
   writing and 215
Engler, Rita de Castro 28 n.4
enlightened false consciousness 83
entanglement 85, 97–8, 100, 123, 125–7, 276
entropy 3, 44, 60, 85, 104, 139 n.15, 178, 264, 281
   nuclear physics and 50, 52–5
   sonic gestures and 236, 237, 239
environment 31, 43, 85, 200, 233, 241
   anti-apparatus and 270–1
   collective 28
   cybernetics and 281
   Dasein and 284
   design/shape and 26–8
   ecology and 287
   linguistic features and 224, 227
   New Weird and 153, 155, 158
   nuclear physics and 49–50
   organisms and 94, 97–100
   pataphysics and 142, 144
   refraction and 165, 167–9
Enzensberger, Hans Magnus 33, 72
epiphenomena 141–8
epistemology 229
Ernst, Wolfgang 107, 243 n.23
Eros 239
"Essays" (Flusser) 128, 221

ethics 20, 21, 69, 104, 166, 315, 318
   ethics and 290–2
   irony and cynicism and 87, 89
etymology 294–6
   as mode of enquiry 294
Everything Quantizes (Brideau) 179 n.1
evolution 27, 105, 132, 199, 209, 247, 270, 298
   demonologies and 118–19
   media 201, 202
   pataphysics and 144, 145
   refraction and 166–8
   of technology 204, 234
   Vampyroteuthis Infernalis and 96, 99–101
Exile and Creativity (Flusser) 18, 269, 309–10
existentialism 5, 71, 85, 86, 182, 201
Experiences in Translation (Eco) 222
Exploits and Opinions of Dr. Faustroll, Pataphysician, The (Jarry) 141, 143
"Exp-perience" (Flusser) 280
expulsion, notion of 18–19, 264
ex-territorialization, of memory 45

fables 287, 293 n.15
face 147, 214, 215, 238
   of Other 290–2
"Factory, The" (Flusser) 26
Faivre, Antonio 253 n.22
false media 188 n.16
fantasy 85, 92, 187, 236, 258, 264
   arch-ideological 84
   automation anxieties and 277, 278 n.10
   demonologies and 114, 115, 117, 120
   narcissistic 238
Farias, Victor 73 n.22
Farocki, Harun 321
fascism 1, 85, 126, 206–7, 218, 295
   Vampyroteuthis Infernalis and 94, 100, 101
fascistoid 206–8
Fatherland 318–19
Faust (Goethe) 70
feedback 32, 34, 135, 142, 155, 257
   automation and 275

cybernetics and   279–81
  demonologies and   118, 120
  Vampyroteuthis Infernalis and   94, 95
Feel Free (Smith)   181
Felski, Rita   264
Felton-Dansky, Miriam   104
Fiktion und Simulation ("Fiction and Simulation") (Kittler) (lecture)   45
filmmaker   136
Finkelstein, Joel   106
Firth, J. R.   228
Fischer, Hervé   31
flânerie   88, 89
flâneur   88–9
Flor, Chris   200
Flusser, Edith   77, 225, 324
Flusser, Vilém   2, 190. *See also individual entries*
  on African descent and Brazil   194
  on Auschwitz   76
  and Baudrillard compared   299–300, 301 n.5
  on biography   5
  Bochum lectures of   294–6, 325
  Bolz on   3–4
  on Brazil as no-man's land   194
  and Buber compared   181–4
  citational minimalism of   128
  diagrammatics of   *310*
  on dialogue   239–40
  and Enzensberger compared   33
  as European Marshall McLuhan   206
  on *Homo Ludens*   59, 61
  and Husserl compared   79
  Latinidad of   192–6
  on McLuhan   207–8
  on media   94, 98–101
  on nationalism   262
  on nuclear physics   49–53
  and O'Grady compared   33–4
  as phenomenographer   79, 80
  as phenomenologist   77
  as philosopher of communication   222
  play with games   64–5
  reading of   309–11
  self-translation practice of   126–7, 202
  on technology   69, 177–8
  at Vienna Secession   2–3
  Weibel and   41
  Wiesing on   79–81
Flusseriana (Pias)   46
Flusseriana (Zielinski, Weibel, and Irrgang)   7, 8
flusserstudies.net (online journal)   210 n.2
Folha de São Paulo (newspaper)   80, 88, 247
Fontcuberta, Joan   5, 61, 62
Forest, Fred   5, 31, 34, 36, 37 n.13
Forman-Barzilai, David   182
Foucault, Michel   8, 33, 45, 69, 272, 273
Fournier, Lauren   193
fractals   44–5
Frampton, Hollis   30, 33
freedom   20, 64, 89, 91, 100, 119, 126–7, 315
  apparatus and   272, 273
  automation and   276, 277
  gesture and   133
  irony and   87
  otherness and   248
  Platonic utopia and   291
Freedom of the Migrant, The (Flusser)   7, 69, 182, 193, 269
freestyle   323, 327 n.14
Freitas, Gabriela   73 n.19
Freud, Sigmund   90, 91, 113–17, 120, 123
Friedrich-Schiller-University   79
From Subject to Project (*Vom Subjekt zum Projekt*) (Flusser)   64, 69, 201
"Frost and Heat" (Caillois)   314
fugitive poetics   186–7
Fukuyama, Francis   103, 108 n.4, 137
Fülöp-Miller, René   318
future science   287

Gabo   312
Gallagher, Rob   63
Gallope, Michael   186
Galloway, Alexander   8
gameplay   63–4
games. *See also* play
  alternative worlds and   62
  communicative structure as   62
  Flusser on   60–1
  language and   57–8, 67
"Games" (Flusser)   59–61

Gänshirt, Christian   28 n.4
gardening, shaving as   147
"Gebrauchsgegenstände" (Flusser)   25, 29 n.12
Gedächtnisse ("Memories") (Flusser) (lecture)   43
"Gegenstände" (objects)   25–6
Gente, Peter   41
German Media Theory   2, 7, 9, 44, 46, 84
German Romanticism   86–7, 203
Gesamtkunstwerk, notion of   204
geste. See gesture
"Gesten auf Videobändern. Für Fred Forest" (Flusser)   36 n.10
gestural inflation   140 n.43
gesture   6, 44, 130 n.23, 167, 199, 226, 324
  communication and   132–4
  definition of   134, 146
  of endings   134–6
  of expulsion   264
  historical   145–6
  intersubjectivity and   123–9
  meaning and significance of   132–3
  of new gestations   136–9
  pataphysics and   142–3
  of paying attention to gesture   132–4
  phenomenography and   80, 81
  photography and   78–9
  of reading Flusser   131–2
  of shaving   147–8
  situationalist   317
  sonic   233–42
  of speculative journalism   143–5
  of writing   130 n.11, 306, 307
"Gesture of Painting, The" (Flusser)   131
"Gesture of Searching, The" (Flusser)   123, 125
"Gesture of Writing, The" (Flusser)   306, 307
Gestures (*Gesten*) (Flusser)   7, 67, 78, 123, 124, 130 nn.11, 23, 143, 145, 146, 148, 234–5, 239
Gharavi, Maryam Monalisa   257
Giedion, Sigfried   26
gigantomachy   264
Gioia, Ted   185
Glissant, Édouard   4, 319–21
global village   207, 209

Gödel, Kurt   43
Godfrey-Smith, Peter   163, 165
Goethe, Johann Wolfgang   7, 70, 250
Goffman, Erving   138
Goh, Annie   240, 243 n.23
"going-along-with", notion of   167
Goldenberg, Paul   107
Goldsby, Jacqueline   277
Greeks, on dialogue   239
"Großdeutschland"   121 n.15
Groys, Boris   264, 321
Grusin, Richard   135
Guattari, Félix   324
Guillotine method   259–60
Gutenberg Galaxy (McLuhan)   207, 208
Gutmair, Ulrich   200

Habermas, Jürgen   99
Hanke, Michael   25, 68
Haraway, Donna   121 n.13, 138
Harris, H. S.   87
Harrison, M. John   151
Hartmann, Nicolai   68
Hassan, Ihab   198
Hayek, Salma   191
Hayles, N. Katherine   280
Heartfield, John   251, 254 n.36
Hegel, G. W. F.   85, 86, 291, 293 n.8
Hegenberg, Leonidas   58
Heidegger, Martin   5, 19, 26, 42, 68–9, 73 n.19, 137, 166–7, 208, 230, 315
  and Buber compared   176–8
heimat   85, 87, 193–5, 197 n.14, 263
  rejection of   194
Heise, Ursula   51
Heisenberg   123
"Herbarium" series (Fontcuberta)   61
Hernández, Daniel   196 n.6
heterochronia   6
Hirsch, Andreas J.   40, 41
historical consciousness   6
  artificial intelligence and   16–18, 21
  digital technology and   217
  disruption of   299
  loss of   51
  objective   100
  shift in   103
  supra-human   18

technical media and 53
writing consciousness and 212
historicity 103, 104, 107, 219. *See also* human
media 108
posthisotrical 107
history 69, 135, 139 n.15, 251
end of 8, 16, 51–3, 55, 75, 103, 135, 137, 152, 201, 299
filmmaker and 136
gesture and 131
human 27
as programmable object 106
"History as a System" (Ortega) 71
"History of Communication Technologies" (Kittler) 107
History of the Devil, The (Flusser) 5, 7, 50, 52, 54, 67, 113, 117, 152, 184, 193, 262
History of the Imagination (*Geschichte der Einbildungskraft*) (Kamper) 325
Hofmannsthal 24
Holz, Hans Heinz 324, 327 n.16
hominization 132
Homo faber 27, 132, 284
Homo ludens (Huizinga) 59
Homo Ludens, concept of 59, 61, 284
Homo viator 280–1
Hoogland, Renée 8
horizontal translation 228
Horkheimer 318
house, as thought 175–6
Hugo, Victor 97, 159
Huizinga, Johan 58, 59
human 3, 4, 6, 34, 45, 76, 108, 125, 152, 263, 290, 308
anti-apparatus and 269–70
apparatus and 146, 147
artificial intelligence and 17, 19
cognition 21, 42, 58, 280
communication 52–3, 100, 139 n.15, 233, 240, 295, 298, 311, 321
design/shape and 26–8
dignity 44
Enlightenment 49
freedom 52, 89, 91, 273, 291
gesture and 131–3, 135, 136, 138
history 3, 26–7, 98–9, 118, 156, 251

images and 51, 57–65
intersubjectivity and 68, 84
irony and cynicism and 86, 88–90
linguistic features and 225, 226, 230
new 25
nuclear physics and 50–5
posthuman natures and 248–50
progress 71
refraction and 164–7, 170 n.2
sonic gestures and 234–6, 238–40
subject 27, 49, 60, 69, 248, 272, 280, 284
technology and 69, 132
vampire squid and interactions with 94–9, 101, 117–20, 152–9, 247–8, 250–2, 269–70
humanism 3, 6, 18, 76, 89, 125, 145, 151, 208, 247
Enlightenment 84, 86
literary 2
humanities 263
"Humanization" (Flusser) 270
Husserl, Edmund 42, 68, 70, 76–7, 123, 125, 129 n.5, 178, 180 n.19, 287
hybrid hegemonies 192
hypernormality 136

I and Thou (Buber) 182
identity 7, 85, 133, 201, 237, 247, 254 n.36, 290
collective 105, 185, 194
games and play and 60, 63
individual 182, 184, 200, 317
language and 223, 228, 315–17, 326
mystical 248
subject 316, 317, 326
synthetic 318–20, 322
ideographic writing, rejection of 212
image and text 135
immateriality 26, 27, 99, 120, 203, 241, 284, 303
immediacy, ethical 290
immediate/immediacy, concept of 94, 100, 101
improvisation 138, 240
archives and 186, 187
critical 182, 185–6
dialogical programming and 185–6

Index

indexicality   230
Infinite Jest (Wallace)   236, 238
infinite monkeys theorem   305
infinity   59–61, 126, 132, 248, 258–60, 326
information theory   71, 295, 297 n.5
Ingold, Felix Philipp   30, 328 n.23
inhuman   4, 6, 83, 88, 108, 185, 237, 247–8, 258, 263
inhumanism   7
Innis, Harold   211, 213
inscription   154–7
"In Search of Meaning" (Flusser)   58, 71
insect model   117–18
Institute Scientifique de Recherche Paranaturaliste (Scientific Institute for Paranaturalist Research)   6
International Anton Bruckner Festival   39, 40
Interpretation of Dreams, The (Freud)   114, 116
intersubjectivity   44, 68, 84, 99, 104, 129 n.2, 251
   Cartesian worldview and quantum physics and   125–6
   demonologies and   118, 120
   design/shape and   25, 27
   religious telematics and   182, 184–6
   significance of   123–4
   sonic gestures and   235, 241
   temporal conditionings and   183
   translation practice   126–8
Into the Universe of Technical Images (Flusser)   5, 7, 22 n.8, 38 n.33, 41, 50–1, 54, 58, 62, 69, 202, 211, 240, 278 n.11, 280, 286, 290–2, 292 n.4, 298, 302
Ionesco, Eugene   141
irony   4, 45, 84, 90, 203, 242, 299
   ecology and   286–8
   flânerie and flâneur and   87–9
   gesture and   131, 134, 135, 138
   of Kafka   70–1
   linguistic features and   226, 227
   New Weird and   154, 157
   Romantic   88
I/Thou dynamic   182

Jabès, Edmond   317, 326
Jakobson, Roman   222
Jameson, Fredric   26
Jarry, Alfred   141
Jespersen, Otto   68
Jewish utopia   184
Johnson, Linton Kwesi   319–20
Joyce, James   159
Jullien, François   316
jurisgenerative grammar   186–7

Kafka, Franz   6, 70–1, 152, 246, 255, 256, 322
Kafka's irony   70–1
Kaizen, William   37 n.17
Kallman, Chester   113
Kamper, Dietmar   319, 325
Kant, Immanuel   229, 326
Kapp, Ernst   95
Kaprow, Allan   33
Kauffman, Stuart   287
Kellner, Douglas   301 n.4
Kepnes, Steven   182
Kimmich, Dorothee   246
King, Nicholas   105
Kirkpatrick, Graeme   63
Kittler, Friedrich   1, 3, 8, 35, 39, 41, 42, 45, 107–8, 137, 319
Kline, Ron   280
Kommunikologie   33, 46, 248, 310–11
Konsult (Ulmer)   307
Kosmologi (Flusser)   209
Kracauer, Siegfried   318
Kraken Wakes (Wyndham)   152, 158–9
Krauss, Rosalind   164
Kronenberg, Kenneth   197 n.14
Kross, Matthias   73 n.19
Kubin, Alfred   151
Kuleshov, Lev   318
Kunstforum (journal)   3

landmark   259, 260
language
   as articulation of covenant   228
   chess metaphor and   225–6
   chronotopic approach to   223, 224
   as city   174–5
   as code   320–2

and design   24–5
digital technology and   211
experience and   228–30
games   67
inflection and   223–4
as magic   248
nature and   249
phenomenology of   225
philosophy and   68, 228, 229
reality and   67, 173, 222, 229
Saussure on   225, 227–8
as social fact   227
spoken   228
as system   225
theory of   198
as trialectic   201
Wittgenstein on   175–6
written   228
Language, Thought, Reality (Whorf)   309
Language and Reality (*Lingua e Realidade*) (Flusser)   5, 67, 127, 184
La pieuvre (Caillois)   97
Latinidad (Ltinness)   190, 196 n.1
  of Flusser   192–6
  whiteness of   190–2
  white supremacy and   197 n.11
Latino Studies (journal)   195
Latinx   190, 191
Latour, Bruno   26, 90–1, 264, 286, 328 n.21
  on design   27–8
Le Guin, Ursula K.   164, 170 n.6
Leibniz   212, 214
leisure   294
Leonardo (periodical)   3
Leruth, Michael F.   37 n.13
"Les gestes du professeur"   31
"Lever Strikes Back, The" (Flusser)   283
Levinas, Emmanuel   290–2, 317
Lévi-Strauss, Claude   322
Le Vivant et L'Artificiel (Living and the Artificial) project   6
Lewis, Wyndham   207, 208
liberal democracy   108 n.4
Liberty   258
  of Kafka   256–7
lifeworld   70, 75, 77, 81, 88, 294
Ligotti, Thomas   151

Limits of Critique, The (Felski)   264
"Line and Surface" (Flusser)   30–2, 299, 310
linguistic relativity   223
Linz (Austria)   39–40
literary humanism   2
Little Red Book, The   316
London Institute of Pataphysics   141
Loos, Adolf   173
Lovecraft, H. P.   151–2
Lovink, Geert   39
Löwith, Karl   315
Luhmann, Niklas   42
Lyotard, Jean-François   159, 262

McDonald, Peter   59
McGurl, Mark   106
McKimmon, Karen   319
McLuhan, Marshall   5, 34, 44, 79, 95, 132, 206–9, 211, 261, 286
McMullen, Tracy   187
Macy Group Processes Conference   58
Madrigal, Alexis C.   242 n.1
Mailer, Norman   208, 209
Main Currents in Modern Thought (journal)   32
Making History (video)   319
Malina, Frank J.   3
Manovich, Lev   40
Man without Qualities (Musil)   325
Manzanares, Raquel Dastre   28 n.4
Marburger, Marcel René   36 n.6
Marcuse, Herbert   318
Mareis, Claudia   23
Marrow, Helen   196 n.7
Marshall, Kate   107, 109 n.29
Martin, Adrian   299
Marx, Karl   90, 91, 166, 178–9, 180 n.20
Marx Brothers   141
mass media, reappropriation of   33
mass techno-image   311
materializing culture   284
Mathews, Antony   271 n.1
"matter of concern"   26, 28
"matter of fact"   26, 28
Mattos, Ricardo Portilho   28 n.4
Maturana, Humberto   97
Mauthner, Fritz   68

Mead, Margaret   123
Mechanization Takes Command
   (Giedion)   26
media   94, 98–101, 207–8. *See also*
   technical image
  ecology and   5, 55, 124, 135, 287
  studies   1, 5, 32, 34, 42, 51, 94, 163,
    165, 238, 309
  thinking   5, 7–10, 33, 42, 46, 49, 261
"Media Are with Us, The!"
   (symposium)   45
Medium Is the Massage, The
   (McLuhan)   206
Meeting the Universe Halfway
   (Barad)   125
Melville   159
memes/memetics   103, 105–7, 214–16
  grammar and   216–17
  visual component of   216
memory   1, 20, 117, 158, 183, 270, 287,
    296, 318, 326
  animal   119
  archives of   182, 185–7
  Ars Electronica festival and   43–4
  artificial   119–20, 241
  as computational system   186
  cultural   44, 155, 250
  electronic   44
  ex-territorialization of   45
  linguistic features and   226, 227
  sonic gestures and   236, 239
  translation and   184–5
  Vampyroteuthis Infernalis and   98, 99
Menninghaus, Winfried   248, 250
Merve-Verlag   41, 42, 45
"Message 'This is Play', The" (Flusser)   58
mestizo whiteness   191–2
metaprogram   284
methodology   145
Metz, Christian   33
Michelet, Jules   97
Miéville, China   151
migrants and unhappy
    consciousness   84–7
migration   31, 95, 144, 192, 193, 195, 245
Milburn, Patrick   37 n.14
minus-sum-game   60
Miranda, Carmen   191

Miyazaki, Shintaro   241
mobile privatization   316
modernism   2, 4, 6–10, 43, 72
  design/shape and   24–8
  irony and cynicism and   85, 86
  language and   25
  New Weird and   151–2, 159
  synthesis and synthetic reality
    and   198–9, 201–2
  totalizing   201
modernity   90, 132, 145, 155, 246, 258
  future science and   287
  inferno of   153
  reflexive   283
  scientific   288
Moles, Abraham   6, 125
"Moon" (Flusser)   288
Moore, Marianne   159
Moravia, Alberto   316
Morgenstern, Oskar   65 n.4
Morse, Stephen   105
Morton, Timothy   84, 87
Moten, Fred   186–7
movement   317, 326–7
Müggenburg, Jan   41, 42
Müller, Adalberto   4
multidimensional codes   307
multilingualism   224
Münsterberg, Hugo   318
Murray, Donald M.   306
Musil, Robert   246, 325
myths   2, 151, 154, 218, 248, 258, 288
  Enlightenment   20
  posthistory and   103, 104, 106
  synthesis and synthetic reality
    and   202–3
  as triggers for history   250

Nagel, Thomas   97, 163
Nappi, Carla   140 n.42
nationalism   69, 262
natural history   248
Natural:Mente (Flusser)   5
Natural:Mind (Flusser) 280, 281, 286, 287
nature
  culture and   245, 247, 249–52,
    282 n.15
  language and   249

nature writing   286
Nazi Psychoanalysis (Rickels)   121 n.15
Negarestani, Reza   262
negentropy   41, 76, 104, 134, 226
Negri, Antonio   273
net dialogue   75
network   5, 7, 21, 35, 70, 94, 136, 225, 264, 300
   Ars Electronica festival and   40, 46
   cybernetics and   279
   etymology and   295
   language and   315–18, 323, 324
   posthistory and   103–7
   posthuman natures and   246, 251
   religious telematics and   183–4
   sonic gestures and   235, 237–8
Network Contagion Research Institute (NCRI)   106
Neumann, Johann von   65 n.4
New Weird and vampire squid   151–2
   disgusting and   153–5
   infernal and   152–3
   perfidious and   155–7
   rapacious and   157–9
New World narratives   194
Ngai, Sianne   154
Nietzsche, Friedrich   23–5, 71, 90, 91, 123, 133, 284, 326
None Like Us (Best)   187
non-zero-sum game   60
Norris, Frank   159
Novaes, Rodrigo Maltez   113, 157, 243 n.23
nuclear physics   49–50, 52
   risk of   51
   technical images and   50–1, 53

"observing observers". *See* second-order cybernetics
Observing Systems (von Foerster)   42
October (journal)   2, 3
Octopus, The (Norris)   159
off-whiteness writing, Spanish   192
Of Grammatology (Derrida)   212
O'Grady, Gerald   32, 33, 36
Ohlheiser, Abby   106
Oldenburg, Claes   256

Omar-i-Chajjam   202
omnibus and pataphysics   143–6
"On Books" (Flusser)   53–4
"On Edmund Husserl" (Flusser)   68, 180 n.19
One Way Street (Benjamin)   251
Ong, Walter   211
"On Language as Such and on the Language of Man" (Benjamin)   249, 254 n.34
online video games   63
"On Science" (Flusser)   49
On the Aesthetic Education of Man (Schiller)   60
"On the Crisis of Our Models" (Flusser)   124, 127
"On the Term Design" (Flusser)   54
"On Three Spaces" (Flusser)   53
"On Three Times" (Flusser)   104
ontology
   American World Literature and   262, 264
   Ars Electronica festival and   43, 44
   intersubjectivity and   124, 126–8
   irony and cynicism and   85–7
   pataphysics and   145–7
   posthuman natures and   247, 249
   religious telematics and   182–4, 187
   significance of   6, 9, 25, 135, 162, 179, 207, 272, 282 n.15, 290, 315
"On Translation" (Jakobson)   222
"On Typography" (Flusser)   179 n.5
"Open Circuits" (conference)   30, 32–4, 35, 37 n.17
open games   60
Oppian   157
orgasm   117, 118, 158
orgon   117
Ortega y Gasset, José   71
Osthoff, Simone   184
otherness   31, 69, 78, 128, 174, 192, 199, 221, 252, 270
   demonologies and   116, 118, 120
   ethics and   290–2
   freedom and   248
   irony and cynicism and   86, 88
   language and   317, 323
   New Weird and   154, 155, 157

refraction and   163–5, 167
religious telematics and   182–4, 187, 188 n.16
sonic gestures and   234, 236, 239
other program, notion of   310

Paeslack, Miriam   89
Paik, Nam June   32–34, 37 n.18
paracinema   164
paraliterature   164
paranaturalism. *See* speculative biology and paramedia
Parikka, Jussi   104–6, 108
park gaze aphorism   88
participatory research   33
Passional Zoology (Toussenel)   97
passivity   89
pataphysics   6
  "Beyond Machines" and   145–6
  definition of   143
  gestes of speculative journalism and   143–5
  gesture and   142–3
  meaning and significance of   141
  phenomenology and   142
  "Shaving" and   147–8
  Speculations and   148–9
pathologos   105
perceptions
  anti-apparatus and   269
  apparatus and   165
  dialogue and   43
  quantization and   173–4
  shape and form and   166
  significance of   3, 20, 43, 51, 79, 97, 142, 153, 211, 224, 277, 281
  sonic gestures and   238, 241
  video image and   32, 34
  visual   174
Perec, Georges   141
Pessoa, Fernando   6, 132
Peternák, Miklós   184, 187
Peters, John Durham   8
phenomena   126
"Phenomena of Human Communication" (Flusser) (lectures)   8
phenomenography   80, 81

phenomenology   42, 68, 123, 158, 174, 233, 240. *See also* phenomenography
  of abstraction   85
  applied   79
  of communication   81, 234, 238
  as disgust   153
  etymology and   294, 295
  experience and   177
  games and   59, 60
  of language   225
  linguistic features and   222, 224
  pataphysics and   142
  of phenomenology   148
  quasi-phenomenology and   76–82
  refraction and   162, 163, 165–7
  relational   182–3
  sociocultural   145
"Phenomenology of Gestures" (Flusser)   146
Phenomenon of Human Communication (seminar) (Flusser)   296
Philip, M. NourbeSe   107, 109 n.28
philosofiction   27
Philosophical Investigations (Wittgenstein)   67, 175
philosophictions   6, 7
Philosophien der neuen Technologie (Merve-Verlag)   42
"Philosophies of the New Technologies" symposium   41
phoneme   226
Photograph as Post-Industrial Object, The (Flusser)   204
photographic universe   68, 83, 298
photography   36, 61–2, 68, 269
  apparatus and   78, 286–7
  automation and   276
  flâneur and   89
  inscription and   154
  lynching of   277
  as philosophical gesture   79
  synthetic synthesis and   202–3
  vampire squid and   157, 270
photomontages   251, 254 n.36
Pias, Claus   46
Pickering, Andrew   279

Picture of the New Man as a Baby (*Bildnis des neuen Menschen als Säugling*) (Flusser)   201
Pilpul   198
Pinocchio Theory (blog) (Shaviro)   299–300
platform capitalism   104
Platonic utopia   19, 291
play. *See also* games
   definition of   59
   gameplay and   63–4
   Schiller on   60
plus-sum game   60
Poe, Edgar Allen   151
Poincaré, Henri   43
polysemy   216
postcritical approach   264
postcritique   89–92
Poster, Mark   9, 18, 22 n.8, 298
posthistory   20, 51–3, 69
   alienation of   85
   authentic   136
   critique and   91
   flânerie and   88
   gesture and   131
   historicity and   103–4, 107–8
   history and   52
   language and   68
   multiplicity of natural worlds and   251–2
   net dialogue and   75
   nuclear physics and   53
   as programmed history   106
   radiation and   54–5
   technical image and   303
   unhappy consciousness and   91–2
   virality and   104–6
Post-History (Flusser)   7, 19, 272
posthuman   25, 132
posthumanism   6, 246–7
postindustrial society   19, 83, 86, 272, 277, 303, 304
postmodern   49, 65
post-process theory   307
Pound, Ezra   6, 207
Prague   200
pre-mediation   135
presence, idea of   186
prewriting   306, 307
Principle of Hope, The (Bloch)   325
Prisms (Adorno)   52
process theory   306–7
progressive humans   101
project   64, 69
projectivity   6, 169
Purdy, Jedidiah   90
purposefulness   145, 146

quantization   172–3, 305
   I-It of technology and   176–9
   perception and   173–4
   Wittgenstein and   175–6
quantum physics   125–6
quasi-phenomenology   75
Queneau, Raymond   141
Question Concerning Technology, The (Heidegger)   69

Rabinovitz, Lauren   89
radiation   50. *See also* nuclear physics; posthistory
radio theory   33
Raindance Corporation   31, 32
Rake's Progress, The (Stravinsky)   113–15
Rapoport, Anatol   60
Ray, Man   141
reactionary humans   101
reality   299–300
   language and   67, 173, 222, 229
   technical image and   302
refraction. *See* speculative biology and paramedia
Reich, Wilhelm   117
relationality   79, 85, 186
   phenomenology and   182–3
relational network   184
religion   86, 88, 145, 209, 260, 290
   telematics and   181–8
religious telematics   181
   improvisation and   185–6
   I/Thou dynamic and   182
   jurisgenerative grammar   186–7
   memory and   184–7
   relational network and   184
   relational phenomenology and   182–3
Remezcla website   191

Remixing Reggaeton (Rivera-Rideau)   191
renaturalization   287, 288
Republic (Plato)   291
Reuther, Walter   281 n.4
Revista Brasileira de filosofia   67
Revolt of the Masses (Ortega)   71
rewriting   306, 307
rhetoric   15, 294
Rilke, Rainer Maria   246, 253 n.14
risk theory   51
Rivera-Rideau, Petra R.   191
robots and alienation   19–20
Ronell, Avital   236
"Roots" (Smith) (poem)   320
Rosa, Guimarães   6
Rosalía   191
Rössler, Otto E.   318
Rötzer, Florian   319
Russell, Bertrand   43, 68, 229

Sabbath   185–6
"Sacred in the Abyss between Words, The" ("Das Heilige im Abgrund zwischen den Wörtern") (Flusser)   198
Salazar, Miguel   196 n.1
Samsonow, Elisabeth von   322
Saussure, Ferdinand de   225, 227–9
Scale Politics of Emerging Diseases, The (King)   105
Schach (Flusser)   225
Schendel, Mira   125, 126, 130 nn.11, 15
Schiller, Friedrich   59–60
Schoenberg, Arnold   322
Schopenhauer   118
Schweitzer, Dahlia   105
science fiction   164
Sconce, Jeffrey   164
Scott, Ridley   76, 121 n.13
Sea, The (Michelet)   97
Seacrest, Ryan   191
second-order cybernetics   42, 43
Seigelman, Jim   281 n.1
Selfish Gene, The (Dawkins)   105
self-translation practice   126–7, 202
self-transposition   166–7
semiotic universalism   258
Serres, Michel   328 n.21

settler colonialism   192–5
Shannon, Claude   71
Shape of Things, The (Flusser)   26, 283
"Shaving" (Flusser)   147–8
Shaviro, Steven   164, 299
Shelley, Mary   87
Shelley, Percy   87
Shifman, Limor   216
signification   104, 168, 257–9, 283, 302–3
silence   185–7
Siloquies, Superloquies, Soliloquies and Interloquies in Pataphysics (Jarry)   143
Simmel   25
Simón, Yara   191
Simulacra and Simulation (Baudrillard)   44
simulacrum/simulacra   299–300
simulations
    literary aesthetics and   45
    surface and   298–300
simultaneous grammar   216
Sloterdijk, Peter   27, 83, 89, 90
smartphones   241–2
smile and emoji, comparison of   214
Smith, Chadwick T.   28 n.4, 264
Smith, Michael   320
Smith, Zadie   181
Snow, C. P.   295
Society of the Spectacle (Debord)   317
software processing   99
solipsism   237
    depressive   236
    human   238
"Song of Myself" (Whitman) (poem)   322
sonic dialogue   240
Sontag, Susan   104
Soziale Systeme (Luhmann)   42
Spain's Long Shadow (DeGuzmán)   192
Spaniards   191
    whiteness of   192
Speculations (Jarry)   148–9
speculative biology and paramedia   162–9
    body and ego-world relationship and   165–6
    para-cinema and   164
    self-transposition and   166–7

speculative journalism 143–5
speech, gesture of 234
Spivak, Gayatri 255
Statue of Liberty 255, 258
Stern, Jonathan 237
Stiegler, Bernard 137, 177
stories and histories, ends of 51–3
Stravinsky, Igor 113, 322
style 130 n.11
subjectivity 6, 64, 123, 138, 169, 276, 296, 303
  irony and cynicism and 85, 89
  language and 315, 316, 322
  religious telematics and 181, 182, 186–7
Sublime Object of Ideology (Žižek) 1
"Submarine, The" (Flusser) 26, 27
Summae (Aquinas) 175–6
superorganisms 100, 119
Supposed/Angenommen (Flusser) 27, 38 n.41
supra-human historical consciousness 18
surface 80, 97, 119, 147, 157, 202, 231 n.11, 302
  simulation and 298–300
surface and simulation 298–300
Surprising Phenomenon of Human Communication, The (Flusser) 239
Suvin, Darko 271 n.10
symbols 225, 229
synchronization 202, 204
synthesis 5, 23, 57, 62, 118, 128, 172, 320
  cultural 200, 201
  linguistic 201
  organic 201
  quasi phenomenology and 81, 82
  synchronization and 204
  and synthetic, comparison of 199, 202
  technical images and 202, 203
  as tripartite form of nesting 202
  writing and 305, 306
synthetic identity 320, 322
synthetic image 153, 156, 203, 204, 242
Szeeman, Harald 33

"Taking up Residence in Homelessness" (Flusser) 85
Tao of Physics, The (Capra) 201
"Task of the Translator, The" (Benjamin) 222, 251
Taylor, Charles 213
technical image 16, 18, 83, 107, 135, 199, 208, 211, 263, 296, 298
  alphabetic image and 16–17
  apparatus and 302–4
  calculated 202, 203
  ecology and 286
  end of history and 299
  future reader and 21
  language and 68
  nuclear physics and 50–1, 53
  as pathways of disorientation 259
  posthistory and 252
  as real and usable 300
  regime of 20
  simulations and 45
  synthesis and synthetic and 202
  video and 30
  writing and 306
  zetetic maneuvers and 310–11
technics 43, 45
technology 176–9. *See also* technical image
  Buber on 177
  evolution of 204
  Heidegger on 177
  Marx on 178–9
  as second nature 246
technology and cultural form 34
telematic aesthetics 290
telematic society 1, 58, 69, 280, 291–2
telematic utopia 19, 20, 292
telephone, communication through 233–5
  authenticity and 237
  connectivity and 234–7
telepresence 35
"Television and the Politics of Liberation" (Enzensberger) (talk) 33
Ten Billion (Emmott) (play) 109 n.29
Tennyson, Alfred 97, 151
Territorium und Technik (Weibel) (lecture) 45
text and image 135

Thacker, Eugene   157
Thenot, Jean-Paul   31
Theory of Games and Economic Behavior (Neumann and Morgenstern)   65 n.4
thermodynamics, second law of   52, 54, 134
thinking   2–4, 34, 59, 90, 104, 126, 152, 176, 209, 264
  artificial intelligence and   17, 19
  conceptual   31, 227, 263
  critical   97, 128, 135
  culture and   223
  cybernetic   279, 280
  deconstructive   237
  design   25
  Enlightenment   172
  experimental   143
  in freestyle   323–5
  historical   103, 129, 296
  imaginative   31
  Jewish   198
  language and   67, 319–22, 326
  media   5, 7–10, 33, 42, 46, 49, 261
  memory as media archive and   185
  modernism and   151, 152
  mythical   218
  nuclear physics and   52–4
  outsource of   137
  posthistorical   53
  post/modernism and   198–204
  quasi-phenomenology and   75, 79
  systematic   300
  technological   218
  tentacular   121 n.13
  typographic   306
  writing and   307
Thorben, Jan   241
Thousand Years of Nonlinear History, A (De Landa)   245
threshold   250
time-stamp. *See* date-mark
Toilers of the Sea (Hugo)   97
tools, as technology   45
Torres-Saillant, Silvio   196 n.7
totalitarianism   27, 88, 91, 239, 270
  cybernetic   273
  programmed   284

totalizing modernism   201
Toussenel, Alphonse de   97
"Toward a Concept of Postmodernism" (Hassan)   198
Towards a Philosophy of Photography (Flusser)   5, 30, 42, 69, 83, 202, 270, 275, 277, 286, 298, 309
Tractatus Logico-Philosophicus (Wittgenstein)   67, 322
Tractatus Philosophicus (Wittgenstein)   175
transference   114, 116
translation   5–7, 68–70, 187, 197 n.14, 303, 321, 322
  codes and   202
  as communication   222, 228
  dialogic exchange and   186
  games and play and   57, 64
  horizontal   228
  indirect   182
  intersubjectivity and   125–8
  language and   184–5, 222
  mnemonic   184
  practice of   126–8
  reciprocal   202
  synthesis and synthetic reality and   198, 201–3
  translatability and   4, 221–3, 228, 230
  vertical   228
transposition   166–7
transversality   104, 105, 107
treatise and essay, difference between   221–2
Treusch-Dieter, Gerburg   319
trialectic language   201
Tripp, Caecilia   319
Tristes Tropiques (Lévi-Strauss)   322
Turning, The (Heidegger)   69
Twentieth Century, The (*Das Zwanzigste Jahrhundert*) (Flusser)   200, 201
Twenty Thousand Leagues under the Sea (Verne)   97, 152, 154, 168
typography   172, 174, 306

Uëxkull, Jacob Von   97, 163
Ulmer, Gregory L.   307
Ulm School of Design   25

"Umbruch der menschlichen
    Beziehungen" (Mutations in human
    relations) (Flusser) 33
Umpleby, Stuart 281 n.5
umwelt, notion of 97
unconditional dialogue 317
unconditioned we 315, 316, 326
Understanding Media (O'Grady) 34
unhappy consciousness
    alienation of 89
    cynicism and 84
    and migrant compared 84–7
    posthistory and 91–2
Unicode Consortium 215
University of Illinois 42
Urrieta Jr., Luis 195
"Use as Philosophy" (Aicher) 176
utopia 27, 115, 201, 209, 235, 241, 280, 290
    anti-mythical 250
    Habermasian 323
    imagination of 119
    Jewish 184
    Platonic 19, 291
    of posthistorical society 76
    telematic 19, 20, 292
    video image and 32, 34

value 145–6
vampire squid and human
    interactions 96–9, 117–20, 152–9,
    240–1, 247–8, 250–2, 269–70
Vampyroteuthis Infernalis (Flusser and
    Bec) 5, 7, 94, 125, 152, 162, 271 n.4
    cow metaphor in 95–6
    ecology and 286, 287
    media and 98–101
    organisms and environment in 94,
        97–100
    significance of 162–3
    speculative biology and paramedia
        and 162–9
    superorganisms in 100
    vampire squid and human interactions
        in 96–9, 117–20, 152–9, 247–8,
        250–2, 269–70
vampyroteuthic communication
    in 99
van der Meulen, Sloukje 206, 208

Van Dyke, Willard 32
"Vanity of History, The" (Flusser) 103
Vasulka, Woody 33, 37 n.27
Vattimo, Gianni 317
Venuti, Lawrence 222
Verne, Jules 152, 154, 159, 168
vertical translation 228
Vertov, Dziga 318
Vian, Boris 141
video, significance of 296
*Videogames, Identity and Digital
    Subjectivity* (Gallagher) 63
video images, dialogic capacity of 30–1
    Open Circuits conference and 32–4
    significance of 34–6
Video-Physiognomic Dysphoria
    (VPD) 238
"Video Troisième Age" 31
Vienna Circle 42, 68
Vienna Secession (1923) 2
Vilém Flusser (Finger, Guldin, and
    Bernardo) 8, 193, 206
"Vilém Flusser's Philosophy of Design"
    (Hanke) 25
virality 45, 103–7
    communicability of 105
Virilio, Paul 72, 299
Visible Sppech (DeFrancis) 212
Vlieghe, Joris 107
von Foerster Heinz 39, 42, 44
    on perceptions 43
Vossler, Karl 230
Vostell, Wolf 31

Waag, A. 68
Wagner, Richard 204
Wagnermeier, Silvia 8
"Waiting for Kafka" (Flusser) 70
Wald, Priscilla 105
Wallace, David Foster 234, 235
Warhol, Andy 115
Warlikowski, Krzysztof 113, 115
Washington Post, The (newspaper) 106
Waugh, Evelyn 159
Weber, Max 295
Weibel, Peter 2–3, 7, 37 n.18, 39, 42, 45,
    301 n.11, 319
    Hirsch on 41

Weiden, Katrin   327 n.15
Weird   151
Wells, H. G.   159
Wells, Kate   185
"We Need a Philosophy of Emigration" (Flusser)   87
White, Simone   188
Whitehead, Alfred North   43, 68
whiteness
    of Latinidad   190–2
    mestizo   191–2
    of Spaniards   191
Whitman, Walt   322
Whorf   5
Whorf, Benjamin Lee   223, 229, 309
Wiener, Norbert   42, 71, 279, 280, 281 nn.1, 3–4
Wiesing, Lambert   79–81
Williams, Raymond   34, 316
Wills, David   138
Winkler, Steffi   44, 48 n.27
"wiring of channels", of communication   80, 81
"Without Firm Ground" (2015–17) (exhibition)   323

Wittgenstein, Ludwig   5, 42, 58, 67, 314, 322
"Wittgenstein's Architecture" (Flusser)   175
writing   305–8, 322
    post-process theory and   308
    process theory and   306–7
writing, future of   211
    and alphabetic and ideographic writing   212
    digital technology and   217–19
    emoji and   214–15
    memes and   215–17
Writing and Difference (Derrida)   213
Wyndham, John   152, 158

xenobath   158

Yoldas, Pinar   168
YouTube   213

Zeitmarke. See date-mark
zero-dimensionality   6, 201
zero-sum game   60
Žižek, Slavoj   1, 2, 200, 319
ZKM (Center for Art and Media) (Germany)   41

www.ingramcontent.com/pod-product-compliance
Lightning Source LLC
Chambersburg PA
CBHW052141300426
44115CB00011B/1470